Augsburg College
George Sverdrup Library
Minneapolis, MN 55454

WITHDRAWN

D1777691

Politics in Israel

Politics in Israel
The Second Generation

ASHER ARIAN
Tel Aviv University

CHATHAM HOUSE PUBLISHERS, INC.
Chatham, New Jersey

POLITICS IN ISRAEL
The Second Generation

CHATHAM HOUSE PUBLISHERS, INC.
Box One, Chatham, New Jersey 07928

Copyright © 1985 by Chatham House Publishers, Inc.

All rights reserved. No part of this publication may be reproduced, stored in a retrieval system, or transmitted in any form or by any means, electronic, mechanical, photocopying, recording, or otherwise, without the prior permission of the publisher.

PUBLISHER: Edward Artinian
JACKET AND COVER DESIGN: Yaron Fidler
COMPOSITION: Chatham Composer
PRINTING AND BINDING: Hamilton Printing Company

LIBRARY OF CONGRESS CATALOGING IN PUBLICATION DATA

Arian, A.
    Politics in Israel

    Bibliography: p.
    Includes index.
    1. Israel—Politics and government. 2. Political parties—Israel.   I. Title.
JQ1825.P3A4   1985   320.95694   84-29300
ISBN 0-934540-38-1
ISBN 0-934540-37-3 (pbk.)

Manufactured in the United States of America
10 9 8 7 6 5 4 3 2 1

In addition to other potential audiences, it was my hope that my children would use this book in their studies. LEOR *(Dukie) was too fast for me and graduated;* AVIV *may get this as a graduation present;* SHELLY *is the only one for whom the original thought is relevant.*

Contents

1 **Introduction**   1
Legitimacy. Identity. Integration. Political Culture.

2 **People of Israel**   11
Periods of Immigration. Emigration. Non-Jews. Sephardim-Ashkenazim.

3 **Political Economy**   25
Prime Movers. Performance and Government Activity. Import Capital. Employment and Distribution.

4 **The Political Elite**   47
Participation and the Elite. A Crisis of Succession. Knesset Members. Politics as a Vocation. Prime Ministers and Presidents. A Sephardi for President.

5 **Political Parties**   71
Alignment Parties. Likud Parties. Religious Parties. Challenge from the Center. Other Parties.

6 **Party Organization**   95
Party Membership. The Iron Law of Oligarchy. Party Institutions.

7 **The Electoral System**   120
Knesset Elections. Constitutional Provisions. Electoral Reform. Electoral Systems. The Yaacobi Proposal.

8 **Electoral Behavior**   133
Voting Participation. Explaining the Vote. The Ethnic Vote. The Floating Vote. Concentration of the Vote.

9 The Knesset, the Government, and the Judiciary 155
   A "Pure" Parliamentary System. Coalition Politics. The Cabinet.
   Knesset Members in Action. Legislation. The Judiciary.

10 Interest Groups and Public Policy 186
   The Israeli Case. Defense. The Histadrut. Agriculture. Religion.

11 Statism, Public and Local Administration 226
   Statism. Public Administration. Local Government.

12 Ideology, Communication, and Socialization 244
   Left-Right Continuum. Left-Right, Attitudes, and the Vote. Political
   Communication. Political Socialization. Democratic Norms and
   Political Tolerance.

   Notes 266

   Glossary 277

   Index 282

   About the Author 290

Tables

2.1	Population of Jews in Israel and the World, 1882-1982	21
2.2	Voting Potential of the Jewish Population in Israel, 1969 and 1981	23
3.1	Distribution of Total National Income, Selected Countries, 1960 and 1970	44
3.2	Gross Income per Household by Continent of Birth and Period of Immigration	45
4.1	Occupations of Knesset Members by Major Parties, 1948-77	60
6.1	Members and Voters in Five Israeli Parties, 1977-79	103
8.1	Knesset Election Results	135
8.2	Determining Factor in the Vote	136
8.3	Party Vote by Age, 1969, 1973, 1977, and 1981	138
8.4	Alignment Portion of Two-Party Vote by Continent of Birth, 1969-84	141
8.5	Stable and Floating Vote, 1973 and 1977	148
8.6	Stable and Floating Vote, 1977 and 1981	149
8.7	Share of 120-Member Knesset by Two Largest Parties, 1949-84	151
8.8	Party Images, 1973 and 1981	153
10.1	Agricultural Settlements by Organizational and Party Affiliation and 1981 Vote	214
10.2	Public Life and Jewish Religious Tradition; Observance of Jewish Religious Law	217
12.1	Parties According to Positions Concerning the Arab-Israeli Conflict	246
12.2	Left-Right Tendency, 1962-84	251
12.3	Political Efficacy by Place of Birth, 1969 and 1981	263

Figures

5.1	Splits and Mergers in the Israel Labor Movement	73
8.1	Alignment and Likud Knesset Seats, 1965-84	150

Acknowledgments

It is a pleasure to acknowledge the influence and aid of many people in preparing this book. Yonathan Shapiro, Samuel Krislov, Yair Aharoni, Aaron Wildavsky, Michal Shamir, Philippa Strum, Giora Goldberg, Yoram Peri, Gideon Doron, Efraim Torgovnik, and Michael Keren were important at different times and in different ways. Yeshayahu Avrech of the Histadrut, Ohad Zmora, and the Social Science Faculty of Tel Aviv University provided encouragement and support. Roslyn Langbart and her staff made the typing process a pleasure. Anthony Grahame deserves thanks for his sensitive and conscientious editing.

POLITICS IN ISRAEL

1. Introduction

A political system must be understood in terms of the people who live under it, their values and ideals, the resources at their disposal, the challenges that face the system, and the institutions developed to meet these challenges. Israel is a fascinating example of a complex system that has developed in a relatively short time (since the 1880s) into a dynamic country that has undertaken enormous commitments in the military, economic, and social fields. There seems to be never a dull moment, with Israel capturing an inordinately large share of the world's attention.

Political scientists who compare political systems find difficulty in fitting Israel into their schema. Discussing political parties, Sartori finds the extended dominance of Mapai exceptional; Lijphart, in his study of relations between major ethnic, religious, and language groups, leaves Israel outside his framework because of its uniqueness; when studying the relations between the military and civilian sectors, Israel is often regarded as special; and discussions of political modernization point to Israel as falling outside many general patterns.[1]

In many senses Israel is unique. Merely by its membership in the exclusive club of democratic nations (in which parties compete for power in free elections), Israel is in a special category. This club has shrunk continually since the Second World War until today only a couple of dozen countries in the world meet the criteria of democracy. Moreover, the defense burden on Israel is unparalleled in other countries, democratic or not. Other countries have large immigrant populations, but proportionate to its size none has absorbed so many immigrants in so short a time as has Israel.

Yet in other senses Israel's political and social experiences are similar to those of other countries. The scarcity of local resources has meant continual searching for foreign sources of import capital, and importing this capital has given the central authorities great sway not only over the economy of the country but over its politics as well. The large numbers of immigrants have facilitated the development of machine politics. Politics tends to be party politics, and party politics tends to be hierarchical. Lacking a majority of one party in the system, smaller parties (usually religious ones in Israel) hold the balance of power in coalition formation.

As Israel enters its second generation of statehood and its second century of development (independence was in 1948; modern Jewish settlement in Eretz Israel began in the early 1880s), it faces problems and issues that are neither new nor unique but will have a strong impact on the system. Through these issues, the politics of the second generation will be played out.

Legitimacy

Almost four decades after independence, the issue of legitimacy still poses a potential threat to the country. Political legitimacy refers to the basis on which the exercise of political authority is established. A system is legitimate when its decisions are generally and widely accepted as just and proper by major groups in the system.

The pre-state period in Eretz Israel (the land of Israel) witnessed the development of a regime that had authority without sovereignty. That is, the population on the whole voluntarily undertook to obey the rules and laws set down by the leadership, including taxation and conscription. This was in addition to the rules set down by the mandatory power that held sovereignty. For our purposes, however, what is important is the perception of legitimacy on the part of the overwhelming majority of the population toward the organized decision-making bodies of the Yishuv (the pre-state Jewish community).

The pre-state period saw both secular and religious challenges to the legitimacy of the Yishuv's decisions. The Revisionists split from the organized Yishuv over issues of policy toward the British mandatory power, arguing that Yishuv institutions and their decisions were not binding on them; in a word, that they were illegitimate. David Ben-Gurion never forgave the Revisionists and their Herut successors for this withdrawal and attempted to deny them legitimacy when he placed them in the company of the communists, the other ostracized group of mainstream Israeli politics in the years following statehood, by declaring that all parties were candidates for his coalition government except the communists and Herut.

In the Yishuv period and for some even in the state period, the ultraorthodox (especially the Naturai Karta group) adopted an anti-Zionist position that denied legitimacy to the laws of the state and the rules by which decisions are made. The basis of their opposition was theological and thus represents potentially a most dangerous challenge to the State of Israel. When religious authorities declare that their divinely revealed law is superior to and in contradiction with man-made law, severe crisis is inevitable. The existence of competing bodies of law to which significant segments of society owe their allegiance is a prescription for disaster. This situation has been avoided to date in Israel because most religious groups accept the legitimacy of the laws of the state (see chapter 10), but the potential for crisis exists, especially if highly emotional issues emerge to divide the public. Most of the Jewish terrorist groups which were revealed in the 1980s were religious and justified their behavior on religious grounds.

The rules by which decisions are made must be perceived as legitimate, and so too must the decisions themselves. One may disagree with a decision yet concede that the decision-making process is legitimate and those who participate in it have the legitimate right to do so. It is important to distinguish clearly between legitimacy and legality. The question is not only whether the decision makers have the legal right to make the decision but whether the decision is generally accepted. If the debate over the future of the post-1967 territories is between returning them and annexing them, it is likely that major groups in the country (military, press, politicians) hold that either or both options are legitimate. The crisis for the political system arises when people are asked to support or act on decisions they perceive to be illegitimate.

Legitimacy in Israel is by no means assured simply because the government has been duly elected and constituted. Sensitive issues have the potential for polarizing the body politic. The future of the territories taken in the Six Day War seems to be such an issue. The population is divided between those who feel strongly about retaining sovereignty over these territories and those who feel that annexing them would change the basic nature of the state and would hence be detrimental. This kind of basic issue holds great danger for a democratic society because a mere majority for either position will not assuage the intense feelings of the other group. In the light of intense feelings, Prime Minister Menachem Begin showed masterful political skill in calling on the Knesset to determine the issue of removing the Israeli settlements from Sinai as part of the peace treaty with Egypt in 1979. By involving the entire political system in the decision, and not just his governing coalition, he won an overwhelming vote supported more by the Alignment opposition than by his own Likud. The coalition of these two groups was more than enough to overcome the fervent opposition of those who wanted to stop the withdrawal from the Sinai.

Identity

Whether or not an individual has a clear conception of the nation-state and his or her place in it is an important question asked by political scientists. The state is the most pervasive object of identification in modern political life, surpassing in importance the family, clan, village, movement, and political party. The Zionist idea was catalyzed into the Zionist movement at the end of the nineteenth century as nationalist ideas and movements were sweeping Europe; Israel was born in a period that saw the emergence of many new states. But Israel calls itself a "Jewish state"; this notion has been expressed in legislative declarations and is fervently believed by most Israeli Jews. When asked, "Are we in Israel an inseparable part of the Jewish people or a separate people?" 85 percent chose the first option.

An overwhelming and growing majority of Jews in Israel identify themselves as both Jews and Israelis. More than two-thirds in 1965 and almost three-quarters in 1974 responded that being Jewish played an important part in their lives. When asked about the centrality of being Israeli, 90 percent of the same samples reported in both 1965 and 1974 that "Israeliness" plays an important part in their lives.[2]

For most Jews in Israel, then, there is no discrepancy between being Israeli and being Jewish. Israel is "Jewish" in the sense that its language is Hebrew, its school curriculum is heavily laced with Bible and Jewish history, and its holidays are Jewish in origin and are set in accord with the Hebrew calendar (although important events such as summer vacation, payday, and even the date when winter uniforms are distributed in the army are determined by the Gregorian calendar). Enormous efforts are expended in the educational system to promote both Jewish and Israeli identities. Politicians have developed a status quo agreement that supposedly freezes the religious issue as it was in the pre-state era — in effect it is the basis for all further negotiations while claiming nothing has changed. Since the Second World War, the Jewish world has almost unanimously accepted Zionism as the top priority on its agenda. It is not surprising, then, that few Israelis feel cross-pressured regarding these topics. To be sure, there have been expressions of support for one end of the continuum or the other. The Canaanite movement of the 1950s held that the geographical expression of its identity as originating from the land of Canaan was more meaningful to its identity than the Jewish identity that included two thousand years of Diaspora; this latter identity was adopted by the Zionist movement. At the other extreme are individuals who reject the national expression of Judaism — the State of Israel — and whose sole identification is with the Jewish religion. For some of them, such as the Naturai Karta group, citizenship in a Jewish state is a secular detail of no religious significance since the state was not wrought by divine decree. For others, it is outright blasphemy to support such a state, and hence it follows that obstructing it becomes laudable.

While the identity issue seems resolved for most Israeli Jews, the system is faced with two crucial issues. The first is the role of the State of Israel for Jews who do not live in Israel. The second is the relation to the state of non-Jews living in Israel.

Introduction

Conceiving itself as a Jewish state has been translated in practice to a policy that makes every Jew a citizen of Israel virtually for the asking. The Law of Return is the concrete expression of the prophetic vision of the "ingathering of the exiles." The statistical fact is that less than a quarter of the world's Jews live in Israel, but the boundaries of Israel's political system are hard to set because the spiritual and material influence of Jews who are not Israelis is often felt. Many Israelis see their national undertaking as providing a refuge for the world's Jews; and many Jews in the world show pride, concern, and anxiety (or other emotions) toward Israel in a manner unusual for citizens of foreign countries. Regardless of the distribution of opinion regarding Israel among the Jews of another country, the question of identity is always near the surface. Sometimes it is asked by Jews themselves and sometimes by those who wish to question the loyalty of the Jews. It is not a new question. If Jews were persecuted in the Middle Ages for having a distinct religion, in modern times this dilemma is compounded by the existence of the State of Israel and the difficulties this raises regarding both religious and national loyalties.

Perhaps the most difficult dilemma is faced by non-Jews living in Israel. For most, the experience raises fundamental conflicts of identity. Let us begin by noting that the Arab population in Israel (in the boundaries preceding the 1967 war) is referred to as the "minorities." What a wonderful example of a Hebrew expression laden with ideological meaning! The Arabs are a minority (some 17 percent at this time) in the formal sense, but this does not accurately reflect the demography of Eretz Israel or the Middle East, nor does it take into account Arab sensibilities. Called upon to support a Jewish state in a period of intense Arab nationalism and when other forces are calling for the establishment of a Palestinian state is a difficult position to be in. Israeli Arabs are not called upon to serve in the army (the Druze are), and this can be seen as a measure of semicitizenship because army service is so important in determining the pecking order of Israeli political and bureaucratic life. The identity of this group is a crucial challenge to the system. On the whole, Israeli Arabs have demonstrated prudence in their dilemma; but it would be shortsighted not to recognize the strains they are under as a potential source of crisis for the system.

Integration

Over a hundred years ago, modern Jewish settlement in Eretz Israel began. The first hundred years were dominated by Eastern European immigrants and their children. Positions of power, institutions, the culture, the economy, and the educational system were in their hands. But a great historical asymmetry occurred. The Zionist movement—based on secular, nationalist European ideas—was not particularly successful among secular European Jews. While most were ready to subscribe to its ideology, fewer were actually willing to live in Israel. In a sense, the Zionist movement generated a leadership but failed to attract its natural followers.

After independence, large-scale immigration of Jews from Arab countries began. The people who arrived tended to be more traditional than their European counterparts who came to Israel or their cousins from Arab lands who did not. They proved to be much more loyal to the Zionist cause as a group. Only 10 percent of the world's Ashkenazi (European) Jews live in Israel compared with two-thirds of the Sephardim (generally from Asian and African countries). The progress of the Sephardim in terms of education and occupation was swift; undergoing extremely rapid development, they were also faced with negative aspects of modernity such as the breakdown of the patriarchal family and soaring crime rates. In the early 1980s, as the Israel-born sons and daughters of Sephardi immigrants became a vocal and numerous factor in Israeli elections, the issue of their integration into the system emerged in a boisterous and sometimes violent manner. On the whole, extreme positions have not been taken, although there have been visible exponents of these. Undoubtedly the Sephardim have lately achieved higher levels of influence and power than they had in the past; whether this will lead to a decline in the intensity of the issue or a call for even faster and more far-reaching change is hard to foresee.

It is clear that the demographic and sociological changes that the Israeli population is experiencing will profoundly affect the political system. The century of Ashkenazi dominance has passed, but it does not follow that we are entering a century of Sephardi dominance. What is more likely is the emergence of a native-born leadership that is more Israeli than Ashkenazi or Sephardi. The children of Israel wandered in the desert forty years before they entered the land of Israel, before a new generation emerged to take on the burdens of nationhood. Israel's fortieth birthday is approaching; by then the new generation of leadership will be about to take over from the generation of the founders.

A problem of integration in another sense is posed by Arabs living in the territories that resulted from the 1967 war. By now, about half of the territories' residents have known no other form of government than occupation by the Israel Defense Force. The dilemma is stark—if the territories are annexed, what is to become of the inhabitants? It is inconceivable that they not be granted full citizenship rights, a fact that would sharply tip the demographic trends and endanger the Jewish state in the sense of having a Jewish majority. Tampering with voting rights would be unacceptable, and depleting the population would be unconscionable. Continuing the military rule is also inappropriate;

as the issue festers, it becomes more difficult to solve. The Begin government's policy of distinguishing between the population and the territory, allowing autonomy to the former while claiming Israeli sovereignty for the latter, has been rejected by Palestinians, Egyptians, and Americans. The existence of more than 1 million people in territory occupied by a country of some 4 million people raises acute questions of politics and morality.

Political Culture

It is important to notice what has been left out. There is no debate in Israel over the importance of security or the continuation of the welfare state. Maintaining strong defenses is the overriding concern of all Israeli governments, and many policies are cast in the name of defense. Even the welfare state is sanctioned because of the importance of providing citizens with minimum standards so that the youth will be fit for army life. Both topics are important in the political system, but it is unlikely that diametrically opposed positions will emerge. In the 1982 Lebanon war the cherished "national consensus" was shattered, especially as the war dragged on and the Israeli army came closer to Beirut. But even while the debate raged, the overwhelming majority of soldiers (many of whom were reservists) obeyed commands. That experience might have been the outer limit, but the system was able to withstand it.

Even in the second generation, various other characteristics are likely to remain. Politics in Israel has been party politics, and party politics has been elite politics. These basic patterns are likely to remain, even though changes occur. For example, the party system has undergone a shift from dominance to competitiveness. The dominant party from the 1930s till 1977 was the Labor party. Herut (Likud), the party once declared illegitimate by the dominant party's leaders, was the largest vote getter in the 1981 elections. At these elections the two parties took 95 of the 120-seat Knesset, with the Likud only one seat stronger than Labor.

While the share of the two biggest parties increased, it seemed that the parties themselves were more and more unresponsive and organizationally frozen. Membership in parties declined, and participation in demonstrations and nonparty movements grew. New groups and new demands found avenues of expression outside the large parties; new parties emerged, and some did well in elections. The party system seemed more open and dynamic than ever before, a record 31 lists competing in the 1981 elections, although only ten of them won the minimum 1 percent of the vote necessary for representation. In 1984, the system was more fragmented: 26 lists ran and 15 of them won representation.

Israel's political system is centralized and hierarchical, and is likely to remain that way. It is centralized in two senses: (1) decisions are made concerning the selection of leaders and the general direction of policy in the chambers of its major political parties; and (2) control of the party that forms the government implies control of the Knesset and control of the major ministries. It is hierarchical in the sense that a party, a politician, and a citizen all tend to know their place in the power structure and rarely overreach themselves. The opposition accepts its relatively powerless role just as a junior coalition power accepts its relatively subordinate role in the calculus of power. Eyes tend to focus on the leader, waiting for the cue. Individuals and groups fit into this structure, and political parties tend to be collections of factions, or nuclei, around leaders, jockeying for position in the pyramid of power. The hierarchical nature of the structure is facilitated because subordinate groups and individuals are likely to be dependent on decisions made at higher levels of the hierarchy regarding appropriations and appointments.

All this fits in nicely with Israel's bureaucratic public life. The centralized economy encourages dependency, with the government controlling 40 percent of the economy's activity and directly influencing 90 percent of the country's economic life. These figures register enormous economic influence and hint at enormous political power. Add to that the fact that almost two-thirds of those employed work in services and that three-quarters of the employed are salaried, and the impact of the control of the centralized economy is clear.

Just as the role of political party and the centralized nature of the economy are likely to retain importance in the second generation, so too with ideology. The style of Israeli politics is ideological. The use of symbols, rhetoric, and coded phrases has always been evident in the Israeli political experience and is not likely to diminish soon. What is also true is that Israeli politicians can be very pragmatic and can review long-expressed ideological formulations if their understanding of political reality so demands. The population on the whole tends to be less ideological, but shows high degrees of deference to the ideological phrases of politicians, just as it does to decisions of the leadership.

Israel's political culture demonstrates a fascinating mix of ideology and pragmatism. The socialist ethic that ruled for decades has withered, although it is still found in preserves such as ideological meetings of the Histadrut (federation of trade unions), in some kibbutzim and moshavim, and in a few youth groups. But the element of nationalism has retained its intensity, if not strengthened. The materialism of many Israelis has been observed often, and it seems to have become the norm; despite very high levels of taxation, the ethos developed is one of seeking creature comforts in the present tense. This materialism does not blunt, and indeed perhaps enhances, high levels of identification with the system by most Jews and a willingness to sacrifice for its preservation and maintenance.

The most enduring feature of the system is likely to be the politician. Israeli politicians tend to be dependent on the party and its institutions for their influence and livelihood. But all of them, except for two or three at the apex of the pyramid, share a generally low level of prestige. In the late 1970s, "Knesset member" was 64th out of 90 preferred occupations ranked by a national sample. A taste of the orientation of the public is gleaned from the story of the Haifa-area resident arrested for attacking his neighbor with a knife. In explaining his behavior he claimed that his neighbor had called him a politician.[3]

The politician and the political system have three distinct spheres of activity, each with its own rhythm and rules. These are electoral politics, coalition politics, and bureaucratic politics. The politician divides his time among the three, but the nature of his investment and his hope of profit are different in each sphere. Electoral politics may be the most important formally because it is the division of Knesset seats as determined by voters on election day that determines the division of political power. Electoral politics is limited to the campaign period, though the press and public (and perhaps politicians as well) think of political life as an unending campaign.

Coalition politics can come up at any time, but usually involves a handful of actors. But since the coalition is necessary to rule, the payoff of the coalition game is high. Coalition politics determines who will control important government ministries, Knesset committees, policies, and budgets. Crisis in the coalition is an effective way of pressuring for more, but there is also a danger that power already achieved will be lost if the coalition crumbles.

Bureaucratic politics is likely to be the major investment of the politician. He must retain or enhance his position within his organization if he is to continue his career. He may well assume that others covet his position; if he is the representative of a group, he may assume that others in the group would like to see him rotate out of office; within his party there are other groups that feel deprived as their groups are denied representation because of one group's success in achieving positions of influence; certainly, outside his party, members of other parties have set their goal to replace him and his party. He must keep the politics of his constituency organization, his party, and the country clearly in mind as he meets, speaks, maneuvers, and negotiates to retain power for himself, his group, and his party. This in-group fighting is the kind of politics that is most hidden from the public eye but the one that probably takes up most of the energies of the politician.

The world of Israeli politics often seems confusing to the uninitiated. One reason is that names of parties and alignments change, and that can be confusing. The basic uniformities are strong, however, and concentrating on major issues and patterns shows that the system often follows a few basic rules. For readers familiar only with Anglo-American politics, a word of advice: Try not to transfer your understanding of politics and its terminology to the Israeli system without adjustment. Terms such as left-right, checks and balances, and even democracy are widely used in Israeli politics. But it would be misleading to accept them in the same way they are used in other systems. Israel is much more understandable to someone who knows political systems in continental Europe. The forms and usages are more directly traceable there. Even then, Israel poses special problems, for its history is unique, and its politics must be understood in that light.

2. People of Israel

A key element in the development of any country, and certainly in Israel, is its population—its size, quality, and morale. It is fitting to focus on the people of Israel for many reasons, not the least of which is the fact that the Zionist movement's overt goal was to change the place of residence of the world's Jews from the Diaspora to Zion. In that sense the Zionist movement has been only partially successful. In 1882 there were 24,000 Jews in Eretz Israel, or 0.31 percent of the world's Jews. One hundred years later, Israel's 3.3 million Jews comprised 23 percent of the world's 14.5 million Jews.[1]

Mass immigration of Jews to Israel continues to enjoy wide support on an abstract level from Jews in Israel and abroad, but the fact is that most Jews do not live in Israel. Any understanding of Israel politics must rely heavily on an appreciation of who came and who did not, when they came, why some left, and how those who stayed became part of the system. We must take into account the relations between the Jews of Israel and the Jews of the world during this 100 years and the impact of the relatively large growth of the Jews in Israel on the Arab population of the country.

The bottom line of the immigration balance sheet is determined by a large number of forces including developments taking place abroad, the attitude of the ruling power, and the psychological predispositions of the immigrating population. These in turn affect the likelihood of successful absorption and the effect of immigration on the political institutions of the country. In general, the following points should be kept in mind:

1. There is no easy explanation for immigration. It is convenient to think of "pull" factors making a country attractive and "push" factors making the country from which one emigrates unattractive. Often these forces work in tandem. Usually there is no similar experience in a normal adult's life parallel to the dependency encountered after immigration to a foreign country. If the "pull" factors outweigh the "push" factors, absorption is likely to be easier. If one is imbued with ideological passion or religious vision, making *aliyah* ("coming up") to Israel will be managed even more successfully. Also, the social context is important. An individual coming alone is likely to have a much hard-

er time than if he belongs to a group, be it family, village, or political group. It is no accident that *landsmenschaft* develop after every substantial immigration. They answer a very basic need of community, roots, and ties to the familiar—things that are usually initially denied the immigrant.

2. While Zionism provided a ready ideology for immigration to Eretz Israel, most Jews who moved and who had other options chose not to come. That was especially true of the mass migration from Russia and Poland to the United States at the beginning of the twentieth century, and it is equally true of those Jews recently allowed to leave the Soviet Union. Note, however, that Jews of North African and Middle Eastern extraction came to Israel in higher percentages when they left their countries.

3. Much immigration is caused by external factors. Large numbers of Polish Jews arrived in Eretz Israel in the mid-1920s because of the double pressures of a general boycott having been declared on Jewish industry and commerce in their country of origin and a simultaneous legislation of quotas formulated in the Johnson-Lodge Immigration Act of 1924 in the United States, which limited access to a desirable country of destination. A record high number of 66,000 immigrants arrived in 1935, about a quarter of them from Germany, as conditions in pre-World War II Europe deteriorated. In 1957 a substantial number of immigrants from Morocco arrived, reflecting anxieties felt by Moroccan Jews as nationalism in North African countries began to emerge. Mass immigration from the Soviet Union could be undertaken only when Soviet authorities granted exit visas.

4. Every immigration has its emigration. Some—especially if they are physically and financially able—are likely to return to their country of origin or to immigrate to another destination. In the massive immigration of many nationalities to the United States between 1908 and 1924, for every 100 immigrants there were 34 emigrants. During the second *aliyah* (1904-14) Ben-Gurion estimated that only one in ten remained (the figure is probably closer to three in ten).[2] Over time, about 10 to 15 percent of Israelis have left Israel.[3] For historians, sociologists, and demographers, this is a natural and well-known phenomenon. To the Zionist it is saddening, since one who believes in the ideological correctness of his cause sees immigration to Zion as a key element in its platform.[4]

5. Earlier waves of immigrants are advantaged compared with those who come later. This tends to be true for both groups and their leadership. By introducing a new group at the bottom of the absorption ladder, the group with longer tenure is "pushed up." The new group generally finds it harder to acclimate itself to the new country than those who preceded it. Especially regarding jobs, housing, and political power, the old-timers are likely to be very jealous of their privileges and suspicious of the demands of new groups. The groups

that perceive themselves as deprived are likely to call for a reallocation of resources to alleviate their deprivation rather than invest large sums on absorbing new immigrants.

Periods of Immigration

For our purposes, the hundred years between 1882 and 1982 can be divided into four categories. Each witnessed an expansion of the Jewish population in Israel, and each had an effect on the politics of the country.

THE FORMATIVE PERIOD: 1882-1924

The formative period saw the smallest immigration numerically, but was the most significant politically. The very limited and select immigration of rather homogeneous populations was the time of the initial emergence of the political leadership that was to dominate Israel's years of creation.[5]

Before 1880, fewer than 25,000 Jews lived in Eretz Israel. They were concentrated in the four holy cities of Jerusalem, Hebron, Tiberias, and Safed and spent their time largely in study and prayer. Sustained by monies collected from Jewish communities outside Eretz Israel, they prayed for the redemption of the land and the coming of the Messiah. Their reception of secular settlers who came to fulfill their prayers without divine help was notably cool.

The settlers of the first *aliyah* (1882-1903), numbering between 20,000 and 30,000, came in reaction to the growing anti-Semitism in Russia. Whereas most of their fellow Jewish immigrants went to the United States, this handful (compared with the 2.5 million Jews who left Eastern Europe between 1880 and 1924) responded to the nationalist awakening among Jews and immigrated to Eretz Israel. Many of them had received ideological instruction in the first organized nationalist Jewish groups known as Hovevei Zion, but were dramatically lacking in funds and agricultural skills. Religious Jewish settlers were especially hostile, seeing the newcomers not only as religious offenders but as competitors for the limited charity sent from abroad. The immigrants were relatively educated, from urban backgrounds, and totally unprepared for the barren wastelands they encountered in Eretz Israel. This brave beginning was rescued from ignominious failure by "import capital," money sent from abroad, a feature of Israeli life that would persist. The efforts of Baron Edmond de Rothschild, a noted Jewish philanthropist, rescued the settlers but installed Rothschild agents as overseers; soon the settlers became accustomed to turning to Paris for help and even sent their children to France to school. Many of them did not return.

The second *aliyah* (1904-14) came out of the ferment of the unsuccessful Russian revolution of 1905 with its attendant ideas of social equality and freedom. Of the 35,000 who came during this period almost all were from Russia, a few thousand from Rumania, and 2000 from Yemen. About 10,000 were pioneers in the sense of abandoning the easy life and comforts of home in order to participate in the Zionist revolution. Reports of malaria and other tribulations received from members of the first *aliyah* did not daunt them, but many proved unable to meet the challenge and left. This is the most important of the original *aliyot* in two senses: (1) Three top leaders of the formative period in Israel's history—David Ben-Gurion, Yitzhak Ben-Zvi, and Yosef Shprinzak, Israel's first prime minister, second president, and first Chairman of the Knesset, respectively—arrived then; and (2) the political organizations they founded would have the greatest impact on the future of the country.[6]

Largely young, single, dedicated socialists, the members of the second *aliyah* proved more innovative than their counterparts in the first. Of course, they had a firmer base on which to work, thanks to their predecessors' efforts. The newcomers were successful in developing new kinds of agricultural settlements and industry, and in promoting Jewish cultural activities. During this period political parties emerged, and the Histadrut was later created by them. These developments occurred naturally in response to challenges and problems faced in everyday living and not as a result of an ideological blueprint.

The interests of members of the first and second *aliyot* soon clashed. The young pioneers wanted to work at physical labor but found themselves shut out of businesses of their natural employers, the members of the first *aliyah*, because indigenous Arab labor was cheaper, more plentiful, and more experienced. Both sides used national-interest arguments, the landowners arguing that they were building a viable economy, the laborers pointing out that Jewish labor was an essential of a viable economy and that in its absence sizable immigration would not be possible. The battle over the "conquest of labor" was begun, and the laborers were successful in winning to their side the World Zionist Organization.[7] They set the tone for Jewish settlement and would ultimately emerge as national leaders. They also won the undying enmity of the plantation and orchard owners, an antagonism passed on from generation to generation in Israeli politics.

The success of the labor leaders was not in their ability to organize the workers nor increase immigration substantially. In fact, most of the laborers were not organized in either of the two labor parties of the day, nor did they work predominantly in agricultural occupations. But they set a course and developed a commonality of cause and internal cohesion, which are preconditions of any politically successful organization.[8]

The years of the First World War saw a cessation of immigration and the ultimate liberation of Palestine from the Ottoman Empire by the British and

Allied armies. In 1917, British Secretary of State for Foreign Affairs Arthur James Balfour sent Lord Rothschild his famous declaration announcing the support of the British government for Zionist aspirations in Palestine. And in the 1922 League of Nations Mandate for Palestine, article 6 stated that "the Administration of Palestine, while ensuring that the rights and position of other sections of the population are not prejudiced, shall facilitate Jewish immigration under suitable conditions."

Immigration to Eretz Israel picked up again at the beginning of the 1920s with the end of the First World War and during the convulsions that swept over Russia in its revolution and attendant civil war. Most of the 35,000 members of the third *aliyah* (1919-23) came from Russia, 15,000 of them identifying themselves as pioneers. This influx of Jews brought the population in 1922 to 85,000, the same as it had been in 1914, counterbalancing those who had left.[9]

The third *aliyah* comprised mostly young, single males from Poland and Russia who had been prepared for their immigration by participation in agricultural training programs in Europe organized by Zionist organizations. They entered a more structured environment than had the members of the first and second *aliyot,* and strong ideological motivation was prevalent among them. Their experiences in Europe taught them the importance of political organization and control, and their nationalism brought them to Eretz Israel rather than America or other destinations. They accepted the authority of leaders already living in Israel (who were only a few years older than they) but pressured for their own goals. Many of them were members of groups, which afforded internal cohesion to their efforts and magnified their influence in the system. They and their predecessors of the second *aliyah* formed the generation of Israel's founding fathers.[10]

We have seen how immigration was shaped by international developments as well as by the motivation of the immigrants. A third factor was the policy of the ruling authorities to immigration. The Turks opposed immigration but because of the system of capitulations under which Europeans enjoyed extraterritorial privileges throughout the Turkish Empire, and because of the ineffectiveness of the officers of the Ottoman administration to police immigration, about 80,000 Jews arrived in Eretz Israel between 1880 and 1914.[11] The British were conscious of Arab sensitivities to the growing Jewish population and were more aggressive in attempting to establish a policy of immigration during their Mandate.

The formula developed by the British was "economic absorptive capacity," and the immigration ordinance of 1920 tried to implement the formula by allowing in Jews of independent means, those with religious occupations, and dependents of residents. Beyond that, only "subsidized immigrants" (that is, those whose maintenance was guaranteed by the World Zionist Organization for one year, later to be redefined as those who had a definite prospect of employment) were admitted, and then only up to the quota set by the authorities. The subsidized immigrant category was specified in the labor schedule that the department of immigration of the Jewish Agency prepared; when approved by the British High Commissioner, labor schedule certificates were issued to the World Zionist Executive, which distributed them according to a party key with each party receiving certificates in rough proportion to its political strength in the country.

1925-48

The period from 1925 to 1948 is the generation of the Mandate, the struggle against the British, the struggle against the Nazis, the struggle for immigration, and ultimately independence.

Quotas were also being set in the United States to restrict the inflow of immigrants in the 1920s, and so when conditions in Poland provided a "push" for many Jews to leave that country, and as the economic depression in Europe worsened, the fourth *aliyah* (1924-30) arrived. Eighty-two thousand Jews arrived in this period, 35,000 in 1925 alone.[12] If the third *aliyah* was Russian and ideological, the fourth was Polish and middle class. Unlike the penniless socialists of the earlier *aliyot,* many of the Poles had some independent means, and their capitalism flourished. But in 1927 there was a severe economic crisis, and the economic foundations of the Yishuv, concentrated in agriculture, could not absorb large numbers of urban-oriented migrants. Unemployment was very high, and starting in late 1926, Jewish emigration gained momentum. Some 23,000 of the 80,000 immigrants of the fourth *aliyah* are estimated to have left the country. In 1927 emigration exceeded immigration.

The fifth *aliyah* (1932-38) reacted to the spread of anti-Jewish activities in Central and Eastern Europe, especially the rise of Hitler in 1933. This was a huge immigration by local standards, numbering some 200,000. In 1935 alone a record 66,000 Jews arrived. The Jewish population of the country more than doubled in five years. The fifth *aliyah,* while often called the "German *aliyah,*" in fact comprised only a quarter of German and Austrian Jews. The biggest group numerically was from Poland, which did, after all, have the largest concentration of Jews in the world at that time; the biggest decline was from the USSR because restrictions on emigration were enforced. These Central European Jews brought with them capital for investment and, along with their middle-class backgrounds, urban life styles and organizational skills.

In the aftermath of the mass immigration of the 1920s and 1930s the local Arab population reacted violently with demonstrations, strikes, and attacks.

By 1939 the Jews, who had made up 4 percent of the population in 1882, had become 30 percent through immigration (see table 2.1 on page 21). Economic difficulties fed Arab resentment. The British reaction was to severely limit the immigration of Jews. In 1933 and 1934 the Jewish Agency requested 60,000 labor certificates; the British allocated less than 18,000. In 1936, 10,695 were requested but only 1800 were approved. The problem could not be overcome easily. In 17 years the Arab population had increased by 50 percent, the Jewish population by 500 percent.

The British introduced political criteria, as opposed to economic criteria, in setting the quota of Jewish immigrants and determined that 12,000 Jews per year would be the "political high level," or upper limit. This figure was more or less achieved for the years between 1936 and 1938, the figure jumping to 30,000 in 1939. Most of the immigrants came from Germany and Austria. As the clouds of war gathered, international immigration slowed to a trickle, but for the first time, Eretz Israel became the major migration destination of world Jewry.

The British White Paper of 1939 limited Jewish immigration to 75,000 for the next five-year period, making the Jews a third of the population and then terminating immigration. By the date the White Paper had immigration ending, only about 50,000 Jews had immigrated. Illegal immigration had existed throughout the Mandate, and since 1934 illegal immigrants were deducted from the quota of Jews permitted to enter Eretz Israel (if the number of illegals could be determined). After World War II, tens of thousands attempted to enter illegally, and many were successful. But after mid-1946, most of these Jewish survivors of European persecution were intercepted and 56,000 of them were imprisoned on Cyprus. Between 1945 and mid-1948 about 75,000 Jews came, most of them illegally.

The organizational efforts required to sustain illegal immigration, preparing the Yishuv for armed conflict with the Arabs or the British by manufacturing or procuring weapons, raising and training an effective fighting force—all this alongside the legal activities of absorbing immigrants, strengthening the economy, and developing a social infrastructure—were enormous. The busyness of the period swept up groups and individuals and generated national enthusiasm and levels of self-sacrifice the loss of which were sometimes bemoaned by later generations who wished to return to "basic values." But on the verge of the symbolic victory of national independence there occurred the greatest modern tragedy to befall the Jewish people—the Holocaust. David Ben-Gurion's political wisdom in navigating these difficult straits raised him to a peak of popularity and general acceptance both in Israel and abroad. It was during this period of the multiplicity of tasks confronting the Yishuv that lieutenants were recognized for their organizational and leadership abilities, and careers in the public sector were begun.

The 1948 Declaration of Independence stated that "the State of Israel is open to Jewish immigration and the ingathering of Exiles." The first order enacted by the provisional government abolished the British restrictions on immigration and defined as legal those residents who had been "illegals" under British rule. Two years later, in 1950, after hundreds of thousands of Jews had come to the country, the Knesset passed the Law of Return which grants to every Jew in the world the right to immigrate to Israel.

1948-54

In 1948 the remnants of the European Jewish society immigrated, but soon after the founding of the state, communities of Jews born in Asia and Africa made up the bulk of the new immigrants. The large number of these immigrants doubled the Jewish population of the country within these years and heightened the already difficult economic conditions faced by the new country. Between 1948 and 1951, 700,000 immigrants were added to the 650,000 Jews already in Israel. Despite the enormous demographic change, the political leadership successfully adapted and remained in power. The Arabs again protested, this time through force of arms, with neighboring Arab states attacking the new state in an attempt to abort its birth. Many local Arabs left, thinking that this was a temporary exodus until the fighting halted, and they became the crux of the Palestinian refugee problem still festering in the region. The reaction of the refugees is familiar: Many German Jews in the 1930s believed that they had left "temporarily" until the Hitler nightmare passed, just as many Iranian Jews 50 years later set up temporary homes in Israel, France, or the United States, convinced that the Khomeini revolution would be shortlived.

After the establishment of the state, waves of immigration came at a fast and furious pace. First came the European immigrants imprisoned on Cyprus and in camps in Europe. Soon after, Jews from Bulgaria, Yugoslavia, Yemen, Aden, and Algeria arrived. In early 1949 there came Jews from Turkey and Libya and the entire 35,000 Jewish community of Yemen. Toward the end of 1949 the doors of Poland and Rumania were opened, and the Jews streamed out, followed the next year by Iraqis and many more Rumanians. The government was hard pressed to absorb, feed, and house the new immigrants. A war was being fought, and resources were scarce. Rationing of foodstuffs was introduced, and demands were made by leaders of the United Jewish Appeal in the United States to slow down immigration for six months in order to balance the budget. Ben-Gurion rejected all such pleas, arguing "economic conditions should be adjusted to immigration volume rather than the reverse."[13] The highest monthly immigration rate was recorded during the first seven months of 1951 when some 20,000 immigrants *a month* arrived in the country, mostly from Rumania and Iraq. This monthly rate was almost as large as the entire first *aliyah*.

1954 TO THE PRESENT

In 1951 the Jewish Agency announced "rules of selection," hoping to reduce the number of people sponsored by the Agency who were chronically ill, nonproductive laborers, or unwilling to settle in agricultural areas. The major realistic sources of potential immigration in the mid-1950s were Turkey and Iran with about 130,000 Jews still living there, and North Africa with half a million. Western countries did not seem a likely source, and the 3 million Jews in Eastern Europe and the Soviet Union were prevented from leaving. Before the restrictions were set, only about 30,000 came to Israel from North African countries, with many of the middle and upper classes making their way to France. It is not clear whether the restrictions prevented larger immigration; what is clear is that after the Israeli economy started to pick up again, after the German reparations began, and especially after the victory of the Sinai campaign of 1956, immigration from North Africa, especially Morocco, began to pick up. After reaching a low annual figure of 18,000 immigrants between 1952 and 1954, the figure reached 70,000 in 1957, with Jews arriving mostly from Morocco, Poland, and Egypt.

The matter of quotas for North African immigrants reached a peak in the mid-1950s, and Prime Minister Moshe Sharett raised the quotas from 2000 per month to 3500. The reasoning behind the government decision was that the economy could absorb no more. The similarity between this and the original 1922 British position is striking. When Ben-Gurion returned to office in 1955 as prime minister, the policy was nevertheless unchanged. The Herut movement consistently opposed all immigration restrictions during these years, while others regarded them as unfortunate but necessary. During its years in power, from 1977 to 1984, Herut's policy was not put to the test, for Israel's problem was a lack of immigration and a growing *yerida* (emigration, or "going down") and not limitations on immigration.

Immigration between 1961 and 1965 reached 230,000, coming mainly from Morocco and Rumania, with some from Argentina as well. By the Six Day War in 1967 the sources of potential immigration had changed. Eastern European and North African reservoirs were largely dried up, leaving Western countries and the Soviet Union. Of the 250,000 Jews given exit visas from the Soviet Union in the 1970s, only 160,000 came to Israel.[14]

The task of dealing with immigration was complicated by the emergence of two competing bureaucracies: the Jewish Agency and the government Ministry of Immigrant Absorption. The fact that politicians and bureaucrats dealing with the issue of immigration were often from different factions or parties made the competition for resources and control of immigration more intense.

Emigration

In Israel every new immigrant is viewed as an important contribution toward the goal of the ingathering of Jews. As a general estimate, about 10 to 15 percent of Israelis have left Israel over time. It is very hard to give an exact number because records are not kept on emigrants. The definition of "emigrant" presents difficulties because most Israelis living abroad, when asked, insist that they are planning to return. Official figures report that over 300,000 Israeli citizens reside abroad.[15]

The early 1950s witnessed the highest rate of outflow in Israeli history. The proportion of emigrants to immigrants was higher (although the absolute number was lower) in the 1950s than in the late 1970s, a period in which problems of emigration concerned the public.[16] Many of those who left in the 1950s spent a few months or a couple of years in Israel after the Holocaust and then left for other countries. For those never involved ideologically with Zionism, Israel was a safe haven in a very long nightmare. For others, living conditions in Israel were too hard.

Jews are known as a wandering people. The Zionist vision was that with a national homeland, certain of the "negative" features of the Diaspora would be expunged from the Jew, including his wanderlust. This has obviously not happened. Not only have most of the Jews not returned to Zion, but many continue in their mobile patterns. This was so even in the time of the second commonwealth, when the Jews made up 10 percent of the Roman Empire.[17] We also know that today, at every educational and income level, American Jews travel more than non-Jews.

Every indication points to the fact that the wandering will continue in the future. When asked whether they are considering emigration, about 14 percent of the adult Jewish population in Israel and about a quarter of those in their twenties report that they are.[18] Patterns of acceptability of this behavior seem stable, indicating that it is likely to continue into the future.

Non-Jews

The Jewish State of Israel has a sizable population of non-Jews. Table 2.1 points up clearly that the picture is not static. The complement of the percent of Jews in Israel is made up of non-Jews. Before the establishment of the state, they

TABLE 2.1

POPULATION OF JEWS IN ISRAEL AND THE WORLD, 1882-1982

Year	Size of population (in 000s)	Number of Jews in Israel (in 000s)	Percentage of Jews in Israel	Number of Jews in world (in millions)	Percentage of Jews of world in Israel
1882	600	24	4.0	7.7	0.3
1922	752	84	11.2	8.0	1.1
1939	1,545	464	30.0	16.6	2.8
1948	806	650	80.6	11.5	5.7
1954	1,718	1,526	88.8	11.9	12.8
1967	2,777	2,384	85.8	13.6	17.5
1982	4,064	3,373	83.0	14.5	22.8
	Including the territories:				
1967	3,744	2,384	63.7		
1982	5,288	3,373	63.8		

NOTE: Population figures up to 1939 are for Eretz Israel. The 1948 through 1980 figures above the line relate to the pre-1967 borders; population figures that include the territories are shown below the line.

SOURCES: Dov Friedlander and Calvin Goldscheider, *Population of Israel* (New York: Columbia University Press, 1979); Dan Horowitz and Moshe Lissak, *The Origins of the Israeli Polity: Palestine under the Mandate* (Chicago: University of Chicago Press, 1978); and various volumes of *Statistical Abstract* and the *American Jewish Yearbook*.

were a large majority. With statehood in 1948 their relative weight fell because the pre-1967 war boundaries excluded most of them. By 1954, after the Jewish population had more than doubled as a result of immigration, the concentration of Jews was at its highest, almost 90 percent. After that, the relative weight of non-Jewish Israelis grew steadily in spite of continued Jewish immigration because the non-Jewish rate of reproduction is higher than that of Jews. In 1982 the non-Jewish community constituted some 690,000 people, of whom 530,000 were Moslems, 94,000 Christians, and 65,000 Druze.[19] Their overall gross reproduction rate was 2.62 in 1980 compared with 1.34 for Jews. The Moslem rate was 2.90, the Christian rate 1.29, and that of the Druze 2.95.[20] If the Arabs of the territories are added to these calculations, Jews make up a smaller majority of the Eretz Israel population (see table 2.1 above).

A lively debate exists among demographers regarding the future structure of Israel's population. Assumptions regarding politics, immigration, emigration, fertility, and morality must be made. Suffice it to say that the demographic factor will continue to be dominant in the political calculations and social realities that develop in the future.

Sephardim-Ashkenazim

If non-Jewish demographic developments are often barely evident in the body politic of Israel, developments within the Jewish community are very evident. The two major developments since 1948 are the growth of Israel-born Jews, who now comprise more than half the Jewish population in Israel, and the halving of the European- or American-born population from more than half to less than a quarter.

In Israeli politics one of the dominant criteria used is ethnicity, not the Jewish and non-Jewish distinction, but intra-Jewish ethnicity. The subject is a complex one, but the major distinction among Jews is between Ashkenazim, who came to Israel from Europe and America, and Sephardim, who immigrated from countries of Asia and Africa. While the terms are commonly used in contemporary Israeli politics, they obscure as much as they reveal because they are borrowed from other spheres. They have their origins in the medieval period of sojourning in the Diaspora of the various communities following different expulsions throughout history.[21] More appropriately, three divisions should be used, consisting of an Oriental (eastern) community of Jews who never left Asia and Africa; the Sephardim, whose language (Ladino) and ethnic culture originated in Spain before the expulsion of 1492; and the Ashkenazim (referring to Germany), whose hybrid language was Yiddish. Sometimes language is suggested as a base of distinction, but today both Ladino and Yiddish are vanishing languages, and in any case they did not penetrate everywhere.[22] Hebrew is increasingly taught to Jews around the world, and the earlier language distinction is failing.

Keeping in mind that we are compressing too much into the popularly used dichotomy of Sephardim and Ashkenazim, we shall also rely on the usage of the government's Central Bureau of Statistics, which reports place of birth and father's place of birth (see table 2.2). There is a very high correlation between the European- or American-born and Ashkenazim, and the Asian- or African-born and Sephardim, and hence we shall use the terms interchangeably. We should remember, though, that differences between Iraqi and Moroccan Jews (both called Sephardim here) are as great or greater than differences between Russian and German Jews (both Ashkenazim). The more recent interaction of these Jews with their host country varied their common heritage as Sephardim or Ashkenazim just as a more distant history varied the common heritage shared by all Jews as they were developing the rituals, traditions, and language shared only by Ashkenazim or Sephardim.

Of the 14.5 million Jews in the world, about 85 percent are Ashkenazim and 15 percent Sephardim. About 10 percent of the world's Ashkenazim live

TABLE 2.2
VOTING POTENTIAL OF THE JEWISH POPULATION IN ISRAEL, 1969 AND 1981

	Percentage in population		Percentage under voting age		Knesset seats[a]	
	1967	1980	1969	1981	1969	1981
Israel-born; father Israel-born	6.5	13.2	62.3	70.7	4	6
Israel-born; father Asian- or African-born	18.7	25.3	81.6	53.7	5	18
Israel-born; father European- or American-born	16.4	16.4	49.1	35.8	13	16
Asian- or African-born	27.8	20.0	11.5	1.7	38	30
European- or American-born	30.6	25.1	3.6	5.1	46	36
TOTAL (number and percent)	2,344,877	3,218,400	31.6%	30.5%	106	106

SOURCES: *Statistical Abstract, 1969*, 42–43; *Statistical Abstract, 1981*, 56–57.

a. Assuming 80 percent participation; 12,000 votes per seat in 1969, 17,000 votes per seat in 1981.

in Israel, compared with about two-thirds of the Sephardim. The Sephardim today make up about 55 percent of Israel's Jewish population, and the Ashkenazim about 45 percent. The composition of the two ethnic groups in terms of place of birth is different from one another. Of Israel's 3,370,000 Jews in 1983, more than 785,000 were born in Europe and America, about 650,000 in Asia and Africa.[23] The number of Israel-born whose fathers were born in Europe and America was a little over 530,000, whereas the Israel-born of Asian- or African-born fathers numbered more than 860,000. An additional 580,000 were born in Israel of fathers who were also born in Israel. At this stage of Israel's development, but not in 15 or 20 years, it is safe to conclude that most of the last group are Ashkenazim, reflecting their earlier arrival in the country.

The reproduction rates of the various ethnic groups are also different, although less so over time. The gross reproduction rate of Jewish mothers born in Asia or Africa was 1.47 in 1980 compared with 2.04 in 1969; for European- or American-born Jewish mothers, it was 1.34 in 1980 compared with 1.32 in 1969. The rate for Israel-born mothers has changed too, from 1.43 in 1969 to 1.34 in 1980.[24] Because the age structure and growth rates of the groups differ, the impact on the political system through the composition of the electorate is not identical (see table 2.2). European- or American-born voters and their Israel-born children constituted a majority of the electorate in 1981 as they did in past elections, but they will soon be smaller in number than the Asian and African voters and their Israel-born voting children. We have seen that the latter group is already a majority of the Jewish population in Israel and that their growth rates are higher than the Europeans. In the 1981 elections the Ashkenazim had a voting potential of 52 Knesset seats, the Sephardim 48. The shrinking of the Ashkenazi base is evident when compared with their potential in the 1969 elections: 59 for the Ashkenazim, 43 for the Sephardim. The potential of the Sephardim will be more fully realized when their children who are under voting age (53.7 percent for the Asian and African children, 35.8 percent for the European and American children) begin voting and when the Ashkenazim, who tend to be older and who have fewer children, make up an increasingly smaller percentage of the electorate.

The shifting mosaic of Israel's Jewish population is likely to persist. That its composition can determine Israel's strength and vitality goes without saying. A country that invests in young people in school, army, and university only to see them set up families in distant lands has an important problem to face. External events and internal conditions in Israel will influence the rate and composition of immigration. While facing the challenges of the next hundred years, the achievements of the first hundred, with their dilemmas and lessons, must be kept in mind.

3. Political Economy

The form of economy in Israel is a mixture of government activity and state planning, along with free enterprise. Israel's economic ideology, regardless of the party in power, is toward an activist welfare state, which in turn condones a high degree of concentration of economic might at the centers of power. The relative poverty of the country in resources and the tremendous expenses of defense and immigration absorption projects have created a highly centralized, overstretched economy. Dependent on the infusion of funds from abroad and dedicated to ensuring minimum standards for its population, a highly institutionalized network of organizations and bureaucracies has developed.

The economy provides an excellent example of many of the major features of Israeli public life.[1] The economy is highly centralized and is characterized by a high level of government influence. It provides the Jewish people living outside Israel with a tangible link with the country and its development. The economy is dependent on loans and grants from foreign countries, especially the United States. Costs of the defense effort make up the single largest expenditure and influence the structure of the entire governmental budget. The economy is a major political resource, and politicians have not hesitated to derive political and organizational benefits from its manipulation. High levels of subsidies for basic consumer goods and public transportation have characterized the policies of both the Alignment and the Likud, but income inequality, while not as high as in other countries, has been growing. Unemployment is kept relatively low, but the inflation rate has been extremely high, mortgaging future generations to the standards of living and huge loans in foreign and local currencies indulged in today. The economy usually skews in favor of the salaried class immediately before elections. Attempts to reform the economy are difficult because of the structures that exist and the political unpopularity of such moves.

Prime Movers

Israel's political economy can only be understood in terms of the historical developments that produced the system. Imagine an economy with few if any raw materials; with great needs for funds to finance political and social projects; with connections to individuals, institutions, and governments abroad interested in aiding it; and with an administrative elite intensely loyal to the overriding goals of the economy yet flexible and ambitious enough to attempt an enterprise that was theoretically not promising. Add to this the need for secrecy, and the result may be something resembling the Israeli economy. These generalizations have held for the entire period of modern Jewish settlement in Eretz Israel, although the details have changed. The need for secrecy, for example, was originally intended to prevent the British mandatory power from discovering clandestine efforts at absorbing illegal immigrants. Secrecy was often justified because of a project's connection with security needs or, later, to allow Israel to deal with firms or countries that did not want these dealings to become public knowledge.

It is useful to think of three prime movers in the Israeli economy: the World Zionist Organization, the Histadrut, and the Israeli government. These prime movers were responsible for fashioning the Israeli economy and for developing it. At different points in the development of the economy of Eretz Israel since the 1920s, economic power has been distributed differently among the three.

NATIONAL INSTITUTIONS

The most important prime mover of the pre-state period was the World Zionist Organization (WZO). After World War 1, development of the economy was spurred by immigrants coming with capital of their own, but mostly it came about because of the activities of the WZO and the monies it collected abroad and expended in Eretz Israel. The WZO was founded by Theodor Herzl in 1897 and now meets once every four years based on elections held by Jews all over the world. Since statehood, the results of the Knesset elections determine Israel's representations to the Zionist Congress. Since 1959, Israel has had 38 percent of the delegates, the United States 29 percent, and all other countries together 33 percent. At the 1982 Congress there were 601 delegates.

The structure of the WZO is pyramidal; above the broad base of the Congress are the executive committee and the directorate. These bodies have representatives in the parties of the Congress, and power tends to be shared, although important functions are kept for the major party if possible. Israeli parties are dominant, and the payoffs and politics of the WZO are often a direct extension of party politics in Israel.

The aim of the Jewish Agency was to assist and encourage Jews throughout the world to help in the development and settlement of Eretz Israel. When the League of Nations established a Mandate for Palestine in 1922, it provided that "an appropriate Jewish agency" be set up to cooperate with Britain, the mandatory power. The Jewish Agency thus derived its name. The executive of the Jewish Agency was the chief decision-making body in Eretz Israel and became the "state in the making."

It was natural upon achieving independence for the chairman of the Agency executive (Ben-Gurion) to become prime minister and the head of the political department (Sharett) to become foreign minister. The political importance of the Agency far exceeded that of local institutions such as Knesset Israel, the Electors' Council (Asefat Nivharim), and the National Committee (Vaad Leumi). It was the Agency that had close working contacts with the mandatory power, and by 1930, as the outlook for the future of European Jewry darkened, it became even more important. By 1935 Mapai had won control of the Agency executive and Ben-Gurion had become its chairman. Such control was important symbolically because the fight over control of the Zionist movement between Jews living in Eretz Israel and those living abroad had gone on for a long time. Even more important were the political implications, for the ascent of Mapai shifted control of the monies collected from abroad to Eretz Israel and from nonsocialist parties to socialist ones.

Two other important organizations of the WZO in the pre-state period still exist, although their functions have largely been eclipsed by the state. The first is the United Jewish Appeal (Keren Hayesod/Magbit), which is the money-raising arm of the Zionist movement. Since it is often less problematic for Jews throughout the world to contribute to a Jewish philanthropic organization rather than directly to the State of Israel, the organization serves important functions, although its efforts are closely coordinated by the finance minister and the government. The ideology of the appeals is that Jews around the world have a responsibility to support Israel and therefore should contribute to it through a worldwide organization. The second important organization is the Keren Kayemet, which was charged with purchasing and reclaiming the land. When the state was formed, many of its functions passed naturally to state authorities. The Israel Lands Administration is caretaker of nationalized land, which comprises more than 90 percent of pre-1967 Israel.

The WZO and the Jewish Agency are still very active in encouraging *aliyah,* in youth and educational work, in settlement, and in welfare work. However, friction exists between the government's Ministry of Immigrant Absorption and the Jewish Agency regarding immigration. As for settlements, different policy preferences have been expressed by senior bureaucrats of opposing parties. The result is conflicting bureaucratic initiatives with personal and organizational interests at stake.[2] The WZO and the Jewish Agency are important sources of income for social projects in Israel, thus freeing the government's budget for other purposes. Also, the continued existence of these organizations allows for activity and involvement by many non-Israeli Jews.

Relations between the State of Israel and the WZO and the Jewish Agency were formalized in 1952. This in effect froze the situation that then existed and recognized the WZO's and the Jewish Agency's continued activity in the fields of settlement, immigration, and education. After independence, the Agency was very active in the economy, owning Raasco (which mainly did construction and had set up 40 settlements), and Bank Leumi, the country's largest bank. In addition the Agency had partial ownership and control of Mekorot and Tahal, which develop water projects; Amidar, which provides and manages moderately priced housing developments; El Al, Israel's national airline; Zim, Israel's major shipping line; and the *Jersualem Post,* the country's major English-language newspaper. This partial list, along with a series of affiliated corporations, indicates the wide scope of the Agency's activities and its role in the economy. The WZO and the Jewish Agency are still active in the economy and are important political plums in Israeli politics.

THE HISTADRUT

The clearest organizational expression of political and economic power in the pre-state period was the Histadrut. Formed in 1920 by socialist parties to further the economic, social, and cultural interests of the Jewish worker in Eretz Israel, it became an important power base for socialist parties.[3] Apart from representing workers in the negotiation of contracts with employers, it also incorporated the important collectivist enterprises of the country, including the kibbutz and the moshav. In addition the Histadrut was a major employer in its own right, supplying social welfare and economic services including education, health, housing, culture, banking, insurance, and sport.

Cooperation between the Histadrut and WZO, and later with the state, allowed a pooling of resources. Bank Hapoalim, for instance, was set up by the Histadrut with the help of the WZO. During the state period the treasury allowed the Histadrut's pension funds to be invested in Hevrat Ovdim, the Histadrut's holding company, giving it a sure source of capital.

The structure of the Histadrut has changed little since the pre-state years, although there are some instances of activities being transferred to or transformed by the state. The Histadrut holds elections among its members every four years, using a list system, in which most of the political parties of Israel compete. In 1981 there were close to 1.5 million members, more than 80 percent of the employed working force of the country. The Alignment has always won an absolute majority in Histadrut elections and has thus completely controlled this important source of power and patronage. The Histadrut's economic activities were historically significant because it was willing to pioneer in sectors that would not attract a capitalist investor. Since the ideology was developing the economic base of the homeland and creating a class of Jewish workers in Eretz Israel, its economic behavior was often prone to take risks.

The Histadrut's role in the economy can be divided into four categories. First, there is the administration, which involves bureaucrats and functionaries of the central administration; the executive committee, workers' councils, trade unions, Kupat Holim (the sick fund), pension plans, social welfare funds, *Davar* (the Histadrut's newspaper), and the *Jerusalem Post* (the English-language newspaper jointly owned with the Jewish Agency). The most important of these is Kupat Holim, employing almost 29,000 people in 1982 and a major consumer of medical supplies and other commodities.

Second are the economic enterprises, which include Sollel Boneh, Koor, Shikun Ovdim, Hasneh, and Bank Hapoalim, to name the major ones. Each is a leader in its field, and each has an important impact on the economy.[4] Sollel Boneh, for example, conducts 20 percent of the building activity in the country and employs more than 17,000 workers (not including workers abroad). Koor has more than 100 industrial firms, some 100 commercial firms, and 50 administrative and financial firms including pension funds whose monies finance many other projects. It is listed in *Fortune* magazine's list of the 500 largest companies in the world.[5] Koor is the country's largest industrial exporter and in 1981 employed almost 30,000 workers. The details can be expanded, but the point remains the same: The Histadrut is a key economic and political force of power in the country.

Third are the cooperative organizations set up to facilitate cooperative marketing for members. This includes Hamashbir Hamerkazi department stores, Tnuva, and supermarkets. Tnuva is the country's largest supplier of fresh produce; in 1980 it supplied two-thirds of the country's fresh agricultural produce.

Fourth is the cooperative economy, which encompasses the kibbutz, the moshav, and other cooperative ventures. In this area work some 21,000 workers, but less than 10,000 of them are members of the cooperatives. Difficult ideological problems are faced because the norm is against exploiting hired labor. Egged and Dan, for example, transportation cooperatives that account for 80 percent of the country's passenger movement, are periodically plagued with tensions between drivers who are cooperative members and drivers who are salaried employees. Another example is the 11 regional enterprises set up by the major kibbutz movement; of the 6000 workers, 1200 are kibbutz members. The perceived exploitation by these enterprises of the surrounding (largely Sephardi) population in development towns became symbolic in the 1981 elections of the ethnic tensions that dominated the atmosphere.

The kibbutz and moshav are prime examples of Israeli inventiveness and adaptation. They continue to perform agricultural miracles and have become active in industrial enterprises, which now account for half their product. But during the pre-state and early state periods these agricultural settlements—especially the kibbutz—were the focus of political and ideological power as well as economic success. This role of moral leadership has been eclipsed, and the decline of the kibbutz in the public mind is both cause and effect of the decline of the Alignment. But its economic achievements stand.

The roof organization of the settlement movements is the Agricultural Center. It represents 650 agricultural settlements, 385 moshavim and 265 kibbutzim. They are dominant in most fields of agricultural endeavor, and in some fields (such as milk or flowers) they control almost all production. In all, the agricultural sector affiliated with the Histadrut produces 84 percent of Israel's produce.

The economic power of the Histadrut is a major factor in the Israeli economy. When it and the government are controlled by the same group, the potential political and economic power is awesome—and that was the case between 1948 and 1977. Even with the ascent of the Likud, the Histadrut continued to play a major role in the economy, and political charges notwithstanding, there was no evidence during its years in power of the Likud's trying to use its control of the government to weaken the economic strength of the Histadrut. The challenge to the Histadrut was at political and ideological levels.

THE GOVERNMENT OF ISRAEL

The government is by far the largest actor in the Israeli economy, and its role is growing. The public sector can be divided into three categories: units that provide governmental services, business enterprises of the state, and state-owned corporations.

The first category, units that provide governmental services, is the most extensive of the three. Activities are undertaken by governmental ministries or special units set up by the Knesset and financed by the public treasury. The category includes defense; ministries concerned with promoting certain aspects of the economy (energy, agriculture, atomic energy, transportation, industry and commerce, tourism, communication) or activities important to the economy (subsidizing credit and supporting public transportation); ministries concerned with the social welfare (education, health, labor, immigrant absorption, religious affairs, building, and housing) and activities related to public welfare (aid to the broadcasting authority, subsidizing basic food articles, and agricultural production); services of a general or administrative nature (the president, the Knesset, the prime minister's office, the ministries of finance, interior, police, justice, foreign affairs, the state controller, financing political parties); and municipal and local government arrangements for firefighting, water, and sewage.[6]

The second category is the business enterprises of the state, such as railroads, lands administration, the port of Jaffa, the government printer, and the arms industry. These sell services and goods, and finance their operations largely by these sales. Another area of government activity is the statutory authority, established by law, which overlaps with activities already mentioned. They include the commissions for production and marketing in the various agricultural areas (citrus, vegetables, tobacco, milk products), Magen David Adom (the Israeli Red Cross), Yad Vashem (the Holocaust memorial organization), the national social security institute, local authorities, the Bank of Israel, the council for higher education, the employment service, the ports authority, the airports authority, religious councils, the broadcasting authority, and the national sport lottery. This list does not have to be exhaustive to underscore the point that the government is active in many facets of the Israeli society.

Government corporations, the third category, operate in areas such as natural resources, development, and tourism. The Goverment Corporations Law identifies a government company as one with at least 50 percent government ownership or 50 percent participation in its direction. Using this definition there were almost 200 such corporations at the end of the 1970s. But if we add the subsidiaries of these companies and joint ventures between government and private owners and the more than 120 corporations set up by municipalities, the real scope of the activity becomes clearer. Some of Israel's most important government corporations include El Al, Israel Chemicals, the aircraft industry (with 20,000 employees), and the Dead Sea Works, a subsidiary of Israel Chemicals.

Government corporations allow the government more flexibility of action in the marketplace than is usually the case with units under strict public scrutiny and financed by the treasury. But all countries face the problem of these corporations becoming empires unto themselves, either not responsive to public demands or too dependent on the politicians who set up the corporations. In Israel each corporation is responsible to a minister, but the diversity and complexity of the corporation demand unusual talents to direct them effectively.

The picture of the Israeli economy painted in the preceding pages heavily emphasizes the structures created by public institutions both before and after the founding of the state. While the public sector is undoubtedly very influential, the private sector must not be ignored.[7] With all its centralization and the influence of the government on its economy, Israel has encouraged private investment and economic activity. Many of these undertakings have proved beneficial to the investor and the economy alike. Corporations such as Klal or Hevra Leisrael were set up under very favorable terms in order to attract investment by Jews abroad. Bank Discount, Israel's third largest bank (after the Jewish

Agency's Bank Leumi and the Histadrut's Bank Hapoalim) has its roots in the private sector. Important local and international figures have invested in the Israeli economy, often with the encouragement and sometimes in affiliation with public-sector enterprises. Both the socialist Alignment and the nationalist Likud have made efforts to encourage this kind of investment, offering loans, collateral, or tax rebates as incentives.

Performance and Government Activity

The enormity of Israel's economic achievements is not to be downplayed. By 1982 its gross national product was almost $22 billion. Between 1950 and 1976 the GNP increased by nearly 9 percent a year in constant prices and by 4.7 percent a year on a per capita basis. After that, growth stagnated (as it did in the rest of the world), GNP increasing by 2 percent in constant prices in 1975 and by only 1 percent in the late 1970s.[8] Nevertheless, when calculated on a per capita basis, this gave Israel a standard of living higher than that of Italy. On an absolute basis Israel's gross national product was higher than that of Egypt, although Egypt has a population more than ten times the size of Israel's. This fact is even more impressive when we take into account that the Israeli economy was about 40 percent that of Egypt's GNP after independence in 1948.

The government has played a very active role in the Israeli economy. Its control of the budget, the rate of exchange, the money supply (nominally controlled by the Bank of Israel), and the granting of licenses, loans and grants make it the single most important actor in the Israeli economy. So enormous is its influence that Yair Aharoni, a close observer of the Israeli economy, estimates that the impact of the government and its policies on the economy's performance is 90 percent. Almost any subject discussed will find the government's activity. The government is the country's biggest employer and its largest customer. It controls important economic resources: land, money, raw materials, water, and the right to grant or deny the use of these and related potential sources of income. The government determines subsidies, wages, and taxes, and in effect determines the standard of living for the bulk of the population.[9] Most imported foodstuffs are imported by the government or by government license, while food production is regulated by public commissions on which the government has major representation. Many raw materials are imported by government monopolies. Wage guidelines are set for salaried workers in consultation with the government; cost-of-living increases, so important in a country of three-digit (or more) inflation, are also determined after government consultation. Prices can be fixed by the appropriate ministry on goods deemed vital or on goods that enjoy the status of monopolistic commodities. Capital formation, investment programs, and the licensing of banks are other areas of government influence and activity.

The key ingredient in the government's influence over the economy is that for all practical purposes it has monopolized the capital market. Israelis save at a very high rate, mostly through retirement funds partially financed by employers, through investment plans, and through the stock market. Most of this activity is supervised by the finance ministry by way of issuing licenses to banks, or financial institutions under the control of the banks, that conduct such investments. Although this supervision is ostensibly to protect the public, in effect it allows the ministry tremendous leverage on the economy; the ministry controls the investment activity of the banks and financial institutions. In practice most of these monies are channeled into projects in tune with the priorities and goals of the government budget. For example, the finance minister, with the approval of the finance committee of the Knesset, can approve bond issues with tax reductions that obviously have a great influence on how the public invests its money. Other bonds are issued for institutional investments, thus creating a mechanism to absorb the very large amounts of money in pension funds.

The key to Israel's political economy is dependence and influence rather than outright control and direction. With its power to control prices and provide licenses, with its monopolization of the capital market, and with its subsidizing of foodstuffs, transportation, land, and housing (in certain areas), most actors in the Israeli economy are influenced by and many are dependent on government policies. This dependency makes the economy highly sensitive to changes in personnel and policy. It also makes the positions of leadership of the finance ministry potentially powerful. But this dependency lowers the likelihood of change in the system because radical change breaks the dependency relations that are so important to both sides. It is easy, for instance, to raise wages before elections; it is extremely difficult to cut them back afterward.

The ministries that deal with economic matters are aided by the Knesset's penchant for delegating to the appropriate minister many of the details of legislation. This transfer of legislative activity to the executive branch allows the Knesset to deal in principle while the ministries deal with details, but in reality it means that enormous economic and political power is concentrated in the economic ministries. What is even more notable from a political point of view is that economic decision making in Israel ultimately leads to the government, and within the government to the finance ministry, especially to the minister and the director of the budget. Enormous power rests in these positions in the Israeli system, the finance ministry usually having an "agent" participating in key deliberations throughout the public sector *before* budgetary decisions are made. Having the information beforehand prevents the finance ministry from being surprised by an enterprising governmental unit and gives the ministry an effective veto for all plans and projects.

The use of the term "veto" is important because it would be incorrect to foster the impression that the finance ministry, its minister, or the budget director can easily bring about a revolution in the economic arrangements of Israel. The Israeli economy is simply too complex, and the interests and organizations at work are too many to be easily bent to the will or policy of determined men. For example, in 1980 Yigael Hurewitz talked gloomily of the Israeli economy not being able to continue at its rate of government activity and expenditure, but he was forced to resign when the political calculations of the government brought in very different conclusions. It can be asserted, though, that when the top political leadership is united in attempting to achieve a goal, the chances of achieving it are greatly enhanced. And if the Histadrut and the political leadership are together, the chances increase accordingly. But when there are disagreements, the most likely outcome is that things will go along pretty much as they had before the issue came to the fore.

The political-economic leadership has more power preventing developments they see as negative or unnecessary than making drastic changes in the regular order of things. Most change that can be effected is incremental in nature. The system is simply too enmeshed, the interests too variegated, and the force of habit too great to allow for sweeping change. Furthermore, sweeping change demands much more political and bureaucratic clout than most political-economic leaders have had or have wanted to expend. The rule of thumb gleaned from Israeli political history is that finance ministers have usually been left to do their own thing, the prime minister being either too unknowledgeable or too preoccupied with other issues to involve himself in the economy. Nevertheless, other ministers quickly become spokesmen for ministries they are charged to lead and fiercely resist cuts in their budgets or perceived infringement on their turf. The high degree of concentration of Israel's economy should not be misunderstood to mean that structural changes can be brought about overnight. The actual meaning of the phenomenon is that almost all enterprises in the Israeli system see in the finance ministry the source of support or funds for expansion in good times or salvation in bad ones. And these, of course, are political and not exclusively economic issues.

An extremely important source of power for the finance minister and his advisers is their ability to determine the appointment of key figures in the economy. Many industries and economic units are directly tied in with government, and others are dependent on it. If the politicians who head the finance ministry desire to do so, they can influence the composition of a board of directors in the public sector by placing people loyal to them or by placing party activists in key positions throughout the economy. This practice stems from their power or their perceived power. More than that, their influence is not always needed; often appointments will be made in anticipation that they will find favor in the eyes of government leaders. This is the sure test of power because anticipatory behavior is a sign of a very large measure of influence and control.

It is little wonder that the finance minister is considered to be one of the most powerful persons in Israeli politics. In the 29 years of Alignment rule, finance was one of the few ministries never to be held by anyone but a Mapai member. Even the defense ministry was given to Rafi after 1967 (first to Moshe Dayan and then to Shimon Peres), but the powerful leaders who served as finance ministers (Eliezer Kaplan, Levi Eshkol, Pinhas Sapir) were all Mapai leaders, as were two weaker personalities but important Mapai functionaries (Zeev Sharf and Yehoshua Rabinowitz) who also held the post. It was natural for the Likud in 1977 to give its top post to Prime Minister Begin and the role of finance minister to Simha Ehrlich, the leader of the Liberals, the other major party of the Likud. He was followed by Yigael Hurewitz of a smaller Likud party, then by Yoram Aridor, and later by Yigael Cohen-Orgad, both dedicated Herut members. In the National Unity Government of 1984, the finance minister was Yitzhak Modai of the Liberal party.

For certain financial decision-making cases, such as the setting of salaries for Knesset members, ministers, and judges, or the amount to be paid to political parties for financing their activities or the activities of government corporations or special allocations, the approval of the Knesset Finance Committee is also needed. This committee reflects the composition of the governing coalition and usually presents no problem (see chapter 9). The cooperation of the chairman of the finance committee is essential, making him one of the most powerful people in Israeli politics. Close cooperation between the finance minister and the chairman of the finance committee can mean an enormous concentration of power.

An idea of the direct involvement of the government can be gleaned by the development of the economy by sectors. While it is not easy to measure these things, it is widely agreed that the relative size of the government sector in the economy is growing. It is customary to speak of three sectors of the Israeli economy: the private sector, the government sector, and the Histadrut sector. Working on data for the first 15 years of statehood, Haim Barkai concluded that the public sector (government) and the Histadrut sector accounted for about 20 percent each of the net domestic product and that "the share of the government sector in net product has been growing since 1953."[10] Barkai's calculations did not include the activities of the Jewish Agency and were made before the increase of military spending that occurred after the Yom Kippur War of 1973. For 1969, based on employment figures, the public sector employed 33.6 percent of salaried workers, the Histadrut sector 18.1 percent, and the private sector 48.3 percent.[11] Using economic figures of the early 1980s (not employment statistics), Yair Aharoni estimates that the private sector accounts for about 40 percent of economic activity in the country, the Histadrut 20 percent, and the government 40 percent.

One legacy of Israel's unique history was the expectation that any problem worthy of solving would be financed by the government or one of its agencies. Also, most projects could be presented in a way that would appeal to leaders anxious to implement Israel's priorities of security, economic development, social justice, and full employment. Loans would have to be guaranteed to attract industry; settlements would have to be built to enhance security; communication and transportation could be important in time of emergency; scientific and technological excellence must be pursued; housing must be provided; health services and hospitals must be improved; and so on. Few activities were outside the scope of government. There were political consequences to these economic activities. Regardless of the motivations of the leaders who initiated the projects, they led to a tremendous concentration of power and resources in the hands of a very small number of politicians and civil servants. And when new immigrants widely perceived that their promotions and even their jobs depended on retaining the present bosses in power (as was the case through the 1950s and perhaps later as well), these perceptions could be translated into electoral victories and power perpetuation.

Direct government activity is very high; the national budget in 1980 represented more than 95 percent of the gross national product. This would be unimaginable if it were not for sources of income outside the country. When government activity is calculated on the basis of total resources, it comes to about 50 percent.[12] The defense budget spent in Israel was 17.3 percent of the GNP in 1980, and the total defense budget (including expenditures abroad, mainly for weapons purchase) was 16.0 percent of total resources (GNP plus foreign sources). The defense spending was almost a third of the government's budget. Servicing debt took another third, and everything else another third. These figures point clearly to the major role played by import capital.

Comparable figures for the United States has defense as 21.0 percent of the national budget and 4.5 percent of GNP; for the United Kingdom the two figures are 14.0 and 5.0 percent respectively, and for France 7.0 and 2.7 percent.[13]

The government budget supposedly reflects the priorities of the government. In Israel this is so only indirectly because much of the budget is based on monies generated and spent abroad, and because activities supported by the government need not be directly financed by it (Jewish Agency activities, for example). Calculating the budget as a percent of the GNP may be a misleading figure because transfer payments are not included in the gross national product. Thus, for example, when the National Insurance Institute supports a retired person or gives a family allowance, these payments are not incorporated in the GNP, although they play an important role in the nation's economic and social policy. Similarly, subsidies paid by the government are not calculated as part of the GNP. The sums involved are very large; transfer payments are as high as 40 percent of the GNP in Israel.

Lest we lose focus because of the details, it is important to remember that the structure and statutory arrangements of the economy provide the government in general and the finance minister in particular with large measures of responsibility regarding the national economy, and tempting possibilities to utilize power to further economic and political ends. But the finance minister is not omnipotent. His major resource lies in his ability to direct, develop, suppress, or reduce the activities of the public and private sectors. But as the economy has developed, complete dependence on the government has been reduced; in the 1950s employment and housing were almost completely dependent on government activity, but this is not the case now. At the same time, powerful groups and institutions within the economy have emerged—largely thanks to government policy. Large unions within the Histadrut, important financial institutions, and major investors have the potential for opposing government policy in an effective manner.

Import Capital

Israel's achievements would not have been possible without import capital. Just as other countries have imported foodstuffs, raw materials, or automobiles, Israel, in addition, has imported money. The most consistent sources of this money have been the Jews of the world, who have regularly contributed to Israel through donations, loans (Israel bonds), or investment. Between 1948 and 1978, collections (not including loans or investments) reached more than $5.7 billion, nearly two-thirds of it from the United States.[14]

What has become even more important than the support of the Jews of the world is the support given Israel by other governments. Two important cases that must be stressed are West Germany and the United States. Reparations paid by the West German government to the government of Israel in the 1950s aided Israel in overcoming one of its earliest and most difficult economic periods. Food was rationed as hundreds of thousands of new immigrants continued to pour into the country. By 1978 over $4 billion had been received from the Bonn government, of which $836 million was reparation payments to the Israeli government for Nazi actions in World War II (these payments ended in the 1960s). In addition, personal restitution payments to Israeli citizens for acts against them during the Nazi rule continued; in 1980 restitution payments amounted to $468 million.[15]

The bulk of Israel's import capital in recent years has come from the government of the United States. By the early 1980s Israel was receiving $2.2 billion a year from the Americans. About two-thirds of it was for defense and one-third for economic aid. More than half the total was in the form of grants, and less than half in the form of loans (which obviously must be paid back).[16] The dramatic nature of the rise in American aid is well illustrated by the fact that in 1970 U.S. aid to Israel totaled $71 million, of which $30 million was military aid, and only $1 million of the total was in grants.

Since its creation and until 1982, Israel has received some $23 billion from the American government.[17] Foreign aid allows policy makers to avoid decisions regarding the country's priorities; since expenses need not be reduced, programs that otherwise would not be funded are continued. In 1982 the gap between imports and exports (deficit in the balance of payments) was almost $5 billion, compared with about $450 million in 1967.[18]

Israel's total foreign debt in 1980 reached almost $22 billion. More than half that sum were government liabilities payable in foreign currency, a result of the long-term independence and development bonds sold mostly to Jews abroad; an additional $85 million was owed by the government but payable in local currency.[19] Developments regarding this topic are striking and unmistakable: a sharp rise in the public foreign debt and a lowering of the role of debts to Jews (bonds) in the equation. In 1955 the total national debt payable in foreign currency was $491 million with the government owing $398 million of it; $198 million, or almost 50 percent, was owed to bondholders. By 1980, bondholders made up a little over a quarter of the total foreign debt of the government payable in foreign currency. This even while the size of the debt to bondholders increased 14.5 times in the 25 years between 1955 and 1980, while the total foreign debt of the government increased by double that rate, 28 times.

Israel's yearly debt, however, is greater than the support it receives from the United States. In 1982 Israel was pledged to repay $3.2 billion. About 14 percent of the GNP was expended on servicing the yearly debt! In 1982 about $1 billion was spent returning principle and servicing the interest on the first large loans given by the United States in 1973.[20]

As U.S. support jumped after 1973 and then stabilized, the proportion of Israel's needs supplied by the contributions of world Jewry shrank. The amount contributed by world Jewry was not large compared to the billions supplied by the American treasury. In the United States less than half a billion dollars a year was donated by American Jews to the United Jewish Appeal, which must finance local activities as well as programs in Israel. The sale of Israel Bonds in the United States in the same period was over a quarter of a billion dollars a year.[21]

Moreover, as Israel proved itself militarily strong, many Jewish communities began to rethink the tradition of putting Israel's needs before communal ones. Slowly a shift in priorities developed, and the share of contributions sent to Israel tended to decrease. The development coincided with the passing of the older generation of American Jewish community leaders whose formative years were spent while the Holocaust was raging and while the State of Israel was being formed. For the younger generation of leaders, Israel was a fact of life, and other needs of the Jewish community had also to be attended to. Jews continued to contribute, but their proportionate share in Israel's import capital tended to be lower.

The relation between economics and politics is especially interesting from this perspective. This chapter has argued that because of the government's ability to influence much of the economy of Israel, it has a potent tool to increase its political power. Yet this does not seem to be the case with the influence of the Jewish fund-raisers abroad in influencing the policies of the Israeli government nor of the major government supporter of the Israeli economy, the United States. We must seek the explanation to this difference in the ideology of supporting Zionism on the one hand and the practicalities of trying to influence a sovereign power on the other.

Being dependent on someone else's money is not the best recipe for independence of action. The Jews of the world, while often politely listened to, were excluded from policy decisions in Israel. This folk wisdom followed Ben-Gurion's thinking that one who wants to influence Israeli policy should live in Israel. The strains that have resulted from the attempted division of labor, which has Jews outside Israel collecting the money and leaders within Israel deciding how to spend it, has existed for a long time.

In the 1920s the WZO tried to influence social and economic development within Eretz Israel from its headquarters abroad; this brought about a series of conflicts with the pioneers, especially socialists. When Mapai became the dominant force in the World Zionist Executive in 1933, it acted to consolidate its control over the inflow of monies. Since then, tensions between donors and receivers have been mitigated by consultation and by passing out honorific titles without allowing economic power to be translated into political power by outsiders to Israeli politics.

The massive dependence of Israel on American funds has been cited by Arab states as proof of American complicity in Israeli policies. It is clear to them that economic power can be translated into political influence, and American protestations notwithstanding, the Americans are not serious in altering Israel's foreign policy course. The Americans have indeed used their economic weapon, usually in Israel's favor. They have generally been careful to avoid putting pressure on Israel by cutting off aid, although more subtle devices such as withholding a shipment of purchased material or failing to approve suggested increases in aid have been used. How a big power influences a smaller power is a complex and fascinating topic; what seems clear is that the options open to the big power are not unlimited. Short of cutting off aid completely, history has shown that translating economic aid into political obedience is a difficult task. But there are intermediary steps, such as making the flow of money more difficult. One of the arrangements that advantages the United Jewish Appeal in the United States, for example, is that it is recognized by the authorities as a charitable organization and hence, according to U.S. tax law, contributions to it can be deducted from one's income tax. It is sometimes "cheaper" for Americans to donate to the UJA (or other charities) and thus put themselves in a lower tax bracket. Should these rules change, a different atmosphere, psychological and economic, might be revealed.

While import capital—loans, grants, contributions—has always been important in the Israeli economic equation, much of the burden has fallen on Israelis themselves. Israelis are very highly taxed. Like any other government, Israel has tried to finance its activities by absorbing capital from the Israeli public. By 1978 about 45 percent of the total government income came from domestic sources, with 55 percent collected abroad.

Employment and Distribution

Because Israel's economy is so dependent on foreign capital and because the defense budget is so large, the government's role is central. But it is also central because Israel is a country of immigrants, and dependency relations could develop easily. Lacking land, capital, and a profession (or the opportunity to work in their profession), many who came to Israel found themselves dependent on the various bureaucracies for all their needs. The kind of labor market that developed accelerated the economic concentration delineated earlier in the chapter.

Two basic facts pinpoint the economy's high degree of vulnerability to centralized control: (1) most employed persons are salaried, and (2) most employed persons work in services. This means that the government, by virtue of its economic policies and its primary role in setting wages and prices, has enormous power in determining the public welfare.

In 1982, 78.6 percent of those employed were salaried, and that figure has been growing.[22] More than 75 percent of the working population tend to be in a dependent financial situation and within relatively easy grasp of the tax authorities.[23] A very large majority of salaried people are directly affected by the wage policy of the government. In 1982 there were 87,321 government employees excluding teachers and employees of government corporations.[24] A former civil service commissioner, Avraham Friedman, estimates that the government's wage policy directly affected 430,000 of the country's 1,250,000 workers in 1981. In other words, a third of the nation's employed people worked in jobs for which the government was either the direct or indirect employer, including the armed forces, teachers, employees of municipalities and local authorities, the Jewish Agency, workers of government corporations, Kupat Holim, and civil servants. This figure does not include workers in industry such as the Histadrut's Koor, whose salaries are influenced by a national wage agreement that does not need the approval of the finance ministry. This makes the Israeli economy somewhat immune to the fluctuations and crises of the international economic system that affect most of the industrialized world, but dependent on the ability of its leaders to procure the budget needed to keep this service sector operating.

A second important feature of the labor market is that most of the employed work in the services sector. Of the 1.3 million employed persons in 1982, 5.7 percent worked in agriculture; 30.2 percent worked in industry including mining, manufacturing, electricity, water, and construction; and the remaining 64.1 percent worked in such service occupations as commerce, hotels, communication, finance, and business. More than 30 percent of the total, half of those working in services, were employed in public and community services.[25] These figures support the image that working in industry does not provide the status or economic rewards that working in services does. But it also means that a great many jobs are dependent on government and public budgets, not on the productive capacity of the economy.

When broken down by nationality and sex, the magnitude of the trends changes a bit. For Jews, the figures in 1982 were 5.1 percent in agriculture, 29 percent in industry, and 65.9 percent in services. The non-Jewish figures reflect the difference between the two sets of numbers with non-Jews more active relatively in agriculture and industry and Jews more in services. Women are also more concentrated in services.

The problems of constructing a modern industrial society with a population whose largely middle-class backgrounds give them inadequate preparation for such a task are evident. Most important from a political point of view is that the leadership was (and is) willing to provide employment by creating jobs even if some of them were redundant or unnecessary. One of the direct results of such high levels of government concentration is that social and political goals (and not only economic ones) can sometimes guide decision makers in their deliberations. For example, industries may be located in developing areas for reasons of dispersing the population or to provide employment for people sent to inhabit these areas, even if the location makes little economic sense. But with such grave military problems and with reserve service in the army ranging from 30 to 60 days for most men until well into middle age, Israeli leaders, regardless of party, have tended to rank full employment very high on their list of policy goals. And on the whole they have been successful in preventing unemployment. Unemployment reached 5.0 percent in 1982, a figure higher than had existed since the 7.2 percent rate in 1955, but very low on an international basis.[26] While scores of millions were unemployed in the 1980s in the West, Israel avoided this situation.

The mechanism of setting wages underscores the central role of the government. The process begins with negotiations between officials of the finance ministry, the Histadrut's trade union division, and the coordinating committee of the employers. The result of the negotiations is a national wage agreement. The government's role is usually one of arbitrator because the workers want more and employers want to pay less. The government is not only a major employer but is also elected by the largely salaried electorate and, no less important, is responsible for the national economy. After the guidelines have been set, attempts are made to reach specific agreements in the various economic sectors and later in individual plants. This long and extended process means that labor issues are almost always in the news, and many contracts are signed long after previous ones have expired. The Histadrut and the government are influenced by political and economic considerations; both are major employers, and the leadership of both must stand for reelection. When both the Histadrut and the government were headed by the Alignment, cooperation was the rule, although arguments, even heated ones, did occur. But their solution was generally achieved through intraparty committees or discussions. When the Likud headed the government and the Alignment controlled the Histadrut, an attempt was been made by the government to limit the role of the Histadrut to economic matters and diminish the Histadrut's role in decisions with political importance.

The point of major interest is that the wage policy of the country, not just of civil servants, is monitored by the center. Industrial enterprises are bound by general guidelines determined in wage negotiations, municipal workers are bound by the dependency of the municipalities on national budgets, and so on. The Civil Service Commission was recently relieved of its role in these wage negotiations, and power over this sensitive area was transferred to the salary-controller, who is more closely under the control of the finance minister.

The finance ministers of Israel have used their power in this centralized wage structure for political benefit. The clearest proof of this is seen when we examine economic indicators and their relations to the elections. It is a well-documented fact that the relative growth rate of nondefense spending is largest in election years and that the largest increase in real wages occurs in election years. Using figures through 1973, Ben-Porath brings data that convincingly show the growth of average annual per capita consumption in the year preceding elections compared to generally low levels in previous years.[27] Changes in real general income grow slowly, reaching a crescendo during election year. Using long-term data, Gideon Doron and Boaz Tamir calculate that in the first year after the election the average wage change is 0.9 percent, followed by 1.8 percent in the second year after the election and 4.2 percent in the third.[28] The peak is reached in the fourth year when the average wage change is 6.5 percent. Extra-economic factors are at work here. Using this kind of analysis, it is less surprising that the Labor Alignment held power through eight elections and that the Likud could use its economic clout in 1981 to perpetuate its power. In a sense it is more surprising that the Alignment lost political power at the polls in 1977 than that it held it for so long.

The economy has generally not been a major political issue in elections because the government strives to make people feel as good as possible about the economy before elections. The most startling example of economic interference was Yoram Aridor's policy of decreasing excise taxes on goods such as color television sets before the 1981 elections. Aridor's policy came on the heels of Finance Minister Yigael Hurewitz's resignation and his dire predictions of catastrophe for the Israeli economy. The subjective change in mood probably did as much as anything else to turn around the Likud's poor performance in the polls and get it moving in the "right direction"—their slogan as they went toward election day.

The turnover of 1977 can be partially understood by the policy of the Alignment in the mid-1970s to cut government nonmilitary spending and services and increase taxes, especially among that portion of the population with higher income. It was precisely that group which defected most from the Alignment (although not only because of the tax increase) and gave their votes to the DMC, in this way accelerating the ascent of the Likud. The Bank of Israel reported that real available income per capita dropped between 1973 and 1976 by 8 percent. For the lower classes this was but another reason to vote Likud and not Alignment, but for upper classes that wanted to vote for neither the Likud nor the Alignment, the available alternative was the DMC. To be sure, the economic downturn was related to the Yom Kippur War and the upswing for the Likud had begun earlier and had been associated with demographic changes within the population, but the inability of the Alignment to fashion an economic policy consistent with vote getting was another sign of its deterioration and another reason for the turnover.[29]

The tendency toward centralization may be curtailed, but only as long as this is tolerated by the political center. There has been, for example, a movement toward the establishment of some government services (telephone and postal service) as independent corporations. One incentive to the workers has been that this would allow more flexibility in the wage structure. Like all Israeli salaried employees, they were involved in the popular Israeli sport of comparing salaries and wanting to be "linked" to the wages of other groups. The government wanted the change to remove entrenched anomalies in these service areas; the workers were counting on higher wages. While the structures might be altered, the locus of power was not. A more vexing case is a strong minister

TABLE 3.1

DISTRIBUTION OF TOTAL NATIONAL INCOME, SELECTED COUNTRIES, 1960 AND 1970

	Percent of national income received by:			
	Lowest 20 percent of income recipients		Highest 5 percent of income recipients	
Country	1960	1970	1960	1970
Venezuela	3.0	2.0	27.0	40.0
Mexico	4.0	4.0	29.0	36.0
Colombia	3.0	4.0	36.0	33.0
Turkey	4.0	3.0	33.0	32.0
Brazil	5.0	5.0	23.0	27.0
India	4.0	5.0	27.0	25.0
Iran	4.0	5.0	32.0	25.0
Netherlands	4.0	3.1	23.6	22.0
Denmark	5.0	4.0	16.9	22.0
United Kingdom	6.0	6.0	15.7	15.0
Yugoslavia	7.0	7.0	17.0	15.0
Canada	6.5	6.4	14.0	14.0
United States	4.0	6.7	16.0	13.3
Israel	7.0	8.0	13.0	13.0

SOURCE: *Social Indicators, 1976* (Washington, D.C.: Office of Federal Statistical Policy and Standards, U.S. Department of Commerce, 1977), 478.

or mayor or director who achieves benefits for his employees that are a function of his political strength and against stated policy. The center then appears weak because it cannot, or has chosen not to, confront the issue of irregular salaries and benefits.

While the ethos of the country is egalitarian, and indeed distribution is more equal in Israel than in many developed countries and certainly most developing countries, gaps do exist. Perfect equality (Gini coefficient 0.0) does not exist, but in Israel it is relatively low (0.222 in 1982). About 10 percent of the households accounted for the lower two deciles of income, while the upper decile accounted for 17.7 percent of the income.[30] Table 3.1 provides comparative data for other countries. When looked at by continent of birth and period of immigration, however, it is clear that Ashkenazim who immigrated before the declaration of independence and immediately thereafter are favored (see table 3.2). Those Europeans who came before 1948 had an index of 115.6 in 1980 with 100 being the index of all Europeans. Sephardim who came after 1961 had the lowest, an index of 75.7, meaning that their gross money income

TABLE 3.2

GROSS INCOME PER HOUSEHOLD BY CONTINENT OF BIRTH AND PERIOD OF IMMIGRATION

Base: Born in Europe or America = 100.0

Continent of Birth and Period of Immigration	1965	1970	1975	1979	1980
Jews, total	90.1	90.0	94.2	93.4	91.5
Israel-born Jews	108.6	103.3	102.5	99.0	93.8
Asian- or African-born Jews	71.7	73.9	82.2	81.0	80.1
Immigrated: to 1947	90.3	83.6	92.7	80.8	89.0
1948-54	71.5	75.8	84.8	85.5	83.1
1955-60		72.4	81.7	75.8	75.8
	63.7				
1961-		63.2	72.5	74.7	75.7
European- or American-born Jews	100.0	100.0	100.0	100.0	100.0
Immigrated: to 1947	120.5	111.3	116.6	106.2	115.6
1948-54	91.0	98.6	101.7	103.8	102.2
1955-60		92.5	94.3	104.7	97.1
	79.5				
1961-		77.2	84.9	91.6	88.8
Non-Jews	—	61.1	86.9	73.2	64.9

SOURCE: *Statistical Abstract, 1981,* 293-94.

was only three-fourths that of the Europeans. But it is also clear that longevity in the country is a major factor in improving one's condition economically, although no Asian-African group reaches the level of the European-American groups. Non-Jews fare even worse, with an index of only 64.9. A similar analysis by years of schooling clearly shows the larger earning ability over time of those with added years of education.

Inequality exists in the society at a lower rate than in many other societies but at a higher level than the egalitarian ethos of the country allows. Although this gap had existed in the past,[31] it became politically more important when subjective gaps of wealth and power failed to be closed. Under the Likud the psychic satisfaction of lower-class voters to rule over the upper classes seemed to be satisfied, as were subjective feelings of "never having it better." But using objective indicators, social and economic gaps were not closing, leaving the social structure relatively unchanged. This situation will probably not continue without some political repercussions.

4. The Political Elite

Politics in Israel is party politics, and party politics is elite politics. The Italian political sociologist Gaetano Mosca, writing at the end of the nineteenth century, accurately described the situation in Israel 80 years later:

> In all societies . . . two classes of people appear—a class that rules and a class that is ruled. The first class, always the less numerous, performs all political functions, monopolizes power and enjoys the advantages that power brings, whereas the second, the more numerous class, is directed and controlled by the first.[1]

The character of society and the direction it is taking can be understood in terms of the composition, structure, and conflicts of the ruling group.

Implicit in the unequal distribution of political power in a democracy is the realization that voting and elections are not the only avenue of expressing political preferences and getting them adopted. Instinctively we know that some individuals have more influence than others. In organizations the hierarchy of ranks clearly identifies those who have a higher likelihood of having their decisions implemented in general; a teacher has more power than a student, in the army an officer is more powerful, in a plant the manager determines what the worker will do, and in the home usually the parents decide what is to be done. In democratic situations equality is the rule. Each of us has considerable power because our vote is equal to everyone else's and—no less important—everyone else's vote is equal to ours.

But in reality, a ruling elite emerges. Even if we are able to change elites by voting in the opposition party at the next election, even if we are able to limit them by the constitution (written or unwritten) the country has developed, effective political power is never in the hands of the people. Moreover, an elite is not usually a collection of isolated individuals but is likely to be homogeneous, unified, and self-conscious. Individuals in the elite know one another well, have similar backgrounds, and share values, loyalties, and interests, although they may have differences of opinion on political issues and their personal ambitions may lead them to clash with one another.

It is important to appreciate that the preceding generalization regarding the unequal distribution of political power is a universal phenomenon. Only an extremely small proportion of the citizens of any country has any real chance of directly influencing national policy. Most people most of the time do not have the resources, access, or interest to involve themselves in policy decision making. In matters of curbing inflation (because the issue is so complex) as in matters of peace and war (because the issue is so sensitive), small groups of decision makers make decisions that affect all of us. This is true in all countries and at all times.

Participation and the Elite

Patterns of political stratification tend to be pyramidal in shape throughout the world;[2] it may well be that the Israeli political pyramid is higher than that found in some other democratic countries and its slope more sharp, but the general contours are the same. Most of the population does but one political act and that is to vote. This public is extremely crucial to the politician, but as individuals the voters have very limited influence. Voters have one important collective political resource: numbers. In Israel the ranks of *nonparticipants* are very thin; voting participation is very high. Among Jews, those who fail to vote do so almost universally for technical reasons; there is more purposive abstention among non-Jewish Israelis, but even among this group the majority participates.

The *attentive public* is composed of those who have the skills and resources to become activists, who follow politics intently, but who take no active part other than voting. Data on very high levels of news consumption in Israel, as expressed by reading newspapers, listening and watching news on radio and television, suggest that the size of the attentive public may be greater than in other countries (see chapter 12).

Activists may be party members, middle-level bureaucrats, or educators. They may be classified as those who take some active interest in politics by talking occasionally with a politician or writing a letter to a newspaper, but usually their action is limited to the issues to which they react.

The *influentials* are turned to by leaders and decision makers for advice. Their opinions and interests must be taken into account because their potential sanctions are feared. This stratum may include party officials, journalists, university professors, army officers, labor union officials, high-level bureaucrats, industrialists, financiers, kibbutz leaders, religious leaders, and leaders of Jewish groups abroad. This group is even more limited in numbers but is likely to react to a broader spectrum of issues of public policy.

The second highest stratum consists of the *proximate decision makers,* those individuals directly involved in policy making, usually ministers and senior administrative officeholders. At the apex of the pyramid is the group of *top leaders,* which in Israel may consist of the prime minister and perhaps another two or three individuals. The symbiosis between the two highest strata is extremely important, for while proximate decision makers provide support, legitimacy, and organization for top leaders, top leaders in their turn provide proximate decision makers with ideological direction, backing, and considerable status and power. People in the second stratum are anxious to sustain the top leadership because their own careers may depend on the continued success of the leadership and their own ambitions may be based on succeeding to the top leadership when the time comes.

At the apex of the pyramid, the top leaders have the final say *if* issues reach them. In Israel many issues of foreign and security policy are regularly brought for decision to the top leadership, while matters of internal and economic policy are not. In foreign affairs the top leadership tends to be the decision makers; in internal matters it tends to act as a final court of appeal if lower levels of decision makers cannot reach agreement among themselves.

The entire political system of Israel is stratified in terms of power, and so are the Knesset and the various political parties. The single member of the Knesset has relatively little power unless he is joined by many others, and this generally implies coalition support for his positions. In turn, the government can almost always block unfavorable motions in the Knesset, and since it also has control of the government ministries, it controls the administration as well as the legislation of policy. Moreover, the individual Knesset member is almost always dependent on his political party for his reelection, and so he is likely to gauge his behavior accordingly.

A Crisis of Succession

An indigenous Jewish political elite emerged in Eretz Israel only after the establishment of the British Mandate in the 1920s. Before then, political activity was circumscribed; Zionist politics, on the whole, was conducted in Europe. Herzl spent little time in Eretz Israel, Jabotinsky had his headquarters in Europe, and many leaders spent a good deal of their time abroad eliciting support and attending meetings.

With the second and third *aliyot,* the political organizations and the leaders of the country for the next generation and a half emerged. They were imbued with the ideals of socialism and collectivism that had become fashionable in the Russia they left after the unsuccessful Russian Revolution of 1905. They were composed of two major groups: those born in the period between 1885 and 1890 and those born at the turn of the century. These groups represented two distinct generational units in Israeli politics. The first group immigrated as part of the second *aliyah* between the years 1905 and 1912 and was instrumental in setting up the major political organizations of their day: the Ahdut Haavoda party in 1919 and the Histadrut in 1920. These organizations were to dominate much of the political and economic activity of the Jewish community in mandated Palestine. The leader of this group, David Ben-Gurion, became Israel's first prime minister. He held the post, with brief interruptions, until 1963. The younger group arrived in the third *aliyah* (1919-23) and was greatly influenced by the Russian Revolution of 1917.[3]

Both groups came from Poland and Russia, both were highly motivated ideologically and politically, and both constituted a small fraction of the Jews who immigrated. These groups set up the important organizations in a political void. They were young, energetic, and self-sacrificing, and their successful efforts meant that they would be the leaders of the State of Israel when it was founded in 1948.

An implicit symbiosis developed between these two groups. Those in the older group were statesmen, making the grand decisions and setting policy. The younger group controlled the party machine, was faithful to the leadership, depended on it, and worked for it. The younger group thus ensured the perpetuation of the power of the older group because in the last analysis the leadership was also dependent on the party machine. With the acknowledged leadership fading from the scene in the 1970s, a crisis of succession loomed. The informal hierarchical relations that had been such an important part of the division of labor within the generational units of the party could not be easily transferred. The long years of shared experience and the generational solidarity that this produced prevented the flow of young, new leadership into the ranks.

A fascinating case in point is the political career of Moshe Dayan. After Dayan left the army as chief of staff in 1957, Ben-Gurion wanted to make him a government minister. The major objections came, as one might expect in a hierarchical system in which political apprenticeship is very long, from the second stratum of the ruling elite. Golda Meir and Zalman Aranne pointed out that Dayan should be trained as a politician in more humble surroundings than the government. By trying to bypass the third *aliyah* group of Mapai leaders, Ben-Gurion infuriated the party machine.

Ben-Gurion had no choice but to relinquish power to the third *aliyah* group, but upon leaving office he became a bitter critic of this group and ultimately split with the Mapai party he had founded. In 1965, Rafi was set up by Ben-Gurion along with some of the bright "young Turks" he had fostered in the defense establishment, such as Dayan and Peres. The new party appealed to many young Israel-born supporters who resented the perceived fact that the party machine prevented adaptability to changing problems and blocked access to positions of power. Many, however, were torn between two long-standing allegiances: between the former leader of the party, Ben-Gurion, and the traditional leaders of the party machine.

The party machine was revitalized quickly by Pinhas Sapir, then minister of the treasury, before the 1965 elections. Sapir was younger than many in the leadership of the machine group, and as minister of finance was able to hold the machine together by setting policies that favored groups and individuals supportive of the party and its clients. As long as the structure of the party machine was hierarchically autonomous, career aspirations centered on the apex of the power pyramid. Now the key positions of the party machine were less attractive for ambitious politicians than were key posts in the national government. They strived to be in the Knesset or a government minister. The symmetrical relationship of the machine with the top leadership was broken. Machine leaders were suddenly dependent on the top leadership for career advancement. They could no longer trade off its support and activity for influence on ministers and policy. They were also less effective as brokers between the leadership and the followers. With the ascension of the third *aliyah* group to power, the party organization suffered, and it was eventually to be felt in the voting results.

The leadership attempted two methods of solving the crisis of succession. One was to ally themselves with other parties, thereby gaining depth of leadership. Before the 1965 elections they formed a joint list with Ahdut Haavoda, whose leaders had split from Mapai in 1944. Preceding the Six Day War in 1967, Mapai exhibited a lack of leadership in foreign and security policies. These were, after all, areas in which Ben-Gurion had predominated. After some hesitation, Dayan was made defense minister and Rafi was included in the National Unity Government. In 1968 the Mapai leadership consolidated this process by forming, along with Rafi and Ahdut Haavoda, the Israel Labor party.

The second method of solving the crisis of succession was by introducing new elements into the party leadership. Before the 1973 elections (and war), Sapir and his party decided to appoint former army heroes to positions of importance in the government. This move was a characteristic "social force." Gaetano Mosca writes that "as civilization grows, the number of the moral and material influences which are capable of becoming social forces increases. For example, property in money, as the fruit of industries and commerce, comes into being alongside of real property."[4] The social force in this case was that it became natural for those who had been endowed with success in the military field to play an active role in politics. Their backgrounds did not prepare them for party politics, however, let alone the intricacies of running a party machine.

Between 1973 and 1977 a fascinating process of differentiation began to develop in the ruling elite of the Labor party. Cabinet members who had primary responsibility for security and foreign affairs (Yitzhak Rabin, Shimon Peres, Yigael Allon, Israel Galili, Aharon Yariv earlier) tended to be from a military background *and not* historically associated with Mapai, while some who dealt with internal matters were also those whose political careers *had been* dependent on the Mapai party machine (Yehoshua Rabinowitz, Avraham Ofer, Aharon Yadlin, and Moshe Baram). A sense of common purpose never developed between the two groups. Rabin's leadership failed to bridge conflicting interests, styles, and backgrounds. The party's lack of accepted leadership was the backdrop against which the details of the political drama were played out: the competition between Rabin and Peres for the right to head the list (Rabin won), Rabin's resignation from first on the list because of his wife's personal foreign currency problems, and Peres's ascension to first place a month before the election in 1977. It is little wonder that the military heroes were not successful in running their party. They were the victims, not the causes, of the crisis of leadership succession and the attendant passing of dominance from the Labor party.

The emergence of the Democratic Movement for Change (DMC) reflected the crisis of succession discussed above. The DMC provided an alternative channel of upward mobility for leaders (political, military, economic, and university) who disdained the opportunity of competing for positions in the disreputed Alignment. The setting up of a new party reflected the disarray of the party system in 1977; both party leadership and electoral support was in flux. A bold move might create a party that would have a pivotal position in coalition calculations. While the DMC did not succeed in being pivotal (the Likud and the religious parties could rule without them), their achievement of winning 15 seats was impressive in Israeli political terms.

In an important sense Begin represented continuity with the Alignment leadership, for he was the last of the older generation still active in politics. Begin's undisputed leadership of the Herut and the Likud was facilitated by the loyalty of his colleagues from the pre-state underground years. The Liberal party chose ministers to the Likud government, but none of them challenged the supreme leadership role of Herut's Begin. When Begin relinquished power and was followed by Yitzhak Shamir, it was unclear if this was an interim premiership or if Shamir could win control of the Likud and the Herut movement. The crisis of succession is likely to erupt as leaders of the younger generation (such as David Levy and Ariel Sharon) try to take control.

Following Mosca's analysis, the social forces in a society indicate the reservoir of potential talent to be tapped for the ruling elite. The young pioneers who set up the dominant political organizations in the 1920s were at the peak of their careers in the 1940s when their children came of age and began seeking their own way. Most of these children did not find politics an attractive career because the best jobs were filled by relatively young people. Moreover, a clear "social force" had emerged: defense. The army, the security establishment, the procuring of arms for the Jewish community, and service with the British armed forces in the Second World War—all these activities attracted the bright young men and women of the 1940s. By the 1960s two processes overlapped: the aging and retirement of the traditional political leadership and the retirement in their mid-forties of a generation of defense and army leaders due to the early retirement policy of the Israel Defense Force. The apex of the political pyramid was vacated just as the apex of the military pyramid was being rejuvenated. It was only natural for experienced army officers who had succeeded in a field that was clearly a "social force" to assume positions of responsibility and authority in politics.

This horizontal movement from the apex of one elite pyramid to the apex of another is called in Hebrew "parachuting." Instead of climbing to the top of the political hierarchy the way a foot soldier would, a general is parachuted in, bypassing the customary apprenticeship of years at the lower levels of the national party hierarchy. It is not suprising that the objections to bypassing traditional channels of advancement came from those who had been serving as second-stratum leaders, waiting their turn to assume the role of top leaders.

The problem was, and is, one of leadership succession. In the Israeli case, parties are crisis-prone concerning succession because terms of office are not limited, and the incumbent usually becomes entrenched in office. In the case of a Ben-Gurion or a Begin, this affords the respective party years of sure leadership. When the crisis starts, however, it is usually very intense.

Both the Alignment and the Likud have experienced an influx of political leaders with army backgrounds who have vied for the top spot. In Herut, both Ezer Weizman and Ariel Sharon tried unsuccessfully to unseat Begin or at least to share power with him. Both men had impressive army careers before entering politics. Both figured prominently in the Likud's creation and victory in 1977, but Begin's role as top leader remained unchanged.

The one party that appeared to successfully pass political leadership to the second generation was the National Religious party (NRP), but, paradoxically, political power seemed to be slipping from its grasp. The average age of the 12 Knesset members they elected in 1977 was considerably younger than those of the other major parties. Political leadership seemed to be shared by the Youth Faction headed by Zevulun Hammer and Yehuda Ben-Meir and the older Dr. Yosef Burg who headed the party list. This development was very impressive because it was accomplished by outmaneuvering a veteran political activist, Yitzhak Rafael, who had run the NRP machine for years.

By careful coalition building and adroit use of parliamentary procedure, the Youth Faction was able to prevent Rafael's inclusion on the party list for the 1977 elections. In another important political move, the party placed Rabbi Haim Druckman in second place on the list. Druckman was widely identified with the Gush Emunim movement, and his inclusion was probably decisive in winning the votes of many young religious voters. While it was not yet at the head of the list, the Youth Faction was moving to the head of the party.

But by the mid-1980s, the picture clouded. One of the young leaders, Aharon Abu-Hatzeira, split from the NRP and set up Tami before the 1981 elections. Then Rabbi Druckman split from the NRP after the election and set up his own Knesset delegation. The ethnic issue raised by Tami and the nationalist issue raised by Gush Emunim plagued the NRP's ability to win votes. Thus, although the NRP (1) had impressive bases of power in the religious education system and the interior and religious affairs ministries, (2) had a platform of intense nationalism that tended to be in tune with the nation's mood, and (3) had determined their political succession, yet they were weak electorally, winning only four seats in 1984 compared to six seats in 1981 and 12 in 1977. The continued friction between Burg's group and the leaders of the Youth Faction weakened the party from within and prevented it from answering the challenges presented to it.

Knesset Members

Knesset members are an easily identified positional elite that has often been studied by political scientists. The average age of Knesset members has varied a good deal. In the first 20 years of Israel's history the average age of Jewish members of the Knesset tended to become older and older, from 49.4 in 1949 to 54.3 in 1965; but this trend has moderated.[5] The explanation for this is that many of the original Knesset members continued their parliamentary careers for a number of years, blocking entrance to the Knesset by younger members. As these older members faded, a more normal distribution was generated. Even this pattern varied from party to party, depending on size. A small party with a tight-knit leadership that perpetuated itself over the years (Mapam, Agudat Israel) tended to have a higher average age from Knesset to Knesset. A larger party (Alignment, Likud) could retain its old leadership and introduce new blood at the same time. The aging of the Knesset is likely to be cyclical, especially if members pursue the parliament as a way of life and if the election results are relatively stable. Age-based parties have never won representation in the elections, however, although both a pensioner's party and a youth party have stood for election. The major parties are aware of the importance of appealing to these large age groups, but the rule is that parliamentarians in Israel begin at middle age and hold on if they can.

The sex composition of the Knesset has shown little change. Women have never been numerous; in the eighth and eleventh Knessets there were ten women, and in the ninth and tenth Knessets, there were eight women. The Alignment has always been careful to provide representation for women. Even though it dropped from 52 to 32 seats in 1977, the percentage of women in its delegation dropped only from 13.7 percent to 12.5 percent: seven in the outgoing Knesset, four in the incoming. In absolute figures the NRP's increase was most impressive, from none to one. The Likud increased from one to two. All this indicates that women are still very far from achieving equality with men. In 1984, six of the ten Knesset women were from the Alignment. In the 1973 elections Marsha Friedman was elected to the Knesset on Shulamit Aloni's Civil Rights Movement list; at that time, Friedman was leader of the Women's Liberation movement. In 1977 and 1981, a women's list ran and failed to achieve representation. The woman who achieved greatest power in the system was Golda Meir, who was prime minister at the end of her colorful and eventful career. She was an important Labor party leader who happened to be a woman. It would be historically inaccurate to picture her as "representing" women in her many roles.

The political system of Israel was developed by new immigrants from Eastern Europe, especially of the second and third *aliyot,* and it was only natural that these elite members would continue to dominate during their lifetimes. As the percentage of East European-born in the population diminished and the percentage of native-born increased, the incidence of native-born Israelis in the Knesset increased. But in an important sense this datum is misleading because the overwhelming tendency was for the second generation of Israeli Knesset members to be the sons of the East European-born first generation. The frequency distribution in the country of birth category may have changed, but the focus of political power and membership in the positional elite in the Knesset in the hands of individuals with a European background was maintained. Sephardim were grossly underrepresented in the Knesset; the political power of the country was firmly in the hands of Europeans and their children. This was not a matter of chance. The political institutions of the country were established by this group, and it was natural for them to favor those who were more like them, as well as consciously trying to perpetuate their power and that of their party's.

The dominance of East Europeans is demonstrated dramatically when the place of birth of the 37 signers of Israel's declaration of independence are analyzed. They were members of the National Committee and later the Provisional State Council that served up to the first general election of 1949. Of these "founding fathers," 29 came from Eastern Europe and six from the rest of Europe. One was born in Eretz Israel, one in Yemen.[6]

As in any new endeavor, those who are the founders—and especially if they are young—are likely to persist and dominate the endeavor for many years. This was the case with the Histadrut. When it was founded in 1920, many of its leaders were in their twenties.[7] The same applied to the Provisional State Council. It was natural that there should be significant carryover from this body to the first Knesset elected in 1949. Indeed, 27 of the 40 members in the expanded Provisional State Council were elected to the first Knesset; 20 years later, in 1969, ten of them were still members of the Knesset. The dominance of the East European elite is evident in other areas, such as the judiciary, the army, and mass media.[8]

Change appears to be taking place in the system because the preponderance of Israel-born Knesset members continually increases. This is an artifact of the changing demographic composition of the country rather than a real switch in the division of power. European-born Knesset members made up more than 85 percent of the house as a result of the first three elections, 79 percent in the next two, and 68 percent in the sixth Knesset elected in 1965. By the seventh election the percentage of European-born members had fallen to 63 percent, then to 56 percent in the eighth and 38 percent by the ninth.[9] On the other hand, both Israel-born and Sephardi Knesset membership was increasing. The Israel-born rose from 11 percent in the first Knesset to 14 percent in the fourth (1959) and to 24 percent by the seventh (1969). In 1973 they comprised 38 percent, 50 percent in 1977, and 60 percent in 1984. Seven members of the Knesset elected in 1984 were Arabs or Druze.

Knesset members of Asian and African birth have also increased steadily and now replicate more accurately their relative strength in the population. From 3 percent in the first Knesset to 8 percent in the fifth (1961), there were 12 percent in both the eighth and ninth (1973 and 1977), 25 percent in the tenth (1981), and 20 percent in the eleventh (1984). Added to Israel-born Sephardim, this shift indicates a gradual strengthening of the representation of the Sephardi community.

The bias in favor of persons of European origin can be seen even more strongly in the composition of the governments in Israel. From independence until April 1974, 58 of the 70 ministers were born in Europe, North America, and South Africa, compared with only four born in Asia and Africa. In the

Likud government of 1977 as well, the vast majority of ministers were of European extraction. Of the 19 ministers in 1981, three (Aharon Abu-Hatzeira, David Levy, and Moshe Nissim) were Sephardim. Of the less important category of deputy minister, three of the nine were Sephardim.

Apologists for the system explain that Sephardi Jews have not had the experience with democratic institutions and therefore have not been adequately prepared to take their proper role in the running of the country. Their day will come. Protesters argue that Sephardim have been consistently discriminated against in many spheres of life and that the political sphere is the most obvious area of this discrimination. Both sides point to the emergence of Sephardi political leaders in the politics of local government to prove their point. Apologists point to examples of successful politicians as proof that they are learning the rules and will ultimately emerge. Protesters respond that these leaders are already capable of much more important roles and are given busywork at the local level to harness their energies and coopt them into the major party frameworks.

It is important to note that ethnic groups in Israel have rarely been successful in winning elections on an ethnic basis. There was a Sephardi list in 1949 that won Knesset representation *before* the massive influx of Sephardi voters in the early 1950s, and Tami in 1981. The Progressives/Independent Liberal party had large measures of support in its early years from German immigrants and was largely dominated by them, unlike almost all the other parties (even the Arab-based communist Rakah party), which were dominated by East European Jewish political elites. More important, there is no clear evidence that ethnic groups strive for ethnic representation in the Knesset. In a national survey conducted before the 1981 elections, a representative sample of the population was asked about groups they would like to see have more representation in the country's parties. Thirty-four percent responded young people, 12 percent said intellectuals; in third place, just before women with 10 percent, came Sephardi Jews with 11 percent. There seemed to be no great demand for more representation, even among the half of the population that was Sephardi.

Politics as a Vocation

The emergence of a popular leader enhances the chances of any party. But in addition to the top leader, a party must be endowed with additional strata of leaders and activists who will carry out the day-to-day tasks of running the party and the organizations in its control. Max Weber made the important distinction between those who see politics as a vocation and those who see it as an avocation, those who live *off* politics rather than *for* politics.[10]

Weber suggested that a system dominated by those who live off politics will tend to be conservative and static. A system dominated by those who live for politics has a better chance of generating innovative political leadership that will present new ideas and directions largely because they would be free of the party and its vested interests. This analysis applies well to Israel. After an initial period of ideological and organizational creativity, the political elite became conservative and its institutions static. In the popular idiom, the politician became more concerned with retaining his seat than convincing others of his position.

The best way to understand this distinction is to contrast the *apparatchik* with the *cincinnatus,* as Zbigniew Brzezinski and Samuel Huntington do in their book *Political Power: USA/USSR.*[11] The *apparatchik* is the bureaucrat-politician commonly found in the Soviet system. He has devoted his life to the party and has progressed from one bureaucratic post to another and from one agency to another. His socialization, his livelihood, and his career are all dependent on hierarchical relationships, on slowly climbing the bureaucratic ladder, on doing the job well but in the framework of the organization, its demands, and its ideology. The *cincinnatus,* on the other hand, dominates the American political system. He is the "distinguished citizen who lays aside other responsibilities to devote himself temporarily to the public service." He is likely to be more independent in thought and action than his Soviet counterpart because he is less dependent on the party and its affiliated organizations for power, status, or livelihood. In fact, an American businessman, banker, or lawyer who agrees to go into politics or accept an administrative appointment with the government usually takes a very substantial cut in salary. But he is likely to be on the job only a few years, lacking experience in government bureaucracy when he enters service and leaving with his experience when he exits.

The Israeli system has been dominated by the *apparatchik*. This was especially true during the period between 1948 and 1977 in which the Alignment parties dominated the government. Then, of Israel's 77 ministers, 52 had spent most of their professional lives in bureaucracies. It is reasonable to suppose that their promotion stemmed from their success in learning to survive in that kind of organizational setting (including military and religious bureaucracies). The figures for the Likud governments between 1977 and 1981 show a more nearly even split between the two types. But the concentration of the *apparatchik* is especially great among those six ministers of the Likud period who also served during the Alignment period (Menachem Begin, Moshe Dayan, Haim Landau, Yosef Burg, Zevulun Hammer, and Ezer Weizman).[12]

Politics for many politicians in Israel is not only a way of life, it is also a way of earning a living. This point sheds important light on the mechanisms of control of the party over its political activists. With the gradual growth of activity on the part of the Jewish community in the pre-state period, the number of offices expanded, as did the number of individuals for whom politics was their primary, if not exclusive, endeavor. The parties were able to attract talent not only because of their ideological appeal but also because public service was rewarded by a salary. Of the 82 political leaders of the pre-state period studied, 42.5 percent earned their living from party-related activities.[13] When these findings are broken down by political party, a significant pattern emerges: Leaders of the parties of the labor movement were much more likely to be on the party payroll than were leaders of the center and right parties. Of the pre-state leaders, two-thirds of the left party leaders and one-third of the nonleft party leaders were salaried by party-sponsored organizations.

Yet another 20 percent of the labor movement leaders were members of kibbutzim. They could be assigned party work in order to fill ideological goals and political-economic interests of the kibbutz movement without any financial sacrifice or risk on their part. Their needs were provided for by the kibbutz, and they were free to devote themselves to public service. This is one of the important explanations for the overrepresentation of kibbutz members and kibbutz interests in Israeli politics.

The material dependence of politicians on political organizations did not cease with the establishment of the state. This dependence—with all that it implies regarding conformity, timidity, and loss of enterprise—continued to be the pattern in the large parties, especially those of the labor movement. The structure of these parties and their vast administrative networks, most clearly seen in the myriad activities of the Histadrut, provided a training ground for ambitious members to try to fill the ranks of the party leadership. When the occupations of the 374 Knesset members who served from 1949 through 1977 are analyzed (see table 4.1 on page 60), we find that the distribution of Knesset members by source of livelihood is similar to the pre-state period, and that the parties of the left are much more likely to be represented by *apparatchiki* than are the parties of the right and center.[14] Activity in the movement and the party was seen as an expression of a commitment to a way of life. As public servants they identified with the party and put themselves at its disposal. This was a great source of strength for the party, which could easily be reinforced, especially during the 40-odd years when the parties of the labor movement were in control of the national institutions as well as the Histadrut. These psychological and economic dependencies accelerated oligarchical tendencies in these parties and assured support for the established leadership.

The Center *(merkaz)* of Mapai, the legally constituted decision-making body, was dominated by people in the party's employ.[15] Most of the members

TABLE 4.1

OCCUPATIONS OF KNESSET MEMBERS BY MAJOR PARTIES, 1948-77

Party	Politician N (%)	Other N (%)	Total (N)
Mapai (incl. Rafi)	99 (63)	58 (37)	157
Ahdut Haavoda	15 (94)	1 (6)	16
Mapam	25 (78)	7 (22)	32
NRP	20 (58)	14 (41)	34
Agudat Israel	4 (57)	3 (43)	7
Poalei Agudat Israel	2 (50)	2 (50)	4
Herut	16 (36)	28 (64)	44
Progressives/Independent Liberals	7 (50)	7 (50)	14
General Zionists/Liberals	7 (18)	33 (82)	40
Communists	6 (75)	2 (25)	8
Others	4 (22)	14 (78)	18
TOTAL	205 (55)	169 (45)	374

SOURCE: Guttman and Landau, "The Israel Political Elite," 227.

had no independent means of support. As we go up the power pyramid, the higher the stratum, the higher the concentration of individuals dependent on the party.[16] This dependence on the party could be translated into political obedience if necessary. When engaged in battles with other parties or in gathering votes, the internal cohesiveness and esprit de corps were high. When faced with internal dilemmas, party bosses could usually count on the loyalty of party activists.

The Alignment parties were most likely to generate the *apparatchik* pattern. This was evident, for example, in the 1977 elections. Twenty of the Alignment's 32 Knesset members worked for the party as its representatives in the outgoing government, Knesset, or in party-related enterprises and local government. The 43-member Likud delegation was much more varied in terms of the occupational structure of its members. Only six Likud members were primarily involved in political life. It is not surprising that the Likud had a much less intense organizational life since it had been in opposition throughout most of its existence and never had control of the bureaucracies that the Alignment led. The DMC was the least *apparatchiki* of all. Of its 15 members, only one reported that he was a party worker. Looking at this dimension only (while not ignoring the differences of ideology and personality which existed), it is not surprising that the DMC did not remain intact throughout the session of the ninth Knesset. The DMC leaders could "afford" to break up their organization, both in the sense that the organization was very young and had few vested interests and that the leadership had prestigious careers other than politics to which they could return.

Prime Ministers and Presidents

Two roles in Israeli politics stand out as being at the head of the pyramid of power and prestige, that of prime minister and that of president. They are fundamentally different in nature. The prime minister's position is of supreme political importance, and the various networks of political struggle usually end up on his desk or close to it. The prime minister is not only head of government but is also head of the cabinet, and as such, head of the coalition that rules the Knesset. As head of his party he also wields great political power, which enhances his powers as prime minister. On the other hand, the president's role is largely honorific and symbolic, although he is formally head of state and plays a role in the establishment of the government.

Short biographies of the people who occupied these positions give an excellent indication of the structure of the Israeli political elite. Eleven of the 14 were born in Eastern Europe and two of them (Rabin and Navon) in Jerusalem. Rabin's father was a Mapai activist whose background was similar in many important ways to the East European leaders. Although ultimately Zionist leaders, many of them came to Eretz Israel, left, and returned again, spending many years abroad in the interim. Although all, with the exceptions of Begin and Shamir, were identified to one degree or another with socialism and the labor movement, many of them trained to be lawyers, a very bourgeois profession. This provided good training for politics and for dealing with the Turkish and British imperial bureaucracies; it also foreshadowed the formalistic, legal character of Israeli politics both in internal and foreign policies.

Ben-Gurion was the undisputed leader and Sharett a substitute prime minister. Only after Ben-Gurion's withdrawal from office did two of his close associates, Eshkol and Meir, achieve office. Rabin was the personification of the second generation of Israeli politics: Israel-born of European origin, military career, no political experience. Other candidates of his generation were denied by the Mapai party leadership because they were associated with other factions of the labor movement—Dayan with Rafi, and Allon with Ahdut Haavoda. Rabin was selected, at least in part, because the others were rejected. Begin's victory in 1977 brought the last political leader of the founding generation to the prime ministry. Born in Poland, a Knesset member since the beginning, a lawyer by training, Begin twice led his party to electoral victory after eight unsuccessful attempts. After his retirement, Shamir became prime minister succeeded by Peres as the head of the National Unity Government in 1984.

Of Israel's eight prime ministers, six (with the exceptions of Begin and Shamir) were associated with the labor movement, seven (with the exception of Rabin) were born in Eastern Europe, seven (with the exception of Rabin) achieved the prime ministry at an advanced age after a long career in party-related political work. Five of them (Sharett, Rabin, and Shamir are the exceptions) were also the head of their political party, and all of them could be considered professional politicians (or *apparatchiki*) in that none of them had a profession or means of support outside the bureaucratic structures of the party and the state.

The symbolic presidency, as we would expect, leaves more room for exceptions and deviation from the generalizations presented above. Three of the six (Weizman, Ben-Zvi, Katzir) were intellectuals and academics. Navon was the only Sephardi among the 14. He was an active and effective Labor party politician although he was elected to the presidency after the election of 1977, which brought the Likud to power.

PRIME MINISTERS

David Ben-Gurion, first prime minister of Israel, was born in Poland in 1886. In 1906 he came to Eretz Israel as part of the second *aliyah* and as a leader of Poalei Zion. In 1908 he returned to Russia to join the army, and in 1912 began studying law in Constantinople. With the outbreak of World War I he returned to Eretz Israel, to be expelled by the Turks to Egypt. In 1919 he was one of the initiators of the establishment of Ahdut Haavoda. In 1920 he was active in setting up the Histadrut and the first assembly of the Jewish settlers in Eretz Israel, called Knesset Israel. Between 1921 and 1935 he served as the general secretary of the Histadrut. In 1930, when Mapai was founded, he was considered its leader. Between 1935 and 1948 he was the chairman of the Jewish Agency Executive. In 1948 he announced the establishment of the State of Israel and was its first prime minister and defense minister. He served in these capacities from 1948 to 1953 and from 1955 to 1963. By 1965 he left Mapai and founded Rafi to compete with his former party. After most of Rafi returned to Mapai in 1968 to form the Labor party, Ben-Gurion set up the State List before the 1969 elections. Ben-Gurion retired from political life in 1970 and died in 1973.

Moshe Sharett, second prime minister of Israel, was born in the Ukraine, Russia, in 1894. He immigrated to Eretz Israel with his parents when he was twelve. He studied law in Constantinople and served in the Turkish army in World War I. After the war he joined Ahdut Haavoda. In 1920 he went to London to study and became active in the World Zionist Organization. Between

1925 and 1931 he was editor of *Davar,* the Histadrut newspaper. In 1933 he was appointed head of the political department of the Jewish Agency in place of Haim Arlozoroff (who had been murdered). Sharett retained this post until independence; in effect, he was the foreign minister of the state-in-the-making. When Ben-Gurion resigned in 1953, Sharett was chosen prime minister. He lacked the political and bureaucratic skills of Ben-Gurion, and in policy matters he tended to be more moderate and less activist than his predecessor. He set up Israel's diplomatic service and retained the post of foreign minister while he was prime minister. In 1955 Ben-Gurion became defense minister in place of Pinhas Lavon in Sharett's government, and before the 1955 elections, replaced Sharett as prime minister as well. In 1956, four months before the Sinai Campaign, he resigned from the government, objecting to Ben-Gurion's activist policies. Sharett remained active in public affairs until his death in 1965.

Levi Eshkol, Israel's third prime minister, was born in Russia in 1895. He immigrated to Eretz Israel in 1914 where he toiled as a worker and was one of the founders of Degania B, the kibbutz of which he was a member until his death. In the 1920s he was sent to procure arms in Europe and at the end of the 1930s was a member of the national command of the Haganah (the Yishuv defense force). In 1937 he initiated the establishment of Mekorot, the Histadrut's water company. He was secretary of the Tel Aviv workers' council in the Histadrut; in the 1940s he managed the Haganah's treasury. He was appointed by Ben-Gurion as the first director general of the defense ministry. From 1949 he was a member of the Jewish Agency Executive and head of its settlement department. In the early 1950s he was treasurer of the Jewish Agency, and minister of agriculture and development. Between 1952 and 1963 he was minister of finance. By the 1950s he was a major figure within Mapai. In 1961 he formed the government that was headed by Ben-Gurion; later Eshkol was Ben-Gurion's chief opponent in the Lavon Affair (see chapter 5). When Ben-Gurion resigned in 1963, Eshkol took over the posts of prime minister and defense minister. His conciliatory nature (and political considerations) led to an alignment between Mapai and Ahdut Haavoda before the 1965 elections, the formation of the National Unity Government before the Six Day War in 1967, and the merger of Mapai, Ahdut Haavoda, and Rafi to form the Labor party in 1968. He died in 1969.

Golda Meir, Israel's third prime minister, was born in Russia in 1898. When she was eight, her family moved to Milwaukee, Wisconsin. In 1921 she immigrated to Eretz Israel as part of the third *aliyah.* She was a member of kibbutz Merhavia until 1924. In 1925 she joined Ahdut Haavoda; in 1928 she was elected secretary of the women's workers' council; and in 1933 became secretary of the Histadrut's executive committee. When many Mapai leaders were detained by the British on the "Black Sabbath" in June 1946, she ran the political section of the Jewish Agency. Before independence, Sharett ran the political section in the United States and at the United Nations, and Mrs. Meir ran the department in Jerusalem. In 1947 and 1948 she held secret talks with Jordan's King Abdullah. After independence, she served as head of Israel's first mission to the Soviet Union. She was minister of labor and national insurance (social security) between 1949 and 1956. Upon Sharett's resignation in 1956 she became foreign minister, a position she held until 1965. In the Lavon Affair she opposed Ben-Gurion. In 1966 she was appointed secretary of Mapai. She resigned from most of her positions in 1968, only to be called back to active political life in 1969 at age seventy-one, after Eshkol's death. She served as prime minister until 1974; during this period the Labor-Mapam Alignment won its biggest plurality (56 seats in 1969), and the Yom Kippur War of 1973 shocked the country. In the aftermath of the war and the criticism made of her and her government, she resigned in 1974. She died in 1978.

Yitzhak Rabin, Israel's fourth prime minister, was born in Jerusalem in 1922. His parents came from Eastern Europe and were active in the Histadrut and Mapai. He was a leading officer of the Palmach during the war of independence; by 1953 he was made a general, and between 1956 and 1959 he served as commander of the northern front. In 1964 he was appointed chief of staff and led the army during the Six Day War. In 1968 he was appointed Israel's ambassador to Washington. He ran on the Alignment list in the 1973 Knesset elections, and in 1974 was appointed minister of labor in Golda Meir's last government. When Mrs. Meir resigned a month later, Rabin was earmarked for the prime ministry by the Mapai kingmaker, Finance Minister Pinhas Sapir; Rabin was chosen because of his connections in the past with the labor movement, his famous military record, and because he was not involved in the military mistakes of the Yom Kippur War. Rabin won the job after a close vote in the Labor party center against Shimon Peres, the first time there was a contested election for the post in Labor party's history. Rabin was the first native-born prime minister and the first to lack a strong political background. For three months he led a minority government without the participation of the NRP in the coalition; by October 1974 the NRP reentered the coalition. In 1977 he again beat Peres for the leadership of the party, this time in the party convention. But in April 1977 foreign currency infractions by his wife were discovered, and Rabin removed himself from first place on the Labor list and was placed in the 20th spot. After the 1984 elections, he became minister of defense.

Menachem Begin, fifth prime minister of Israel, was born in Poland in 1913. Until he was thirteen he was a member of Mapam's youth group (Hashomer Hatzair). When he was sixteen he joined Beitar, the Revisionist youth group. In the 1930s he studied law and was active in the Revisionist movement. In 1939 Jabotinsky appointed him head of Beitar in Poland, the chief concentration of power of the movement. In 1940 he was arrested by the Soviets and sentenced to eight years' imprisonment for Zionist activities. He was sent to Siberia but released because he was a Polish citizen. After his release, he joined the Polish army and at the same time was appointed head of Beitar in Eretz Israel. He arrived in Eretz Israel in 1942 and became head of the Irgun in 1943; he led the Irgun until independence in 1948. A £10,000 bounty was offered by the British for his capture, but he evaded arrest. After the Irgun was disbanded and the Israel Defense Force established, Begin was the natural candidate for leading Herut. He became the leader of the opposition, objecting strenuously to reparations from Germany and arms sales with Germany. In 1965 he ran at the head of the Gahal list, a joint list of Herut and the Liberal party that was further expanded in 1973 and named the Likud. Between 1967 and 1970 Begin served as minister without portfolio in the National Unity Government. After eight unsuccessful attempts, Begin's Likud won a plurality of the votes in 1977 and 1981. Begin was the first Israeli prime minister to sign a treaty of peace with an Arab state, the 1979 treaty with Egypt. Although there were occasional challenges, Begin's control of his party was essentially unopposed. Begin resigned in 1983.

Yitzhak Shamir, the seventh prime minister, was selected by the Herut faction of the Likud to succeed Prime Minister Begin in 1983 and served until 1984. Shamir was born in Poland in 1915 and came to Eretz Israel in 1935. He joined the underground movement fighting the British in defiance of the official Jewish policy of self-restraint. He joined the radical Lehi (Lohamei Herut Israel – the Israel Freedom Fighters), also known as the Stern Gang, and was widely considered to have played an active role in planning the assassinations of senior British officials. After statehood he worked for Mossad, Israel's intelligence agency, and later became a Herut member of the Knesset. He served as Chairman of the Knesset after the Likud's ascension to power in 1977 and as foreign minister after Moshe Dayan resigned that post in 1980. In 1979 he opposed the peace treaty with Egypt, but since he was Chairman of the Knesset at the time, he abstained rather than vote against it. In 1984, he became foreign minister in the National Unity Government headed by Shimon Peres.

Shimon Peres, the eighth prime minister of Israel, was born in Poland in 1923. He immigrated to Israel in 1934. When he was twenty, he was elected head of the youth group associated with Mapai. In 1947 he became active in the Haganah procuring arms. During the war of independence he served in the defense ministry and after the war was the ministry's representative in the United States. Between 1953 and 1959 he served as director general of the defense ministry. He was elected to the Knesset on Mapai's list in 1959 and served as deputy defense minister until 1965. He was one of the architects of Israel's nuclear energy program and the cooperative efforts with France in military and political spheres. In 1965 he left Mapai and followed Ben-Gurion to form Rafi. He served as secretary general of Rafi but broke with Ben-Gurion when Rafi decided to form the Labor party in 1968 along with Mapai and Ahdut Haavoda. Between 1969 and 1977 he served at various times as minister of immigration absorption, transportation, communication, information, and defense. In 1974 and 1977 he competed with Yitzhak Rabin for the Labor party's support for the role of prime minister but was defeated. In 1977, after Rabin removed himself from the top spot, Peres headed the Labor list in the election. Between 1977 and 1984 he headed the opposition to the Likud governments. In 1984 he headed the National Unity Government.

PRESIDENTS

Haim Weizman, Israel's first president, was born in 1874 in Russia. He studied in Germany and Switzerland and received his doctorate in chemistry in 1899. In 1898 he participated in the second Zionist Congress, and before the fifth Congress in 1903 he was among the founders of the Democratic party. In 1904 he accepted a position at Manchester University in England. In 1907 he visited Eretz Israel for the first time but decided not to settle there. In 1910 he became a British citizen. He emerged as a Zionist leader after World War 1 as a result of his connections with the British establishment. During the war he had aided the war cause through his scientific work, and in 1917 his diplomatic efforts brought about the Balfour Declaration promising the establishment of a Jewish national home in Eretz Israel. Weizman was then head of the Zionist Federation in England; with the Balfour Declaration he achieved political stature throughout the Zionist movement. In 1919 he signed an agreement with King Feisal regarding cooperation between Arabs and Zionists. In 1921 he was elected president of the WZO and continued sporadically in that position, occasionally losing to the socialists, who often opposed him. In 1937 he settled in Rehovot in Eretz Israel. His pro-British policies were rejected by the Zionist Congress in 1946. In 1947 he settled in New York and was active in recruiting the support of President Truman to the Zionist cause. In 1948 he was elected president of Israel; he continued in this post until he died in 1952.

Yitzhak Ben-Zvi, second president of Israel, was born in the Ukraine in 1884. In 1904 he came to Eretz Israel for a few months; in 1905 he began studying in Kiev. During the 1905 pogroms he was active in the Jewish self-defense movement. In 1907 he again came to Eretz Israel, this time as part of the second *aliyah*. He was active in socialist organizations. In 1910 he began studying law in Constantinople but was interrupted by the First World War. He was arrested and expelled along with Ben-Gurion. He was a founding member of Ahdut Haavoda and a member of the secretariat of the Histadrut's executive committee. When the National Committee of the Yishuv was formed, he was elected to its directorate. In 1931 he was elected chairman of the national committee's executive and became president in 1945. The National Committee dealt mostly with local matters, leaving the important international matters to the Jewish Agency and the Histadrut. After independence, he was elected to the Knesset but was never appointed a minister. In 1952 he was elected president, and was reelected twice until his death in 1963. He was widely regarded as a historian and intellectual, dealing mainly with various Jewish ethnic groups.

Zalman Shazar, Israel's third president, was born in Russia in 1889. In 1912 he immigrated to Eretz Israel as part of the second *aliyah*. He studied in Europe until the First World War and worked as a historian. In 1920 he returned to Eretz Israel as a member of a study mission and finally settled there in 1924. He became a member of the secretariat of the Histadrut's executive committee and a member of *Davar*'s editorial staff. He was given various missions for Ahdut Haavoda and later Mapai. He was a founding member of the Knesset and was appointed minister of education and culture in 1949. In 1951 he resigned from the government to head Israel's mission in Moscow, but the latter appointment did not materialize. In 1963, at the age of seventy-four, he was elected president. He continued in this post until his death in 1973.

Efraim Katzir, Israel's fourth president, was born in the Ukraine in 1916. When he was six, he immigrated to Eretz Israel with his parents. His studies were completed in Eretz Israel with the granting of his doctorate by the Hebrew University in 1941. In 1948, at President Weizman's invitation, Katzir joined the Weizman Institute for Science in Rehovot and headed its biophysics department. His career was academic and not political. He was elected president in 1973 and served until 1978.

Yitzhak Navon, Israel's fifth president, was born in Jerusalem in 1921 of a Sephardi family that had lived in Eretz Israel for generations. He studied Hebrew literature and Islamic culture at the Hebrew University and taught at a local high school. Between 1946 and 1948 he was head of the Arab section of the Haganah. From 1952 to 1963 he served as an aide to Ben-Gurion, and in 1965 was a founder, along with Ben-Gurion, of Rafi. In 1965 he was elected to the Knesset on the Rafi list and was later elected on the Alignment list. In the eighth Knesset, he served as chairman of the foreign affairs and security committee. In 1978 he was elected president; he served until 1983. In 1984, he became minister of education and culture in the National Unity Government.

Haim Herzog, Israel's sixth president, was born in Ireland in 1920. His father was the chief rabbi of Ireland. He immigrated to Eretz Israel in 1935 and studied law as well as attending the yeshiva in Hebron. He served in the British army in the Second World War. He served as head of intelligence in the Israeli army, as military attaché in Washington, and as Israeli ambassador to the United Nations. He was a member of Rafi and then of the Labor party, and was elected to the Knesset. In 1983 he was elected president.

A Sephardi for President

While political power has stayed firmly in the hands of East Europeans and their descendants, more Sephardim and others have achieved positions of prestige and influence over the years. Symbolically the most important office in Israel is the presidency of the country. While it wields some power in the area of forming the government, it is largely a nonpolitical task. Formally the president is elected by the Knesset by secret ballot for a period of five years and may serve no more than two consecutive terms in office. The election is by majority vote after the candidates have been nominated by at least ten Knesset members, with the agreement of the candidates. On the first two ballots an absolute majority of the Knesset (at least 61 votes) is needed for election; after that, a plurality is sufficient. The president may be removed from office if three-fourths of the Knesset members so vote. The president's role is nonpolitical with important moral, symbolic, ceremonial, and educational functions. He also has powers to grant pardons, which he usually does only after careful consultation. While his election is certainly political, on the whole his functions are not.

In 1973, after the death of Zalman Shazar at the age of eighty-four, a popular candidate for the presidency was Yitzhak Navon. The son of an old Sephardi family in Jerusalem, he had a long career in public affairs, having served with Sharett and Ben-Gurion. The party machine, and especially Golda Meir, opposed Navon's candidacy for political rather than ethnic reasons. Navon had been disloyal to Mapai by aiding Ben-Gurion, Dayan, Peres, and others in forming Rafi in 1965. Many thought that her opposition was an act of anti-Sephardi discrimination when in fact it penetrated to the real heart of the matter—political loyalty. Mrs. Meir added another (nonethnic) dimension to the issue when she declared that she would find it inappropriate to have Ben-Gurion's aide ask her in his new capacity of president to form a government. Efraim Katzir was ultimately elected to the post. It was a blow to many Sephardim since they were keen on Navon's election, but the Labor party machine won the day and had a distinguished scientist as president.

When Katzir's term ended in 1978 and he declared that he would be unwilling to be reelected, Prime Minister Begin announced that it was his intention to elect a Sephardi as president and said that Yitzhak Navon of the Labor party would be an appropriate candidate. What followed was a valuable lesson in how politics seeps into many areas of Israeli life: the election of the president, increased sensitivity to the growing Sephardi population, the desire to grant Sephardim representation at the highest symbolic levels of the state, and the inability of the Likud to elect its own candidate to the presidency. After the elections in 1977 (which brought them to power after 30 years of opposition) their major factions could not agree on a candidate. In addition, and in a more general sense, the case points up the dilemma known as the Arrow Paradox of Voting.

The paradox is named after the economist Kenneth Arrow and occurs in a democratic setting when the voters (in a country or in a committee) have more than two alternatives and order their preferences in such a manner that no majority outcome is possible. The election of Navon in 1978 is a demonstration of the dilemma presented by the paradox. When Begin announced his support of Navon, he had not fully taken into account the reaction of the Liberal party, which was anxious to elect Elimelech Rimalt, a long-time Liberal leader. Navon, supported by the Alignment and the DMC, was strongly opposed by the Liberals. Since Begin was adamant about the importance of electing a Sephardi as president, he proposed the candidacy of Yitzhak Shaveh, an obscure physicist, for the post. Begin's Herut supported the prime minister's candidate, as did La'am. The Alignment wanted Navon, but preferred Rimalt to Shaveh. The following situation developed: Shaveh had the support of 41 Knesset members from Herut, La'am, and the NRP; Rimalt won the support of 47 Liberal and Alignment Knesset members; and Navon was supported by 52 members of the Alignment, DMC, and smaller parties. Equally important, the preferences of the groups differed:

(1) Alignment and others	(2) Liberals and others	(3) Herut and others
Navon	Rimalt	Shaveh
Rimalt	Shaveh	Navon
Shaveh	Navon	Rimalt

At a crucial moment Navon announced his unwillingness to continue as a candidate. It was clear that in the situation as it developed Rimalt would be the winner. As Shaveh would not be elected, he too withdrew his candidacy, and then Navon returned to the fray as an alternative to Rimalt. Begin's group preferred the Sephardi candidate—even though he was an Alignment politician—to the candidate of the Liberals. Despite the fact that Herut and the Liberals were the major factions in the victorious Likud, Herut joined the Alignment and the DMC in voting for Navon for president. Navon received 86 votes and was elected in April 1978.[17]

5. Political Parties

The basic division of the Israeli party system, easily understood in the light of the 1984 elections, is between the parties of the Labor-Mapam Alignment (44 seats) and the parties of the Likud (41 seats). The division in the Knesset has shifted over the years; the parties of the Likud have grown greatly; and the notion of two blocks is handy in thinking about Israeli politics. Add to this a third cluster of religious parties and the picture is complete except for some loose odds and ends of small one-candidate and one-issue parties.

In Israel's proportional representation system of elections, many lists and parties compete. The record was set in 1981 when 31 different lists ran; in 1984, 26 lists competed. It is important to distinguish between lists and parties. A list is precisely what it says it is: a list of candidates prepared for the elections sponsored by a group of people banded together for that purpose, or by a political party or by a group of political parties. The list of Soviet immigrants and the women's list are examples of the first; Tehiya or Shinui are examples of the second; and the Labor-Mapam Alignment on the one hand and the Likud on the other are examples of the third. While a party sets up a list for the elections, not all lists have parties behind them. A party is an ongoing institution that seeks power within the established rules of elections; a list is the technical name given to those running for office together and says nothing about their institutional relationships.

In discussing Israel's parties in the 1980s it is best to refrain from terms such as *left* and *right*. First, the left-right continuum is a complex tool of analysis; after all, the left today represents the workers less than it has in the past, and the right initiated and approved major territorial concessions. Moreover, religious parties are very hard to place in the simplistic two-dimensional world of the continuum. Second, the major parties of Israel have been undergoing a fascinating metamorphosis, which has culminated with the emergence of two large amalgamations of political power, the Likud and the Alignment. Not only has each encompassed three or four traditional parties but these two groups have won a large share of the vote (see chapter 8).

The two major concepts needed to understand what has happened are *dominant party* and *political legitimacy*.[1] Both terms are discussed elsewhere, but for present purposes suffice it to say that a dominant party is one that wins a plurality of the vote for an extended period of time; is central to any coalition calculation; is identified with a crucial event in the nation's history, thus providing it with spiritual dominance; and is supported by diverse groups throughout its policy—for example, Mapai of the pre-state and immediate post-state periods. Legitimacy has to do with the perception of appropriateness, of fit, of dominant groups in society toward a party or leader. Thus, Mapai was perceived as legitimate, Herut as illegitimate. The weakening dominance of Mapai and Labor and the achievement of legitimacy on the part of Herut and the Likud sum up the political history of Israel since statehood.

Alignment Parties

The key group in understanding Israel's political system is the Alignment. This is true even though the group lost two Knesset elections after winning eight and barely won the eleventh. It is true because the history of Alignment parties and their leadership is closely tied to the history of the pre-state years, the period of independence, and the first three decades of statehood. It is true because the organizations set up by the Alignment—the Histadrut, Kupat Holim, kibbutz, and moshav—are mainstays and still largely under Alignment control.

THE PRE-STATE PERIOD

Ahdut Haavoda was established in 1919, bringing together various organizational undertakings begun under Turkish rule. With the defeat of the Turks by the British in World War I, organizational developments gained momentum. In 1920 the Histadrut was set up, forming a structure to further the social, economic, and cultural interests of the workers. The socialist leaders of Ahdut Haavoda were an integrated group of militants imbued with shared goals; aware of traditional Jewish culture, values, and scholarship; and open to the revolutionary movements and ideas sweeping Europe. Their ideological world was a confluence of the urges for social justice, class awareness, and Zionist aspirations. The instinct of their leadership indicated that their goals of national independence and social justice could be achieved only if the requisite political and organizational work was adequately done by them. Their varying brands of Marxist analysis all led to the conclusion that economic foundations had to be laid for the Zionist enterprise and that the Jews in Eretz Israel had to undergo a radical social transformation in order to realize the Zionist goal of a new Jewish nation.[2]

The 1920s saw the expansion of the Histadrut and its activities, although it was increasingly threatened by a largely bourgeois immigration, which failed

Political Parties

to join its ranks, and later by the severe economic crises of 1927 during which major enterprises, including the Histadrut's Sollel Boneh, went bankrupt. By 1930, faced with new issues, Ahdut Haavoda merged with a former rival party in the Histadrut and formed Mapai, led by Ben-Gurion, who was at the time secretary-general of the Histadrut. By 1935 Ben-Gurion was chairman of the WZO Executive and thus the leader of all Jews in Eretz Israel. As Ben-Gurion and the leadership became ever more preoccupied with national concerns, their socialism waned and became more pragmatic in nature.

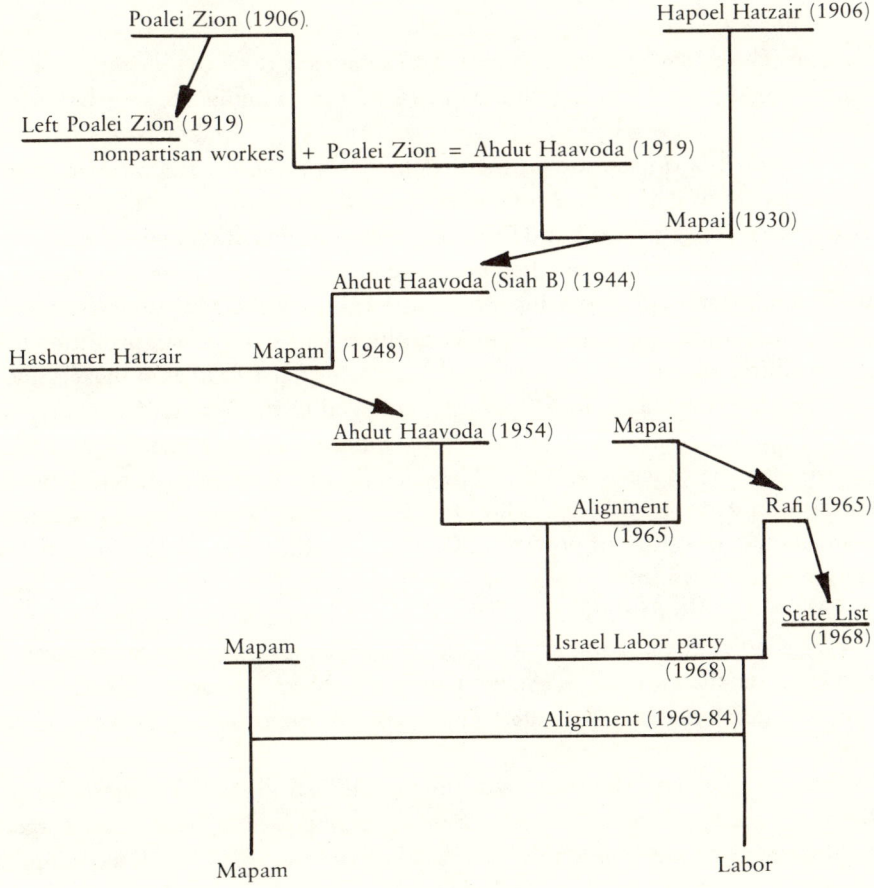

FIGURE 5.1

SPLITS AND MERGERS IN THE ISRAEL LABOR MOVEMENT

SOURCE: Aronoff, *Power and Ritual in the Israeli Labor Party.*

NOTE: Straight connecting lines indicate mergers; arrows indicate splits.

As the old Ahdut Haavoda moved to the right with the formation of Mapai, an active left-wing opposition emerged both within and outside the party. The left favored a less centralized and less powerful Histadrut and called for the strengthening of local units, especially the kibbutzim. The left-wing opposition was led by Hashomer Hatzair, the ideological center of the kibbutz Haarzi, although it refrained from declaring itself a party until the mid-1940s. The group endorsed a vision of Jews and Arabs living together in a binationalism, pursuing the class struggle for the mutual benefit of all. It was strengthened in the 1930s with the arrival of immigrants trained in its vigorous youth movement abroad.[3]

The left-wing opposition within Mapai took up the cause of the kibbutzim, which resisted the enhancement of the authority of the Histadrut. Kibbutz Hameuhad, a left-wing kibbutz movement, was influential in urban matters as well, its faction winning a majority in the local labor council of Tel Aviv. The leftist opposition was active in 1935, preventing the ratification of an agreement reached between Ben-Gurion and Jabotinsky regarding cooperation between the Histadrut and the trade union movement set up by the rightist Revisionist party. Ben-Gurion had negotiated the agreement without consulting the second stratum of leadership, and most of those leaders opposed the agreement. They were not prepared to compromise with a rival organization that stemmed from a party that had aroused extreme negative feelings in the Yishuv.[4]

The left opposition in Mapai fully emerged in the Mapai Conference in 1941, calling itself Siah B. It opposed the change in Zionist policy that called for the creation of a Jewish state. The left opposed plans for the partition of Palestine and also opposed statehood. Instead these leaders called for socialist control of all positions of power in the country and further settlement and development. The Biltmore Program, named after the New York hotel in which the American Zionist Organization endorsed the goal of Jewish statehood in 1942, became official Zionist policy in November of that year. Siah B, more favorably inclined toward the Soviet Union and Marxism, demanded recognition within Mapai as a separate faction with the right to veto majority decisions.

At the party conference in 1942 all internal factional activity was banned. But when the opposition faction persisted in its opposition, Ben-Gurion staged a showdown at a meeting of the Histadrut executive in 1944. Siah B left Mapai, renaming itself Ahdut Haavoda to indicate that Mapai had abandoned the ideals of the old party and that they were being carried on by the new one.

In 1948 Hashomer Hatzair and Ahdut Haavoda formed Mapam. Each component group had a kibbutz movement, which dominated it (Haarzi and Hameuhad, respectively), but these movements were not combined or integrated. This

Political Parties 75

enlarged left attempted to remind Mapai of its socialist origins even if it could not win power on its own. In 1954 Ahdut Haavoda left the merged party to emerge under that name. Hashomer Hatzair had persisted in its pro-Soviet policy, which was unacceptable to many in Ahdut Haavoda. Moreover, the Ahdut Haavoda leadership, especially the high concentration of the group that had served as officers of the Palmach, demanded a more activist foreign and defense policy than was acceptable to the Shomer Hatzair faction of Mapam.

Socialism is the major conflict theme running through the history of the Alignment parties. Some of them opted for orthodox Marxist-Leninism; others preferred a Marxist-Zionist brand or a humanistic social-democratic orientation with emphasis placed on nationalistic Zionism. Today, Mapam tends to favor the second version, the bulk of the Labor party the third. Differing international conditions reflect the line-up of parties at any given time. For example, immediately after the Russian Revolution of 1917, some parties urged following the path of class struggle. After the defeat of Nazi Germany in 1945, some followed the Soviet model, while others opted for a brand of Western European social democracy. On issues specific to the country, extreme leftist parties often take a binational position, whereas others take a much tougher line regarding the Arabs. Differences have developed within the Alignment over the eventual resolution of the status of territories taken in the Six Day War in 1967; some are prepared to return most or all of them, others none.

THE STATE PERIOD

In the years immediately following independence Mapai epitomized the dominant party. The largest vote-getter, the key ingredient of any government coalition, the standard-bearer of the society's goals, and the articulator of its aspirations, Mapai also had the tremendous political advantages of a united and integrated leadership; a broad-based, well-functioning, and flexible political organization; no serious political opposition; and control over the major economic and human resources flowing into the country. But Mapai failures, especially internal disputes over political leadership and ineffective party organization, were as important in explaining its eventual decline as was the gradual strengthening of the Herut movement and the Likud.

The point to start in seeking the seeds of decline is the notorious Lavon Affair.[5] When Ben-Gurion decided to retire (temporarily) from political life in 1953, Foreign Minister Moshe Sharett was appointed prime minister, Pinhas Lavon became defense minister, Moshe Dayan chief of staff, and Shimon Peres director general of the defense ministry. The latter two appointments previewed the emergence of the "young Turks" in Mapai; along with Ben-Gurion, they would oppose the old guard.

In autumn 1954 undocumented reports circulated that Israeli intelligence ordered a cell of Egyptian Jews to engage in bombing and arson against American installations in Cairo in order to harm relations that were at this time improving between Egypt and the United States. The group of 13 was detained; and two of them were hanged by the Egyptian authorities. An Israeli retaliation raid into Gaza, killing 40 Egyptian soldiers, could not wipe out nagging questions about the degree of training and readiness of the spy unit and the political wisdom of the plan. More critically, Minister of Defense Lavon claimed that he had not given the order for these acts and that his signature on the order had been forged. Isolated, he was compelled to resign.

The issue was revived in 1960 when Lavon received evidence that, in his opinion, cleared him. Ben-Gurion declined to exonerate him, reasoning that since Lavon had not been convicted, he could not be exonerated. Dissatisfied with this, Lavon infuriated Mapai by bringing the matter before the Knesset Committee for Foreign and Security Affairs, and the story leaked to the press. Since Lavon was also reported to have called into question the integrity of Dayan and Peres, the developing split within the party along generational lines was brought into sharper focus.

The findings of a committee headed by Justice Haim Cohen were not conclusive. Next, efforts made by Levi Eshkol brought about a statement by Sharett, acceptable to Lavon, that had the evidence placed before the Cohen committee been available in the middle 1950s, it would have brought a different decision concerning Lavon's role in the affair. A ministerial committee was appointed to study the matter, and it concluded that Lavon was free of responsibility. Nevertheless, Ben-Gurion insisted that as Lavon had evidence that imputed guilt to others, only a court of law could undertake the exoneration.

Ben-Gurion resigned as prime minister on 31 January 1961, thus bringing about the resignation of the government. New elections were held in August 1961 with Ben-Gurion heading Mapai's list for the last time. The party closed ranks for the elections, and only four seats were lost compared with the 1959 vote. But the party would never be the same again. Ben-Gurion was defeated by his former disciples on an issue that he considered one of principle. Moreover, unlike the situation when Ben-Gurion resigned ten years earlier, his colleagues realized that they could assert themselves and run things without him.

Conditions were ripe for Ben-Gurion's split from the main corps of second-stratum leaders in Mapai. These developments forecast tensions in the party for years to come. Ben-Gurion and the young guard he had promoted opposed the alignment with Ahdut Haavoda. The old guard favored it, regarding the Ahdut Haavoda leadership as a counterbalance to the appeal of the young guard and an alternative source of future leadership if the young, ambitious pretenders to leadership actually split from Mapai. More important, by neutralizing the young guard, the leaders of the third *aliyah* would be able to continue their rule. At the 1965 party convention the alignment with Ahdut Haavoda was approved by a vote of about 60 to 40. At the same Mapai party convention the delegates rejected Ben-Gurion's demand that the next government headed by the party reverse the government's decision to approve the recommendation of the ministerial committee exonerating Lavon by a vote of about 40 to 60. The emergence of Rafi occurred when Ben-Gurion simply announced the formation of a separate list. Six weeks later, the party expelled those members who had set up the new list; soon after, a reluctant Moshe Dayan joined the Rafi ranks. The Lavon Affair thus split Mapai, fostered the aspirations of the young guard, and gave the leaders of the third *aliyah* their chance to rule.

The decade between 1963 and 1973 was one of third *aliyah* leadership. Eshkol, the general conciliator and finance minister under Ben-Gurion, served as prime minister from 1963 to 1968. He was also defense minister until 1967 when, before the outset of the Six Day War, a National Unity Government was formed that included Rafi and Herut, with Moshe Dayan as minister of defense and Menachem Begin as minister without portfolio. Begin, head of the Gahal faction (Herut and Liberals) in the Knesset, was instrumental in having the National Unity Government formed. He even suggested that his old nemesis, Ben-Gurion, be recalled to power to head the new government. As the prolonged crisis that preceded the war simmered, the old-time leaders of Mapai, led by Eshkol, finally acquiesced. Eshkol's government was expanded to include Dayan and Begin.

The three years of the National Unity Government (1967-70), including the period of the Knesset elections of 1969, were most important in changing the perceived illegitimacy of Begin and Herut in the system. Eshkol agreed even before the war to a proposal (that Ben-Gurion had rejected) to have the body of Zeev Jabotinsky, the Revisionist leader and Begin's mentor, reinterred in Israel by formal decision of the government. After the war, even Ben-Gurion relented in his intense animosity toward Begin and Herut, and the two leaders maintained correct, if not warm, relations until Ben-Gurion's death in 1973.

The National Unity Government symbolically presaged future developments. In 1968 Dayan and most of Rafi returned to Labor, and along with Ahdut Haavoda and Mapai, formed the Israel Labor party. Begin and Herut remained in the unity government until the summer of 1970; they withdrew when the government decided to consider the proposals of U.S. Secretary of State William Rogers for a settlement of the Israel-Arab conflict. Begin's participation in Eshkol's government did more than anything else to legitimize the former leader of the outcast Irgun as a respectable, and ultimately alternative, leader.[6]

Golda Meir was the second member of the third *aliyah* to serve in the role of prime minister (1968-74). Selected by Mapai on Eshkol's death, she served through the Yom Kippur War and the 1973 elections. Soon after, she resigned. She left an Israel weakened by war, in increasing political isolation, with an enormously inflated defense budget, and a Labor party that would have difficulty overcoming the shocks of the experience.

When the Labor party was formed in 1968, its constituent parties comprised its institutions on the basis of the following formula: 57.3 percent Mapai, 21.35 percent each for Ahdut Haavoda and Rafi. The remnants of these three parties were partially intact six years later when the issue of succession arose. The candidate who had the support of the old-time leaders was Pinhas Sapir, an effective finance minister and party kingpin. Even in 1974, 54 years after the Histadrut was established, it was clear that the older generation could dictate the choice of prime minister to the party institutions if they had an agreed-upon candidate. While formal power had passed to younger hands, the old guard had the influence and the votes to determine the outcome. Yigael Allon and Shimon Peres were unacceptable to the majority Mapai group because they came from Ahdut Haavoda and Rafi, respectively. That they were now all in the same party and that these candidates were admittedly loyal leaders of the new party did not shorten the memories of an old guard trained in the tradition that the first rule of politics in Israel is loyalty to your faction. Yitzhak Rabin, chief of staff during the Six Day War and ambassador to Washington until a short time before the Yom Kippur War, became the choice of the convention; his political background was less clear than those of the others, and he had no obvious factional affiliation that could be used to veto him.

Rabin served as prime minister between 1974 and 1977 with Shimon Peres as defense minister. Before the 1977 elections, Peres contested for the top spot with Rabin and was defeated. Shortly before the elections, word was released of an illegal foreign currency account held by Rabin's wife. Rabin left the prime ministry and abandoned his plans to be number one in the Alignment's list for the elections. Peres was named in his place, and it was his misfortune to lead the party into opposition. Although ideological differences between Rabin and Peres were minimal, competition between the two continued. After the 1984 election, Peres became prime minister as part of the agreement that set up the National Unity Government.

Mapam was the junior partner of the Alignment between 1969 and 1984. In this period, it lost some of its distinguishing features. While it retained its own party institutions, it appeared subservient to Labor's policies and interests, and some voices within Mapam occasionally called for breaking up the Alignment. Its kibbutz attachment remained very strong, although for the first time in its history, a nonkibbutz member, Victor Shemtov, emerged as the leader of the party. When the Labor party agreed to form a coalition with the Likud in 1984, Mapam left the Alignment.

Likud Parties

The Likud group has three major components. The most important politically and ideologically is the Herut movement, set up by former Irgun leader Menachem Begin in 1948.[7] The second major partner in the Likud is the Liberal party, a bourgeois party that is the political continuation of the General Zionists of the pre-state and early state years. The third is La'am, a remnant of the Rafi faction of Mapai that refused to return to the Labor party camp in 1968 when the united party was formed. After Ben-Gurion's death, La'am joined the Likud.

As with the Alignment parties, the period of amalgamation began in 1965. Gahal was a bloc of the Herut movement and Liberal party and competed in 1965 with the Mapai-Ahdut Haavoda Alignment and in 1969 with the Labor-Mapam Alignment.[8] In 1973 the Likud was formed, joining the Free Center and La'am to Gahal.

Formally, such matters as nominations to the Knesset list, decisions regarding who would be the party's ministers in the government, and positions on ideological issues were resolved in each party individually. Since 1981, a movement to unite the Likud has been gathering momentum, although representatives of vested interests and ideas in the various parties have reacted apprehensively.

HERUT

The Herut movement is the direct ideological descendant of the Revisionists, a party founded in 1925 by Vladimir (Zeev) Jabotinsky. The movement's name derived from the party's belief that the policies of the Zionist Organization had to undergo immediate revision if the goals shared by all Zionists were to be achieved. Opposing the paths of conciliation and gradualism advocated by the socialists, the Revisionists demanded militancy in achieving their nationalistic goals. Jabotinsky offered a myth of martial strength to compete with the myths of the conquest of the land offered by the socialists and *tora veavoda* (religious law and toil) offered by the religious. Not by the patient accumulation of another cow and another *dunam*, but by blood and iron would the country be won. The Revisionist youth movement, Beitar, was named after Joseph Trumpeldor, whose heroism and labor ideology made him a hero in both revisionist and labor camps.[9]

Jabotinsky, a fiery speaker and original thinker, had been active in Zionist circles for years before resigning from the Zionist Executive in 1923 and conceiving the idea of forming a political party and youth movement. At first, the Revisionists worked within the frameworks of the General Zionists and the WZO, but Jabotinsky's ideas were seen as too militant and were unacceptable to the leadership. In the 1931 elections to the local Electors' Council, the Revisionists won 23 percent of the delegates, the second highest, with only Mapai's 42 percent having a larger share. In the 1931 elections to the Zionist Congress outside of Eretz Israel they did even better, winning 21 percent compared to Mapai's 29 percent. But by 1933, with the advent of Hitler and the murder of Haim Arlozoroff, Mapai surged to 44 percent and the Revisionists slipped to 14 percent. By 1935 the Revisionists had given up hope of taking over the WZO and formed their own New Zionist Organization. It was precisely during this period that Ben-Gurion and Mapai consolidated power in the WZO, with Ben-Gurion named chairman of the Zionist Executive. Jabotinsky's refusal to cooperate with the organized Yishuv headed by Mapai would earn him Ben-Gurion's political enmity to the end.

With participation in the organized Yishuv voluntary, there was no possibility of coercing dissident groups. The Revisionists were outside the organized Yishuv and were stigmatized by the establishment, which effectively denied them legitimacy. They were branded as irresponsible opportunists, unworthy of support and likely to pose a danger to the Zionist cause. Three incidents left a large layer of ill will: Arlozoroff's murder, the "season," and the sinking of the *Altelena*.

In June 1933, Arlozoroff, a prominent leader of Hapoel Hatzair and a gifted thinker and writer, was gunned down at the age of thirty-four at the seashore near Tel Aviv. The leadership of Mapai was convinced that the Revisionists were behind the murder.[10] The young immigrant Revisionist arrested and convicted of the murder was later released for lack of evidence. While Histadrut leaders were certain that Arlozoroff's murder was a Revisionist plot, the Revisionists were equally sure that the trial was the product of a conspiracy between Mapai and the British police. Years later it was revealed that two Arabs had confessed to the murder but had been silenced by British authorities so as not to force the police to admit that they had falsely charged the Revisionist. In 1982 an official commission of inquiry was established to look into the matter, indicating that memories and passions have not faltered that much.

The "season" occurred at the end of the 1944 and beginning of 1945. It amounted to cooperation by Jewish authorities with the mandatory power in rounding up members of the Irgun and Lehi.[11] The Irgun Zva Leumi was the major nucleus of Herut; it was formed in 1937 after Jabotinsky negotiated a return to the Haganah command structure of dissidents who had formed Haganah B in 1931. These dissidents numbered 100 at the time of formation and 3000 at the 1937 reunification. They were more militant than the Yishuv leadership and feared what they considered the pacifist policies of Histadrut leaders.

In 1940, after the Second World War had broken out, the Irgun was faced with the issue of cooperation with the British in fighting the war. The Yishuv adopted Ben-Gurion's formulation of fighting the war as if there were no White Paper (severely limiting Jewish immigration) and fighting the White Paper as if there were no war. Jabotinsky called for a truce with Britain, giving priority to waging war against Hitler. Abraham Stern rejected this path, and immediately after Jabotinsky's death in 1940, Stern took the majority of Irgun members with him in establishing Lehi (Lochamei Herut Israel). Stern's plan was to trade Europe's Jews for Lehi's support in defeating Britain and aiding the Germans to capture Palestine.

The Haganah, the military force of the organized Yishuv, had long operated an intelligence unit to follow the activities of other underground organizations, but rounding up and turning in fellow Jews to the hated British was an unusual act. The willingness of the leadership to participate in this activity followed the assassination in Cairo of Lord Moyne, the British minister of state in the Middle East, by two Lehi agents. This high point of the campaign of terror against the British helped Yishuv authorities agree to cooperate with the British security forces in detaining Irgun and Lehi "freedom fighters." This was often done in a clandestine manner in order to ease the troubled conscience of a Jew turning in another Jew—and this at the height of the European nightmare. The "season" successfully dampened the activities of the nonestablishment underground, but it did not extinguish its fire. Its leader, Menachem Begin, successfully avoided capture, and young new enthusiasts volunteered, filling the ranks thinned by arrest.

Some six weeks after independence, less than a month after the establishment of the Israel Defense Force and a few days into the truce worked out by the United Nations, a third trauma poisoned relations between the nationalist right and the socialist left.[12] The *Altelena* was a ship procured by the Irgun and carried some 800 volunteers, 5000 rifles, and 250 machine guns and ammunition. Irgunists claimed that the government knew about the shipment and that negotiations were under way for its distribution. Ben-Gurion did not disabuse his cabinet of the impression that the shipment was against the law and meant to arm the Irgun's men, thus defying the authority of the government. The ship was scuttled by army fire with the loss of the much-needed ammunition. After the public agitation died down, Ben-Gurion appeared to be the victor. He had upheld the rule of law and had crushed possible defiance of the primary rule of the modern state—that it is to have a monopoly on the use of violence. The Irgun disbanded, and many of its members reorganized as the Herut party. The traditions, leadership, and values of the Irgun and Lehi were transferred to Herut, but the new organization clearly accepted the supremacy of governmental decisions.

The images the leaders had of one another and the groups they led lingered for decades. Fissures were so deep that only time could heal them. This is why Herut's achieving legitimacy and eventual power was so long in coming. Ben-Gurion and Mapai understood that to deny legitimacy to another enhanced their own. The causes of the antagonisms have faded, but the mutual recriminations and passionate expressions of political views have been passed on to the next generation.

Menachem Begin was thirty years old when he became commander of the Irgun in 1943; five years later, he set up the Herut movement in which was to be found many features of the Revisionists, the Irgun, and Lehi. Most obvious was the role of the leader. Begin was still "commander"; his former staff became his aides. He tended to surround himself with his "fighting family" (former members of the Irgun and Lehi) and retained the fiery rhetoric and tough posture that had characterized his underground life. His first years in Herut were as stormy as the Irgun days. Immediately after the sinking of the *Altelena* and a round-up of Irgun and Revisionist party members, Begin declared that the State of Israel had become a totalitarian police state. During the debate over German reparations in 1952, he said that there should be no negotiations with Germany under any conditions. Mobs influenced by Begin's stance attacked the Knesset, and the future of Israel's parliamentary life seemed imperiled. A less intense furor took place seven years later when the issue of the sale of Israeli arms to Germany came up.

Ben-Gurion declined to call Begin by name, referring to him in Knesset debates as the man seated next to Dr. Bader. Ben-Gurion called Begin a fascist, a particularly weighty word in Israel right after the Second World War. Political passion was never higher, nor was Ben-Gurion's popularity. The combination of the two forced Begin to bide his time. His efforts were mostly parliamentary, attempting to provide the Israeli Knesset with a dynamic opposition; this he effectively achieved, especially on matters dealing with Israeli and Jewish honor and defense.

In the early 1950s Begin removed himself as head of Herut after the party lost almost half its Knesset seats in the 1951 elections, but he soon returned to head the party with added gusto. In 1965, after the newly formed Gahal did more poorly in the elections than anticipated against the newly formed Mapai-Ahdut Haavoda Alignment headed by the lackluster Levi Eshkol, a challenge was mounted against Begin's leadership of Herut by a group led by Shmuel Tamir, an Irgun veteran and a prominent criminal lawyer. After a bitter fight, Tamir lost and was suspended for a year by a party court. Perhaps taking his cue from the "young Turks" in Mapai, Tamir split with Herut to form the Free Center.

Because of the party's relatively poor showing in the 1969 elections, Ezer Weizman tried to wrest control from Begin. Weizman too was defeated by Begin's superior control of the party's institutions. Weizman went into political limbo to return as architect of the Likud's electoral victory of 1977 and as minister of defense in Begin's cabinet. After Weizman resigned in 1980, arguing that the government was not pursuing the peace treaty with Egypt energetically enough, and even voting against the government on a no-confidence vote sponsored by Labor, he was expelled from Herut.[13] He returned to head a list called Yahad in 1984. This list won three seats; Weizman joined the Labor Alignment and became a minister in the National Unity Government.

The Tehiya party emerged from Herut movement leaders (Geula Cohen and Moshe Shamir) who opposed the peace treaty with Egypt, which demanded Israeli withdrawal from the Sinai. This challenge to Begin's authority was also overcome within Herut, although other prominent Herut leaders such as Yitzhak Shamir and Moshe Arens abstained and voted against the peace treaty, respectively.

As Herut's electoral fortunes improved, the visibility of its leadership cadre increased. The pattern was not that different from the one experienced by the Alignment parties: first, the "fighting family" leadership; next in prominence, former generals; and finally, politicians with special representational qualities, such as Sephardim. The post-Begin period may introduce instability to Herut until the political succession is sorted out. Shamir's ascension to leadership in 1983 was the first time since 1940 that the major rightist group had been led by anyone except Begin. It is not clear that Shamir will be able to consolidate his grip on Herut and the Likud. If no consensus develops regarding Shamir or his successor, the Likud may well be in for the same kind of difficult and unstable period that faced the Alignment in the 1970s and early 1980s.

Herut's basic ideological plank on foreign policy has changed little over the years. At first it expressed Israel's claim over all of Mandatory Palestine. It refused to recognize the 1949 borders as legitimate, arguing that this would prevent Israel from taking advantage of circumstances if war was forced upon it. When the Herut movement formed Gahal with the Liberals, no changes were needed; each party retained its own platform. Herut supported the idea of *shlamut haaretz,* an undivided Eretz Israel, and after the Six Day War its platform stressed the importance of continued Jewish settlement in Judea, Samaria, Gaza, Sinai, and Golan. Immediately after the 1967 war, Begin, along with the rest of the National Unity cabinet, agreed to return Sinai to the Egyptians as part of a peace treaty. The Arabs refused; a decade later, Sadat and Begin agreed to the same thing.

A nationalist party, Herut's social and economic planks favored free enterprise, but not in a dogmatic sense. If government activity or intervention was needed to achieve national goals, this was ideologically permissible. The socialists and Mapai were anathema to Herut for historical, organizational, and ideological reasons. The Histadrut was perceived as a tool of the socialists to exploit the workers, and strikes were seen as a poison in the nation's system. After the General Zionists did so well in 1951, jumping to 20 seats from seven seats in 1949, Herut attempted to appeal to General Zionist voters by adopting a more liberal-bourgeois economic and social platform in 1955. While not a religious party, neither was Herut anticlerical, as the socialists were purported to be. The platform said, as did the original statement of the New Zionist Organization that Jabotinsky set up in 1935, that the movement would "implant the eternal values of Israel's heritage in the life of the nation."

LIBERALS

The Liberal party was the successor to the General Zionists. The General Zionists represented the core of the World Zionist Organization; their goal was to remain politically united for the common purpose of achieving Zionist programs. In the 1920s the General Zionists split into two factions. Faction A was led by Haim Weizman, then president of the WZO, and had a prolabor policy supportive of a conciliatory approach to the mandatory powers. Faction B, which was more bourgeois and middle class, supported private enterprise in Eretz Israel and had a more activist policy against the British.

Faction A, bolstered by the German immigration of the 1930s, came to be called the Progressives; Faction B retained the name General Zionists. By 1961 the two factions merged and formed the Liberal party, but the merger was short-lived. They again split in 1965, this time over the issue of electoral cooperation with Herut.

The Progressives retained their gradualist ideology and favored cooperation with Labor, a position they regularly achieved over the years by participating in Labor governments (even joining the Alignment in 1982). The majority of the Liberal party opted for the formation of the Gahal list, and the party split. The Liberals (former General Zionists) retained the name Liberal; the Progressives called themselves Independent Liberals, which seemed to refer less to their independence of thought or action and more to their independence from the General Zionists and Herut.

Clearly parties such as these were at a disadvantage compared with the ambitious and well-organized parties of the left and the religious groups whose members were in networks that extended beyond the political dimension of life and encompassed social, cultural, and often economic dimensions as well. As their name proclaimed, they were interested in the generalized goals of the movement and less so in the specifics of the project. They supported free enterprise and tended to disdain grass-roots organizational work, believing that their enlightened ideas would carry the day. The General Zionists and the Liberals tended to resemble middle-of-the-road European parties believing in limited government, a constitution, and free enterprise. They believed that if each individual was allowed to pursue his or her own goals, it would be to the advantage of the nation as a whole. Their prominent role in the WZO afforded them close ties and organizational advantages with important organizations such as Hadassah, Maccabee, and WIZO; but the General Zionists never developed patterns of party control over these organizations as did the parties of the left and the religious parties over organizations within which they were dominant. The General Zionists did not identify with the class politics of the left stressed by Mapai; they perceived the importance of the economic and agricultural enterprises undertaken by the socialist parties of the Histadrut in national terms and not in sectoral or political party terms.

The Liberals in the Likud have always been relegated to second place. Because no leader of national stature ever emerged from the party, its decision to accept Begin's leadership made political sense. The relations between Herut and the Liberals in the Likud are governed by rules set up over the years to divide power and jobs, by the practices that develop, and by compromise. The Liberal leader Simha Ehrlich was "kicked upstairs" from the job of minister of finance to the deputy premiership when the economic policies he introduced after the 1977 elections not only liberalized the economy but brought about an inflation rate of more than 130 percent a year. As he was the leader of the second major partner in the Likud, firing him outright would have been out of the question. Ehrlich's opposition to the appointment of Ariel Sharon as minister of defense, after Ezer Weizman resigned, prevented the appointment before the 1981 elections. Once the elections were out of the way, Begin could overcome Ehrlich's implicit threat of the Liberals rocking the Likud boat and appointed Sharon. The Likud council had decided that Begin would have the right to appoint ministers to his government, and so Ehrlich's and the Liberal's veto power were overcome formally. This was one more indication of the weak political role of the Liberal party. In 1984, Herut leaders tried to reduce drastically Liberal representation in the Likud list. After a tense period of negotiation, a moderate reduction of Liberal strength was agreed to.

The Independent Liberals have largely lost their position as the party at the center in Israeli politics. After achieving a handful of votes for years, their fortunes were cruelly dashed when the Democratic Movement for Change (discussed later in the chapter) reduced their power to one Knesset seat in 1977. By 1981 even that had disappeared. Their economic and settlement organizations, especially Haoved Hatzioni, will probably sustain them in existence. In 1984, they opted not to run independently and accepted a place on the Alignment's list.

Religious Parties

If there was ever an example of a political group whose power is greater than its strength in the country, the religious parties provide it. Consistently the third largest winner in Knesset elections, they have served as coalition partner to the biggest winner. To the big winner this makes good sense. It is better to pay the smaller price demanded by the third biggest winner than to pay the higher price that the second biggest winner could demand. With the exception of a number of months in 1958-59 and a number of weeks in 1974, the largest of the religious parties, the National Religious party (NRP), has always been a coalition partner, whether that coalition was formed by the Alignment (1949-77) or by the Likud (1977-84). In the 1984 National Unity Government, most of the religious parties participated.

The parties of the religious group are the NRP, Tami, Agudat Israel (the Aguda), Poalei Agudat Israel, Shas, and Morasha. The NRP is made up of two major former parties, the Mizrachi and Hapoel Hamizrachi. Tami split from the NRP in 1981 and Shas from the Aguda in 1984 over the issue of ethnic representation. The religious parties have adopted various forms of electoral cooperation in the past. In 1949 they all ran together as the United Religious Front, and in 1955 and 1973 Agudat Israel and Poalei Agudat Israel ran together on a joint list as the Torah Religious Front.

The best way to differentiate the religious parties is by their willingness to cooperate in the Zionist enterprise.[14] The most willing is the NRP, as its name attests. Its cooperation with the secular parties of Zionism in building the Jewish state has been complete with their sons (and some daughters) serving in the armed forces and their party being a member of the "historical partnership" with Mapai and Labor in the formative years and then a member of the government coalition with the Likud. Tami and Morasha, offshoots of the NRP, also fit into this category.

At a lower level of cooperation are the Aguda, Poalei Aguda, and Shas. They maintain separate organizational and social structures, although they agree to limited political participation. They do not consider themselves Zionists and see their role in influencing the Israeli government as similar to their role of influencing the local government in Boston or Brooklyn where they have large numbers of adherents. To ensure their support Israeli governments (led by both the Alignment and Likud groups) have allowed them unusual privileges, such as exempting their sons from army service while studying in yeshivas (daughters are completely exempt) and allowing them to maintain an "independent" school system partly funded by public monies but not controlled by the ministry of education. Although the Aguda has participated in government coalitions, its participation has been restricted since 1952. Until 1977, Aguda leaders often cooperated with Alignment policies but refrained from assuming cabinet positions. This pattern continued after the ascension of the Likud in 1977, with the Aguda formally agreeing to support the Begin government but not accepting a cabinet appointment. Aguda leaders were awarded chairmanships of important Knesset committees.

Religious separatists, including the Eda Haharidit and other extreme elements (some of whom are in the Aguda), pursue a policy of noncontact with Zionists, seeing in them a threat to religious purity. Naturai Karta, a small group of a few hundred families in Jerusalem and Bnei Brak (a religious suburb of Tel Aviv), refuse to recognize the legitimacy of the State of Israel to this day and accuse those who do of blasphemous behavior. There have even been reports that they have conspired with elements in the Arab world to rid themselves and their Jerusalem of the Zionist oppressors.

On the whole, religious groups came to terms with Zionism late, if at all. Although religious motifs, groups, and leaders were affiliated with Zionism from its inception, the most vociferous opposition to Zionism among Jews came from religious circles. It is therefore not without its irony that these religious groups should prove to be the most stable, organizationally, of the groups competing in Israeli politics. As a group, the religious camp has always won some 12 to 15 percent of the vote. The percentage in 1981 was lower than usual because the Tami split from the NRP evidently caused confusion, and the elections witnessed an unusually high level of voting for the biggest parties. It is likely that some former religious votes went to the Likud and Tehiya, a much smaller number going to the Alignment. Also, Poalei Agudat Israel's votes were "wasted" because the party came close but did not achieve the minimum 1 percent needed for representation. In 1984, five religious lists won 13 Knesset seats.

The passion for pioneering that characterized the left in the first half of the century is now found among the Gush Emunim religious movement. Gush Emunim sprang from the ranks of the NRP. Its members have brought to the project of settlement and redeeming the land of Israel the same kind of youthful excitement, dedication, and self-sacrifice that early generations identified with the kibbutz movements.[15] This is especially ironic since the kibbutz movements have continued to settle, and the Alignment-led government until 1977 and the Likud-led government after 1977 have supported settlement in many ways. But the public mind identifies settlement with Gush Emunim. Part of the reason is that Gush Emunim has broken with past practice and has settled in Arab-populated areas of the territories taken in the 1967 war. Another reason is that the Alignment parties settled so long ago and so successfully that their continued settlement was simply not news. A third reason was that the Alignment-led government did not want to flaunt its settlement policy, but to keep it under wraps. The Likud-led government had neither the personnel nor the organization to undertake similar tasks even when its government was in control. It was pleased to identify itself with Gush Emunim pioneers. The NRP benefited from this development; the Youth Faction and others strongly supported this behavior; still others, such as the religious kibbutz federation, were more cautious. Also, the shift of policy in the NRP in support of an activist settlement and foreign policy coincided with the structure of opinion and changing demography of the country. Gush Emunim, with the implicit and often explicit support of the NRP, could capitalize on the religious claim to the land of Israel, and the national and security importance of the territories, while using forms of settlement developed in earlier times.

In 1981 and 1984, the NRP lost strength to nationalist lists such as Tehiya and Morasha. Morasha was set up by Rabbi Haim Druckman, a former NRP Knesset member and Hanan Porat, a former Tehiya Knesset member, both Gush Emunim leaders. When they failed to set up a joint list with the NRP in 1984, they formed one with Poalei Agudat Israel and won two seats. The nationalist challenge on the one hand, and the Sephardi one on the other, has weakened the established NRP and Aguda.

The religious parties in Israel today are the clearest cases of total interpenetration of social, cultural, and political, and often economic life. Their members tend to live in religious areas, send their children to religious schools and youth groups, read religious party newspapers and journals, pray together, and vote together. In the pre-state period this interpenetration existed among socialist groups as well; there are still strong remnants of this, especially in kibbutzim. One of the last sizable communities in which political life is still so intertwined with social life is the religious neighborhoods. The educational activities of the religious parties are much more clearly identified organizationally and in terms of social and political values with their parties than is the case in parallel secular situations. Their youth groups are more successful in recruiting and conveying a clear social, cultural, and political message. The unifying effects of national sovereignty have only partially penetrated their value structure. Whereas "statism" (see chapter 11) tended to blur differences among parties in the secular camp, especially in schools and youth groups, members of the religious parties retained a central core of religious belief that differentiated them from the general population. This particularistic orientation was reinforced by the social, educational, and political structures that existed in their environment.

The existence of separate communities is reflected in the dress of the adherents. In modern Israel it is likely that a man whose head is covered (unless he is in the sun) is religious and supports a religious party. But the differentiation is likely to be even more fine. A knitted *kipah* (a skullcap) has become a symbol of the NRP and especially of its Youth Faction and movements; a nonknitted *kipah,* by extension, is likely to indicate support for the religious point of view but not necessarily for the NRP. The more traditional garb (common to Jews in Poland in the Middle Ages) of long-flowing robes and fur hats identifies the dress of the Aguda and their supporters and separatists. Different subgroups also have different colored socks, gowns, and other identifiables. The above is a rough measure only, raised here to point out how complete is the penetration of the community into the lives of the adherents, including the clothes (uniform) they wear.

As one would expect, the competition within the religious parties is intense. Each group grades the other in terms of categories important to it. The Aguda argues that the NRP is not religious enough, finding fault with the NRP's record of compromise and cooperation with secular governments and policies. The NRP emphasizes its record of contribution to the Zionist cause and education, arguing that a separatist Aguda can have no impact on the larger society and its values. The rabbis of the Council of Torah Sages, the spiritual and ideological guide of the Aguda, take to task the chief rabbis of Israel, associated with the NRP, for their interpretations and scholarly exegesis of the Halakah. This competition is made possible because both sides accept the same basic texts, the Bible and the rabbinical teachings, as holy and binding. All ideologies face the issue of interpreting dogma (witness Marxism), and all use the argument of ideological orthodoxy to bolster their interpretations.

Challenge from the Center

The Israeli political party system is firmly rooted in its historical origins. It is perhaps difficult for the electorate or outside observers to understand, but the party leaders of the Alignment and Likud parties perceive themselves as representing the left and the right, respectively. Their ideas, vocabulary, organization, and imagery come from the first half of this century and not the second. Their political world is one with a strong and leading socialist party and a beleagured but persistent right.

And so it came to pass that the two serious challenges to the established parties since independence came from within the left establishment and attempted to fill the void perceived to exist between the dominant Alignment and the revisionist right. The first challenge emerged in 1965 with Rafi, the second in 1977 with the Democratic Movement for Change (DMC).[16] Both lists appeared only once, but in their single appearances they were more successful than many long-established parties had been. Rafi won ten seats and the DMC 15. Both parties consciously attempted to fill the political and ideological middle ground between what they saw as a decaying Alignment and an irresponsible and out-of-touch Likud. Both tried to project the image of a centrist party. As the major groups were amalgamations of smaller, more ideologically oriented parties, it was not always easy to perceive the differences between the Alignment and the Likud. The insertion of a center party into the formulation allowed the larger parties to continue thinking of themselves as left or right. Both new parties perceived themselves as parties of the future, rejecting the Alignment and the Likud, which they considered parties of the past. Both took their major leadership and electoral strength from the Alignment camp, returning most of these resources to the Alignment after the aborted experience ended.

But there similarities end. Rafi split from Mapai, and with the exception of Ben-Gurion and the renegade La'am group, returned to it. As time passed, former Rafi leaders played a more and more important role in the Labor party and in the country. Shimon Peres was to become prime minister, both Moshe Dayan and Peres were to serve as defense minister, roles previously reserved for the Mapai leadership. Yitzhak Navon and Haim Herzog were to serve as president of the country. Ben-Gurion's bright "young Turks," impatient in their youth with their likely rates of ascent up the ladder of political power in Mapai, achieved positions of importance in Labor despite their disloyalty to Mapai. This was all the more likely because of the lack of alternative leadership in Mapai itself.

If the Rafi challenge came from the heart of the party system, the DMC challenge came from its periphery. The existing parties could ultimately ignore the challengers because the threat could not be sustained over time. Their leadership was ad hoc, without the bonds of mutual respect and understanding necessary for sustained political action. Rafi returned to the fold, the DMC disintegrated. Neither was characterized by effective organization at the grass roots. Neither was especially effective among the lower class, the workers, or the Sephardim (groups that often overlap). The appeal for good government

Political Parties

and to "throw the rascals out" worked in certain middle-class and professional groups, but could not compete with the organization of Mapai in 1965 nor the shift to the Likud in 1977 among many Sephardi voters.

The 12 years between the Rafi and DMC challenges to the prominent parties saw two important wars. In both Israel was victorious militarily, but in the latter Israel suffered terrible political and psychological blows, which shook national self-confidence. The Rafi campaign was a direct challenge to the leadership of Mapai and hurried the process of party amalgamation by bringing about the Mapai alignment with Ahdut Haavoda and, in reaction, the Herut bloc with the Liberal party. Rafi featured a young generation of political leaders straining to assume major roles of power sponsored by a charismatic political patron (Ben-Gurion) who felt wronged by the party he had set up. The generational effect was central to its appeal for efficiency, modernity, and reduction of bureaucracy in the face of a ruling power that spawned bureaucracy and was perceived to equate the good of the party with the good of the nation.

The DMC also had a reformist air about it, but the conditions that led to its creation were dramatic and troubling. The 1973 election took place weeks after the Yom Kippur War, and the lists submitted before the war were still in effect. The 1977 elections, then, were the first elections at which the terrible frustrations of the war and its aftermath could be expressed. The protest groups that had grown in strength and volubility after the war had largely disappeared (except for Shinui). The Labor party had also witnessed cases of corruption by key officials and even the suicide of a minister, Avraham Ofer, who evidently feared that he was being investigated. The unrest within the Labor party was at its height, and many leaders felt that the organization was too brittle to be able to change in any meaningful way.

The differences notwithstanding, the common plank in the Rafi and DMC platforms was electoral reform. The Israeli penchant to see cultural and political problems in procedural terms was again expressing itself. Change the method and you change the system, this point of view argues. Whether this truth is ever put to the test in Israel or not, neither Rafi nor the DMC was successful in bringing about this change, although the electoral achievements of both were impressive.

The DMC leadership disintegrated along with the movement during the tenure of the ninth Knesset between 1977 and 1981. Never an integrated leadership group to begin with, it attempted to set up a party with democratic structures, and this presaged its downfall. The three major components of the DMC were the Democratic Movement, led by Yigael Yadin, former chief of staff of the Haganah and a renowned archeologist; Shinui, headed by Amnon Rubinstein, who had been dean of the law school at Tel Aviv University and was a prominent newspaper and television personality; and part of the Free Center, led out of Herut by Shmuel Tamir. Preparations for the organization of the movement were rushed, partially because Prime Minister Rabin surprised the country by having elections in May instead of in the fall. The DMC decided on an open primary for determining its Knesset list, and for the first and only time in Israel political history, some 30,000 citizens participated in setting up a Knesset list. Allegations of noncollegial behavior, heard even before the results were counted, stemmed from practices of recruiting members and arranging deals to vote for (or not vote for) certain candidates. But the enthusiasm of the volunteers and the vocal public support pushed these concerns to the background as the excitement of a new, reformist party prepared for election day. The DMC determined the conditions for their participation in the government, most of them procedural and constitutional, the most important being an immediate revision of the electoral law and a call for new elections.

After the elections, it turned out that Begin could form a coalition without the DMC. He did so, relying on the coalition-wise NRP and Aguda parties. Realizing that they did not hold the balance of power, many DMC leaders pressed for participation in the coalition anyway, feeling that their constituents expected action and not loyal opposition. The call to join the Likud-NRP-Aguda coalition split the party, and Shinui withdrew. Some DMC leaders attempted to curb the excesses of Likud policy, especially regarding further settlement in the territories during the negotiations with the Egyptians and the Americans after Camp David, but on the whole their role was marginal. By the end of the term, Yadin returned to the Hebrew University and his archeology, Tamir tried unsuccessfully (despite Begin's acceptance but lukewarm support) to return to Herut, and Minister of Welfare Israel Katz joined Dayan's largely unsuccessful (two seats) Telem list in the 1981 elections. Thus ended one of the most promising, yet disappointing, chapters in Israeli politics for those who wanted to see new blood and new ideas reinvigorate the business-as-usual atmosphere of intrigue and personality-groupings. Shinui persisted and won two seats in the 1981 elections and three in 1984, a quiet echo of the clarion call for change heard in 1977.

With both Rafi and the DMC we can detect a reluctance on the part of the electorate to support the challenging party. We can see this by comparing the results of the party in Knesset and Histadrut elections. The two parties ran in both elections, and in both cases they did relatively better in the first of the two elections. In 1965 the Histadrut elections were held before the Knesset elections; Rafi won 12 percent of the votes of the Histadrut members and 7.9 percent of the votes to the Knesset. This is surprising since a new, young party should have been especially attractive to the emerging professional mid-

Political Parties   93

dle class, many of whose members were likely not to be Histadrut members. Making some liberal estimates, we may conclude that Rafi barely held its own between the Histadrut elections and the Knesset elections. About two-thirds of Israelis are members of the Histadrut, and Rafi's 80,000 votes in the Histadrut elections are almost two-thirds of the 118,500 votes it won in the Knesset elections. In other words, Rafi was unable to pick up a disproportionate share of the non-Histadrut voters or, alternatively, was unable to keep the loyalty of those who voted for it in the Histadrut elections till the time of the Knesset elections. Mapai's political machine worked overtime in 1965 to try to overcome the appeal of Ben-Gurion and his Rafi list. Judging from these figures, the machine was at least partially successful.

The DMC case in 1977 reiterates some of these points. In their first Knesset election the DMC won more than 200,000 votes, or 12 percent of the total. In the Histadrut elections six weeks later, it received only 8.1 percent, with about 75,000 votes. That is less than 40 percent of the votes it won at the Knesset election. We can again use the alternative explanations we used with Rafi — that the DMC was unsuccessful in picking up an unusually large share of Histadrut members; or that the Alignment was successful in returning voters to its fold by the second vote. Both explanations are partially true. Parties of the center that have emerged from the Alignment have not been able to attract masses of Histadrut members' votes. There appears to be a homing mechanism that works in favor of the Alignment when faced with this kind of challenge; many Alignment voters return to the fold and leave the new party with a feeling of only a victory and a half instead of two complete ones.

Other Parties

The parties that today make up the Likud and the Alignment, plus the religious parties, have always been important in Israeli politics. They have the greatest number of adherents and have figured in coalition calculations. Occasionally small parties become crucial to the system because of their contribution to government stability in the Knesset. Two examples of this are lists whose leaders were once in bigger parties but who broke off and ran in elections on their own.

Shulamit Aloni was elected to the Knesset on the Alignment list in 1969 but antagonized the party leadership by her outspoken stands in party and Knesset debates. It was clear that she would be relegated to a low position on the 1973 list, making her reelection very doubtful. Before the 1973 election (and war), she presented a list along with a women's group and a group advocating electoral reform. Her Civil Rights Movement (CRM) list won three Knesset seats with support from voters who wanted to punish the Alignment for its mishandling of the opening phases of the war but who were not willing to vote for the Likud. In 1974 her three seats became crucial in Rabin's attempt to form a government without the National Religious party. The CRM was in the government until the NRP joined it, at which time the CRM withdrew.

Aharon Abu-Hatzeira's Tami party found itself in a similar position in 1981. The list was set up after the leader withdrew from the NRP a short time before the deadline for submitting lists to the Central Elections Committee. Abu-Hatzeira was annoyed at the lack of support he received from the NRP leadership during his trial on charges of accepting bribes and because of the lack of representation in the NRP of Sephardi Jews. (In the 1981 trial he was acquitted because of insufficient proof; in a different trial involving misuse of public funds, he was found guilty and sentenced to serve a three-month prison term.) The three votes Tami won were instrumental for Menachem Begin in setting up his 61-vote coalition.

Barring a role in coalition politics, small parties lend local color (and at times comic relief) to Knesset deliberations, but their political role is insignificant. Individual party members may play an important educational or moral role, and the work of individual Knesset members may be important on Knesset committees, but since we are talking about political arrangements in which votes count, the small party is almost always at a disadvantage. Examples of colorful Knesset members whose presence enhanced the visibility of the Knesset were Uri Avneri, editor of *Haolam Haze* and head of a list by the same name; Meir Pail, who represented the New Left and Shelli; and proclaimed representatives of lower-class Sephardim, such as Charlie Biton. Arab voters are afforded symbolic representation by having delegates in the Knesset. The communist Rakah party and the Progressive List for Peace allow expression of Arab nationalist goals. Rabbi Meir Kahane's rabid anti-Arab positions added a tense dimension to Israeli parliamentary life.

A growing phenomenon has been the list headed by a leader who has split with his party. Moshe Dayan headed Telem in 1981. In 1984, four examples are Ezer Weizman's Yahad; a list headed by former Likud finance minister, Yigael Hurewitz; one headed by former Labor party secretary-general, Lova Eliav; and Likud minister and former Dayan running mate, Mordecai Ben-Porat. It is not clear from the 1984 experience if running alone is good electoral strategy: The first two won representation, the second two did not.

While Israel's electoral system encourages small parties, its political and cultural traditions do not provide them with a role in governing. They are given a platform for their ideas in the Knesset, if they know how to use it. There is no constitutional barrier to a small party's using this platform as a springboard to grow into a major party. While this has not happened, it could.

6. Party Organization

The party is the focus of contention for politicians ambitious to run the country or at least be on the fringes of power. It is the forum where ideological issues are raised, if not ultimately and formally decided. It is where electoral lists are drawn and approved, an act that determines the roster of personalities who will be in the Knesset, the natural reservoir of those with increased probabilities of attaining significant levels of power. Most crucially, the political party selects the person who will be prime minister of the country.

A political party is a group organized for the purpose of achieving power and holding office within a political system. This distinguishes it from a pressure group, which is intent on influencing policy on a certain issue. Israeli politics can be thought of on three levels: *electoral politics, coalition politics,* and *bureaucratic politics.* All three levels are associated with the political party. The electoral list is composed by the party, and voters perceive elections as a contest among parties; coalition decisions stem from the strength the parties have won at the polls and the decisions of party leaders; the efforts of the politician to achieve advantage in his organization by increasing influence and concentrating resources is a basic characteristic of bureaucratic politics, and the major locus of this behavior is the political party.

Political parties fill many functions. They set the political agenda; they select candidates and choose leaders; and they contribute to the process of political socialization of the electorate by transmitting political values and information to voters. They are also a force for unification in the divisive Israeli political system, for while the campaign is usually intense and the interelection period is marked by stinging attacks, the democratic contest among parties has generally been conducted within the rules. This controlled competition tends to bridle antagonism and stresses shared goals and ideals as much as it highlights differences among the parties.

Simply counting the number of parties in a political system does not reveal enough about the functioning of the system. While Israel has always had many political parties, for much of the pre-state era and for the first 29 years of independence, political power was centered in one party. Since the subject of politics is power and not merely formal, legal, or constitutional issues, two additional dimensions must be added to the analysis: the *competitiveness* of the system and the *rotation* between parties.

In Israel we have an example of a democratic system in which competition was allowed and free elections took place, and yet the ruling party was not rotated out of power. Certain states in the United States have also been known to continually elect members of one party (e.g., the Democrats in the South and the Republicans in the Midwest), even though competitive politics is allowed.

An attempt to come to grips with the dilemma of competition without rotation in a democratic system was proposed by Amitai Etzioni in what he called "an alternative way to democracy."[1] His argument was essentially that a nonrotative system could be democratic if the internal organization of the ruling party was open to competition among its constituent elements. Moreover, the party could be responsive to shifts in public opinion in the country by revising its formula for coalition formation. Having a plurality, not a majority, of the seats in the Knesset meant that the government was always formed by a coalition of parties. This meant that power was diluted, at least to some extent (see chapter 9). Etzioni's data extended only through the 1955 Knesset elections, but his basic argument could be applied up to 1977.

At first glance the Israeli political system seems to fit the multiparty pattern. But on closer reflection the multiparty model with its implicit assumption of instability is inadequate. At least until 1977, the Israeli case is an important example of a dominant-party political system. A dominant-party system is characterized by one party winning a plurality of the votes over a long period of time. But most important:

> [A] party is dominant when it is identified with an epoch; when its doctrines, ideas, methods, its style, so to speak, coincide with those of the epoch. . . . Domination is a question of influence rather than of strength: it is also linked with belief. A dominant party is that which public opinion *believes* to be dominant. . . . Even the enemies of the dominant party, even citizens who refuse to give it their vote, acknowledge its superior status and its influence; they deplore it but admit it.[2]

In the years immediately following independence, Mapai was presented with an opportunity shared by few parties in democratic polities—that of presiding over the creation of the constitutional and political order. As a consequence, it was closely identified with the new state, and it was the party of those segments of Israeli society most involved with those heroic years. It was able to translate this identification into an organizational network that complemented and amplified the advantages conveyed by its image. Furthermore, most of this network consisted of channels maintained largely at the expense of the state, with the result that party and government tended to merge in the popular mind. The role of governmental personalities in this image building process was most important, and until 1977 almost all were from the Alignment parties.

The strategy of the dominant party vis-à-vis other parties in the system thus has two principal goals: (1) to keep the party near the center where the action is, and (2) to mobilize and demobilize segments of the population selectively in relation to the needs and absorptive capacity of the party. In the development of this strategy the party benefits from its symbiotic relationship with the society in that its dominance ensures it a major role in the definition of where the center is. Moreover, its orientation toward power encourages it to move with long-term shifts in public opinion regardless of its ideology. Party strategists labor under obvious and not so obvious handicaps in moving the party in new directions; there is nothing inevitable about their success, just as nothing is inevitable about the continued dominance of the party. Wrong interpretations of public opinion, inadequate attention to the demands of major groups, misjudgments concerning the importance of marginal groups, poor organizational work—all can lead to disaster. As long as the dominant party performs intelligently, the opposition can do little that is effective. As Maurice Duverger has written: "The dominant party wears itself out in office, it loses its vigor, its arteries harden. It would thus be possible to show . . . that every domination bears within itself the seeds of its own destruction."[3] Even bad decisions by the dominant party are not disastrous unless the opposition is in a position to take advantage of them, which is seldom the case. And it is not in such a position because the dominant party has systematically excluded it and its leadership from positions of control and from the symbols of legitimacy.

As a result, the dominant-party system is remarkably stable. Disorder and even violence may be recurring features of the system, but they are surface disturbances that lead to little change. The opposition cannot replace the dominant coalition. The frustration of the opposition leads only to superficial instability. Although governments may not last long, the same parties and usually the same men continue to dominate the coalition. The faithful are rewarded, the opposition is shut off from power.

As in other dominant-party systems, in Israel the role of centralized hierarchical structures (especially bureaucracies) in the society is very important. The democratic internal processes that often exist in two-party systems are absent here.[4] The apparatus of mobilization typical of single-party systems is likewise negligible as a base of power, though it exists. Society tends to be held together by hierarchies that serve as the principal links between government and citizen. Indeed, these lines of communication, extended and humanized by networks of personal ties, are the true instruments of control in society, and they are either coopted or controlled by the dominant party.

Mapai and Labor were identified with an epoch and its values, and provided the leadership and ideology of the first 30 years of independence. With the passing of Labor from its position of dominance in 1977, it was clear that the Labor leadership had failed to remain attuned to changes within the society. All the problems are discussed at length elsewhere but listing them here is instructive: A new generation of leadership was not groomed after the old guard passed from the scene; the passing of the old guard coincided with a blow to Israel's military, political, and psychological prowess in the Yom Kippur War of 1973; the party's organization had grown lax, and nasty evidence of corruption had surfaced; the steady change in the demographic structure of the country was not responded to in a convincing way. In sum, not only had the opposition become convinced of the dominance of Labor, but Labor leaders themselves had fallen into the reassuring trap of believing in perpetual dominance. This was the start of their undoing.

What follows a dominant-party era? The question is not easily answered. Some Labor supporters assumed that in 1981 Labor would return to dominance after its temporary setback in 1977. This was not to be. Another possibility is rotation between the two large parties. For this, however, Labor's organizational work and structural change was not yet adequate; there were few signs that Labor had regained the support of the working-class voters it once claimed to represent. Even Labor's return to power in 1984 showed that many of the symbiotic relationships that characterized the first generation of Israeli politics had withered. As Israel entered its second generation of politics, many characteristics of the earlier era changed.

A third possibility was that the Likud would emerge as Israel's new dominant party, and thus the dominant-party system would continue but with a new dominant party. But just as the loss of dominance is not an abrupt matter, so too the establishment of dominance is a process rather than a moment. If the Likud is to emerge as a dominant political group in Israel, it must overcome the lack of organizational contact with the citizenry on an extended basis. Likud parties never had the organizational strength possessed by Alignment parties, a factor that facilitated the Alignment's dominance. On the other hand, the Likud possesses three characteristics that would be important to it on its road to dominance: (1) a major national turning point, the peace process with Egypt; (2) the broad support of growing sections of the population, the young, and the Sephardim; and (3) the absence of serious ideological opposition on the part of the Alignment. These three are necessary, but perhaps not sufficient, conditions for the emergence of a new era of political dominance.

As power shifts in a society, so does the organization of the political party change. In a society run by the nobility and clergy, politics was confined to the shifting coalitions in the king's court. When elections determine the division of power, it becomes politically advantageous to organize the electorate better than your opponents do.

A thorough categorization of the elements of party organization is provided by Maurice Duverger in his book *Political Parties*.[5] It is worthwhile to dwell on its contents, for his schema, perhaps more than any other, provides us with important insights into the workings of the Israeli party system.

Duverger divides parties into three kinds, which correspond with different historical periods. The cadre party was the party of limited suffrage when the leadership was made up of notables and the appeal was to middle and upper classes; the mass party was introduced by the socialists between 1890 and 1900; shortly thereafter, the fascists and communists introduced the devotee party.

The mass party concerns us most because this is the form followed by most Israeli parties. Adopted by parties of the left, secular and religious, mass forms quickly spread out among other parties in an attempt by the latter to imitate the success of the former. The basic organizational unit of the mass party is the branch, and the working class is the major focus of organizational efforts. Organization must be conceived in a broad sense; not only the attainment of office is at stake, but it is also necessary to transform society and the minds and lives of the workers organized in the parties.

The mass party generally has a socialist orientation, one in which centralization and discipline are strong. Properly motivated individuals do not need explicit instructions about how to act in their jobs or their public lives. The good of the party incorporates notions of the good of the state and individual good as well. Leadership tends to be oligarchical; elites of mass parties are developed by the parties themselves. This is perhaps one of the few instances in history in which political power can be obtained through organizational skill alone, rather than in conjunction with military, commercial, or ecclesiastical skill or office.

Membership in a mass party is very important, for the party needs not only sources of financial support but must also promote class consciousness among the membership. The number of members desired is very large, and the enthusiasm expected of the membership is high. Doctrine is important in a mass party to keep enthusiasm high, to stir class consciousness, and to suggest that the political and social payoffs for the party's strivings are attainable in the near future.

The proliferation of party-related bureaucracies in Israel followed neatly from the conception of the organization of a mass party and from the special conditions that existed in the country. Not only was there a scarcity of social services but the country lacked the basic economic infrastructure of roads, docks, and energy that are a prerequisite for economic growth and development. In the case of the Yishuv, the situation was basically unique because the political elite preceded the bulk of the population in arriving in the country and making plans for its future. Political organizations, then, provided some services and much ideological instruction, as they did in many European parties; in addition, the socialist parties of the Yishuv were key agents of socialization as new waves of immigrants arrived in the country. The immigrants were dependent on these parties, which absorbed them not only in the sense of party members benefiting by their party's activities but also in the sense of immigrants grateful to the absorbing authorities.

The development of parties of social integration stemmed from ideological and organizational needs. Peter Medding described the reality well when he wrote:

> . . . the activities in the party branch embraced much of the member's social life and were his major source of information and guidance in political and social affairs. His employment, friendships, cultural interests and leisure hours were all deeply influenced by his party membership focused on the local branch. Attempts were also made to encourage the member to live in politically homogeneous Histadrut housing developments. In addition, he read the Histadrut newspaper, *Davar*, which because of Mapai's control of that body, was in reality a Mapai paper, and subscribed also to one of the party journals, such as *Hapoel Hatzair*. A Mapai member could, if he so desired, lead his life in a completely party circumscribed environment, hardly coming into major political contact with outsiders, and barely subject to competing political influences or conflicting sources of information.[6]

It was inevitable that the large scale of membership-oriented activity should lead to drives for more budget, larger membership, and an ever increasing bureaucracy. Larger bureaucracies also meant more political control because more people were dependent on party activities for a livelihood. These people could easily be mobilized when demonstrations or elections took place. Larger bureaucracies also meant more jobs in the cities for an immigrant population that was on the whole of urban origin and was not anxious to fulfill the ideological imperative of agricultural settlement. And so the clerks, bureaucrats, and apparatus members involved in the delivery of health services, culture, economic activities, and education grew in number as the parties grew in power and control. As the bureaucracies expanded, more programs were sought, and the role of the bureaucracies and their leaders in the party strengthened.

The devotee party is also evident in certain communist and fascist party organizations in Israel. There is a basic justification in grouping these two forms of party organizations together, for despite the ideological differences, there is a basic similarity in the kind of individual to whom these parties appeal. Both parties demand fanatical devotion to the party and discipline to the dictates of the party. There must be a basic acceptance of the notion that, whatever the behavior, the party is working for the good of the class and the state; blind adherence to the leadership must be forthcoming. While communists may be considered on the extreme left of the social and economic continua and fascists on the extreme right, there is a sense in which they are very close to one another. In figurative terms, the continuum must be bent and the extremes joined as the continuum becomes circular. Then it is clear that in psychological terms the values and attitudes of both communists and fascists tend to be authoritarian, antiliberal, and closed-minded, unwilling and unable to put up with the frustrations and compromises necessary in a democratic form of government.

Perhaps the greatest similarity is in the extreme authoritarian structure of leadership within these two forms of party. The leadership is developed by the party, but fundamental obstacles to rotation are built into organizational structures; stable, if not always inspiring, leadership tends to emerge. Stability lasts as long as the leader lasts. After that, the crisis of succession is often severe.

Characteristic elements of the devotee party were in evidence in the Israel Communist party and Mapam, especially the feature of democratic centralism in the former and ideological collectivism in the latter, in which party members were required to accept the decisions of the party's decision-making bodies as ideologically binding. Debates and division of opinion are appropriate only until the party's authoritative bodies have ruled; after that, the membership must acquiesce in the decisions adopted.

Elements of devotee organization were evident in the Revisionist movement and its successors. Jabotinsky was given absolute power by a referendum of the membership in 1933; the leaders Ahimeir and Yevin openly advocated a totalitarian party led by a dictator.[7] The underground military organizations of the Irgun and Lehi continued this tradition, which also answered the needs of a secretive fighting unit. The values of discipline and obedience were exalted, and the use of ceremony and pomp was familiar to those who followed developments on the continent of Europe during the 1930s. In Herut, Begin was called the "commander" by members of the "fighting family" who followed him from the Irgun to Herut. When he arrived at a Tel Aviv outdoor election rally in the early 1950s, flanked by uniformed motorcycle guards, the imagery for many was indelibly imprinted.

The major organizational difference between the forms of organization outlined above have to do with the basic organizational units used by each party.

For the communists it is the *cell*—a secretive, small group of party members organized at the place of work. The location of organization was an important innovation of Lenin, emphasizing the Marxist analysis of the importance of economic factors in the life of the individual and the state. The cell can fill functions of encouragement, disruption, intelligence, or dissemination of ideas, all according to the needs of the moment. The branch of the mass party is connected with an individual's place of residence, thus making party activity an after-work enterprise. The branch therefore concentrates on providing individual services as well as cultural, educational, and instructional activities because members lack a common place of work. The branches of mass-membership Israeli parties, especially in the heyday of party activity, filled all these functions and were augmented by a complementary organization of the workers at the place of employment by the Histadrut. There, the political and occupational work of the parties could be pursued. The *militia* was the form developed by fascist parties as the unit of organization. Recruiting mainly from middle and lower-middle classes (as opposed to the working-class appeal of the socialists and communists), the fascists used the militia with its overtones of army discipline and patriotic symbolism to increase levels of allegiance of members.

It is fascinating to consider the implications of a high and a low membership-voter ratio. A party would obviously want its ratio to be high and steady over time. This would mean great appeal and a high likelihood of stability in power in the future. A party that registered a high number of voters but a low number of members could celebrate for that one election, but would have to suspect that its performance over time might be unsteady. It would not be unusual for a party in this position to begin a campaign for new members immediately after the election. If the number of members was nearly the number of voters, the party would have a firm nucleus of voter support but may have exhausted its potential because it was not successful in recruiting voters who were not members.

Table 6.1 lists the number of voters for 1977 and the number of members estimated or reported as of 1979. The ratio of voters to members was best for the NRP and was influenced by the relatively clear ideology of the party and the socially identifiable network that supported the commitment of the NRP. While the high ratio was probably influenced also by years of relative organizational stability within the NRP, it was unable to signal in advance the split that occurred in the NRP in 1981. The Alignment was also a mass-membership party, and its ratio indicates that. The Labor party's 1980 census counted 262,871 members; its 1981 vote was 708,536. The Likud, less than a mass-membership party but more than a cadre one, has a relatively low voter-membership ratio. Its appeal must be beyond organizational attachments; the Likud provided this

Party Organization

with a popular leader in Begin and by broadcasting a negative image of the Alignment. The DMC mushroomed nicely from its relatively small groups of leaders and militants to a party that was the third largest in the 1977 elections. The ratio alone could not predict that the DMC would not be around for the 1981 elections, but it was clear that the party would face organizational problems different from those of, say, the Alignment.

TABLE 6.1

MEMBERS AND VOTERS IN FIVE ISRAELI PARTIES, 1977-79

	Likud	Alignment	DMC	NRP	Independent Liberals
Estimated membership, 1979	100,000[a]	250,000	35,000	100,000	3,000
Voters, 1977	583,968	430,023	202,265	160,787	20,621
Approximate ratio	1:6	5:8	1:6	5:8	1:7

a. This estimate is based on 60,000 members of Herut and 40,000 members of the Liberal party.

A party would want to have many voters and just about as many members. But while voting has become more concentrated and less fragmented in Israel, membership has been in decline. The leadership of a party must keep in mind the three separate categories: activists, members, and voters. Appeals to each group must be timed differently. Ideally these three groups should overlap at the highest numerical level possible, but most people do not become members, let alone activists.

Party Membership

The development of political party organization in Israel is highlighted by a tendency toward mass-membership parties with extreme oligarchical tendencies. The tone was set by the parties of the left, both secular and religious, and the other parties followed. We might have expected that a bourgeois party with centrist ideological inclinations, such as the Liberal party (General Zionists), would have organized differently, but at least at the formal level, many characteristics that occur in the more successful parties of the left are copied by the Liberals. There is obviously an attraction in political life to mimic success, and this seems to explain why, at least on paper, most parties in Israel seem to resemble one another.

A closer analysis indicates that this is not really so. Take membership, for example. While formally all Israeli parties want members, this becomes more important in parties whose ideologies demand political and educational work in the electorate, whose program calls for party activities that demand budgets and bureaucratic organizations, and for outlays of funds otherwise unattainable. Obviously, these characteristics better correspond to socialist parties than to the General Zionists. This was especially true before the state was founded, for then much of the activity was based on party-related organizations, especially the Histadrut (to which the General Zionists did not belong).

In the pre-state period membership was very important for a number of reasons. First, in order to raise money. A steady stream of funds flowing in from the payment of dues was an organizational innovation of extreme importance in the history of political parties. But it was predicated on the assumption that parties did something, that they provided services. All Zionist parties engaged in fund-raising activities abroad, and none of them relied exclusively on membership in Eretz Israel to fund their activities. But the General Zionists and Revisionists had two advantages: (1) The level of their activity in Eretz Israel was much lower than that of the other parties, and (2) the extent of their success at fund-raising abroad was higher abroad than it was in the Yishuv. Members' dues in Eretz Israel for the socialist mass-membership parties were relatively more important.

Second, parties provided important services that were available only to members. The polity of the Yishuv was a voluntary structure, and few services were available on a universalistic basis because no central authority existed. The party (often through the Histadrut) could provide housing, employment, and health, cultural, and educational services. Being a member of the "right" party could enhance the probability of receiving these services.

Third, membership was important because it was believed that in the political struggle each additional member raised the likelihood of success. Membership was not conceived of as a passive role entered into only to receive material benefit. Membership was perceived to indicate agreement with the party's ideology and the efforts of the party's leadership. The party played an important role in educating the public through the education of its members.

Fourth, the assumed relationship between voting and membership was always at the back of the minds of party leaders. Growth in membership indicated growth in the potential of votes at the next election. Besides granting the leadership important psychological support, added members seemed to indicate that the party's program was growing in acceptability.

Fifth, the party machine, its bureaucracy, was very interested in members as a sign of its success. Short of elections, no clearer indication of organizational success was available than membership. Another incentive for the bureaucrats was that with each jump in membership, additional programs, and hence additional funds and additional jobs, must be added.

An important distinction to be made is between direct and indirect membership. A direct member applies directly to the party and is accepted on an individual basis. In most Israeli parties during the period when strong ideological divisions seemed to separate the parties, an applicant had to be recommended by a party member in good standing, in addition to accepting the party's platform and paying periodic dues. A much more practical arrangement in terms of the party organization is indirect membership. In this form one becomes a party member by virtue of membership in another organization, most often a trade union. Not only is the member offered a social support system within the party, but he is represented in party affairs by the same leaders who represent him in union affairs. In reality, as we can imagine, the worker is not overly aware of his party membership because he joins automatically when joining the union.

The conveniences for the organizational bureaucrats are clear. They can count on a steady income from the dues of the union's membership deducted from the worker's salary and forwarded directly to the party by the union. No more uncertainty regarding membership funds; no more fear that party positions will alienate members and bring about large-scale resignations. Another aspect of this same "benefit" from the point of view of the party bureaucrats is that they can now deal with trade union bureaucrats on political matters and no longer have to deal with the members themselves. The two sets of bureaucrats are likely to have similar backgrounds, goals, and life styles; hence they will probably get along quite well with each other.

An example of indirect membership comes from the National Religious party. When the Mizrachi and Hapoel Hamizrachi merged in 1956 to form the NRP, the merging organizations were not disbanded. Hapoel Hamizrachi handles issues of labor, agricultural settlement, the protection of rights of workers, and the development of labor and pioneering values. Members of Hapoel Hamizrachi have access to Histadrut sick-fund facilities on the basis of an agreement drawn up in the 1920s. Hapoel Hamizrachi members (but not all members of NRP) are provided services by the Histadrut, while their organization transfers a percentage of their dues to the Histadrut sick fund. These individuals are not members of the Histadrut, although they pay the same dues as do Histadrut members. They are members of Hapoel Hamizrachi, and by virtue of indirect membership, NRP members as well. This complex arrangement allowed Hapoel Hamizrachi to continue providing these services to its members without renegotiating the agreement, and allowed them to merge with another party to form a new one and retain their original organizational identity.

Since statehood, the importance and incidence of party membership have been slipping. Surveys find that the percentage of respondents who report that they are party members falls from 18 percent in 1969 to 16 percent in 1973 to 13 percent in 1977, 10 percent in 1981, and to 8 percent in 1984. The fall is gradual but consistent. The causes of the decline in party membership provide us with important insights into the problems facing Israel's party democracy.

The three most obvious causes of decline in party membership are the contraction of the roles played by the political parties, alternative sources of income for the parties, and the growing role of the mass media (especially television) in the Israeli polity.

The description provided about the roles of the party in the Yishuv period became outdated after independence. Many of the roles played by the party in defense, education, and employment were transferred to the state. Inevitably the citizen was less dependent on the party than before, and although habits persist, these new realities were perceived over time. The fact that the party leadership (especially in Mapai) became the national leadership reduced the perceived importance of party membership. Affinities were shifted as services were no longer undertaken by the party leadership (see chapter 11).

Up to 1969, much of the parties' budgets had come from their political organizations abroad or from groups and corporations affiliated with them or anxious to support them. An alternative solution of financing parties and their election campaign expenses by the government treasury was developed in 1969. This legislation mandated payments to the parties in proportion to their representation in the Knesset. The party receives one "unit" for each Knesset member, the amount being set by the Knesset's finance committee. In 1983 the "unit" was about $12,000 per Knesset member per month — or a total of some $17 million per year. The rationale is democratic because parties are central to a functioning democracy; the outcome is that the biggest winners are also the biggest earners for their organization's ongoing expenses. Special payments are also made for election periods; lists are granted a proportion of the funds based on the size of the delegation in the outgoing Knesset. If they do better in the new elections, they are reimbursed; if they lose strength, they may owe the treasury. The generous payments made by the public treasury to the political parties have introduced some oversight and scrutiny in the affairs of the parties, but each important party is connected with so many other economic units that it is clear that the controller-general is not apprised of all money transfers undertaken by the party or for its purposes. Since 1969, organizational efforts to recruit members to Israeli parties have declined.

The third cause of decline in party membership stems from the technological revolution of mass communication. No more are precinct workers or party bosses immediate and reliable sources of political information and encouragement. No longer are large crowds anxious to hear a party leader speak on the

Party Organization

issues of the day. No more are political relations cemented by a social visit or other informal behavior. For the vast majority of the population, the message of the television signal fills the functions of sizing up the leadership and comparing competing images.

Party membership answered important organizational problems for a certain kind of party at a certain point of development. One of the secrets of the socialist parties in Israeli politics was that they adopted, adapted, and perfected organizational forms that were developing when the pioneers came to Eretz Israel at the beginning of the century. Toward the end of the century the socialist parties face a dual problem: The other parties have learned many of their methods and have imitated them; the days of their organizational success have become increasingly outdated. Membership has become less important as the party offers less and less ideological direction and material benefit. The fact that the news carries nightly the comings and goings of party leaders and organizations takes much of the mystery and power out of the hands of politicians and places them in the hands of those who provide the news (see chapter 12).

In the internal life of a political party, membership may become a source of strife. This is the case when a census of the membership is taken. In a faction-based party such as the NRP, the census determines the relative strength of each faction in the party institutions and the party bureaucracy. It is not only a matter of prestige; it is a source of power and patronage of utmost importance. In the Labor party the size of the delegation to the party's convention is determined by the size of the branch or district; thus, signing up as many members as possible becomes a crucial resource in the internal struggles of the party.

By extension, preventing members from joining may be a method of struggling against a faction within the party. A classic case occurred before the 1977 elections when the issue of holding new elections in the NRP to determine the size of the factions came up. At that time Yosef Burg, the party's head, felt challenged by Yitzhak Rafael and the Youth Faction headed by Zevulun Hammer. The procedural debate that ensued placed the issue of membership at the center of the factional manipulations on both sides and showed how larger membership within the party could be perceived to be a threat to the faction's interests.[8] Burg's Lamifne faction had 28.8 percent of the votes in the party according to the last party election, which occurred in 1972. The faction headed by Rafael (which included Aharon Abu-Hatzeira) had 24 percent, the Youth Faction had 20 percent, the faction headed by Zerah Wahrhaftig had 13.7 percent, the moshavim had 8.8 percent, and the religious kibbutzim had 2.8 percent. When Wahrhaftig's faction merged with the Youth Faction, the votes that Hammer could command became greater than Burg's and caused Burg to have second thoughts about how secure his leadership actually was. Even more threatening to Burg was the likelihood that as a result of new elections in the NRP, it would be Rafael's faction that would emerge as the largest faction.

This outcome was likely because Rafael, as minister of religious affairs, had pampered the yeshivas belonging to the Aguda in Jerusalem and Bnei Brak. Their budget rose by a factor of eight in the first years of Rafael's tenure as religious affairs minister. The goal of increasing support to yeshivas is not in itself difficult to understand on the part of an NRP minister in charge of religious affairs. What must be clarified is how support for Aguda-related yeshivas could possibly be to his advantage in his struggle in the NRP.

The answer lies in the special arrangements in the NRP with regard to Hapoel Hamizrachi and relations between Hapoel Hamizrachi and the Aguda on the one hand and Hapoel Hamizrachi and the Histadrut on the other. Again we come back to the question of health services. Like other citizens, Aguda members want the best health services they can afford at a reasonable price, and as a rule they are found in the Histadrut's sick fund. It is not surprising, then, that Aguda members became members of Hapoel Hamizrachi—not to join the NRP, but to take advantage of the health services provided by the Histadrut (which is dominated by the Labor party). If the organizational arrangements are complex, notice that they result from rational behavior on the part of groups and individuals alike. Rafael's call for immediate elections without a previous membership drive threatened both the Burg and Hammer factions. But for different reasons. The Youth Faction wanted to open a membership drive that would net the party 10,000 new members. Their calculations showed that 90 percent of these new members would support the Youth Faction, likely making it the strongest in the party. Burg wanted to avoid both new members and new elections, feeling that in either case his position would be weakened: by the Youth Faction in the case of new members, and by Rafael's in the case of new elections. Burg's dilemma was adding 9000 new votes to the Youth Faction or facing the undiluted impact of 25,000 votes of the Aguda yeshivas to the Rafael faction.

The end of the story was the introduction of an amendment restricting eligible voters in the NRP elections to those members who did not participate in the internal elections of another political party during the past year. This "objective" rule could only be aimed at Rafael and his Aguda supporters, for it was the only party (for the first time in 22 years) to conduct internal elections that year. But elections were never held, and the competing factional elites in the NRP acceded to the organizational imperative that prefers to work things out among themselves without the "interference" of the rank and file. In 1977, in a stunning confirmation of the corollary that Robert Michels's iron law of oligarchy is suspended when the leadership is not united, Rafael was ousted from power. A coalition of elites ganged up on him as the list for the Knesset was being prepared. But that is another story.

The Iron Law of Oligarchy

Michels's iron law of oligarchy is one of the most insightful concepts in the study of political parties and is worthy to be described here at some length.[9] The notion is especially relevant to the reality of Israeli politics; Michels might have been writing about Israeli political parties and not German ones. Although he died twelve years before Israel was declared a state, Michels wrote (not about Israel) almost prophetically that "the social revolution would not effect any real modification of the internal structure of the mass. The socialists might conquer, but not socialism, which would perish in the moment of its adherents' triumph."[10]

The iron law of oligarchy posits that true democracy in any organization is impossible. Autocratic tendencies in an organization are neither accidental nor temporary, they are inherent in the nature of organization. "He who says organization, says oligarchy" sums it up well. Michels details the reasons that the masses are unable to control their destinies. There are technical reasons, such as the difficulty of assembling in one place or the need to make quick decisions on complex issues that demand great expertise. There are psychological reasons, including the fact that most people are apathetic about public issues, not knowledgeable enough nor engaged enough to participate in decision making. More important, argues Michels, most people want to be led.

Which brings us to the crux of the matter. Michels distinguishes between the mass of members in an organization and the leadership. The many financial, political, diplomatic, and informational tasks that must be performed cannot be performed by all. Organization implies a division of labor and a hierarchy of command. Whenever something *must* get done, someone has to do it; someone must see to it that this thing is done. Leadership necessarily arises in an organization and will act independently of the will of the masses. The leaders will likely speak in the name of the masses and of a democratic ideology, but Michels would counsel that we pay very little attention to what the leaders say and instead look at what they do.

One indicator of the psychological dependence that develops between the leadership and the mass is a phenomenon that might be called the customary right to office. Although formally a leader can be replaced when new elections are held, the fact that he has held office is thought to give him a moral claim on that office or some other leadership post in the organization. Playing on these sentiments may lead politicians to threaten resignation. This is generally very threatening—to the masses because it causes uncertainty and denies security, and to other leaders because it may lead to unpleasant confrontations and disclosures—and tends to be avoided, with the proper concessions made to the threatening leader. There is always the chance that the resignation will be accepted, and the prudent politician assesses these probabilities before he undertakes the gamble. On both grounds—the customary right to office and the use of resignation—Michels would be quite comfortable in Israeli politics. Ben-Gurion, Golda Meir, Yitzhak Ben-Aharon, among many others, successfully used the threat of resignation as a powerful tool to force their will on the group.

As Machiavelli pointed out, when the mass is deprived of its leadership in time of action, "they abandon the field in disordered flight."[11] This happens in politics and organizations as well. This need for leadership on the part of the passive masses makes them dependent on leaders and grateful for their efforts; concomitantly, it makes leaders of mass parties or the state extremely busy people. Soon the leaders as a group are perceived by the masses, and perceive themselves, as indispensable to the organization. The leadership develops power independent of the mass membership and is constituted as an informal subgroup. This is clearly evident in the salaries, expense accounts, and fringe benefits they vote for themselves from organizational funds—amounts that are larger than the wages of the workers they represent. This they justify by their enormous efforts and indispensability to the organization; the members, after rightly protesting this autocratic maneuver, approve the increases.

The leaders develop a sense of group superiority with regard to the masses, and soon the leaders themselves change. This drive for power is not only self-seeking but is also based on the belief that for them to continue in power would most benefit the organization because of their superiority, sacrifice, and indispensability. The extreme form of the development is that stage in which the leader "identifies himself completely with the organization, confounding his own interests with its interest. All objective criticism of the party or nation is taken by him as a personal affront. . . . If, on the other hand, the leader is attacked personally, his first care is to make it appear that the attack is directed against the party or nation as a whole."[12]

Peter Medding has written an important book on the role of Mapai during the first 20 years of statehood. Robert Michels would have immediately recognized the situations and manipulations. For example, Medding writes that "Mapai stood at the apex of a whole interconnected network of organizations and institutions which it controlled and directed from within" or that "the party was thus left as final referee, arbitrator or decision maker."[13] Medding writes that the party displayed a wide latitude in conducting the affairs of institutions it ran on behalf of the party—it was rarely upset by "lack of concern with constitutional formality [which] led to centralization of control in the hands of narrower executive bodies, and the inevitable lessening of the influence of the wider representative bodies." Strangely, after all this and more, Medding concludes that "the internal decision making process as we have analysed it provides impressive evidence against Michels's theory of political party organization." Since many decisions were made in Mapai in many committees and institutions, and not all were made by the handful of major leaders, Medding concludes that Mapai was an example of "consensual power relations: the views of many groups were put forward or taken into consideration, and bargaining and mutual compromise characterized the discussions." Medding's analysis confronts the iron law of oligarchy with essentially trivial exceptions to the thrust of Michels's argument. Mapai was an excellent example of Michels's iron law of oligarchy, and Medding's thorough research chronicles an oligarchical party at the height of its power.

Party Institutions

The major feature of internal party structures in Israel is indirect representation. This is "an admirable means of banishing democracy while pretending to apply it."[14] Its major characteristic is simple: Members cast their ballot only once for the broadest-based institution of the party. This broadest-based institution elects the next-highest-level institution, the members of the third tier are elected by those in the second, and so on. This arrangement facilitates control of the party by a group or groups of activists while professing concern with the demands and wishes of the broader membership. Indirect democracy can be thought of as a many-layered pyramid with each layer distilled to form the layer above it until the topmost layer is finally reached. Each layer is called upon to select only the layer directly above it, but all higher layers can commit the party as a whole, unless specifically prevented from doing so by the constitution.

Anyone with experience with adminstration will recognize the pattern and will even applaud its logic and appreciate its potential efficiency. If something is to be done, endless debate and mass decision making can be disruptive and time-consuming. On the other hand, this special version of democracy prevents the sustained control of the organization by the rank and file and lends itself to control and manipulation by groups of activists.

The typical structure of an Israeli party is a multitiered one that includes a broad-based convention, a narrower-based central committee that elects an executive committee, which in turn selects a secretariat. While the number of tiers and their respective sizes may change, the general principle applies. As a rule, the more tiers between the mass membership and the leadership, the more unlikely direct democratic control or, if you prefer, the more indirect the form of representation.

There is a great temptation in this setting to perpetuate the power of your supporters and friends and shut out the opposition—the very essence of oligarchic organization. As Duverger notes: "Party congresses are just like a meeting of employees facing their employers: obviously the former will tend to keep in office the latter, whose creatures they are." The major parties in Israel were all constructed on the basis of indirect representation. In 1979, for example, the Labor party had a 3000-member convention, which elected a center of 880 members, which selected a leadership bureau of 61 members, which elected a smaller executive. Obviously power becomes distilled to a very refined degree in this situation. The selection of the center becomes crucial in controlling the party, and great efforts are made to achieve a list of center members that will be selected by unanimous consensus. Because so many competing groups struggled for representation in the center in 1981, the Labor party simply enlarged the number of center members to 1150. This allowed many groups to feel politically satisfied, made many activists proud to be center members, and maintained the proportionate power relations within the party.

Mapam's convention had 901 members, its council 601, its center 401, and its executive 101. In addition, it had a 25-member committee and a select committee made up of the general secretary, the political secretary, and the center secretary. Mapam used a method of rotating members of the council in order to afford greater participation. The membership of the Mapam convention was so constructed that 45 percent of the members were from Kibbutz Haarzi, 45 percent from urban branches, and 10 percent from moshavim and Arab sectors.

The Liberal party has also seen changes in the number of people in its various institutions. In 1979 the Liberal convention numbered 801, the council 429, the center 196, and the executive 35. Herut had 1300 members in its convention and 700 in its center.

The NRP's structure took account of the fact that both the NRP and Hapoel Hamizrachi are represented in its formal decision-making bodies. Its joint convention had 902 members in 1979, the center 688, and the united executive committee 264. This last organization was the joint meeting of two separate executive committees of the NRP and Hapoel Hamizrachi, each committee having 76 members. When the two groups sat in joint meeting, 110 additional members were added. Democrats might say that this increases representation; political analysts would point out that this also increases honorific appointments while lowering the probabilities that key decisions will be made.

Party conventions are the supreme governing bodies of parties, but they provide imperfect examples of democratic practice. The most important point is that most party conventions do not result from secret elections by members of the party. Elections in many parties for the convention turn into an act confirming the existing leadership of the branch. In all the Israeli parties the vote for a convention delegate is for an individual, with the exception of the Liberals and the NRP in which the election is by list. While it may be possible for an opposition group to organize successfully in a district or two or in a few branches, it is almost inconceivable for an opposition group to pose a serious challenge to the leadership of the party at the convention because of the enormity of the organizational task facing it. If one must canvass hundreds of branch members in order to be elected, let alone elect enough convention delegates around the country with similar views, the advantage obviously lies with established party leaders and local activists. This is why successful opposition to the established leadership is rarely fielded from the grass roots. What is more likely is for dissension among leaders to galvanize the grass roots.

Often, local elections are dispensed with altogether. For Herut's party convention in 1975, only 11 out of 100 party branches held elections, the others being appointed by agreements worked out by local activists. This arrangement has characterized the Independent Liberals as well.[15]

Yet another limitation of the democratic nature of the party convention lies in the fact that additional members are often appointed to the convention by the convention without undergoing election anew. For example, it is customary to elect *en bloc,* as delegates to the new convention, notables of the party such as ministers, Knesset members, and members of the outgoing central committee. This serves the dual function of adding more establishment votes and avoiding the embarrassment of having a national leader lose his election to the party's convention. Usually there is an upward limit to the number of additional members permitted in this fashion, and often they serve in an advisory capacity to the convention without the right to vote.

The more supreme a political body, the less authoritative it is. This cynical point of view sums up the general assessment of party conventions in Israeli politics. Party conventions are large, unwieldy affairs needing careful control. This control is almost always provided by the party leadership. Usually conventions are staged for public relations and attempt to portray a party characterized by harmony, cooperation, and common cause. There have been notable exceptions to this: The 1942 and 1965 Mapai conventions predated the splits in the party, and the 1981 convention was the site of Peres's victory over Rabin for head of the party. It was at the Herut convention that Geula Cohen attacked Begin for the Camp David agreement, left the party, and set up Tehiya.

But, on the whole, party conventions are orchestrated demonstrations of organizational control and political compromise.

Party leaders generally promote a "central list." In the case of Mapai, and later Labor, this list usually included leaders of the local labor councils who were members of the party, leading party figures in the municipality or local council, and key members of the secretariat of the local party council. When contests develop, they tend to be over personalities and not over national or party issues. In the 1964 election for Mapai delegates, only six out of 84 branches had hard-fought contests, and these were related to personality clashes. And this at a time when the nation was agonizing over the Lavon Affair and Ben-Gurion's call for a judicial investigation.

The convention delegates, elected and appointed, are usually individuals dependent on the party and the leadership. Sometimes this dependency is material, as when large numbers of delegates are employed in party or party-related jobs.[16] Sometimes the debt is political, as when a delegate's continued political success is dependent on a good relationship with the party hierarchy and leaders. Often the dependency is psychological because individuals can develop feelings of organizational loyalty and solidarity with the party. Regardless of what the dependency stems from, its existence makes convention delegates instruments in the hands of party leaders and not active representatives of the rank and file.

Party leaders feel they have the power to commit their membership regardless of the loose linkage they have with members. This is clearly seen by the fact that the founding convention of newly merged parties in Israel has never been preceded by an internal election among the membership for convention delegates called upon to ratify the merger. This was true of Mapam in 1948, of the NRP in 1956, of the Liberals in 1961, and of the Labor party in 1968. The composition of the merged party's convention was arrived at through negotiation with leaders of the merging parties, and delegates were appointed by agreement. Should we be surprised that the conventions meekly ratified the mergers?

The key body in determining the smooth operation of the convention is the standing committee. This committee has had total control over the convention in the Mapai and Labor parties, controlling the agenda and the preparation of the convention. It generally has presented proposals to the convention that were adopted unanimously. The control of the standing committee has been the crucial element in controlling the convention and those bodies that determined its composition. Once the control of the committee was gained, the rest was a matter of detail. Myron Aronoff, who details these matters, stresses the ritualistic, ceremonial nature of Mapai and Labor conventions.[17]

Party Organization

The frequency of the convention is also a sore point of Israeli party democratic practice. The NRP's constitution, for example, calls for a convention once every fourth year (although the constitution does allow for the postponement of the convention). In reality, conditions are much worse; NRP conventions were held in 1956, 1963, 1969, and 1973. All conventions except that of 1973 were "agreed" conventions with the leaders' factions determining the delegates to the convention among themselves without holding elections in the party.[18]

The convention, the supreme body of most Israeli parties, provides an imperfect link with the membership because of the shortcuts used in its elections. The committee then becomes the agent that embodies the principles of indirect representation by selecting the party's center. The center, a smaller group than the convention, meets more often and plays a more central role in the ongoing life of the party. Often the center approves the party's platform and list of candidates, and debates important policy issues. As we have seen, much effort is made to select for a convention those who will conform to the leadership's wishes. The efforts extended regarding the selection of the center are no less great. The selection of the center is the focus of great political activity on the part of political activists and party hacks because the best way to determine the outcome of a vote is to control the composition of the electing body. On the surface the procedure is smooth enough with a nominating committee presenting a suggested list to the convention, a list that is almost always unanimously approved. The real action is behind the scenes in the nominating committee where intense political and personal pressure is often applied to increase the membership in the center of this or that group. It is the job of the nominating group (whether that be a special committee, the standing committee, or a small group of party leaders) to accommodate competing demands and end the process of selection of the center with a show of party unity. The factional parties, the NRP and Liberals, see to it that the factional division in the convention is simply perpetuated in the center.

The center tends to number a few hundred members and meets no more than a dozen times a year, if that. Generally it has the last word in electing the secretary-general and approving the party platform. In most parties it rubber-stamps its approval of the list of candidates for the Knesset, although in Herut its role is more active.[19] Party constitutions may have special provisions for the Knesset list, such as special quotas for women, Sephardim, and the young in the Labor party. But the nominating committee, controlled by the party leadership, puts these provisions into operation; the center approves.

The center is a microcosm of the convention whose importance is as symbolic as it is practical. What the center does is to choose the body next up in the hierarchy, whatever its name. This is a smaller group and hence a more powerful one. This rule is partially suspended when the party is in power. Then the leaders that made the small-party institution powerful by their presence and personal authority are concentrating their efforts in other matters. When most of the leaders are government ministers, their consultations become crucial not only for national policy but for party policy as well.

Another modifier of the rule of the inverse relationship between size and power of party committees is that the top party leaders must be involved. During the years that Herut was in opposition, the practice of the party was for the parliamentary party to decide the party's stand on issues and report to other party institutions. The dominance of the parliamentary party assured that its path would be followed by the party. When in power, the parliamentary party was overshadowed by the government and its Herut/Likud leaders.

Ben-Gurion's interest in party affairs shifted when he became secretary-general of the Histadrut and then leader of the Jewish Agency. As prime minister he had even less time for party affairs, and much of the real decision making regarding party policy shifted to the Mapai ministers in the government. This process became even more acute in 1954 when the executive of the party was increased to 19 members in order to accommodate pressures from ministers, parliamentarians, Histadrut officials, party branches, women, young members, ethnic groups, kibbutzim, moshavim, and workers in *moshavot* (smaller agricultural towns). Moshe Sharett, then prime minister, instituted meetings that consisted of Mapai ministers together with the secretary-general of the Histadrut and in effect bypassed the executive. Sharett was anxious to have the support of his colleagues and needed this form of collective leadership, especially after having followed the charismatic Ben-Gurion in office. When Ben-Gurion returned to office, he continued the meetings of this informal, extraconstitutional device.[20]

Once decisions were made in this forum, the participants were expected to follow the line in public and see to it that it was adhered to in decisions made by the party and governmental bodies. Such an informal network is infinitely stronger than formal constitutional provisions, but it relies on a very high degree of group solidarity and common purpose. A leader who finds himself at the head of such a network is blessed; he can utilize the formal arrangements in a much more successful manner.

Developments in Mapai continued in the same direction; after Secretary-General Lavon of the Histadrut stopped participating in the meetings in 1959, Sharett's committee became a committee of cabinet ministers. The executive had grown to 30 members, and since no real power was at stake, more groups could be given representation. And so, as we should have come to expect by now, another, more compact group was selected. This was the leadership bureau, and in establishing it (without any constitutional sanction) the executive abdicated much of its own authority.

This is not the place to document the ins and outs of intraparty politics, but the general picture is clear. Groups jockey for power, and the organizational structure is accommodated to the tides of battle. Control over the party is at stake, and resources are not spared in the effort. The mass of members is generally not brought into the fight—probably most of them do not know of it. Temporary truces are reached, usually giving time to marshal forces for the next battle. When a leader emerges whom the party can rally around, his authority can be brought to bear if he is willing to alienate one side in order to find favor in the eyes of the other. The infighting consumes enormous amounts of time and energy. While the politicians' ambitions and future careers are at stake, it is also important because the winners will be the ones to determine policy.

A larger number of tiers generally means that effective control is that much farther from the rank and file. Additional tiers are usually introduced to solve organizational problems, as we saw in the case of Sharett, and not to introduce antidemocratic tendencies into the organization. The proliferation of tiers usually has its origins in a desire to settle problems or distribute representation among the groups, sections, leaders, officeholders, pretenders to power, and bureaucracies that make up the party.

The impression should not be given that the internal life of a party is static, held in control by the ruling oligarchy. Often the contrary is the case with the oligarchy striving mightily to keep diverse elements of the party satisfied. Turbulence occurs especially when a group thinks that it should be stronger in the party hierarchy than it actually is in terms of positions, representation, or prestige. Sometimes it can be bought off easily by being provided with more jobs for its people or by having its leader appointed to a honorific position. Sometimes it can be coopted. Cooptation is a process by which dissidents are included as a minority in decision-making bodies, making them privy to deliberations and responsible for decisions without there being a real possibility that their points of view or program will carry the day. Sometimes there is no other choice but to accommodate them by granting them real power; because replacing members of existing bodies would likely upset other fine-tuned relationships, one strategy would be to bypass existing groups by setting up yet another body within the decision-making structure of the party.

Efficient structure or neat textbooklike organizational charts are not goals of political parties; control and political success are. Even if the organizational structures are messy, the questions we should ask ourselves as political scientists must center on political effectiveness, control, collegial relations, and the generation of an image of unified leadership. The latter will likely count for far more in the end than conforming to the abstract, and unproven, rules of rational adminstrative science. Party structures become more, rather than less, complex because changes tend to be made to existing bodies. It is unusual to start from scratch. Solving a problem by patching an already barely understandable structure tends not to clarify that structure but to make it even harder to understand.

Once the process is entered into, the momentum toward oligarchy increases quickly. Defenders of the form insist that it provides a satisfactory solution to the conflicting demands of democracy and organizational efficiency, allowing the membership to vote and yet concentrating power in the hands of the party leadership. Critics of the system identify this structure as one of the prime resources in the hands of the party leadership, which allows it to perpetuate its control over the organization. For if enough members of the broad-based convention can coalesce around a candidate or point of view, they can see to it that their view prevails in the smaller tier above the convention. In that body, the majority point of view of the convention can also be perpetuated when selecting members for the next highest tier, and so on. Power is not only perpetuated but is likely to be distilled and made stronger. As the body becomes smaller, the proportion of those with divergent views is likely to shrink. This, critics say, is the ultimate result of the system and its principal fault.

The system does not ignore lower, broader-based bodies but tends to convert them to rubber stamps. Decisions or nominations are sometimes brought before these larger groups and are approved by near-unanimous votes; the authority of the leadership is often brought into play, and the convention is not about to upset the precarious compromises worked out in late-night sessions. The convention feels a sense of responsibility to the party and its leadership, and typically abdicates its authority. This very understandable, very human, reaction still causes critics of the system to question whether the party must remain as centralized and hierarchical as it typically is in Israel.

It should be pointed out very clearly that this is not a problem invented by the Zionist movement or even by Israeli politicians. This is a fundamental problem in the life of organizations and is faced by kibbutzim, labor unions, university councils, voluntary organizations—by any organization that considers it a positive value to order its internal life in a democratic manner.

To those who despair of democracy in view of the inevitability of oligarchy, Michels's words are important. He expresses that famous dictum about democracy compared with all other forms: "If we wish to estimate the value of democracy, we must do so in comparison with its converse, pure aristocracy.

The defects inherent in democracy are obvious. It is none the less true that as a form of social life we must choose democracy as the least of evils." His view of the role of scientific observation is an important one. Democracy is to be desired, but oligarchy will always remain. The goal must be to put some limit on the absoluteness of oligarchy. For this we need detachment and objective analysis. "Nothing but a serene and frank examination of the oligarchical dangers of a democracy will enable us to minimize these dangers, even though they can never be entirely avoided."[21]

Israeli political life, as exemplified by its parties, its organizations, the Knesset, and the government, is highly oligarchical and hierarchical. But change can and has occurred. Politics, especially in its democratic form, means hard work, frustrations, and setbacks. Those who work within the existing parties must learn the rules of representation and the secrets of organization. Those who despair of the existing parties and attempt to set up new structures must take into account that past history and the laws of social science indicate that their new organization will not be immune from the rules of oligarchy described here.

7. The Electoral System

The voting act is conditioned by influences and pressures brought to bear on the citizen and by political arrangements that characterize the system within which the vote takes place. Electoral laws have political consequences, hence many constitutional issues in the realm of elections — reapportionment, extension of suffrage, financing elections, type of ballot, use of voting machines, single-member district as opposed to proportional representation, rules of party and candidate eligibility, and formulas for distributing the leftover vote — are matters that provoke the politician's serious concern and attention. The multiplicity of electoral arrangements is clearly a monument to the ingenuity of political man and a manifestation of his striving for power. Far from being objective rules to regulate the game, electoral laws are never neutral; they favor one political rival at the expense of another.

Legal arrangements are not the only constraints on the system of political competition. Social and historical factors can be just as powerful in limiting the range of potential outcomes the development of a system may produce. These factors may not be causal in determining who shall rule for how long, but they set parameters on the political struggle and its possible outcome.

Knesset Elections

Elections in Israel are held every four years unless earlier elections are called. Only the Knesset (Israel's parliament) can call early elections; the executive cannot disperse the Knesset, as can the monarch in Great Britain. There is no fixed date for elections other than the general instruction that they be held no less often than once every four years.

The tenure of the Knesset has been substantially shortened three times, in 1951, 1961, and 1984. The previous elections had been held in 1949, 1959, and 1981. In 1973, when elections were scheduled for the end of October and the Yom Kippur War broke out at the beginning of that month, elections were postponed for only two months. There is no history of the ruling party manipulating the election date for political advantage in Israel. The shortened Knesset time resulted from political crises. After the Six Day War in 1967 and at certain

The Electoral System

stages of the peace negotiations in 1978, the Alignment and the Likud, respectively, probably could have benefited from early elections, but they were not called. One explanation is that elections must be called well in advance. A Knesset law mandates a 100-day cooling-off period for a civil servant if he wishes to run in the elections. Since many parties infuse their political ranks with fresh blood from the military, diplomatic, or administrative services, it is customary to set the date for elections well past the 100-day period. A politician knows that in three and a half months his rosy prognostication might well change, and he might regret the move.

Israel's is a proportional representation list system of elections. Any list that receives 1 percent or more of the vote wins representation in the 120-seat Knesset. To present a list of candidates for the Knesset one needed 2500 signatures (in 1984) and a deposit of about $2000. The list of names is represented by a letter or group of letters, and the citizen, on entering the voting booth, chooses from these letters and places the slip of paper with the letter of his choice into an election envelope. Votes are counted on a nationwide basis and Knesset seats allocated in direct proportion to the strength of the list at the polls.

The list must be submitted a month before the election. The list cannot be altered; a voter chooses a list and cannot change the ordering or delete candidates, as is possible in some electoral systems. If 30 seats are won by a party, for instance, the first 30 names on the list become members of the Knesset. If during the Knesset's tenure a seat is vacated, the next person on the list automatically fills it. Neither by-elections (as in Great Britain) nor appointments (as in the United States) are permitted.

The Central Elections Committee, made up of representatives of the various parties in proportion to their strength in the outgoing Knesset, is headed by a justice of the Supreme Court and is responsible for conducting the elections. This committee must also approve the letter symbols of the competing lists. Each party chooses a Hebrew letter or group of letters, and campaigning and voting are conducted using these letter symbols. An interesting sidelight of the campaign is the symbolism involved in the parties' choices.

The letter combination the Alignment requested and was assigned was AMT—*aleph, mem, taf*. A good argument could be made for this combination, since the *aleph* (revealingly, the first letter of the alphabet) was traditionally the letter of Mapai, the *mem* the symbol of Mapam, and the *taf* that of Ahdut Haavoda, all of which were in the Alignment. But this special combination of letters was more than a throwback to the days when these parties ran as separate entities. For AMT (pronounced *emet*) means "truth" in Hebrew. And who can be against truth?

The letter *B* used by the NRP and the *D* used by Poalei Agudat Israel, both religious parties, have both been used in campaign rhetoric in highly symbolic and suggestive ways.[1] So was the *Z* (besides the name of the letter, the male sexual organ) used by the Black Panthers, a group of Sephardi Jews who felt they were discriminated against by the authorities, indicating succinctly that they were being "screwed."

Constitutional Provisions

The Basic Law: Knesset states that "the Knesset shall be elected in general, national, direct, equal, secret and proportional elections" (sec. 4). These six requirements are the legal basis for the relatively "pure" form of proportional representation practiced in Israel.[2]

General, allowing no discrimination among qualified voters. Every Israeli citizen eighteen years of age and older is entitled to vote. The issue of suffrage was a major scene of political battle in Western democracies. Israel was spared these battles, always opting for universal suffrage. In the Yishuv period, religious groups demanded the exclusion of women from the list of voters because, the argument ran, women have no role to play in public affairs. So furious was the debate that some groups boycotted the elections of Yishuv institutions because of the rules of women suffrage in the election. Others permitted only males to vote and then had the weight of the male vote doubled in order to compensate for the lack of women votes.[3]

National, that votes will be counted on a national basis, although administrative provisions are made for conducting elections and reporting results on regional, city, district, subdistrict, and precinct levels.

Direct, that each voter must complete the voting act by himself or herself. No delegation of authority or absentee balloting is permitted.

Equal, that each voter has the same amount of influence as every other voter. This ideal is probably unattainable in the real world because in all electoral systems some votes are "wasted," and the voters of "wasted" votes have less influence on the election results than do other voters. But, on the whole, the Israeli system approaches this ideal. While there are two reservations to this generalization (discussed below), even in spite of them, the Israeli system receives high grades for equality.

Secret, that it not be possible to identify the vote of the voter.

Proportional, that each list be represented according to its strength in the electorate, providing that it achieves at least 1 percent of the vote.

The reservations regarding the equality principle stem from the fact that, ultimately, the result of the electoral process is to select the Knesset. The 120-

member Knesset is selected by determining the "quota" of each seat. If there are 1,200,000 valid votes, a list will win a seat in the Knesset for each 10,000 votes that it gets. But reality is not that neat. Parties do not win votes in increments of 10,000; rather, one party wins 9994 and the other 14,968. What is to be done?

The first reservation regarding the generalization of the equality of the Israeli electoral system is that the minimum needed for winning a seat is 1 percent of the valid voters. That is, for the first seat in our hypothetical example, 10,000 votes would not be enough. One percent of 1,200,000 is 12,000, and 12,000 votes, not 10,000, would be the minimum needed to win a seat. By Israeli law, a higher price must be paid for the first seat than for those following it. (Technically, then, the second seat is cheapest.)

The second reservation concerns the distribution of the "surplus vote." Between 1951 and 1969 the party with the largest remainder won the vacant seat or seats. In 1949 and since 1973, the d'Hondt system has been used. Widely used in Europe, in Israel the method was popularly known as the Bader-Ofer Amendment, after the Likud and Alignment politicians who sponsored the bill and saw it through the legislative process.

The d'Hondt system provides for a floating quota after the original allocation of seats takes place. Each list has its quota recalculated in order to allocate the surplus votes; the new quota is the number of votes won by a party divided by the number of seats already allocated to that party plus one. Inflating the denominator in this manner obviously works in favor of larger parties to the detriment of smaller ones.[4]

The method works as its proponents desired. Of the three additional seats allocated in the 1973 elections, the Alignment won two and the Likud won one using the Bader-Ofer calculation. In 1977 the three largest parties (Likud, Alignment, and DMC) won a total of five additional seats compared to the largest remainder formula, the middle-sized NRP did not win or lose, but five small parties lost five votes among them.[5]

Proponents of this deviation from the principle of equality argue that the relative size of the electorate that supports a list must also be taken into consideration in determining the allocation of seats. A party supported by a million voters must be treated differently from a party supported by 20,000 voters. The d'Hondt formula expresses this preferential treatment. Opponents argue that this is a case of the majority legislating against the minority; indeed, all the small parties in 1973 banded together, regardless of ideology, to oppose the passage of the Bader-Ofer Amendment. In a system in which the multiplicity of opinion and political organization is legitimate and even encouraged, it is unfortunate that the two large parties "ganged up" on the smaller ones, even if the overall damage to the principle of equal representation is relatively slight. In order to safeguard the principle of majority rule, the new law stated that a party will not win a majority of the seats in the Knesset if it fails to win a majority of the valid votes in the electorate. This contained, slightly, the hue and cry that the amendment generated.

Electoral Reform

Debate over electoral reform has become a regular feature of Israeli political life. The interest shown by the press and the involved public stems from the belief, strongly rooted in the Israeli political system, that changes in the law can change behavior, that the formal rules of the game are central in determining the nature of the game and the way it is played. In a sense this is correct because the electoral laws ultimately determine who is elected and how much support they will have. But the debate regarding electoral reform is usually cast in much more general terms. Reform is championed as the way of changing the nature of the political system, making the member of the Knesset responsible and responsive to voters and altering the very moral climate of the country.

Electoral laws are as much a result as they are a cause of the political culture of a country. They project the political values and interests of the times and the ruling groups. Like other laws, they benefit certain interests and groups at the expense of other interests and groups.

The important point is that electoral laws have political consequences. They provide no magic formula for curing the ills of the nation. The laws are incapable of making politicians honest, officeholders responsible, or voters wise. In a simplistic sense, when officeholders perceive that it is in their or their party's interest to be more responsive to the demands of the electorate, they are likely to be so. A change in the electoral laws may also coincide with this perception, but the change in behavior (responsive officeholders) cannot be attributed solely to a change in the rules. The system is much too complex and the interrelations too many to use a simple mechanistic model to expect change in the political system as a result of legislation.

Electoral Systems

Two major democratic systems of elections—the single-member district system and proportional representation—provide us with a framework for considering the pros and cons of various electoral systems, making comparisons among countries, and inspecting criteria for judging electoral systems.[6]

The single-member district system (SMDS) is associated with government stability, while proportional representation promotes democratic representation. The first is widely used in Anglo-Saxon countries, the second is more prevalent in continental Europe. In SMDS, the candidate who wins a majority of the vote is elected. That is the "pure" case. Variations include electing the candidate who receives the most votes even if he fails to receive a majority, or electing the candidate who receives the most votes provided that it is more than a certain amount (say, 40 percent, as in the election of mayors in Israel).

Proportional representation provides for the election of representatives in proportion to the strength of the competing groups in the electorate. Usually individuals do not compete in this system, although in some variations the voter may rearrange or delete names on the list presented by the party or even choose candidates from different lists. Other details also vary from one example to another. For instance, the country may be one electoral unit (as in Israel) or may be divided into districts with competition taking place in each district according to the rules of proportional representation (as in Italy). Another limitation may be the minimum percentage needed in order to win representation. It may be a single arithmetic function of the size of the group to be elected and the number of voters (1 percent of the 120-member Knesset, as in Israel), or the number of votes needed for winning a seat may be fixed. Regardless of variation, the principle of representation according to electoral strength is the key.

The size of the electoral districts is the critical factor in approximating the ideal of proportional representation: The larger the electoral district in terms of seats, the more proportional the representation will be.[7] This is why the 120-member Israeli system is considered a "pure" version of proportional representation. This is why the NRP, a party that has traditionally opposed electoral reform to a constituency system, argued for dividing the country into five large districts; and why the DMC, whose platform heavily stressed electoral reform, opted for 16. The DMC reform would have increased local visibility of the constituency's representative at the expense of proportionality.

Since there is no perfect system and since electoral reform is not a magic formula to cure the ills of political or social systems, what does electoral reform try to achieve? Put another way, in order to make up your mind regarding electoral change, it is important to know what goals you are trying to reach. What are the important criteria for judging electoral systems? What is the experience of other democratic countries? Which system tends to be associated with which results? Four important criteria are system stability, democratic representation, the link between the elected and the electorate, and the role of the party.

STABILITY

In a parliamentary system in which the executive is elected by the legislature and the parliament is fragmented into many parties, the probability of instability rises. No clear majority is achieved by any party, coalitions are necessary for organizing the parliament and for legislation, and no easy agreement can be reached as to who should serve as prime minister. This condition has prevailed in many countries in Europe—in France before the Second World War and in Italy after it. The British system is more stable because only two or three large parties are in parliament and the leader is more clearly discernible. In Britain, coalitions are rarely needed and stability is the rule.

In presidential systems such as in the United States, France, and Mexico the identity of the head of government is determined by vote and is not decided by parliamentary coalitions. This is the meaning of the direct election of the head of government. The presidential system provides for stability of the executive and the government but does not ensure that the executive's relations with the legislative branch will be trouble-free, especially if the legislature is in the hands of another party. This development is very unlikely in a parliamentary system, for the stability of the executive is predicated on control of the legislature because the parliament chooses the prime minister.

Israel, despite its system of proportional representation, has not suffered from governmental instability. When Shimon Peres took office as prime minister in 1984 it was at the head of Israel's 22nd government. This was for 36 years and 11 elections. Italy, in contrast, had some 44 governments in the same period. Stability is not only a matter of numbers. The parties of Israel's prime ministers have been in firm control of the political situation for the most part. There has rarely been a feeling of lack of stability, despite the fact that Yitzhak Rabin headed a minority government in 1974 and that coalition problems have always been a factor in Israeli politics. In fact, Prime Minister David Ben-Gurion's problems in the early 1950s with religious party partners in his government coalition led him to suggest the adoption of the British electoral system of single-member constituencies. The central committee of Mapai adopted this position in 1954, and since then electoral reform has been a constant issue of Israeli politics.

DEMOCRATIC REPRESENTATION

The premise of proportional representation is that opinions in the legislature accurately reflect opinions in the population. This is unlikely if only because many people do not have firm opinions on many issues of public importance, and even those who do are unlikely to follow the "party line" on each of them. Furthermore, many voters are influenced by matters peripheral to the central issues, such as the candidate's television appeal, the persuasiveness of the campaign, or some emotional attachment with one party or another. The modern political party should not be understood as the mechanism for reflecting distribution of opinion in the population; it is more accurate to think of the party as the mechanism that transfers votes into public policy and political power. What the voter "really" meant is always a matter of interpretation. Proportional representation must be understood in terms of proportional political party representation and not in terms of proportional representation of public opinion or policy alternatives.

On the whole, proportional representation may not produce an identical image of the electorate in the legislature, but the distortion is not nearly as great as it usually is in the constituency system. Choosing someone to represent a district may pinpoint responsibility, but it denies representation to all those voters who did not support the person elected. The ideal of proportional representation is the faithful representation of all shades of opinion. This is a profoundly democratic notion and is in fact relatively modern. The idea of a single-member constituency originated in predemocratic days when legislators were expected to represent corporate bodies such as localities, universities, and economic corporations rather than individual persons. The British idea of constituency representation grew out of its feudal heritage and has remained the dominant political expression of the British system. Significantly, the British are now studying the possibility of electoral reform to a proportional system.

THE ELECTORATE AND THE ELECTED

A third criterion for the assessment of electoral systems is the proper relationship between the electorate and the elected. Two classic models are the free agent and the delegate. A free agent will vote his conscience regardless of the interest of party or constituency; the delegate will do as he has been instructed to the best of his ability. Modern representative government arose out of the proper relationship between the representative and his constituency. The free agent model assumes that the representative is only remotely attached to his constituents and that his understanding of the national interest will guide him.

In the Israeli system, an oft-heard criticism of the electoral system is that voters do not know who represents them. The party, especially the large party, is too anonymous for many voters. Technically there is no representative who can protect interests, hear pleas, or present proposals. Yet, in a broader sense, many Knesset members are selected by their parties precisely because they represent an important ethnic, occupational, geographical, or ideological group. Also, many Knesset members are often approached by interested parties to promote legislation or solve a personal problem. The fundamental question is on what basis groups are represented. The SMDS promotes geographical representation. Proportional representation promotes functional representation. In England or the United States a representative is identified because of his (or her) association with a given district or state. In Israel he is identified by the fact that he is Moroccan (or Polish), lives in a city (or development town), is for an aggressive settlement policy (or against it), and so on, *regardless* of where the representative lives. Obviously in SMDS it is simpler to identify your representative.

But the facts also indicate that even in constituency systems many individuals do not know who their representative is, let alone come in contact with that person for political purposes. We should not be misled into thinking that if we know who our representatives are, we suddenly become better citizens by participating more in debate over public issues. In Great Britain about half of the population does not know the party of their district's representative in Parliament, let alone the representative's name. In the United States the parallel figure is even lower. The proper relation between the electorate and its elected representatives is an extremely important issue, but it will not be determined simply by legislating a constituency system.

The Israeli voter has almost nothing to say about the selection of candidates for the party's list to the Knesset.[8] He or she must indicate a preference among the lists offered without the possibility of adding, subtracting, or changing the order of the names that appear on the list. Contact with the candidate is minimal both before and after the election. While the argument can be made that exposing the candidate to the judgment of the electorate would make him more responsive, the other half of the dilemma is that perhaps responsiveness to the momentary whim of the public is not in the national interest—in short, is not a responsible act. We return to the dilemma of the free agent and the delegate; it, in turn, leads us to the next major topic.

THE ROLE OF THE PARTY

The fourth criterion is the proper role of the party, especially the role of the party machine. Israeli parties have tended to be hierarchical, and small elite groups have tended to appoint the candidates for the party's list. While this loosened up somewhat in 1977, it is still the rule. These party leaders themselves were not elected by the public and yet, in effect, they are kingmakers. A very serious question of democratic politics is whether it is appropriate to have unelected leaders select candidates for high office, which, in effect, limits the choice of the public come election day.

One answer to this question is that it is a free country. Anyone who dislikes the way a certain party selects its list can either vote for another party or set up another list. As long as competition is open and unhindered, proponents of this view argue, there is no damage done to the democratic ideal. Alternatively, they argue, individuals who feel this way can involve themselves in the party and change the rules. The general argument in Israel has been that parties are keepers of an ideology, and as such they are in the best position to determine who is qualified to serve that ideology in the Knesset.

Indeed, basing itself heavily on the criticism of the role of machine politicians in other parties in choosing the list, the DMC in 1977 held a primary election among its 30,000 members to determine its list for the Knesset. Paradoxically, but not suprisingly, the most well-known candidates received the most votes. If democracy implies free access to decision-making positions, it was not attained by the DMC's primaries. The list of the DMC, chosen most democratically, was most heavily peopled by luminaries; the list of the Labor party, selected in a smoke-filled room by party stalwarts, was much more representative.

This raises yet another troubling dilemma: In Israel's parliamentary system, the party needs party discipline in order to govern. Party discipline demands Knesset members who are willing to be "delegates." On the other hand, it is important to attract to the Knesset individuals with skill, ambition, and talent. Is a talented person likely to want to play the role of party faithful and be disciplined when matters of importance are at stake? Will party interests always, or even often, meet the criteria of personal or national responsibility? Will a dynamic, thinking individual meet the test of acceptability that a party nominating committee is likely to use? Troublemakers and backbenchers are not looked upon kindly by nominating committees and are likely to be left off the list or placed in low spots the next time around. And yet these are the people needed by a dynamic, creative party. The dilemma is that discipline enhances stability, but also stagnation and a lackluster effect. To recruit first-rate people to the Knesset means allowing them more creativity; this works against the power of the machine bosses and the stability of the system.

This is not a problem unique to Israel. Some countries try to solve it by allowing alterations of the list presented by the parties, others by allowing the constituency to select its candidate pending approval of the central office (as in Britain). The primary held by the DMC in 1977 was a natural way of determining the place on the list of the competing leaders; while it was technically possible that they would not be elected, none doubted that the top leaders would be high on the list—the only question was where.

With these four criteria in mind—stability, representation, link, and role of party—we face the question of electoral reform. Different priorities will generate different systems. If democratic representation is considered more important than a direct link with the representative, perhaps proportional representation will be preferred. If government stability is considered more important than underrepresentation of minority viewpoints, then perhaps a form of constituency system will be preferred. All criteria cannot be fulfilled equally; some ranking of priorities will inevitably occur.

The Yaacobi Proposal

Many proposals have been made for electoral reform in Israel, but only one will be developed here.[9] Gad Yaacobi of the Alignment proposed to have Knesset members elected by two systems: The majority would be selected by district, the minority by the existing proportional system. An early version of his proposal was that there would be 18 five-member districts accounting for 90 members, 30 others to be elected proportionally. As this seems to be the most widely accepted version of electoral reform proposed, it is important to consider it carefully.

First, notice that the reform would add districts but exclude direct elections of representatives. In other words, all Knesset members would still be elected on a proportional basis, but instead of having one national constituency, there would be 18 smaller constituencies and one national one. In effect, the proportional nature of the district elections would still allow considerable control to be retained by party influentials and would not fully transfer power to the people's choice. Evidently each party would submit 19 lists, 18 five-person lists and one 30-person list. The person elected would be determined by the number of votes won by the *party* in the district and not the candidate. The voter would not be able to directly identify his or her representative nor be able to influence the party's choice of candidates.

Second, the minimal price paid for each seat would increase dramatically. Under the present system the minimum is 1 percent; under the reform legislation it would in effect be 20 percent in the districts (one in five) and 3.3 percent for the national list.

Third, the problem of differentiation would remain. It is unclear whether the voter would be permitted two ballots or one. That is, would he (or she) be able to split his ballot between an attractive district list of the Likud, say, and still vote his national preference by casting his ballot for the Alignment? Or would he be allowed but one vote that would serve both functions? In municipal elections the voter has two ballots, one for mayor and one for the municipal council. This would seem very appropriate in national elections too if reform is undertaken. Otherwise, the power of the electorate to influence a party to choose responsive and attractive candidates would be severely limited.

The Electoral System

Fourth is the problem of gerrymandering, or drawing arbitrary districts, in order to benefit the party that controls the apportionment process. An example would be putting predominantly religious neighborhoods in with four or five religious kibbutzim in order to dilute the strength of the Labor party and assure the election of the religious candidates. In fact, while gerrymandering comes to politicians easily, it is not too difficult to prevent. If a nonparty body, say, headed by a Supreme Court justice, were to be in charge of apportionment, it would likely be above reproach. In the Yaacobi proposal the districts envisaged are relatively equal in size and contiguous in land area in order to avoid gerrymandering.

There has been a tremendous groundswell in favor of electoral reform. Yaacobi's Rafi party stressed electoral reform as one of its chief planks in 1965. Yigael Yadin was active in the electoral reform movement long before he entered national politics in 1977. Rubinstein's Shinui group and the DMC all spoke enthusiastically of electoral reform, although most politicians preferred to speak in generalities and avoid details. The evidence of public support for electoral reform was striking. In 1972, 32 percent of a sample reported support for a mixed proportional-district system; by 1977 that figure had almost doubled to 59 percent.

Politicians, faced with this groundswell, were forced to react, and almost all parties indicated some degree of support for electoral reform in the 1977 elections. But in reality party politicians were very uneasy about electoral reform because it would add yet another element of uncertainty to their already precarious occupation. The footdragging could be clearly seen in negotiations among the Likud, the NRP, and the DMC to expand the coalition government set up after the 1977 elections to include the DMC. The DMC had an ideological belief in and had made a public commitment to electoral reform. The NRP, as a middle-size party with most of its voters in a few concentrated geographic areas, had every reason to oppose reform. The Likud, and especially Herut and Prime Minister Begin, were never enthusiastic supporters of reform, but had committed themselves to it in the election campaign.

The lines of argument were classic with the NRP wanting five districts of 16 members each (we must recall that large districts increase the chances of approximating proportional representation) and the DMC arguing for many districts with few delegates since their plank had been one of district representation. The problem was solved in a typical Israeli way: A decision was made not to decide. The parties agreed to set up a committee that would bring a proposal within a certain time. That period passed and no recommendation was made. The lack of enthusiasm on the part of most politicians was hard to hide. Electoral reform had not yet come about.

Whether electoral reform should take place is a matter of belief, preference, and evaluation. Whether it will take place is a matter of politics. Public support was unquestionably more in favor of electoral reform in 1977 than was the support among the political leadership. The small parties have everything to lose and nothing to gain, the medium-size parties are wary, and the large parties are unanxious. If the electoral system is reformed, the politicians are likely to back into it with their eyes closed, and the public will be surprised that even after the change, things will seem amazingly familiar.

8. Electoral Behavior

The distribution of political power in a democracy is determined by the electoral rules employed, by the party system and the actions of parties, by political events, and by the behavior of the voters (see table 8.1 for election results).

Voting Participation

Voting turnout in Israel has always been high; about 80 percent of the eligible voters voluntarily cast ballots on voting day. The highest rate of participation was in the first Knesset elections in 1949, in which 86.8 percent of the eligible population voted.[1] The lowest rate was in 1951, with only 75.1 percent participation. The number of eligible voters between the two elections increased by 70 percent as a result of large-scale immigration; the dislocation as a result of this immigration probably explains the lower participation rate. By 1955 the rate was back up to 82.8 percent. With the possible exception of the Bedouin tribes, voting participation is not associated with levels of modernization. The Bedouin 1977 voting rate was only 64.3 percent, much lower than other groups, but high by the standards of other countries.

Non-Jews also have had high rates of participation in elections. Even in Arab cities where protest is strongly felt and the antiestablishment Rakah won 70.8 percent of the vote in 1977, the voting rate was 77.4 percent. By 1981, however, the participation rate for non-Jewish settlements had fallen to 69.7 percent and the rate for Bedouin tribes to 53.3 percent. But by 1984 it returned to about 80 percent.

The motivation for nonvoting in Jewish and Arab sectors seems different. Few Jews abstain for political reasons; their reasons are generally technical in nature, such as illness, improper registration, or lack of identification. Among non-Jews, the dominant reason for nonvoting is that they prefer not to vote; in 1973, 54.6 percent of the non-Jews gave purposeful abstention as the reason for not voting, compared to 12.8 percent of the sample of Jewish nonvoters.[2] This explanation seems fortified by the 1981 elections. Because of the dilemma in which these elections placed non-Jewish voters, a record percentage simply did not vote.

Explaining the Vote

Besides asking whether people vote, political scientists are concerned with why people vote as they do. The answer to this question is usually complex but can conveniently be thought of in terms of (1) the political socialization an individual has undergone, (2) the major issues of the campaign, (3) the candidates offered, and (4) the voter's socioeconomic position.[3]

As a rule, people learn political symbols and values in much the same way they learn other values—through the family, the school, and peer groups. In the case of an individual whose political learning is reinforced by all the socializing agents with which he or she comes in contact, the result is likely to be high levels of belief and behavior consistent with the expectations of the environment. A good example is the voting behavior of kibbutz members. Their vote for the party with which their kibbutz federation is associated is generally very high. The pressures for voting for the party are rarely opposed by significant others. Just as most Israeli Jews accept their Judaism as a matter of course, so too most kibbutz members accept their socialism and identification with a political party as a matter of course.

The situation is more complex when cross-pressures come to bear. Among residents of a city, for example, where levels of political organization are much lower, socialization into political life or into voting for a specific party is likely to be lower and less intense. Voters who were affiliated with party-sponsored youth groups *and* internalized the values and identity of the party *and* were reinforced by the home environment in this learning are obviously more likely to continue voting for that party in later years.

It is almost impossible to know why people *really* vote the way they do. One way of trying to assess the vote is to ask voters what factor was most important in determining their vote. Another way is to ascertain what factors are associated with voting for one party and not another. In both cases we must take into account that factors we have not tapped are also at work.

Israeli voters tend to report that ideological considerations are important in motivating the vote. The Israeli political system is, and is perceived to be, ideological in nature; one is tempted to say that this is the ideology of the system. This is so even when strong, popular leaders are running for reelection (Golda Meir in 1969 and Menachem Begin in 1981). In none of the four surveys (see table 8.2) does the candidate carry as much weight with the voters as the platform of the party. This datum seems to be challenged by observers who note that the candidates for office in Israel are very important in attracting voters or, on the contrary, in detracting voters. Also, this datum of the centrality of the party platform or ideology flies in the face of the observation that ideological differences among parties are not great, although their style, emphases,

TABLE 8.1
KNESSET ELECTION RESULTS (120 SEATS)

Election Year	1949	1951	1955	1959	1961	1965	1969	1973	1977	1981	1984
Mapai[a]	46	45	40	47	42	45	56	51	32	47	44
Ahdut Haavoda[b]	—	—	10	7	8						
Rafi[c]	—	—	—	—	—	10					
Mapam[d]	19	15	9	9	9	8					
Liberals[e]	7	20	13	8	17	26	26	39	43	48	41
Herut[f]	14	8	15	17	17						
NRP	16	10	11	12	12	11	12	10	12	6	4
Aguda parties[g]		5	6	6	6	6	6	5	5	4	8[l]
Arab lists	2	1	4	5	4	4	4	3	1	—	2[m]
DMC	—	—	—	—	—	—	—	—	15	—	—
Independent Liberals[h]	5	4	5	6	—	5	4	4	1	—	—
Communist	4	5	6	3	5	4	4	5	5	4	4
Others	7	7	1	—	—	1	8[i]	3	6[j]	11[k]	17[n]

NOTES: *a.* Joined with Ahdut Haavoda in 1965 and the other labor parties in 1969. *b.* See note *a. c.* Ben-Gurion's party; joined the Labor Alignment in 1969 minus the State List. *d.* Ahdut Haavoda included in Mapam in 1949 and 1951. *e.* Until 1959 known as General Zionists; joined Herut to form Gahal in 1965, and part of the Likud in 1973. *f.* Jointly with the Liberals since 1965 and part of the Likud in 1973. *g.* Poalei Agudat Israel and Agudat Israel. *h.* Included in Liberal party in 1961 and independent again since 1965. In 1984, part of Alignment. *i.* Includes the State List (4 members), the Free Center (2 members), and Haolam Haze (2 members). The first two joined Herut and the Liberals in 1973. *j.* Includes Shlomzion (2 members), which joined the Likud after the elections, Shelli (2 members), the Citizens' Rights Movement (1 member), and Flatto Sharon (1 member). *k.* Includes Tehiya (3 members), Tami (3 members), Telem (2 members), Shinui (2 members), and the Civil Rights Movement (1 member). *l.* Including Shas (4 members), Aguda (2 members), and Morasha (partly Poalei Agudat Israel, 2 members). *m.* Progressive List for Peace. *n.* Including Tehiya (5 members), Shinui (3 members), Civil Rights Movement (3 members), Yahad (3 members), Tami (1 member), Hurewitz (1 member), and Kach (1 member).

and images may be. The reported importance of identification with the party is growing even while membership in parties is decreasing. While the role of the candidate is growing in the television-dominated election campaign, and party differences are made to seem larger than they really are during the campaign, the fascinating point is that Israelis report that their voting decision is dominated by ideological considerations. The Israeli voter has internalized the expectation of democratic theorists that voters make their decision by virtue of rational, cognitive processes. Obviously other factors are also at work, but this is the way Israelis present themselves to others.[4]

TABLE 8.2

DETERMINING FACTOR IN THE VOTE

"Which is the most important factor in influencing a person to vote for a particular party?"

	1969	1977	1981	1984
Identification with the party	17%	26%	31%	32%
The party's candidate	21	15	18	10
The party's platform/ideology	37	46	38	53
The party being in government or opposition	7	6	7	4
Other reason; no answer	18	7	6	2
N =	1314	1372	1237	1259

Voting behavior in Israel must be understood in terms of the dominant party that was at the heart of the political system for 30 years. Mapai, now Labor, found support among all groups, but especially among those who identified with the epoch in which the party rose to its peak and to the epoch's dominant values. The highlight of Mapai's (Labor's) achievements was the gaining of independence. All the projects undertaken by the Jews in Eretz Israel—immigration, building the land, security—were highlighted by achieving independence. After the founding of the state, these undertakings were continued, sometimes within different organizational settings and institutional arrangements, but with much of the same symbolism and ideological justification. One who lived through the independence epoch in Israel was more likely to identify with the dominant party. In the process of having party and movement values permeate the society, the distinction between party and state was often blurred. Achievements of state accrued to the benefit of the party. Jews who immigrated to Israel before independence and immediately thereafter continued to support the Alignment heavily. The rate fell off for those who immigrated after 1955, and for Israel-born voters.

Much of the program and appeal of the dominant Labor party at the time of independence must be seen in the light of the social and political realities that the Labor leadership knew in Eastern Europe in the first decades of the twentieth century. The precarious position of the Jew, the restrictions on economic and political activity, the unbalanced nature of their occupations, the spread of nationalist feeling, the undermining of traditional religious belief and behavior—all these things led to the creation of the socialist-Zionist experiment. The Labor leadership, almost exclusively of East European origin, developed a party and an ideology that answered the needs of the nation as they saw them and experienced them.

The Likud saw the problems of the country from a different ideological perspective and consequently found its support from different groups. The Alignment was notably successful among earlier immigrants and among those born in Europe and America. Likud appealed more to the native-born than to any immigrant group, and more to the Asian- or African-born than to the European- or American-born. The symbols the Alignment used to evoke the epoch of independence and nation building were more effective among the old than the young, more effective among those who came before independence than among those who came after independence or were born in Israel, and more effective among those born in Europe than those born in Asia or Africa.

The opposition Likud, of which the right-wing nationalistic Herut movement and the bourgeois Liberal party are major components, gave the appearance of being broadly based in its electoral support (as was the Alignment). But much of this spread was an artifact of the difference between the Liberals and Herut. The Liberals are a bourgeois party that received most of its support from middle-class and upper-middle-class merchants and businessmen. Herut, on the other hand, was a party that appealed disproportionately to the lower-class and lower-middle-class workers, and to Israelis born in Asia or Africa. Since the followers of the Liberal party had higher levels of education than did supporters of Herut, the spread evident for the Likud was a balancing of two countertendencies; thus it is misleading to read into the data that the Likud before 1977 was beginning to generate the appeal characteristic of a dominant party.

The support of the Likud came heavily from the young, from native Israelis, from Israelis of Asian or African background, and from those with lower education and income levels. Undeniably, many of these cleavages overlapped with strong differences in political opinion. To give but one example, the same groups that tended to support the Likud tended to have hawkish opinions on foreign and defense policy. Those who were older, had more education, and from a European background tended to hold more flexible views.

TABLE 8.3
PARTY VOTE BY AGE,
1969, 1973, 1977, AND 1981

1969

Age	N	Alignment	Likud[a]	Religious[b]	Other
			(in percent)		
24 and less	210	40	36	15	9
25-39	414	54	30	9	7
40-49	272	61	25	10	4
50 and above	461	62	21	14	3
TOTAL	1357	56	27	12	5

1973

Age	N	Alignment	Likud	Religious[b]	Other
			(in percent)		
24 and less	154	39	44	6	11
25-39	277	37	44	7	12
40-49	135	48	35	7	10
50 and above	310	54	23	13	10
TOTAL	876	45	35	9	11

1977

Age	N	Alignment	Likud[c]	Religious[b]	DMC	Other
			(in percent)			
24 and less	144	20	51	4	21	4
25-39	336	25	34	11	27	3
40-49	156	38	29	10	20	4
50 and above	314	53	23	8	15	1
TOTAL	950	35	32	9	21	3

1981

Age	N	Alignment	Likud	Religious[d]	Other
			(in percent)		
24 and less	191	27	51	4	18
25-39	410	35	43	6	15
40-49	147	35	55	1	8
50 and above	277	50	37	7	7
TOTAL	1025	38	45	5	13

a. Including Gahal, the Free Center, and the State List. They formed the Likud in 1973.
b. Including the National Religious party, Agudat Israel, and Poalei Agudat Israel.
c. Including Ariel Sharon's list.
d. Same as b; in 1981 including Tami.

The religious parties, especially the National Religious party, regularly received about 10 percent of the vote and were the consistent coalition partner of the Labor party. Its support came from traditional Jews from Asian or African backgrounds with low income and low education levels; highly educated intellectuals from European origins; and Israel-born educated youth imbued with religious ideals through formal schooling in the state-supported religious schools. On the whole, the religious parties were relatively more successful among those with lower levels of education. The picture was more complex when support for the religious parties was considered in the light of both education and place of origin. Among the European- or American-born, support for religious parties tended to decrease with educational attainment. The Israel-born provided the opposite picture, with religious party support increasing with additional education. The pattern for the Asian- or African-born was harder to ascertain since so few respondents in this category had more than a high school education. What was clear, though, is that between the first two categories of educational achievement there is a sharp decrease of support for religious parties among Asian- or African-born as education increased.

The growing strength of Likud over time is well documented in table 8.3 where party vote by age is displayed. The direct relationship between age and Alignment support and the inverse relationship between age and Likud support are remarkably persistent over four time periods. The oldest group changes its rate of support for the two parties only little, especially between 1973 and 1977, and the same again in 1981. It is in the youngest voting group that the significant change comes about. The Likud, always strongest among this group compared to other age cohorts, proceeds from 36 percent support in 1969 to 44 percent in 1973 and 51 percent in 1977 and 1981. The Alignment loses half its support in this youngest age group between 1973 and 1977, the same amount of support that the DMC attracts. The Alignment more clearly than ever becomes the party of the older, more conservative voter; the Likud, the choice of the young, even though the DMC was the party of young adults. In 1984 the Likud continued to do better among the youth than did the Alignment.

The Ethnic Vote

While age and education are associated with the vote in Israel, the most striking correlation is between ethnicity and the vote. Simply put, the Likud is heavily supported by voters of Asian or African background, and the Alignment is heavily supported by voters of European background. Although this was very pronounced in the 1981 an 1984 elections, the relationship between voting and origin is not a new one in Israeli politics. Such a correlation was found in the

1950s and 1960s,[5] but it has become more pronounced. Moreover, due to demographic processes characterizing Israeli society, the effect of this ethnic voting behavior on the ethnic composition of the parties is different today.

In the 29-year period since independence in which the Alignment in its earlier versions (Mapai, Labor) was dominant in the system, it regularly won support from most groups in the society. This was especially true of new immigrants, who were often in awe of the "miracle" that had returned them to the land of their fathers. These immigrants were dependent on the bureaucracies of the establishment for the whole gamut of economic, educational, health, social, and cultural needs. Even though an increasingly large share of the electorate was of Sephardi origin, Mapai maintained its dominant role as the largest plurality party and the leader of every government coalition. More than that, attempts to appeal to the Sephardi population at election time by lists set up by Sephardim largely failed. It was only before the mass immigration of the early 1950s that representation to the Knesset was achieved by any lists manifestly linking themselves with Sephardim and Yemenites.

Table 8.4 presents the percent supporting the Alignment vs. the Likud from 1969 to 1984. The data support the claim that as early as 1969 Ashkenazim tended to vote for the Alignment more than Sephardim did, and Sephardim tended to vote more for the Likud. But this tendency has become more pronounced, beyond the general trend of the Likud's growth and the Alignment's decline. Today we find more ethnic voting among the Israeli public: Ethnicity discriminates or predicts better the vote for the Likud vs. the Alignment. In 1984 the preference ratio for the two parties among each ethnic group was about 3 to 1, with the Sephardim preferring the Likud, and the Ashkenazim the Alignment.

The fortunes of the Likud and the misfortunes of the Alignment are evident along generational lines as well as ethnic and demographic ones. The Likud does even better among the second generation of Sephardim than it does in the first. The Alignment's support is greater among Ashkenazim who immigrated than among their children who were born in Israel (see table 8.4). The Likud has gained most among the youngest and fastest-growing groups; the Alignment, losing support within all groups over time, does best in the group that is oldest and is shrinking rapidly.

In the 1981 and 1984 elections the term "ethnic party" was used often. It was supposed to portray the support of Jews from Asia and Africa and their children for the Likud. The fact is, the Alignment was as close to being an "ethnic party" in this sense as the Likud was. About two-thirds of the Alignment's voters were Ashkenazim, and a similar percentage of the Likud voters were Sephardim. This had not always been the case. In the past the bulk of

TABLE 8.4
ALIGNMENT PORTION OF TWO-PARTY VOTE BY CONTINENT OF BIRTH, 1969-84[a]

Respondent born	Israel	Israel	Israel	Asia or Africa	Europe or America		Sample size[b]	Total sample size
Father born	Israel	Asia or Africa	Europe or America	Asia or Africa	Europe or America	Total		
Date of poll								
Sept. 1969	70	77	83	79	90	84	698	1315
Oct.-Nov. 1969	40	62	73	68	81	74	1026	1825
May 1973	60	51	57	66	79	70	1066	1939
Sept. 1973	57	22	42	62	75	63	287	548
Dec. 1973	41	24	41	43	77	52	274	530
March 1977	37	26	50	41	71	52	639	1372
April 1977	39	31	42	43	68	49	180	497
May 1977	53	32	38	35	61	49	198	485
June 1977	29	10	30	33	56	37	255	465
March 1981	46	47	68	48	71	57	765	1249
April 1981	46	31	68	33	71	51	585	1088
June 1981	43	27	55	35	64	46	797	1237
July 1984	58	31	80	28	86	54	763	1259

a. Surveys were conducted by the Israel Institute of Applied Social Research, except for March and June 1981, and July 1984, which were conducted by the Dahaf Research Institute. b. Respondents giving "Alignment" or "Likud" party answer to question about intended vote are included here.

both the Likud's and the Alignment's support came from Ashkenazim; after all, the Ashkenazim comprised a majority of the electorate. Polls going back to the late 1960s indicate that then too about two-thirds of the Alignment vote was from Ashkenazim, even though Sephardim also voted for the Alignment often (see table 8.4). In the late 1960s both parties were predominantly Ashkenazi; by 1981 the Alignment had stayed that way, and the Likud had become predominantly Sephardi. The turnabout seems to have occurred in 1977 when a majority of the Likud vote was Sephardi for the first time.

The question may also be turned around by asking how members of the two ethnic groups divided their votes in 1981 between the two large parties. Again we get a mirror-image answer. About 60 percent of the Ashkenazim voted Alignment, about a third Likud. About 60 percent of the Sephardim voted Likud, about a third Alignment. By 1984, the Ashkenazi vote was more concentrated in the Alignment than the Sephardi vote was in the Likud, about 70 percent for the former, about 60 percent for the latter.

If indeed the two major parties in the 1980s may be defined as ethnic parties, it is only in terms of their electorate. One has to keep in mind that about one-third of each ethnic group voted for "the wrong party." Neither party organized to further specific ethnic ends or along ethnic lines. Both the Alignment and the Likud were run by Ashkenazim, as has been the case with most parties in Israel. In fact, the Alignment tried to deal with its problem of lacking appeal among Sephardi voters by placing Sephardim in places assured of election on its list. By any mechanical measure of representation the Alignment did this more successfully than the Likud. Of the members of the 1981 Knesset elected by the two parties, the Alignment had 14 Sephardim, the Likud nine. Both parties were led by men born in Poland, but both put Sephardim in the number-two slot. The Alignment had a Sephardi woman, Shoshana Arbeli-Almozlino, as its second candidate. She was born in Iraq and had been a very effective parliamentarian in the outgoing Knesset. The Likud put David Levy as number two. Minister of Housing and Immigrant Absorption, and the Likud's candidate to head the Histadrut, Levy was born in Morocco and lives in Beit Shean, a development town in northern Israel that manifests many of the social and economic problems with which the underprivileged population must contend. In 1984, Shamir and Peres, both Polish-born, headed the lists. Two Sephardim, Levy and Navon, were in second place. But representation was not the issue, and the images were different. The Likud and the Alignment were thus ethnic parties in the 1980s in one sense only: The social basis for voting for each of them was more than ever before related to ethnicity.

There was an ethnic list or party in the 1981 elections, in the full sense of the term. That was Tami, Minister of Religious Affairs Abu-Hatzeira's party, which won three Knesset seats. Abu-Hatzeira had been cleared of charges of bribery soon before the election and had split from the National Religious party on the grounds that Sephardim were not adequately represented in the NRP and the other political parties. Abu-Hatzeira also managed to recruit a former agriculture minister from the Alignment, Aharon Uzan, who then relinquished his place on the Alignment list in order to run on Tami's. Together with other visible leaders they presented a Sephardi list with special appeal to North African voters. The North African Jews are the largest Sephardi group in the country and are disproportionally concentrated among its lower classes. The North African community that arrived in Israel in the early 1950s did not come as a complete community; many of the leadership preferred to emigrate to France rather than Israel. Unlike the Iraqi community, which arrived with its political, economic, and cultural leadership intact, the North African community was the slowest to achieve higher status and positions of influence. Lacking any identifiable leadership and with lower levels of skills, education, and resources than other groups, some voters were receptive to Tami's arguments. Abu-Hatzeira also capitalized on his being a scion of a prominent rabbinical family in Morocco, and so for some his political plea turned into a religious cause as well. Tami was and is an ethnic party in terms of its electorate, the issues it has raised, its appeal, its goals, and its leaders and activists. But in the 1984 elections, Tami fell to only one seat. Shas, on the other hand, an ethnic spinoff of the Aguda, captured four seats.

The emergence of lists trying to tap ethnic resentment is not new; what was special was its partial success in the 1980s and its appearance during campaigns charged with ethnic tension. Tami's 45,000 votes (2.6 percent) in 1981 was the clearest, most authentic expression of ethnic political organization to have appeared in these elections. But its appeal must also be measured against previous efforts. In past elections ethnic lists had competed, and while they did not win representation, they came close. In 1973 the Black Panthers and Avner Shaki's list, which split from the NRP, received almost 25,000 votes between them; and in 1977 Ben-Porat (an Iraqi who was to be number two on Dayan's list in 1981) headed a list that won almost 15,000 votes. Despite Tami's gains, the rule remains that most voters, Sephardim and Ashkenazim, tend to support the mainstream national lists.

In an April 1981 survey, respondents were asked to conceptualize the ideal party they wanted to see in power and to describe it as Sephardic or Ashkenazi on a scale from 1 to 7. Among the Ashkenazim, 79 percent wanted a party in the middle, not Ashkenazi and not Sephardi. Among the Sephardim, this figure was 74 percent. The Israeli public, Ashkenazi as well as Sephardi, does not want an ethnic party. The historical sociological analysis of Hanna Herzog of the ethnic lists in Israeli leads her to the conclusion that the ethnic political organizations are marginal in Israeli politics, but that "ethnicity" is a resource in politics.[6]

Among the plausible explanations for the association between the vote and ethnicity is the continued identification of the Alignment as the party of the establishment despite the fact that it had been out of power since 1977. Sephardim, especially their Israel-born children, tended to reject the Alignment because of the persistent inequalities these voters perceived. Ashkenazi voters tended to reject the populism of the Likud governments and longed to return to a more familiar and pragmatic past. The hawkish image of the Likud also correlated with attitudes prevalent among Sephardim. While most Israelis have hawkish attitudes on foreign and defense policies, Sephardim have them at a higher rate. The fact that the Likud was more clear and united in expressing these attitudes worked in its favor among Sephardim. Another factor is that Sephardim tend to be more traditional about religion than Ashkenazim in Israel today. Begin (although not the Likud party generally) was very successful in 1981 in utilizing the symbols and language of religion; the Alignment, in attacking the religious parties and their disproportionate gains through coalition bargaining, appeared at times to be antireligious.

The chances for the continued success of a democratic regime rest in part in having social groups overlap. In Israel of the 1980s we are witness to a heavy overlapping of social cleavages, so much so as to point to a possible danger to Israeli democracy. When the polity is polarized and one group concentrates within it the religious, Sephardim, and less educated and lower-status workers voting for the Likud, and the other group has a disproportionate share of secular upper-class Ashkenazim voting for the Alignment, the chances of intolerance, lack of communication and understanding, and violence grow. These patterns are not immutable and it may be that with changes in the leadership of the two major parties the system will become very fluid, and new affiliations will emerge.[7]

The Floating Vote

Despite social and economic change, the political system of Israel seemed on the surface to be remarkably stable until 1977, with one party (Mapai, later Labor) consistently receiving a plurality of the votes. But the Israeli political system was hardly static. Appearances notwithstanding, it would be misleading to depict the election results as robotlike behavior on the part of the public, election after election. To sustain this kind of analysis, we would have to make herculean assumptions about the unimportance of population change due to the exit of some from the voting public (death, emigration) and the entrance of others (coming of age, immigration). The anomaly of the Israeli case stemmed from the very large change in voting publics (primarily due to immigration) from election to election, and the apparent stability of the voting results. Part of the effect was illusory: Votes changed but the government did not.

The proportional representation system and the emergence of a dominant-party system in Israel prevented the translation of voting change into government change until 1977. Changes in the vote, however, were accurately reflected in the size of the delegations that represented parties in the Knesset.

Between 1965 and 1969, 25 percent of the respondents reported that they voted for different parties in the two elections. A stability rate of 74 percent is very similar to the results obtained in Britain in a study that concluded that "electoral change is due not to a limited group of 'floating' voters but to a very broad segment of British electors."[8]

Prior to 1973, a good deal of the change of vote in Israel was among factional groupings. For example, the parties of the left lost voters to one another. We have seen that the individual party may be exposed to a substantial swing in its votes from election to election. But when examined in terms of factional groupings, a much more stable picture emerges. Parties of the left (including the communists) never won fewer than 64 nor more than 69 seats in the 120-seat Knesset in the seven elections through 1969.[9] In 1973, they won 59 seats. The center parties ranged between 27 and 34 seats (43 in 1973), and the religious parties between 15 and 18 (15 in 1973). Smith has divided the parties into six such groupings and has calculated the average deviation for each grouping from 1949 through 1969. The average deviation from the 1949-69 average vote for the parties in the Labor grouping (excluding the communists) was only 1.0 percent. The average deviation for the center and religious groupings was even lower: 0.8 and 0.6 percent, respectively. The overall strength of factional groupings was relatively stable. Changes were occasioned by mergers and splits, alignments and divisions that characterized the relationships among the parties within factional groupings. But these swings should not obfuscate the basic fact that the parties of the Labor grouping, especially Mapai, dominated the voting results and politics of the entire period.

The period following the Yom Kippur War of 1973 is best thought of in terms of a realigning electoral era. In a realigning election (or a critical election, in Key's phrase), a new party balance is created. Key characterized an election as critical when "more or less profound readjustments occur in the relations of power within the community, and in which new and durable election groupings are formed."[10] Many thought that the 1973 war could be seen as a turning point in Israeli politics because it shattered so many myths and previously held conceptions. The publication of the 1973 election results soon after the war provided a rare opportunity to compare the voting behavior of large segments of the population. Since much of the population was serving in the army on election day, the results were especially informative, for the army is rather homogeneous in its composition—predominantly young and male (although women and the not-so-young are also represented).

If the experience of the 1973 war was to have had far-reaching effects in the future, it would have been best to search for signs of these effects in groups directly involved in the war and among those whose political beliefs and partisan attachments were still relatively flexible. If the army went Likud by a large majority, we might interpret the war as a shared experience of the generation then reaching maturity that would have an impact on the politics of the future. The new tendency would be different from the dominant one in the previous generation; the younger generation, which comprised a larger share of the electorate and was raising its children in a new climate of opinion, would eventually prevail.

The election results did not indicate that the voters behaved very differently on election day from the way they had behaved before. The army results gave the Likud 41.28 percent of the vote, as opposed to 39.54 percent for the Alignment. In the general population the division was 30.2 percent and 39.6 percent, respectively. (In 1977 the results were even more dramatic in the army: 46 percent Likud, 22 percent Alignment, 16 percent DMC.) It is true that the Likud outpaced the Alignment in the army returns. But even before the war it was well known that the Likud was strong among younger voters. The Alignment won from the army voters the same share as it did from the general population. Using this indicator, it was inappropriate to conclude that the 1973 elections were critical; at most, tendencies already in process were accelerated as a result of the war. There was no clear large-scale shift of group allegiances from one party to another. Previous patterns were accelerated; no new patterns were obvious.

In a dominant-party system it may be more useful to discuss a "realigning electoral era" rather than a critical election. During such an era the dominant-party's electoral support slips from its grasp. Maurice Duverger has pointed out that each period tends to have a doctrine that is dominant. A dominant party identifies itself with the doctrines, ideas, methods, and style of the epoch.

As time passes, as "dominant doctrines" shift, the power base of the dominant party may well be eroded. No one act or failure is enough to explain this decline.[11] The Labor party, the pivot of all government coalitions until 1977, became entrenched in office. Socialist values notwithstanding, it became conservative. It was anxious to preserve the gains it had won for the state, for the citizenry, and for its functionaries as well. Many of the revolutionary socialist ideals that were part of Labor's legacy became only verbal goals.

The fact that Labor had difficulty in attracting the votes of the young — the generation that had grown up since independence — indicated a partial short-circuiting of the party's claim to dominance. This decline was evident in the voting results.

The 1977 elections ended the realigning era by deposing the dominant party. As we would expect in a dominant-party system, the opposition itself did little to depose the ruling party. The Likud's strength increased steadily; demographic and ideological forces were harnessed behind it. The Alignment's greatest loss was to the Democratic Movement for Change. Alignment votes that went to the DMC determined the fall of the Alignment and the rise of the Likud. It may be that in future elections the Alignment will win again, but it will not automatically regain its position of dominance. Dominance is a set of power relations, and a state of mind. Dominance is difficult to deny to the party that has it and extremely hard to rewin for the party that has lost it. The results of the 1981 elections strengthened the impression that a basic change in Israeli politics had come about as a result of the critical election era. Despite its relative success compared with the 1977 election, the Alignment was unable to stymie the continued growth of the Likud. In 1984, although the Alignment won more votes than any other party, it was far from a position of dominance and had to share power with the Likud in a National Unity Government.

In 1973, after the postponement of elections as a result of the Yom Kippur War, the rate of vote stability remained remarkably high. To be sure, the Alignment was weakened and the Likud strengthened. The Likud won 8 percent of the 1969 Alignment vote while it lost only 1 percent of its own 1969 vote to the Alignment. But when the overall rate of stability is calculated by dividing the number of stable votes in the two elections by the number of voters who reported a 1969 vote, the stability rate is 68 percent. The religious parties' voters were most loyal, with 79 percent reporting identical votes in 1969 and 1973. Only two-thirds of the 1969 Alignment voters reported that they voted for the Alignment in 1973, with 17 percent reporting a vote for the Likud and 4 percent for the Civil Rights Movement list.

The 1969 lists that formed the 1973 Likud were not uniformly successful in delivering their 1969 votes to the joint 1973 list. Gahal's success was greatest, with 84 percent continuity. Only about a third of the Free Center and State List voters went Likud in 1973; many Free Center respondents did not answer the 1973 question, and many State List voters voted Alignment in 1973. The Independent Liberals had trouble in keeping the faithful, with 37 percent voting Independent Liberal again, but an equal number voting for the Alignment. This is particularly interesting because the Independent Liberals managed to retain their 1969 strength, indicating that they attract votes but lack a hard core of loyal voters who habitually support the party.

If the rates of stability and floating vote were not all that different in 1973 from what had occurred earlier, what was different was the unbalanced nature of the tradeoff. Usually the floating vote is a multisided affair with the losses of one party made up by the gains it wins from another. Many of the losses sustained by the Alignment this time were net gains for the Likud. Perhaps this is the uniqueness of the 1973 results—not in the scope of this shift but in the relatively uniform movement of its direction.

In 1977 the rate of voting change was very high. If between 1965 and 1969 it was about a quarter, and between 1969 and 1973 about a third, between 1973 and 1977 it was half of the sample; between 1977 and 1981 it fell back to about 40 percent; and between 1981 and 1984 it retreated to a quarter. Most of the change was among those who had supported the Alignment in 1973 (see table 8.5). Of those (44.5 percent of the sample), less than half voted for the Alignment again in 1977 with 20 percent going to the Likud and 18 percent to the DMC.

The 1973 Likud voters remained loyal on the whole, with some 8 percent supporting the DMC in 1977. Those who did not vote in 1973 gave the Likud 40 percent of their vote, the DMC 16 percent, and the Alignment a scant 4 percent. The DMC received two-thirds of its voters who had participated in the 1973 elections from the Alignment, and the Likud almost 30 percent of its 1977 vote from the same source.

TABLE 8.5

STABLE AND FLOATING VOTE, 1973 AND 1977
(in percent)

1973	1977						
	Likud	Alignment	DMC	Religious	Other	No answer	Total
Likud	19	0.5	2	—	0.5	2	24.0
Alignment	9	20.0	8	0.5	1.0	6	44.5
Religious	2	—	—	5.0	—	—	7.0
Other	1	—	2	—	1.0	2	6.0
No vote	5	0.5	2	0.5	0.5	4	12.5
No answer	—	—	—	—	—	6	6.0
TOTAL	36	21.0	14	6.0	3.0	20	100.0

$(N = 465)$

NOTE: Based on June 1977 survey; stable vote in box.

In 1981, a very tense and polarized campaign led to low levels of tradeoff among the Likud and Alignment voters of 1977 (see table 8.6). Most of them stayed with their previous choice with the Alignment picking up 3 percent of the sample from those who had voted Likud in 1977, compared with 2 percent of the sample who had voted Alignment in 1977 and shifted to the Likud in 1981. The major movement was the DMC vote, which was overwhelmingly won by the Alignment at a ratio of 4 to 1 compared with the Likud. Some 1977 Likud voters voted for other parties, especially Tehiya. But the most crucial datum regarding the future, which again appears clearly in table 8.6, is the attraction of the Likud among these who did not vote in 1977 (mostly young voters): The Likud outdraws the Alignment among this group by a ratio of 2 to 1.

TABLE 8.6
STABLE AND FLOATING VOTE, 1977 AND 1981
(in percent)

1977	1981						
	Likud	Alignment	Religious	Other	No vote	No answer	Total
Likud	27	3	1	3.0	4	1.0	39.0
Alignment	2	18	—	1.0	2	1.0	24.0
DMC	1	4	—	2.0	2	—	9.0
Religious	1	—	3	0.5	—	0.5	5.0
Other	1	1	—	1.0	—	—	3.0
No vote	4	2	1	2.0	1	—	10.0
No answer	3	2	—	1.0	2	2.0	10.0
TOTAL	39	30	5	10.5	11	4.5	100.0

(N = 1203)

NOTE: Based on June 1977 survey; stable vote in box.

In 1984, 23 percent of the total sample repeated their 1981 vote for both the Alignment and the Likud. Four percent of the 1984 sample who voted Likud in 1981 switched to the Alignment; 5.5 percent to other parties. The Alignment lost 0.5 percent to the Likud, 2 percent to others. Among the army voters, the Likud and Tehiya won about 50 percent, the Alignment, Shinui, and the Civil Rights Movement about 40 percent.

The factors associated with consistent voting are the same factors associated with a "conservative" vote. Age, for example, has always been very powerful. The older one is, the more likely one is to retain old patterns of behavior, including the vote. Education is also related to voting stability: the lower the education, the higher stability of the vote. Voters with higher education change

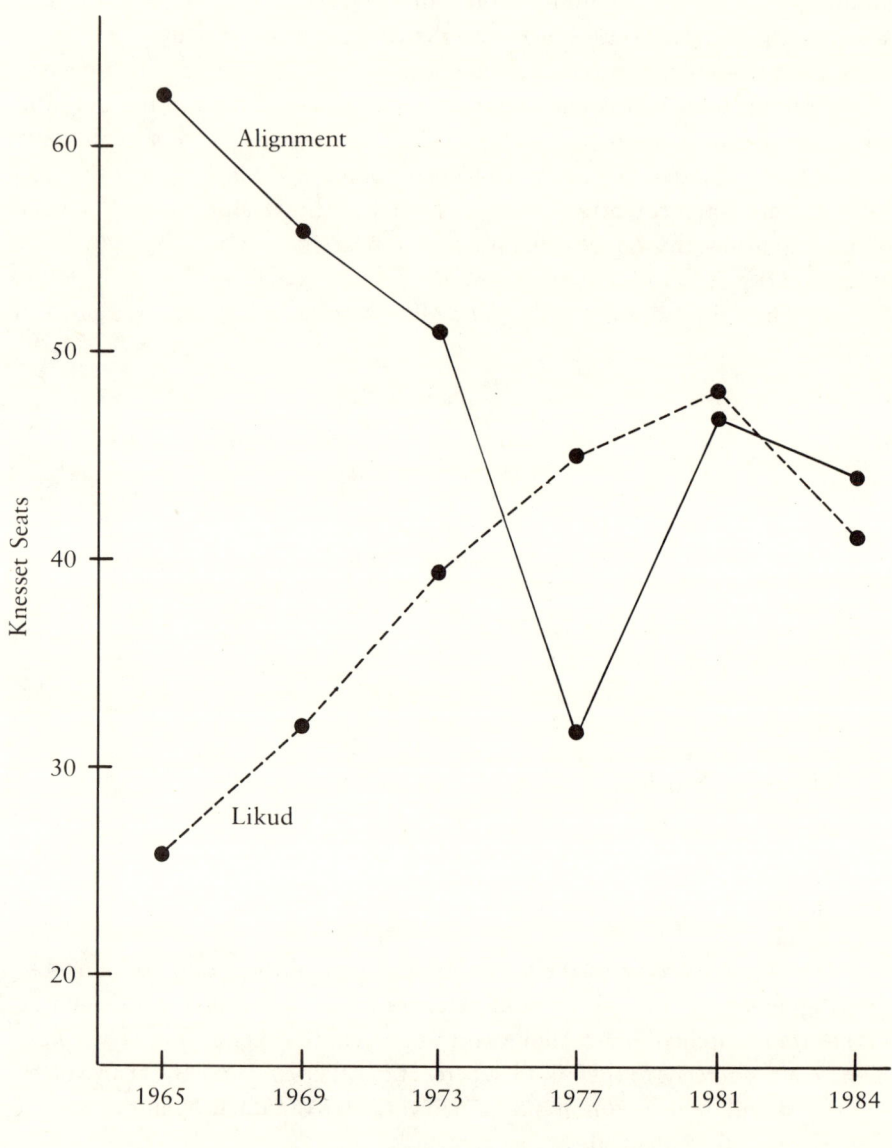

FIGURE 8.1
ALIGNMENT AND LIKUD KNESSET SEATS, 1965-84

NOTE: Alignment includes Rafi and Mapam in 1965. Likud includes State List and Free Center in 1969; and Sharon in 1977.

their vote more often and vote less often for the larger parties and more often for smaller ones.

Concentration of the Vote

The impact of the many individual decisions of voters has been an increase in the size of the two major parties and a concentration of the votes between them. The trend toward bigness began in 1965 with the emergence of the Mapai-Ahdut Haavoda Alignment and the Herut-Liberal Gahal, and reached a new height in 1981 (see figure 8.1 and table 8.7). It is not an unrelated fact that growth of the two-parties' share of the vote coincides with emergence of amalgamations of parties, that is, lists set up by a combination of parties. In 1965, in reaction to the split in Mapai caused by the setting up of Rafi by Ben-Gurion, Dayan, Peres, Navon, and others, old-time Mapai leaders formed an electoral coalition with Ahdut Haavoda in order to avoid political defeat. By 1968 Rafi, Mapai, and Ahdut Haavoda had formed the Labor party, and in 1969 Labor joined Mapam in the Alignment. Meanwhile, the right Herut and center Liberals were forming an electoral bloc for the 1965 elections, expanded in 1973 under the pressure of Sharon, with the acquiescence of Begin, to form the Likud.

TABLE 8.7

SHARE OF 120-MEMBER KNESSET BY TWO LARGEST PARTIES, 1949-84

	Biggest winner	Second biggest winner	Total	Competitiveness ratio[a]
1949	Mapai: 46	Mapam: 19	65	.41
1951	Mapai: 45	Liberal: 20	65	.44
1955	Mapai: 40	Herut: 15	55	.38
1959	Mapai: 47	Herut: 17	64	.36
1961	Mapai: 42	Herut: 17	59	.40
		Liberal: 17		
1965	Alignment[b]: 45	Gahal[c]: 26	71	.58
1969	Alignment[d]: 56	Gahal[c]: 26	82	.46
1973	Alignment[d]: 51	Likud[e]: 39	90	.76
1977	Likud[e]: 43	Alignment[d]: 32	75	.74
1981	Likud[e]: 48	Alignment[d]: 47	95	.98
1984	Alignment[d]: 44	Likud[e]: 41	85	.93

NOTES: a. Competitiveness ratio = second biggest winner/biggest winner.
b. Mapai and Ahdut Haavoda.
c. Herut and Liberals.
d. Labor and Mapam.
e. Herut, Liberals, and others.

This kind of arrangement affords party activists many advantages. Their quota of parliamentary seats is fixed through negotiation with the other partners in the amalgam, reducing the organizational and personal tensions usually associated with elections. The relative strength of a partner in one of these arrangements is fixed; if the list does well, the absolute number of representatives in the Knesset increases. This arrangement also affords the politician ideological benefits. Whereas he (or she) can be extreme (or moderate) in the councils of his own party, he can also explain to his party that in order to reap the benefits of the larger amalgamation, his position must be flexible in negotiation. It is not clear whether this is the cause or the effect of the general de-ideologization of Israeli politics, but it is increasingly prevalent.

The appearance of a breakaway third party has tempered the trend of two-party vote concentration. In 1965 Rafi won ten seats, and in 1977 the DMC won 15. Most of these votes were at the expense of the Alignment; without their appearance, the trend would be even clearer. A related trend is the growth of the Likud. The advent of the Likud in 1977 was aided mightily by the emergence of the DMC because the DMC took many votes away from the Alignment, lowering the Alignment to the second largest party. But had it not happened in 1977, it probably would have happened at a future date. Judging from the projection of trend lines and the ability of the Alignment to reform itself, Likud would sooner or later have won power. The surprise of May 1977 was in the timing rather than in the fact of the Likud victory.

By 1981 the race between the Likud and the Alignment was very close; between them they won almost 1,500,000 of the almost 2,000,000 votes cast, but only 10,405 votes separated them. Within the Jewish population the Likud was a bigger winner, since Arabs accounted for more than 40,000 of the Alignment total. The Likud continued its steady growth and added more than 100,000 votes to its 1977 total. The Alignment bounced back from its 1977 trauma and grew by 50 percent. But comparing the 1981 results to the Alignment's more glorious past leads to the inevitable conclusion that despite the good 1981 showing, it remains a party in decline. The difference between the 1969 and 1981 votes for the Alignment, for example, was a mere 75,000 votes, whereas the Likud in the same period added more than 375,000 votes to its total. The number of voting Israelis grew in that same period by more than half a million. In 1984, the Alignment added less than 15,000 votes to its 1981 total of nearly 750,000 votes, while the Likud lost more than 50,000 votes. While the Alignment won, it did less well than many had expected and the Likud lost less than others had expected.

There are many reasons for the change in fortunes of the two parties; some of them—the passing of leadership, weakening of dependency relations, and

Electoral Behavior

demographic changes—have already been discussed. All these changes are connected with images of parties within the electorate, and to that topic we turn.

Just as a social myth is a convenient way of ordering reality, the party's or leader's image is no less important than the actual opinion or personality. While reality is usually complex, myths and images have a simplifying quality about them. They are easily grasped, widely accepted, able to convert masses of detail into an understandable whole. If Peres is thought of as insincere or Begin as unstable, conflicting evidence can easily be put aside in favor of the widely held image, which allows one to grasp the essence of the person more easily. And when conflicting images are widely held by polarized groups, beliefs tend to be held and expressed all the more strongly.

TABLE 8.8
PARTY IMAGES, 1973 AND 1981

1973, N = 1939	Ideal	Alignment	Likud
Strong/weak	87/4	83/8	58/21
Right-wing/left-wing	54/15	37/32	76/9
Old-fashioned/progressive	21/57	44/24	42/26
Middle-class/working-class	33/37	24/49	62/12
Inexperienced/experienced	6/86	10/85	22/61
Young/old	—	19/55	29/38
Sephardi/Ashkenazi	—	14/38	20/28
Honest/corrupt	—	50/27	61/12

1981, N = 1088	Ideal	Alignment	Likud
Strong/weak	93/2	44/33	50/33
Right/left	55/13	28/40	77/7
Old-fashioned/progressive	15/61	48/26	42/31
Middle class/working class	28/32	27/42	55/14
Young/old	52/10	17/51	28/35
Sephardi/Ashkenazi	11/11	6/47	18/25
Worries about itself/the citizens	3/89	43/37	31/45
Inexperienced/experienced	4/86	4/79	45/38
Honest/corrupt	—	35/39	57/18
Cannot/can be believed	—	36/42	32/48

NOTE: Based on a 7-point semantic differential battery. The numbers in the table are the sum of the percentage of the sample identifying the parties with a given characteristic, with the three categories left of the center point being summed and presented left of the slash and the three categories right of the center point summed and presented right of the slash. The size of the middle category is the difference between 100 and the sum of the two reported figures. For example, on the 7-point scale, 55 percent reported in 1981 that their ideal party was either in the first, second, or third category toward the right end of the continuum, while another 13 percent were in the three categories on the left end and 32 percent (100−68) were in the fourth or middle category.

The images of the two major parties, and changes in images over time, are important keys to understanding electoral behavior in Israel. In 1973, before the Yom Kippur War, the Alignment was perceived as a strong, experienced party, relatively honest and working class. The Likud was perceived to be less strong, less experienced, but more honest, less Ashkenazi, and much more right-wing. In the 1980s, the Alignment was perceived to be the establishment party, even though it had been in opposition to the government since 1977. Labor was probably punished in 1981 (as it was in 1977) for its establishment status. The Alignment's negative image is evidenced in that it was perceived to be the party more concerned about its own interests than those of the citizens, and not very honest. The Likud was now closer to the ideal party image; it was perceived as a slightly stronger party, honest, one that could be trusted, and a party more concerned with the citizens than with itself.

There were other differences in the parties' images as well. The Alignment was the opposite of the ideal on the young-old dimension in 1981, the ideal being young, the Alignment perceived as old. The Likud also had an older image, but it was much less extreme than that of the Alignment. While the ideal called for a progressive party, both parties were perceived as old-fashioned, but the Alignment slightly more so than the Likud; yet the two parties won more votes between them than ever. A strong party was wished for: In 1973 that was clearly the Alignment, by 1981 it was the Likud by a slight margin.

On class and ethnic dimensions the differences between the parties and their images were striking. The ideal party in both time periods was almost evenly divided among those who preferred a middle-class party, those who preferred a working-class party, and those in between. The Alignment was perceived as close to that ideal, although more working class; the Likud was very far from the ideal with a high preponderance of middle-class responses. Workers tended to support the Likud and not the Alignment, even though the Alignment is the labor party associated with the socialist movement.

The ethnic dimension reveals that the ideal party was neither Ashkenazi nor Sephardi; yet both parties in both time periods were perceived to be more Ashkenazi than Sephardi. But by 1981 the Alignment was perceived to be much more Ashkenazi than the Likud, or than it was perceived as Ashkenazi in 1973. The establishment image reinforced its association with the dominant ethnic group, facilitating the Likud vote by the Sephardim and the Alignment vote by the Ashkenazim. This polarization led to a high rate of competitiveness in 1981. By 1984, the lingering negative image of the Alignment was that it was an Ashkenazi party and was responsible for the ethnic gap that existed in the country. The Alignment, unable to change its image, failed to penetrate significantly the growing Sephardi population group.

9. The Knesset, the Government, and the Judiciary

The Knesset, Israel's parliament, is the supreme legislative body of the state. It has tremendous symbolic importance as the seat of the people's sovereignty and the most important deliberative council of the nation. The Knesset is born of politics. The composition of the Knesset is determined by the one true expression of mass democracy—the elections. It is organized along party lines, committee appointments are made by party, and even seating arrangements are determined by party. Some aspects of the Knesset can be traced back to the Parliament of Great Britain, other aspects to continental usage and procedure. The Jewish state, deprived of autonomous independence and institutional development for some 2000 years, took up parliamentary forms of the late nineteenth century. The long evolutionary process of the emergence of the supreme Parliament was bypassed, and the acceptance of the Knesset as the omnipotent legislative body was natural. In fact, the struggle for parliamentary dominance in the world's democracies was protracted and crowned with success in England only in the eighteenth century. The lack of this historical perspective makes it more difficult, and more necessary, to evaluate the functions, strengths, and weaknesses of the Knesset.

The nineteenth century can rightly be considered the golden age of parliamentary supremacy. Legislative supremacy was the prevailing tendency in America and Europe, and representative institutions could successfully cope with the relatively simple conflicts of democratic societies. Governmental expenditures were small, and the state tended not to interfere with the economy so that the legislature could delve into the details of budget making.[1] At this point of legislative evolution the Zionist revolution adopted parliamentary procedures. The Zionist Congresses reflected parliamentary life in turn-of-the-century Europe, and this is the legacy of the Knesset. The link between the Congresses and the Knesset was the Electors' Council (Asefat Nivharim) of the Yishuv, which served as the assembly for the Jewish community under the Mandate.

Two interesting structural features of the Knesset indicate the Israeli parliament's affinity to the continental style rather than the English. First, speakers in the Knesset, as in continental parliaments, speak from the rostrum. This encourages prepared speeches and lengthy oratory and decreases the likelihood of sharp interchanges between the speaker and his listeners. In the English Parliament one speaks from one's seat. At one time Israeli practice introduced microphones at the seating place of each member to assure that interlocutions be heard, but this was discontinued. As a rule, the speaker who has the floor now comes to the rostrum and addresses the Knesset from there.

The second feature is the matter of permanent seating and the capacity of the house to hold all the members. The British case is unique in this sense; members do not have fixed seats, and the hall is too small to fit all the members comfortably. In contrast, Knesset proceedings take place in a spacious hall, and each member is assigned a seat. Members of the government sit at an oblong table in the center of the chamber with members of the Knesset around them in a semicircle. They all face the chairman of the meeting and the rostrum.[2]

A "Pure" Parliamentary System

An important school of thought argues that the institutions of constitutional and representative government are central to democracy. One of the central issues determining the viability of a democratic political system concerns the relative merits and demerits of the parliamentary and presidential systems in terms of the relations between the legislative and executive branches of the government, the accountability of one to the other, and the overriding question of separation of powers and checks and balances.

Almost all governments have executive, legislative, and judicial functions differentiated in different branches. Amnon Rubinstein points out that there is often contamination in the functioning of the branches in all systems. As far as the Knesset is concerned, he states that

> ... it fills judicial functions when it discusses, for example, challenges regarding election results; judges fill administrative functions regarding implementation of judicial decisions, the division of land, and bequests. While the deviations of the courts and the legislature may be considered marginal, the deviations of the administration from the principle of division of power are often essential. The administration busies itself with secondary legislation in amounts which surpass the output of the Knesset in primary legislation and administrative justice becomes more important as the degree of intervention of the central government grows.[3]

The Knesset also takes on judiciary powers when it decides to revoke the immunity of a Knesset member or the immunity of the president of the country. More crucial to our interest is that the executive branch in Israel takes on disproportionate importance in any analysis of the system. The legislature is not the equal of the executive, although formally the legislature generates and controls the government. The legislature in Israel does not have the status or the power of the executive. The strong party system on which both rest makes it a political inevitability that the dependent Knesset members support their party leaders, who are also government ministers.

One of the important myths of Israeli political life is that checks and balances exist within the system. This is simply not so. To be sure, the legislature is important, and in some hypothetical situations we could imagine it to be crucial, but in the political sense it must be thought of as a staging ground for the government and the executive branch. Should Knesset members move from party to party, the government could be threatened. But it would be inappropriate to consider spontaneous behavior on the part of representatives as the base for an Israeli version of separation of powers.

Israel is a good example of the parliamentary system: The Knesset is elected by the people, and it in turn selects the executive branch based on its membership. The leader of the plurality party is usually called to form the government and stand at its head. If there is no majority party (as is usually the case in Israel), a coalition government is formed. Confidence in the government is generally assured as long as the coalition remains intact. While the coalition holds, it is almost inconceivable that the government would fail to see its legislative program passed by the parliament. The government ceases its term in office if the Knesset expresses no confidence in it, if it decides to resign, if the prime minister no longer can or wishes to serve in that capacity, or if a new Knesset is elected. In all four situations the outgoing government continues as a caretaker government until a new one is appointed. A caretaker government has all the powers of a regular government and none of the political liabilities. It is hermetically closed (Joshua 6:1); ministers cannot be appointed or replaced. A no-confidence vote cannot be expressed in a caretaker government.

The result of a vote of no confidence, or the resignation of the government or the prime minister, is that the government falls. New elections are *not* a result of any of these developments. The only way in which new elections can be called in Israel is through a law of the Knesset. The president cannot dissolve the Knesset. This is an important point that adds perspective regarding the role of the president of Israel in the political system. Israel is a very pure example of the parliamentary form of government; the president is a figurehead, the head of state but not the head of government. Hypothetical situations may be imagined in which he could grant the task of forming the government to the leader of a minority party. This happened in 1983 when Shamir was asked by the president to form the government after Prime Minister Begin's resignation, even though the Likud's Knesset delegation was smaller than the Alignment's. The person who is to form the government must win a majority of the Knesset's votes, and if the choice of the president was inappropriate, his candidate would be unsuccessful in his task.

But lest we be overly impressed with the Knesset's ability to call for new elections, it must be remembered that the Knesset is made up of politicians and political parties, and the decision to disband the Knesset and call new elections demands a majority of the house, which can be achieved only when the ruling coalition so decides or when a working coalition emerges that cannot agree on the formation of a government but can muster a majority for new elections. For the historical record, no government of Israel has ever lost a vote of confidence and new elections have been called against the wishes of the ruling majority once once. This occurred before the 1984 elections when Tami, although a party in the governing coalition, used its 3 votes to support an opposition motion to hold early elections.

It is an elementary fact of Israeli political life that the government, not the Knesset, is the focus of political power in the country. The ministers of the government are generally the leaders of the political parties in the coalition. As ministers, they not only have political power and prestige, but generally also have the patronage and budget to enhance their political positions and that of their parties. As leaders of political parties that tend to operate oligarchically, the other Knesset members of their party soon realize that is in the interest of the party—and in their personal interest—to toe the line.

The strength of the government is achieved by a process of condensation in which, at each successive stage, the potency of the remaining material increases. Within a voting population of 2 million, the power of an individual voter is not great. Of the 120 members of the Knesset, the relative influence of each one is obviously greater. If members of the government coalition parties number, say, 70, and members of the government 20, power is concentrated even more. Now, if you are one of the 12 who happen to be ministers who are members of the major party and, say, among the ministers of the major party you also happen to be in the dominant faction, of which there are seven members, your power grows greatly. This process of condensation is a major feature of the Israeli political scene and is enhanced by the governmental institutions that have developed. The smallness of the country, the electoral system, the parliamentary system with coalition government and the supremacy of the executive—all enhance the centralization of the system that characterizes Israeli politics.

The Knesset and Israeli government are closely bound to one another in both the constitutional and political senses. The political leadership of the group of parties that can form a working coalition in the Knesset is elected to be the government. Formally, the president of Israel, after consultation with leaders of the parties, assigns a member of the Knesset the task of forming the government. The member may notify the president within three days that he declines the responsibility. If he does not, this government builder has 21 days to form his coalition. The president may grant him an additional 21 days, if needed, or he may turn to someone else to perform the task. If a second Knesset member also fails to form a government, the president may turn to a third, and so on. If the president is unsuccessful in finding a candidate or has acted too slowly, a majority of the Knesset may petition the president to appoint their candidate, and if the candidate agrees to this task in writing, the president must appoint him. In this case he has 14 days to complete his task, during which time the previous candidate's commission is terminated. When successful, the government builder becomes prime minister after he presents his government to the Knesset, announces its policy guidelines, and is granted the Knesset's approval and confidence. Notice that, politically and constitutionally, the entire exercise of forming the executive branch of the government is dependent on the composition of the legislative branch and its acquiescence to the process of coalition formation.

The work of the government demands in many instances the continued support of the Knesset. If ministry assignments are to be changed among the government ministers, Knesset approval is needed. If a new minister is to be added, or if ministries within the government are to be restructured, the government's decision must be announced to the Knesset and must be approved. But notice that while the Knesset can express lack of confidence in the government, it cannot express no-confidence in a single minister.

Coalition Politics

The two words *coalition politics* are almost synonomous. In order to construct winning majorities in committees, organizations, or legislatures, coalitions must often be formed. Forming coalitions comes naturally to politicians, and in parliamentary systems of Europe it has become accepted as a basic characteristic of politics.

As a general rule we would expect coalitions to be formed with the smallest surplus over the resources necessary to maintain a majority in the Knesset. There are costs involved in having another party support your party's platform or your candidate for a minister's post. Obviously, one would try to keep costs down by entering coalitions with as few other parties as possible. The "minimum size" principle applied to the Knesset would lead us to expect that a coalition of 61 in the 120-member Knesset would be formed. In fact, the Israeli experience has rarely adhered to the minimum-size principle.[4] Most governments formed in Israel between 1949 and 1984 have rested on solid majorities in the Knesset, well above the minimum size needed for rule. These comfortable majorities have given the governments more leeway in actions and have intimidated smaller parties from causing coalition crises because by simple arithmetic it is clear to smaller parties that they are dispensable. Of the 22 governments since 1949, only four have had support from fewer than 65 members at the outset. In 1955 the cabinet formed by Prime Minister Sharett was made up of a coalition of only 64 votes, but it lasted only two months.

During the term of office of a coalition its size may be reduced to the point that it is in danger of losing its parliamentary majority. Thus the Ben-Gurion cabinet of 1951 had the support of only 60 Knesset members after Agudat Israel and Poalei Agudat Israel left the cabinet over the issue of compulsory army service for women. As a result of defections from the Likud and the splitting up of the DMC, Begin's Knesset support fell drastically in 1979. After the 1981 elections, Begin set up a government based on the support of only 61 members of the Knesset.

Until 1977 the consistent leader of the coalition was the Mapai-Labor-Alignment. Being the pivot of all arithmetical calculations regarding the coalitions, the dominant party consolidated its position by controlling the key ministries of defense, foreign affairs, finance, education, and the prime ministry. Budget allocations, key appointments, and important matters of policy were all in the hands of the Labor party. With the ascension of the Likud in 1977, the government coalition was constructed for the first time by another party. But its political behavior in terms of forming the coalition was not much different from that displayed by the Alignment over the years.

The basic ingredient of the Likud coalition of 1977 was the same as that used by the various Labor governments—the National Religious party. With 12 Knesset votes, the NRP was attractive to the Likud without being threatening. Moreover, the NRP was experienced in the politics of compromise, which is the essence of coalition politics. The alternative DMC, with 15 seats, had a reformist bent to it and insisted on items in the coalition negotiations, such as electoral reform, to which the Likud preferred to pay only lip service. Once the government was set up it was harder for the DMC to stand by its principles; ultimately it acquiesced in entering the government coalition without receiving the assurances it had sought.

A good working relationship developed between Mapai and the religious parties, although the major crises in the history of coalitions in Israel are often associated with problems of religion. In a country so hard-pressed with security and economic problems, it is enlightening to note that cabinet crises usually center on matters peripheral to immediate concerns of government and pertaining more to matters of philosophy and theology. Perhaps this indicates special cultural attainments of Jews and the Jewish state, but it also means that ruling coalitions are relatively successful in governing; government policy is generally assured of support before it reaches the Knesset, and only on matters on which cleavage cannot be overcome do partners sometimes quarrel in public.

Three examples will suffice. The first crisis in Israeli cabinet history occurred in early 1950 over the religious education of children in immigrant camps. A compromise solution was worked out whereby religious schools would be set up in predominantly religious camps and two systems, secular and religious, would operate in others. By the end of 1950 the issue emerged again; the cabinet recommendations were rejected by a Knesset vote of 49 to 42 with many opposition parties using the opportunity to strike a blow against Mapai as much as support the claims of the religious parties. Ben-Gurion immediately announced the resignation of the government, and new elections were called for July 1951. This crisis gave impetus to Ben-Gurion's assessment that a national system of education must be established, thereby abandoning party-related tracks that had characterized education in the pre-state period. At the government level, he was convinced that effective ways must be found to assure collective responsibility in order to prevent cabinets failing as a result of the defection of coalition members. It also convinced him that electoral reform was needed in order to free the political system from the stranglehold that strong parties had over it.

A second crisis occurred in July 1958 when the two NRP ministers resigned from the cabinet over a directive issued by minister of the interior, Israel Bar-Yehuda of Ahdut Haavoda. Bar-Yehuda's instructions to registration officials stated that "any person declaring in good faith that he is a Jew shall be registered as a Jew and no additional proof shall be required." This infuriated the religious authorities, for the question of "Who is a Jew?" has historically and traditionally been their province. Indeed, it can be argued that the issue is of prime concern to them because matters of group exclusivity are meaningful only in terms of some preconceived notion of the history and destiny of the group. Ultimately, the NRP resigned from the cabinet and experienced the taste of opposition for the first time. The real issue was not "Who is a Jew?" but *who decides* who is a Jew? The most significant political outcome of the crisis was that since 1959, the minister of the interior, who is responsible for registration of citizens, has consistently been from the National Religious party. This pro-NRP conclusion was reached while the party was not a member of the coalition, indicating that even in opposition they had considerable leverage.

The story of the third example of a coalition quarrel began in January 1970 when the Supreme Court ruled that a person's statement that he was a Jew was sufficient to define him as a Jew. The government headed by Golda Meir subsequently amended the Law of Return by defining a Jew as "one who is born to a Jewess or is converted." This is in accord with rabbinical practice and was considered by many a major victory for the religious forces. But the issue soon arose—converted by whom? Conversions undertaken by nonorthodox rabbis were not regarded as valid by the establishment of Israeli religious leaders. The demand was made that the Law of Return be further amended to have conversion valid only if it was performed in accord with Jewish rabbinical law.

Golda Meir's efforts to form a new government after the 1973 elections were held up until March 1974 by this issue. After much effort a formula was developed. The prime minister issued a statement that since the amendment of the Law of Return, "no non-Jew had been registered as a Jew, and the government intended to continue in like fashion." The NRP gave in for all intents and purposes and joined the Meir government in the light of "compelling security considerations" occasioned by reports of the deteriorating situation on the Syrian border. When Golda Meir resigned as prime minister soon after having established the government, however, the process had to begin again. In this second round, the opponents of the coalition, especially the Youth Faction led by Zevulun Hammer and Yehuda Ben Meir, hardened their line and were successful in preventing the NRP from participating in the new Rabin government. By November 1974 the NRP replaced the Civil Rights Movement members in supporting the government without achieving any change in the "Who is a Jew?" issue.

Explanations for this behavior are varied, but among them it is important to point out that the NRP was concerned about losing its powerful base in the ministry of religious affairs, which allowed it to control religious councils and chief and local rabbinates. This had happened in the 1958-59 crisis, and the leadership was afraid that it would happen again. The turnabout can also be understood in terms of the internal struggle for power among the various factions of the NRP. Hammer initially refused the portfolio offered him by Rabin, but many of his young colleagues argued that it was important to be in a position to influence policy in the sphere of security and foreign affairs in order to strengthen the hawkish wing of the government.

Coalition involves a large number of issues, such as ideology, government ministries, programs, and money. Many of these are tied together. Sometimes behavior explained at the public level in one way is really motivated by something altogether different. One way to examine the nature of the payoffs in coalition politics is to examine the ministries assigned to the various parties. This is harder to analyze than it appears, because not all ministries are of equal importance and even the size of the budget is not always an indicator of a ministry's importance. Using government ministries as an index of the payoffs of coalition behavior, we can distinguish between the qualitative and quantitative dimensions. Qualitatively, the important ministries have historically been in the hands of the major party of the coalition. During parts of the terms of office of Ben-Gurion, Levi Eshkol, and Menachem Begin, they were also their own defense ministers. The appointment of Moshe Dayan to the post of defense minister on the eve of the Six Day War of 1967 was important not only because Prime Minister Eshkol relinquished the post but also because it was given to a member of Rafi, a party outside the government coalition before the establishment of the National Unity Government. Moshe Dayan represents another important exception when, after the 1977 Likud victory, Menachem Begin offered him the post of foreign affairs minister, even though Dayan had been elected on the Alignment list.

The second National Unity Government was set up in 1984. It resulted from the stalemate that the election produced. In an unprecedented manner, the Alignment and the Likud agreed that Peres would be prime minister for the first 25 months. Also, most of the other lists elected supported the government, making its promised strength in the Knesset 97 of 120 members. A careful balance was struck between the two large parties over ministries, timetables, and commitments to smaller parties associated with each of the bigger ones.

Besides ministries, many other things are bargained over in coalition negotiations. Policy is a crucial one. The government sets up guidelines that are in effect the government's platform. These are approved by the Knesset when the government is approved, but the guidelines do not have binding status. They reflect promises made by partners of the coalition to each other. Usually, however, no timetable is set on promises for enacting policy, and often such promises can be overlooked. If the coalition is fragile, however, or if the other party must acquiesce in supporting a policy, the payoff may be that the large coalition leader fulfills its promise by enacting legislation or pursuing certain policy goals. The coalition has the resources to do this because the Knesset members can be pressured to follow the party line.

Other chips in the bargaining process include deputy ministers, chairmanships of Knesset committees, and budgets. A deputy minister must be a Knesset member; he enjoys the status of minister and many fringe benefits. Budgets may be promised to kibbutzim or yeshivas or any other favored organization of the party being wooed to join the coalition. The public treasury often pays a high price for the continued existence of the government coalition.

The Cabinet

Formal and informal power rests with the government and its ministers. Obviously there are gradations of power, with the prime minister and those close to him near the top of the scale. While formally all ministers are equal and the prime minister is the first among equals, this legality does not come close to portraying actual relations within the government.[5]

Israeli government can rightly be called prime ministerial government. Ben-Gurion could conceive of and plan the Sinai operation with almost no prior knowledge by his cabinet. Golda Meir's decisions regarding Egyptian overtures in the early 1970s and Menachem Begin's decision regarding the feasibility of a peace treaty with Egypt at the end of that decade magnify the contention that the predispositions and conclusions of the prime minister can have very far-reaching influence in the system. Both leaders were surrounded by colleagues who had differing opinions, but it was ultimately their line that prevailed. The superior position of the prime minister, in law and politics, makes him the undisputed focus of power. While his political acumen, personality, or coalition imperatives might lead him to share his power, and even to be responsive to party or public opinion, the prime minister's near monopoly on power resources is impressive. The incumbent in any political situation has a distinct advantage; in Israel he has a double one. He is both incumbent head of government and incumbent head of party. Used judiciously, the combination is almost irrepressible.

Cabinet ministers are not advisers of the prime minister, nor are they appointed because of expertise in fields controlled by their ministries. Members of the cabinet are there because of their political role as politicians whose parties have decided to join the ruling coalition. The 1984 National Unity Government had 25 ministers; four of them were ministers without portfolio. Ministers need not be Knesset members by law, but usually they are. The fact that some 20 percent of the Knesset are government ministers means that the work of legislation falls on the remaining members. It also means that the coalition parties in the Knesset are usually led by second-level leaders because the first-rank leaders are in the cabinet. And this, of course, weakens the Knesset politically. There have rarely been more than one or two ministers at a time who were not Knesset members. While some have tried to resign from the Knesset after being appointed minister in order to make room in the Knesset for someone lower on the party list, this practice is rare and generally frowned upon. The law now provides that a member who resigns from the Knesset also resigns from the government if he is a minister. This limits the use of this practice to the period between the elections and the installation of the government.

The minister is appointed by his party and is responsible for the voting behavior of his delegation in the Knesset. The prime minister generally does not interfere with the selection of ministers by coalescing parties, although Golda Meir refused to allow Yitzhak Rafael to serve in her cabinet. Until 1981, the prime minister was powerless to fire a minister. To do so would mean a political confrontation with the minister's Knesset delegation, something a prime minister would usually choose to avoid. Since then a new law was passed, making it possible for the prime minister to remove a minister by announcing his intention to the Knesset. Forty-eight hours later, unless the prime minister changes his mind, the minister's appointment is terminated.

The government sets up its own rules of procedure, and most of its official decisions have to do with legislation that the government approves before forwarding it to the Knesset. What really is done in cabinet meetings is a function of the personality of the prime minister and the issues on the public agenda. Unfortunately, little is known in a systematic way about the dynamics and interactions within the cabinet. We know the procedures for asking the various ministries involved for their comments on pending legislation. We are sometimes aware of acrimonious debate that takes place in the cabinet meeting, especially if there is a leak or if the debate continues on the evening's television news or in the newspapers. We also know the quantity of legislation and decisions taken (and we may debate about their quality). But the cabinet and its meeting must be thought of as a rather formalized setting for the continuation of the political game. Matters of coalition politics, electoral politics, and bureaucratic politics can never be far removed from the minds and actions of the ministers and the government. It is important to be sagacious and concerned with the public welfare, and we all hope that ministers are those things. Being first and foremost politicians, however, it is clear that their motivations are complex and do not always flow directly from trying to achieve the greater good. When there is a conflict within the cabinet, things become more focused and then it is easier to determine the lineup of the players and assess why they act as they do and what they hope to achieve. The personalities of the major actors, especially that of the prime minister, determine much of the governing style of the cabinet.

The government sometimes delegates matters to one of its committees of ministers and at times even empowers the committee to make the decision in place of the cabinet. The prime minister may participate in any meeting, and if he so desires, he may serve as chairman of that meeting. Deliberations of the government and the ministerial committees are secret.

The ministers are responsible for the actions of their ministries, and the minister is also responsible for the decisions of the government as a whole.

This means that once a decision is taken in the government, all the ministers must support it, in the Knesset and publicly, even if they opposed it in the cabinet meeting. Ministers must also see to it that Knesset members of their delegation vote for the government's position unless given permission to do otherwise.

In Israeli political history, the resignation of most ministers from the government can be explained in political terms. While there may have been matters of principle or policy at the heart of the issue, the resignation itself must be thought of in terms of its effect on the political structure of the coalition. Parties (and hence ministers) have resigned from the government over religious issues and matters of foreign policy. The examples used earlier in this chapter can be cited as cases of leaving the government on political grounds connected with party principle. Another example would be the exit in 1970 of Gahal from the National Unity Government because it could not agree to the government's position on the Rogers's plan with its acceptance of UN Resolution 242. Rarely does an individual minister resign on issues of principle, as Yitzhak Berman did. He did so in 1982 after the government refused (only to reverse itself a week later) to set up an official commission of inquiry regarding the events in the Palestinian refugee camps of Sabra and Shatilla in Beirut. Government ministers almost never resign out of ministerial responsibility. For example, Prime Minister Meir and Defense Minister Dayan did not resign as a result of the Yom Kippur War, in part because of the support given their view by the Agranat Commission that decisions regarding the war involved the collective responsibility of the entire government.

Knesset Members in Action

Knesset members play more complex roles than simply that of legislator. The Knesset member must be concerned with his (or her) own career and with his ties with those groups within his party or in the public at large that supported him, with the fortunes of his party and with its adherence to his ideals, and the interests that he represents. As legislator, he also is concerned with the public welfare. His hardest task is synthesizing these sometimes competing roles.

The Knesset member is granted immunity by law. By comparative standards the immunity of Knesset members is extensive, if not excessive. The basic concept is to allow the legislator freedom of speech and freedom of action while pursuing his duties. Parliamentary immunity refers to his actions in the legislature. This immunity is irrevocable. A second form of immunity extends to matters not directly connected to legislative work. The Knesset member is protected from criminal proceedings against him for the entire period of his membership in the Knesset, and even for acts committed before he became a member of the Knesset, although this immunity can be removed by the Knesset on recommendation of the House Committee. In the ninth Knesset there were three sensational cases of immunity removal: NRP minister Aharon Abu-Hatzeira was accused of improperly using public funds, and found not guilty; Shmuel Rechtman of the Likud was sentenced to prison on bribery charges; and Flatto-Sharon was accused of illegal campaign practices and later found guilty.

The Knesset may remove a member from its ranks by a vote of two-thirds of the members if he is convicted of a criminal act and sentenced to at least one year of jail. In the case of a sentence that is not yet final, a Knesset member may be suspended until the legal proceedings are completed.

The need to grant special legal status to legislators is recognized by all democratic countries. Representatives must be free to go about their business without harassment by the authorities. But granting them almost blanket immunity—the exceptions are treason and being caught in the act of committing a crime—is excessive. The popular example of the excesses of the law is that Knesset members are immune from prosecution because of traffic violations. This is not only maddening, it could well be dangerous. There are good reasons to protect the independence of the legislator, but it must be done in a sensible manner. In 1982 an addendum to the law of immunity calls for Knesset members to be liable for punishment in the case of traffic violations, but the Knesset member is entitled to ask to have his immunity restored regarding specific violations.

The Knesset member is entitled to serve out his term regardless of his political behavior. This is an important exception to the central rule of Israeli politics that the political party dominates the Knesset. Even if the Knesset member leaves the party on whose list he was elected and joins another party, he remains a member of the Knesset. The resignation of a Knesset member from his list is always an agonizing affair. The list claims that he must resign from the Knesset, because the voters voted for the party and its ideology, not for the individual Knesset member. The Knesset member invariably answers that if he had not been on the list, his former party would not have done nearly as well.

The Knesset is a fairly reliable prism through which the Israeli political system can be viewed, but it is not to be confused with the heart of the system. The composition of the Knesset is determined by elections, and the relative strength of the parties determines the government coalition and national policy. Even the organization of the house is influenced by the party composition of the Knesset. The delegation of a party or list to the Knesset is the major building block of the house's organization. Political calculations in forming the government are based on the size of the delegation. The assignment of committee membership and chairmanships are done by the delegation, and for important debates, speaking time is allocated to delegations who in turn divide it among their members; motions of no-confidence must be made by a delegation; and even office space in the Knesset building is provided to the delegation rather than an individual Knesset member.

The parliamentary delegation is obviously an important political force within its own party. Generally there is overlap between the leadership of the party and the leadership of the parliamentary delegation. Party policies are guides for the parliamentary delegation. If the party is represented in the government coalition, government policy in effect dictates the stand of the parliamentary delegation. Often, then, the parliamentary delegation of the party must accept this state of affairs or be open to the accusation that its party platform has been flaunted by the government. The overlapping membership of an individual in government, parliamentary delegation, and party can be used to pressure the government in a direction more amenable to the party platform. This may happen when, behind the scenes, a minister encourages a stand against a proposed government policy and even has the party issue an ultimatum that its continued support in the government will be conditioned on the altering of government policy. Small and medium-size coalition partners, such as the NRP, Mapam, and the Liberal party, have used this ploy often. In major coalition parties the party leadership is also leading the government, and thus the usual pattern is for the parliamentary delegation and the party institutions to pass declaratory resolutions supporting the government policy and wishing it continued success.

In small, ideological parties (Rakah, Agudat Israel) the primacy of the party institutions over the Knesset delegation appears in the party constitution and in its operative procedures. This situation can be manipulated by the political leader when some outside group superior to him, such as the Council of Torah Sages in the case of Agudat Israel, "demands" that he conform with the group's dictates. The party establishes the identity of the ideological authority, and the Knesset member, as powerful as he may seem, is only a messenger of the ideological party. He too may compromise in the end, as do all politicians, but in the interim he can cite the superior authority of the party's decision to explain his seeming intransigence.

An example of a Knesset delegation being given voting instructions by the party council on a specific issue occurred in 1975 over the Knesset vote regarding the interim agreement with Egypt worked out by U.S. Secretary of State Henry Kissinger. Yaad was a four-member Knesset delegation that thought it would be best to abstain or reject the agreement since it did not go far enough.

The party council, after strenuous debate, requested that the Knesset delegation support the agreement. All four members, against their better judgment, did so.

This example of party control of the Knesset delegation is rare in Israeli politics because usually the party councils and the parliamentary delegations are dominated by the same people. The triangle of relationships—party/Knesset delegation/Knesset member—is the source of many conflicts.[6] Party rules find it necessary to state specifically that the Knesset member is subject to the decisions of the party, generally leaving it that vague. It is clear that in the logic of the Israeli political system hierarchical relations exist among the three with the party usually taking precedence, followed by the desires of the Knesset delegation, and lastly the Knesset member. The member is elected on the party list representing a program or ideology, and he usually decides that his personal career will be better off in the long run if he is a loyal party member. Most Knesset members do not have the financial, organizational, or personal qualities necessary for risking a political career on a given issue. For most members, the Knesset is the culmination of a political career, not the beginning of one.

Party discipline is the only way in which a coalition's program can be passed, argue the advocates. Party discipline promotes mediocrity among Knesset members, who no longer think for themselves, and cynicism in the public at large when parties change long-held views for political advantage and force their Knesset delegation members to toe the line, argue the dissenters. Party discipline even has its expression in the Knesset law that makes the minister responsible for the behavior of Knesset delegation members and can bring about the forfeiting of office because the minister fails to have the delegation's member vote in conformity to the government's decisions on certain issues.

The government coalition has at times permitted abstention on crucial issues by members of coalition parties and has even allowed verbal opposition to its proposals along with abstention on the vote. As a rule, however, members of delegations that participate in the coalition are expected to support government proposals. The major exception applies to issues that the coalition decides are matters of conscience, such as certain religious matters, at which time party discipline is removed. Party discipline may also be rescinded when the government is willing to gamble on its success, as when the Begin government brought the peace treaty with Egypt before the Knesset. Some Likud members opposed or abstained in the vote, but the prime minister correctly calculated that the votes of remaining Likud members and the votes of many more moderate opposition parties would assure the passage of the treaty and support the evacuation of the Sinai. This example notwithstanding, party discipline allows the Knesset to legislate and the government to rule in a stable manner. Party discipline makes meaningful the contention that the Knesset must be understood in political, not ideological, terms.

Two areas in which Knesset members can supposedly influence the Knesset and the government are question time and motions for the agenda. Unlike the British system, in which question time is an opportunity for a sharp exchange between government minister and parliament member, in Israel question time is usually dull. The attention goes to the question submitted and not to the answers, which can take six weeks or longer in coming. Although the answer can be followed by a short oral question to the minister by the Knesset member who asked the question (*if* he happens to be present), the whole procedure is usually lackluster. Motions for the agenda allow matters of public importance to be aired even if no specific legislation is to be debated and even if the government has not requested the debate. At the end of a ten-minute introductory speech, the minister concerned replies. The issue may then be deferred for a general Knesset debate on the matter, rejected, or referred to a committee for examination and report to the Knesset. So as not to clog the house with motions for the agenda and private members' bills, a quota system has been instituted, based on a party ratio, with a slight advantage to the opposition parties. Urgent motions are outside these quotas. The urgency must, however, be recognized by the chairman of the Knesset.

The organization of the Knesset follows party lines. The chairman is almost always from a major faction of the largest party and his deputies are generally chosen from the large parties in the house. Aside from his symbolic and ceremonial importance, the chairman has considerable authority in the routine affairs of the Knesset, because he largely determines the agenda and is responsible for the day-to-day operation of the legislature.

No quorum is necessary for Knesset deliberations and action. Criticism is sometimes expressed by those who believe that a legislator should sit in the house when business is being conducted. Attendance is very low at most times. The contention made by some Knesset members that they do not attend the plenum because they are busy with the Knesset's really important work in its committees is on the whole unfounded. Many Knesset members absent themselves from committee meetings as well, and the importance of the Knesset committees has been overstated. A more plausible explanation is that as politicians their activities are varied and time-consuming; it makes little sense for them to listen to speeches on matters they, or their parties, have already settled. Because of the centrality of the parties, the dominance of government ministries on legislation, and the nature of the profession of politicians, it is difficult to argue that the absence of Knesset members from the debates in the plenum is a major problem of Israeli democracy. It is a symptom, but not the disease.

By law, being a Knesset member is not an exclusive undertaking. Knesset members may continue their private concerns while serving in the Knesset. The only limitation is that their Knesset salary is the only salary they can receive from a public institution. The reason a political party would want a public officeholder to be a Knesset member has a political explanation: For the party organization, it affords control over centers of power; for the individual, it allows utilizing a power base for additional exposure and influence, at the same time allowing the legislator to espouse the interests of his constituency. An interesting exception is the recent rule passed by the Labor party that prohibits representatives from holding more than one elected post. The reason for this ruling is that in opposition, the party had to provide positions for its activists and must therefore limit the number of positions held by each individual. The official reason given was the principle of rotation. However, from the perspective of the Knesset, it obviously weakens the house as a legislative institution. Relegating a day or two a week to matters of the Knesset may be enough for very talented and very busy people, but it also indicates the relatively low stature and importance of the Knesset in the political system. The regulations for cabinet ministers are more stringent. A minister is expected to devote all his time to his job. Rules against professional and commercial conflicts of interest have been established, and while these expressed expectations have proven largely unenforceable, they make clear norms of behavior expected of ministers.

In the Knesset, especially for those more active in the day-to-day operations of the house, a clublike atmosphere develops. Common interests and shared experience bring people closer together regardless of party background. As in other social situations and in legislatures around the world, this esprit de corps is an important social feature of the informal life of the Knesset and Knesset members. It undoubtedly gives many of them an enhanced feeling of purposive behavior in legislating for the nation and its needs. The atmosphere cushions the uncertainties surrounding the decisions to be made and the unpredicable nature of the life of the politician. Being accepted by colleagues is sometimes erroneously translated by Knesset members into feelings of success and satisfaction and invincibility at the polls the next time around. Needless to say, while the clublike atmosphere is functional for legislation and for reducing tensions between ideological opponents, some Knesset members are rudely shocked when they are removed from the club by party leaders or the voters.

Legislation

The formal stages of legislation will be familiar to students of European parliaments. There are three readings of a bill. Most bills are initiated by a proposal introduced by the government. It must be placed on the table of the Knesset 48 hours before the Knesset takes it up for a first reading. The minister responsible for the legislation generally presents the explanation of the bill in the first reading, and a member of the opposition opens debate on the bill. After the debate, the bill is voted on. If returned to the government, it is in effect a defeat for the government because the Knesset chooses not to consider legislation proposed by it. Almost always, however, the first reading ends with a decision to send the bill to committee, which is tantamount to approval.

The committee by which the bill is considered is generally suggested by the minister. His suggestion is almost always accepted. If there is dissent, the matter is decided by the Knesset House Committee. Important matters are certain to end up on the table of a "friendly" committee. No time limit is set on the committee's deliberations, and no mechanism can be used to force a committee to report on a bill, short of the efforts of committee members themselves to have the bill read out of committee.

In the committee the bill is discussed in detail, and amendments to the bill are suggested. Changes may be introduced by the committee, which then reports back to the Knesset with its version of the bill. The second reading of the bill is concerned with the amendments proposed by the committee. If no changes are made in the committee's version, the second and third readings of the bill can proceed immediately. If additional changes were introduced during the second reading of the bill, the third reading is postponed in order to study the ramifications of the changes adopted in the second reading and give the government the opportunity to withdraw the proposed law in view of the changes made.

The bill becomes law after being signed by the prime minister, the president, and the minister responsible for the bill; it is then published in the official gazette. The right of veto does not exist; the three signatures on the bill are mandatory, not discretionary.

About 95 percent of Israel's legislation is initiated by the government. The remaining 5 percent is the result of private members' bills. A private member's proposed bill follows the same procedure except there is a preliminary reading of the bill before it goes to committee to be reported back for the first reading. Many private members' bills fail at this preliminary stage, especially if the proposal is not consistent with government policy.

Most private members' bills are submitted by members of the opposition. One important exception was the private member's bill passed in 1960 known as the Kanovitz law, which intended to regulate the pollution caused by motor vehicles. Shimon Kanovitz was a member of the Progressive party. While the intentions of the Knesset were good, it took two and a half years for the ministries responsible (health, transportation, and interior) to publish the necessary regulations, and to this day the law is a classic example of one not enforced. The fact that execution of the law is no less important than its legislation reinforces the tendency to rely heavily on government ministries for bill initiation. Government-proposed legislation is initiated only after it has been cleared with the various ministries involved, especially the ministries of finance and justice. Since most legislation involves financial costs for additional manpower to enforce the legislation or impinges on other legislation, these ministries are especially active in determining which legislation, and in what form, will reach the Knesset for deliberation. The Knesset, as an institution, has been virtually powerless in the face of this development.

The committees of the Knesset are also formed along party lines. Soon after the elections, an arranging committee headed by a member of the largest party is established to determine the composition of the committees. The work of the arranging committee is quintessentially political since it must balance the size of the delegations with the attractiveness of the committees.

The ten standing committees of the Knesset are the House Committee; the Law, Constitution, and Justice Committee; the Finance Committee; the Foreign Affairs and Security Committee; the Immigration and Absorption Committee; the Economics Committee; the Education and Culture Committee; the Interior Affairs and Environment Committee; the Labor and Welfare Committee; and the State Control Committee. Assignment to committees is done by the arranging committee, and representatives of the various delegations determine for their own parties where they want their stronger delegates placed. They can enhance a Knesset member's career by placing him on an important committee and weaken him by not doing so. Small delegations are faced with a difficult dilemma because they do not have members on all the committees; they must convince their Knesset colleagues to grant them representation on the committees they deem important. Committee appointments are for the duration of the Knesset's tenure. If a member resigns from his party, the place on the committee reverts back to the party, even though he continues to remain a member of the Knesset.

The temporary replacement of committee members who disagree with the government's position is an excellent example of a mechanism of control by the ruling coalition and the passivity of the individual Knesset member. Two important instances of this were the appeal of the government decision regarding the settlement of Jews in Hebron in 1980 before the Foreign Affairs and Security Committee, and the decision to close El Al on the Sabbath and Jewish holidays in the Finance Committee in 1982. In the first case the Likud had agreed to permit the DMC the right of appeal before the Foreign Affairs and

Security Committee on settlement issues. In the second case the courts had ruled that a decision by the government to change the charter of a government corporation was not sufficient unless approved by the Finance Committee of the Knesset. Since the defeat of the first issue and the passage of the second were important to the Likud, and since party discipline did not hold in the Knesset committees, the leadership "temporarily" replaced unreliable coalition members on the committee until the votes were taken. Subsequently, the Foreign Affairs and Security Committee leadership of the major parties agreed that in the future, members would always be substituted for a period of at least three months. But this agreement applied only to that committee and probably only for the period of the ninth Knesset.[7]

Committee chairmen are formally elected at the first meeting of the committee, upon the nomination of the House Committee. The chairmanship of committees has been used in coalition negotiations conducted after the elections for setting up the government. Rather than agree to give a bargaining party another ministry or deputy minister, an important Knesset committee chairmanship may suffice. Coalition parties always have a majority in the committees of the Knesset, although chairmen are occasionally appointed from opposition parties. This depends on the size of the opposition and the importance of the committee. The Economics Committee and the Public Services Committee, which existed until 1977, were often chaired by members of the opposition.

As a rule the chairmanship of important committees is reserved for members of the ruling coalition. Three important committees are the House Committee, the Foreign Affairs and Security Committee, and the Finance Committee. The House Committee is important because it has virtual control over the Knesset and its day-to-day operations. Since the Knesset is often in the public eye and is the formal decision-making organ of the state, the ruling majority must be able to control procedural decisions. In this kind of situation, where majorities are automatic, rules of order can determine how effectively the coalition or the opposition will be able to use parliamentary procedure to its advantage.

A second committee usually headed by a member of the ruling party is the Foreign Affairs and Security Committee. Although its membership is select and the matters brought before it often very grave, its impact on policy is relatively small. The committee has been used as a sounding board or as a mechanism for consulting with members of the opposition on important international matters. This committee provides the government with an opportunity to discuss sensitive security issues without involving the entire house. During the ninth Knesset, its chairman, Moshe Arens, made valiant efforts to increase the committee's role in policy making, but they were largely in vain. Even though the membership included former Prime Minister Rabin, ex-Chief of Staff Bar-Lev, and former Defense Minister Peres, its impact on policy remained relatively small.

The Finance Committee has an active role in policy and has usually been headed by a member of a coalition party. In both the ninth and tenth Knessets the committee was headed by Agudat Israel Knesset members. The Aguda was willing to forego government ministries and agreed to support the coalition on condition that a string of legislation be adopted (including tighter control on abortion, tighter observance of the Sabbath and holidays, and more financial support for yeshivas) and that they be assigned the chairmanship of the Finance Committee. Not being members in the government gave them a certain distance from ongoing government policy; they could support it without being responsible for it. At the same time they could bargain for budget, legislation, and power because these were commodities more easily available to coalition members than ministries. The annual budget is discussed at length in the Finance Committee, and its recommendations to the Knesset on the subject generally are passed. The Finance Committee is also given statutory authority to approve changes in the budget during the fiscal year. The Knesset has allocated decisions regarding the salaries of judges, Knesset members, and ministers to its Finance Committee, as well as the responsibility for setting the amount of money to be allocated for financing political parties.

The committees meet on a regular basis and there are Knesset members who are ready to explain that the major task of a Knesset member is work in committee. This statement must be seen in perspective. The power of the Knesset committees does not come close to approximating the power of committees of the U.S. Congress. There, committees play a key role in the legislative process. In fairness it must be pointed out that the American case is unusual. In Europe as a whole, and even in Great Britain, committees of the parliament do not reach the level of importance reached by committees in the American system.

There are two important reasons for this state of affairs. First, the American Congress is conceived of as the legislative branch of government, *independent* of the executive. As pointed out earlier, the parliamentary notion is different. The parliament *cooperates* with the government it chose, while the Congress may *compete* with the President. The Knesset does not perceive itself operating independently or at cross-purposes to its government. This explains the relative weakness of Knesset committees. They cannot subpoena witnesses or have them testify under oath. They cannot order documents to be brought before them. They can invite, persuade, and cajole, but they have no legal means of sanctioning those who refuse to cooperate. This extends to ministers, civil servants, and senior army officers, as well as to private citizens. The Knesset committee is not perceived as having a role in the legislative process independent of the government and its ministries.

The second reason for the relatively minor role played by Knesset committees in the legislative process is budgetary. To function properly as an independent agency in legislation, a Knesset committee should have a large staff of professionals who could gather information, assess it, and put it at the disposal of members of the committee. Take, for example, the field of education. Almost a third of Israel's population is in school. Overseeing the ministry and collecting, processing, and analyzing data, are just too much even for a conscientious and hard-working member. For in addition to his membership on the Education Committee, he is likely to be a member of a second Knesset committee, he is also a member of a party, and he has a constituency to attend to—in short, he (or she) is a politician whose tasks are numerous and whose time is limited. To provide the Knesset Education Committee with the kind of staff needed to fill this function would be expensive. Besides, there is an easy alternative: The information requested can be provided by the minister and his ministry's staff. They have gathered the information and supposedly have made their policy proposals based on these data. But this is exactly where the independence of the legislature breaks down. Committee members become dependent on the data, experts, and points of view of the ministry and do not exercise their function of overseeing and independent legislating.

Knesset committees do have staff, but not nearly enough. The committees may be granted legal assistance since the conception is that drafting legislation is the job of a lawyer. As a moment's reflection will indicate, this is only partially the case. On occasion the Finance Committee has had economists in a consulting capacity, as have other committees. But a part-time consultant or testimony before the committee by a university professor simply cannot replace staff work done over a long time in a consistent manner. The reason given for the failure to set up independent staffs for the Knesset committees has been the cost of such a proposal. But at the same time Knesset members will agree that being dependent on experts from the ministries weakens the effectiveness of the committees. The point that these Knesset members gloss over is that the matter is fundamentally in their hands. The practice in Israeli government has always been that the government does not discuss or approve the budget of the Knesset. (This is one of the only areas of real legislative independence in Israel.) Since this is the case, and since many Knesset members feel that the committees must be strengthened, they could appropriate monies for this purpose and establish a staff system for the Knesset's committees.

It may be that this is a utopian suggestion, for participating in the legislative process in a significant manner means that the responsibility of legislation will also shift (at least partially) from the government ministries to the Knesset. As members of hierarchical political parties, Knesset members in actuality may fail to take a more active role in the legislative process because they are content in knowing (and keeping) their place in a system that does not encourage conflict between the executive and legislative branches.

The Judiciary

The judicial system provides one of the greatest paradoxes in Israeli civil life. In a culture that is very highly politicized, the judicial system is professional and impartial despite its occasional wavering and despite charges that it is being politicized. Although there is no written constitution, the political system as a whole and particularly the judicial system respect the principle of limitation of government and have exercised self-restraint in many areas. The country has been, almost from its inception, under emergency conditions and hence liable to be run by emergency regulations; yet in many areas of civil liberties (at least in Israel's pre-1967 boundaries) Israel's record is good. The rule of law is much respected as an ideal, although in fact access to justice is stratified by one's wealth, determination, and patience to utilize the judicial system. In a system where most appointees in public life must meet some political requirement, the appointment of judges is widely perceived as generally based on professional attainment and potential. These characteristics make the Israeli judicial system very un-Israeli and hence important as a bastion of Israeli democracy in a sea of forces that would hasten the erosion of its foundations.

A basic notion of a liberal democracy is the limiting of the powers of government through the existence of a constitution. This document sets the outer limits of the permissible and also implies a form of redress through the courts if that limit is breached. Yonathan Shapiro has rightly pointed out that a democracy consists of both the formal procedures of electing governments and the freedoms from government interference that protect minorities and individuals from having their liberties infringed by government action.[8] The Israeli experience has always taken a formalistic approach to its understanding of democracy. This is nowhere better seen than in the fact that the issue of electoral reform is studied in schools and debated at length in the press, while the lack of a basic law that covers human and civil rights is taken for granted as a political necessity. No bill of rights exists in the Israeli system, and although various Knesset members and committees have worked for many years on preparing one, its passage has still not been achieved.

Great Britain also has no written constitution, but Great Britain has a tradition of hundreds of years of guarding civil liberties and developing their meaning. Israel's experience is too fragile to leave the guarding of civil rights to the goodwill of the authorities. The glaring shortfall in the Israeli system is the absence of a written constitution.

The Israeli solution to the lack of a constitution is the stage by stage approach. In 1950 when debates over the writing of a constitution were at their peak, it was clear that the two major bodies of opinion created a standoff. Secularists insisted that Israel must have a constitution like other modern, Western, liberal states. Religious spokesmen claimed that the Torah and its rabbinical commentaries made up the written constitution of Israel and that this was superior to any secular legislation since it was of Divine origin. As consensus is usually an important goal in Israeli politics, especially regarding matters of principle and public concern, it was decided not to attempt to reach a compromise but to put together, stage by stage, legislation that would, at a later date, form Israel's constitution.[9] This solution has been known as the "Harari decision," named after the Knesset member who introduced it. It is also likely that the leaders of the fledgling state did not want the limitations of a constitution to limit their freedom of action. Amnon Rubinstein is critical of the poor record of the Knesset in producing basic laws and thereby completing the work of writing the constitution. The Harari decision called for the Law, Constitution, and Justice Committee of the Knesset to prepare the appropriate legislation. The first Knesset, which passed the resolution, was perceived to be a constitutional convention and was in fact called a constituent assembly. All the basic laws, however, with the exception of the Basic Law: Knesset, were prepared and approved by the government and not by the Knesset Law, Constitution, and Justice Committee. Moreover, most of the basic laws do not have limiting clauses, a condition necessary if the legislation is to serve as a constitutional provision.[10]

The status of the basic laws was intended to be higher than that of regular legislation. This is obvious, among other reasons, because in passing a basic law the Knesset is continuing the work of the first Knesset, the constituent assembly. This is even more clear when entrenched provisions in the basic law require that changes be made only by special majorities. In general, legislation in the Knesset is passed by a simple majority of those present—abstentions not counting. The Basic Law: Knesset has two entrenched provisions. Article 4, which deals with the electoral system, can be changed only by an absolute majority during each stage of legislation. Articles 44 and 45 of the same basic law exempt the law from being changed by emergency regulations unless two-thirds of the members (at least 80) concur. Article 42 of the Basic Law: Government entrenches the basic law from emergency regulations unless a majority (61) of Knesset members agree.

The entrenchment clause in the Basic Law: Knesset was the background for the closest the Israeli judicial system ever came to judicial review. Judicial review is the power of a court to invalidate on constitutional grounds a governmental action whether it be committed by the executive (administrative) or legislative branch. The Bergman case involved the Israeli Supreme Court in a case in which the court declared an act of the Knesset void for violating a basic law.

Aharon A. Bergman had brought an action before the Supreme Court, sitting as the High Court of Justice, to block the implementation of the (Campaign) Financing Law of 1969. Bergman's complaint was that the law unfairly discriminated against new political parties because it provided governmental funds only for those parties already represented in the outgoing Knesset. He argued that the financing law violated the equality required by section 4 of the Basic Law: Knesset, which had been entrenched and could be changed only by a majority of Knesset members. The financing law had passed its first reading in the Knesset by a vote of 24 to 2.

Writing for all five justices who participated in the case, Justice Landau agreed that the financing law was in conflict with the equality required by section 4 of the Basic Law: Knesset. The absolute denial of funds to a new list constituted a major denial of equal opportunity in the democratic electoral process. Justice Landau acknowledged the absence of any provision in Israel's written law that expressly authorized the court to construe statutes in terms of the natural justice principle of the equality of all before the law. "Nevertheless this principle that is nowhere inscribed breathes the breath of life into our whole constitutional system." It was therefore right and just, Justice Landau argued, for the court to use it in interpreting the law. This story of judicial innovation has a political ending. The Knesset enacted the financing law again — this time by an absolute majority — incorporating changes in the light of the court's remarks. The issue of judicial review was skirted and the supremacy of the Knesset upheld.[11]

Despite the need to complete the work of drafting a constitution and despite the fact that the Knesset has the constitution-writing function in addition to that of the regular legislative function, the basic laws do not seem to have a constitutional aura about them. They can and have been changed and amended with ease, and thus lose their strength as limitations on the governing authorities. When in 1979 the coalition parties wanted to appoint a second deputy prime minister in order to solve problems of prestige and coalition formation, the Basic Law: Government was amended accordingly. The basic laws have yet to yield a constitution, nor have they been used by the legislature as a means of training themselves and the public to think in terms of a body of law that limits later legislation and governmental action.

The tension between the limitations on government implied by a constitutional system and the security problems of Israel is best evidenced by the constant state of emergency that has existed since 19 May 1948, five days after the achievement of independence. The legal arrangement is an announcement by the Knesset of the existence of a state of emergency, which allows the government to empower the prime minister or any other minister to issue emergency regulations intended to provide for "the defense of the state, the security of the public and upholding necessary distribution and services."[12] These emergency regulations may modify or suspend existing legislation and can impose or increase taxes. These regulations are for a three-month period unless extended or shortened by the authority making the regulation. In effect, emergency regulations have afforded the government an alternative method of legislation. Legislation that might be time-consuming and controversial can be achieved quickly with the emergency regulations. Emergency regulations are often used in defense matters and in economic matters involving labor disputes or taxation.

The emergency regulations continue the practice of the British mandatory power. Even the legal framework of the regulations rests on mandatory powers. These regulations during the Mandate were subject to fierce criticism by Jewish settlers as arbitrary and infringing the provision of the Mandate that assured the rights of the population. When they turned from subjects to administrators, the Jewish leadership accepted the powers afforded by the emergency regulations and often used them to shortcut the parliamentary process.

ELEMENTS OF THE LAW

Israeli law is influenced by four major traditions: (1) Ottoman law, (2) British common law, (3) religious law, and (4) Israeli law. Each element represents a different historical period or cultural influence in the developing Israeli law.[13]

Ottoman law reflects the impact of the rule of the Turks in Palestine before World War I. It was a composite of Koranic precepts and Islamic customs along with a heavy influence, especially since the beginning of the twentieth century, of French legal models and sources. Ottoman law was not influential regarding personal laws for the Jews, for at that time non-Moslem communities were under the jurisdiction of their own community. But Ottoman law was very influential regarding property law, especially land. The French influence was introduced by the Turks in the nineteenth and early twentieth centuries regarding civil and criminal procedures, and commercial and maritime law. During the Mandate period, the British enforced Ottoman law and practice unless specific British mandatory regulations were issued in their stead. The scope of influence of Ottoman law is constantly decreasing as Israeli legislation replaces aspects of the Ottoman law.

The British Mandate lasted from 1922 to 1948. In this period legislative power was vested in the high commissioner. The high commissioner was bound by provisions of the Mandate but had full power and authority to pass ordinances needed to maintain peace, order, and good government while maintaining complete freedom of conscience and exercise of freedom of worship. He was prohibited from discriminating in any way between inhabitants on the ground of race, religion, or language.

By the time of the establishment of the state the substance of British common law and the doctrines of equity and *stare decisis*—the binding force of judicial precedent—had been firmly established in the judicial system. These principles in particular and the British influence on the Israeli judicial system in general are probably the most significant heritage of the British Mandate.

Personal law is largely under the jurisdiction of the courts of the recognized religious communities—Jewish, Moslem, and Christian. In the Jewish communities this means the orthodox rabbis (see chapter 10), for neither conservative nor reform rabbis are recognized in Israel for performing religious ceremonies. This issue has the potential for creating ill will between the various organizations of Jewry because outside Israel the two latter groups are powerful and growing.

The jurisdiction of Jewish religious courts extends to all Jews in Israel, whether Israeli citizens or not. The religious courts' decision is subject to appeal both within the appellate system of the religious courts and through the High Court of Justice. With few exceptions, such as bigamy and abortion, the Knesset has not undertaken to legislate in the field of personal law. In other matters, Jewish law is often taken into account, but wide-ranging precedents from the Western world are usually dominant in legislative and judicial matters.

Israeli law has developed from the special nature of the country's problems. There are still laws from the Mandate period on the books and occasionally one hears a call to update them. But, as would be expected, the proportion of Knesset-made law is growing over time.

THE COURTS

If the judicial system is based on a complicated legal order influenced by many sources, the court system is much more straightforward. The courts have a hierarchical structure with little overlap among them. The two major systems are the civil and the religious courts; in addition there are special courts for military, labor, traffic, municipal, and juvenile matters, to name but a few. The civil court system has three levels: magistrates', district, and supreme courts. Magistrates' courts deal with offenses that carry relatively light sentences (a maximum of three years' imprisonment) and relatively small money claims. District courts may accept appeals from magistrates' courts; jurisdiction of the former covers civil and criminal matters exceeding the limits of the lower courts. There are five district courts in Israel—in Jerusalem, Tel Aviv, Haifa, Beersheva, and Nazareth.

The Supreme Court is composed of ten to 12 justices and is the country's highest appellate court. In addition, the Supreme Court has original jurisdiction over petitions seeking the grant of relief against administrative decisions that are not within the jurisdiction of any court. In this role the Supreme Court sits as the High Court of Justice and may restrain or direct government agencies or other public institutions by such writs as habeas corpus and mandamus, as is customary under English common law. The Supreme Court and district courts generally hear cases with a panel of at least three justices, although sometimes larger odd numbers are used. No jury trials are held in Israel.

An important explanation for the independence and stature of Israel's judiciary is the special method of selecting judges. This is done on the recommendation of a nine-member appointments committee that consists of the president of the Supreme Court and two other justices of that court, the minister of justice and one other cabinet minister chosen by the cabinet, two members of the Knesset elected by secret ballot by majority vote, and two practicing lawyers who are members of the Israel Bar Association and approved by the minister of justice. The justice minister serves as chairman of the appointments committee; the nominees of the committee are formally appointed judges by the president.

Judges serve for life during good behavior until mandatory retirement at the age of seventy (seventy-five for judges of religious courts). Salaries are fixed by the Finance Committee of the Knesset and are graduated according to the level of the court and tenure on the bench. The salary of the president of the Supreme Court is usually equivalent to that of the prime minister, and the salary of Supreme Court justices equivalent to that of ministers.

While the Israeli experience has shown that justices can be chosen in a manner that neutralizes the highly political nature of the national culture, other considerations are still active. For example, it is customary to have at least one religious justice on the high court, with representation also considered important for Sephardim and women.[14] Previous judicial experience is not required in the appointment of judges. Two-thirds of the 25 Supreme Court justices appointed between 1948 and 1978 had prior judicial experience; of the first five appointed, only one did; of the next 20, 14 did. Of the judges promoted from the district court to the Supreme Court, none had obvious political affiliations.

Others were more visible in the public spotlight; their previous posts included general consul in a diplomatic mission, legal adviser to the government, legal counsel of the Histadrut, and university professor.

The judicial elite of Israel is similar to the political elite discussed in chapter 4 in terms of its demographic characteristics. Of the 25 judges who served on the court during the country's first 30 years, 23 were Ashkenazim. Four, including the two Sephardim, were born in Israel. Seven were born in Germany, seven in Poland, five in Russia and Lithuania, one in England, and one in the United States.[15]

The judicial system in Israel is the foremost guardian of civil liberties in Israel. There is no written constitution and no bill of rights. Most legislation is designed to permit the authorities to limit freedoms by, for example, giving the interior ministry the task of licensing printing houses or giving the police the task of granting permits for demonstrations. The record of the interior ministry and the police has been generally good in protecting the rights of the individual to freedom of the press, speech and assembly, but these rights are *granted* to the individual by the authorities rather than *assured* the individual. It is true that in moments of crisis laws cannot thwart a determined antidemocratic force, yet the existence of a constitutionally endowed right tends to have a limiting influence on enemies of freedom and sets up norms that may be difficult to overcome. To make the point perfectly clear, limiting rights is a matter of interpretation as to whether the public safety is jeopardized; the burden of proof is on those whose rights are being limited. If rights were constitutionally protected, they could of course still be abused, but then the burden of proof would fall on the government that agreed to limit freedom.

In the Israeli judicial system the role of the Supreme Court stems from the ability of the court, when it sits as the High Court of Justice, to act before an action is taken by the authorities. The common-law principle is that damages can be recovered after the act had been perpetrated. Imagine a wall shared by you and your neighbor. The neighbor decides to tear down the wall without any concern for your rights or your house. After your house fell in because your wall was destroyed, you could collect damages. Equity demands the ability to pursue justice even before the act is committed. You are entitled to petition the court to have the neighbor prevented from tearing down your joint wall without your permission. The same principle applies to actions of the authorities. The High Court of Justice can prevent government actions instituted illegally, and that will be harmful to your rights or property. The functioning of the court of justice is well illustrated in cases of land requisitioning in the territories (the cases were based on international law and not Israeli law since the territories are under military rule). The court determined that requisitioning land from its owners could be done only if the proposed settlement was necessary for military reasons. Since the court was convinced that this condition was met regarding Beit El but not Elon Moreh, it vacated the orders for the confiscation of land in the second case and upheld it in the first.[16]

We are presented with a Supreme Court that has acquired, by traditional role and by the abdication of other institutions, the task of major guardian of justice and civil rights in Israel. The court has been reticent in interfering in political issues and its asserting itself in the Bergman case (which might be thought of as a foray into the field of judicial review) was tentative and unsustained. The court in the last decade or so has become more passive and has not developed into the dynamic court some hoped it would be. It has not shied away from questions brought to it, but neither has it extended itself in broadening the meaning of justice throughout the system and in ensuring for itself the role of fearless guardian of inherent rights.[17]

Israel's courts are highly aware of civil rights and respect the tradition of the Enlightenment that sees the individual and his rights at the heart of the society. The role of the court is to protect rights and to limit the authorities in their unwarranted use of power. However, there is no constitution, few laws, and few decisions on which to base this protection. It falls to the court to set the tone of self-control for the authorities in respecting rights. Considering that civil liberties are not firmly entrenched in law and that the system rests on the discretion of the authorities, Israel's record in this field is quite good. The blemishes on the system are the religious requirements that, when applied, restrict certain liberties taken for granted in other liberal systems, and the emergency regulations that transfer to the executive functions that would otherwise demand the public deliberation of the legislature.

Regarding Arabs, the record is more complex. Israeli Arabs are full-fledged citizens, granted all formal rights. They vote and are represented in the Knesset and in municipalities. But since they do not serve in the army (and probably do not want to), they are deprived of access to the whole of the system, including welfare benefits provided for veterans, political access to the highest levels of decision making, and the psychological satisfaction that goes along with the identification of country, religion, and nation. Psychological satisfaction may not be a civil right, but it would be shortsighted to assess the position of Israeli Arabs using only formal legalisms. There may be no easy solution for their dilemma, but denying its existence, as many Israelis do, is no solution either.

West Bank Arabs present a much more difficult problem. Formally they are not citizens of Israel, although they can appeal to the High Court of Justice. If we conceive of them as living in a battle zone, then the Israeli record of dealing with them is reasonable in the history of warfare. But if the judgment is based on the norms of a regular country, the Israeli record is much weaker. Military occupation is difficult under any circumstances, and its chances to be perceived as humane over time are very low.

The court system is slow and inefficient.[18] While the quality of judging is generally regarded to be high, the system lacks the modern staff and equipment that might make access to justice more speedy and less painful and costly. Lawyers proliferate; the system seems so built that only they can manage to navigate in the murky waters of bureaucrats and special regulations. The Israel Bar Association is a statutory body whose tasks include licensing and controlling practitioners.

In general, Israel is a nonpunitive society. Penalties prescribed by law for many crimes are low compared with other countries. The death penalty was applied only once—in the case of the Nazi Adolf Eichmann. The crime rate is increasing and is a topic of public concern, but it has never become a political issue as it has in other Western countries.

10. Interest Groups and Public Policy

It is appropriate for political scientists to concentrate on groups that try to influence public policy. We do well to remind ourselves that policy decisions benefit some groups at the expense of others, that political decisions are made by a small portion of the population, and that groups try to influence decisions.

The right to assemble and organize has long been regarded as a fundamental political right, and that is precisely why it is one of the first rights denied by authorities in periods of tension or upheaval. That like-minded citizens can organize to have their interests expressed in policy is a keystone of the democratic process. Unlike a political party, whose primary function is to aggregate various interests in order to compete in elections with a view to gaining control of the government, the interest group articulates the demands and attitudes (the "interests") of group members in order to bring about policies in line with their views. Whereas the party is primarily concerned with elections and ruling, the interest group is geared to the policy outputs of the system. Political theorists have often taken the existence of a large number of active interest groups as evidence of the vitality of democratic institutions in the country.

The theory of political pluralism posits the struggle among myriad interest groups as a highlight of the democratic process. For a writer like David Truman, the extensive organization of competing groups is evidence that power is widely shared and that no group ever loses completely, although none always wins either. While the pluralist school points to some groups as stronger than others, they also recognize that new groups ("potential groups" in their parlance) can organize and take part in the political process to their advantage.[1]

The terms *interest* and *interest group,* although very pervasive in political science, are also very difficult to employ as analytical tools. What is an interest? The empirical referents of the term are many at best and ambivalent at worst. In the final analysis it appears that most commentators have employed the term interest as synonymous with group activity to achieve desired results. But are we not all characterized by the interests we support? And if we only support interests but do nothing to achieve them, can we be thought of as participating in the political process?

We all have interests. At the most basic level there are the interests of survival and sustenance, but even these "interests" involve policy issues. Are subsidies to be enlarged, reduced, or maintained? Does security demand lengthening or shortening the extent of army service? Are settlements to be expanded or not?

Quickly it becomes clear that interest is often synonymous with politics. What we want is, almost by definition, opposed by others and hence part of the political game. And if there were no groups or individuals fighting over it, if there were no interests, we would not be concerned with it. Years ago, before there was widespread awareness of the limits of our planet's natural resources, clean air was not a political issue. And precisely because there was widespread belief that there were sufficient amounts of clean air for all of us, no interests were felt jeopardized and no groups felt vulnerable. But with the development of greater awareness of the finiteness of the earth's resources and the growing awareness of the role that these matters play in maintaining our quality of life, the issue entered politics. Interests were perceived in maintaining low levels of ozone in the atmosphere or low degrees of chemical concentration in lakes and rivers. Economic "interests" brought on an era of concern with nuclear plants for the production of electricity and the safety of automobiles on the roads, with material fire-resistant enough for making of children's pyjamas, with where to locate electricity-generating plants, and with the carcinogenic character of the foods we eat.

"Interest" is so pervasive a phenomenon, and so closely related to the group organization designed to further it, that it must be used very carefully. It is important to keep in mind that in order to better understand the phenomenon we must characterize two things: the interest and the group. Interests may refer to personal interests or social or general ones. Increasing the minimum wage may stem from personal motivation for a low-paid unskilled worker, or it may be an altruistic goal for greater social equality on the part of a group or political party. One's orientation is likely to be affected according to whether a personal interest is involved. Another helpful distinction may be between sectoral interest, such as business or labor, and promotional groups that have more altruistic goals in mind.

The organization of the group is also a key to understanding the role of interest groups. A loosely coordinated group with part-time leadership and a low budget behaves very differently and most likely has a different impact on the system than a well-organized, bureaucratic group with large budget. The outcome is not a foregone conclusion. The former group and its membership may be sufficiently motivated for a large effort on a relatively short-term basis (stop the war, or lower taxes), while the latter organization is better able to handle long-range protracted contacts with government authorities. A bureaucratized interest group inevitably faces organizational problems of the growing conservative nature of its bureaucracy and a tendency to oligarchy; the other kind of organization may be able to be more dynamic, at least in the early phases.

A popular notion of interest-group activity is that it must be public and loud. This notion must be reconsidered. The most effective pressure groups are those we hear of least. Confrontational politics and long petitions are not necessarily a sign of strength in a system such as Israel's. The popular notion of interest-group behavior in pluralistic political cultures has the lobbyist wage a brave fight in the name of the interests of the masses. But the truly effective lobbyist is the one known only by those he needs to maintain the policies desired by patrons. The basic fact is that most policy matters are indeed decided behind closed doors on issues most of us would not understand or become agitated about. It is the rare issue that excites public passion, and on such issues unusual tactics might be employed. But for most policy matters, interests are expressed, promoted, and transformed into policy in much more subtle and mundane ways.

Some groups have won reputations as effective lobbyists for positions they favor. Politicians are likely to fear the clout of such groups long before they have organized petitions, mass mailings, or demonstrations. In the United States the National Rifle Association (which opposes limiting the right of Americans to bear arms) and the so-called Israel lobby are two examples of groups whose potential is enhanced by their previous behavior and successes. Israeli counterparts to such groups are hard to find because Israeli interest groups are more likely to be ideologically, if not organizationally, linked to a political party or point of view. An appeal by Gush Emunim, Peace Now, or the Histadrut would tend to reinforce existing political divisions rather than add a new dimension to the forces at work on a given policy area. Other groups, such as the Council for the Prevention of Traffic Accidents or various ecological groups, are largely financed by public monies and promote causes rarely embroiled in partisan politics. The call for electoral reform, a call that went straight to the heart and interests of politicians and parties, swelled in 1977 and deflated soon thereafter, after winning the verbal support (but not the votes) of most parties and politicians.

The Israeli Case

An analysis of interest-group activity must begin with a careful consideration of the system to be influenced. The trait that makes the pluralistic model described above not completely relevant to Israel is the relative lack of points of access in the Israeli political system. In a large, decentralized system such as the American one, points of access are many, and the role of the media in launching nationwide campaigns is crucial. With a Congress composed of 435 congressmen and 100 senators and a President whose political antennae are always up, the potential for interest-group activity is great. But in a centralized, bureaucraticized system such as Israel's, it is not at all clear that the same rules apply. In Israel the major focus of policy-oriented pressure must be the few senior civil servants responsible for the area under discussion or the leaders of the two or three important parties in the government coalition. This handful of people is likely to have the political and administrative power needed to satisfy the demands of the group making application.

Israel, a small country whose politics and politicians are thoroughly acquainted by those active in the field, is a case of a democratic system whose interest groups work in a very compacted environment. Groups organize and jockey for power and influence, but because the space is so small and the system so intense and so dense, the interplay that might exist in other countries is not evident. This is so for at least three reasons. First, Israel's system is so centralized and party dominated that there exist only two or three effective access points into the system. The Knesset, as we have seen, is run by a coalition of parties that also controls the government. Most legislation is initiated by the government and is generally assured of passage by coalition parties in the Knesset. Why, then, lobby individual Knesset members? The effective interest group would concentrate on the two or three major parties that make up the government coalition. Within each party there is likely to be a handful of individuals whose support would be critical in bringing the issue on the agenda and having it passed. But since the Israeli system is so centralized, so party dominated and bureaucratic, lobbying can be much more concentrated and even secret. How different from the 535 congressmen and the President who can be lobbied in the American system. Their techniques of sophisticated communication networks and computerized mailing lists become irrelevant in Israel. Having access to the party leadership or the hierarchy of the government ministry dealing with the issue is infinitely more important than fancy organizational techniques developed in and for a different culture.

Second, there is a lack of free-floating issues in the system. Few issues in Israeli public life are not already being processed. It is very hard to find an issue that might raise public attention that is not already being discussed, debated, studied, or researched by a government, public, or semipublic agency. The absence of free-floating issues decreases the potency of interest groups and gives a tremendous advantage to the ruling party if it can regulate the introduction of issues being processed by the system. The timing of the infusion of issues into the system, as much as anything else, allows powerholders to nip in the bud movements that might otherwise gain public momentum and to divert attention to the areas they favor.

The success or failure of the ruling party in managing demands has depended very little on ideological differences between them. Issues of labor relations, wages, and economic policy have been troublesome for any finance minister who has tried to deny the workers what they wanted. Alignment governments might have had a slightly easier time since the Histadrut was also under their control, but the differences have been more of style than of substance. Likud governments have had no control over the Histadrut and hence could be sniped at by this Alignment-dominated institution from time to time. Religious issues have generally been called up by the religious parties according to a political clock that they have controlled. At times, religious issues were raised close to the period in which the coalition they participated in appeared to be in danger and in which their votes were needed to avert its fall. Sometimes the religious issue was propelled into the public sphere by intrareligious competition among various religious parties and factions.

Insertions of issues by groups outside the party system have traditionally been more easily contained. The number of demonstrations and petitions in Israeli politics is high,[2] but this does not mean that they are effective on the whole. What it seems to mean is that an extraparty level is sought for asserting pressure because party channels are either clogged or overloaded. The Wadi Salib riots in 1954 and the Black Panthers in the early 1970s, both examples of the introduction of the ethnic issue into Israeli politics, were handled by setting up a committee, by coopting a number of the leaders, and/or by initiating some policy changes. These groups tended to be small, their efforts episodic, and their achievements in concrete terms marginal.

It is instructive that the largest returns for the lowest effort are always won in the Israeli system by groups affiliated with one of the major parties. Numbers can certainly make a difference, but numbers in themselves are not enough. The fact that hundreds of thousands signed a petition supporting the annexation of the Golan certainly was noted when the annexation was finally legislated. But in and of itself it was insufficient. After all, the petition had been circulating for years; poll after poll and election after election indicated that popular support for the idea existed. Numerical strength, coupled by the appropriate political and diplomatic conditions and the political will of the leadership, preceded the legislation.

The third reason that Israeli interest groups must be understood as existing in a compressed environment is that interest-group leaders are often in a hierarchical relation with the party politicians they are trying to influence. These are not likely to be anonymous callers lobbying for some obscure issue but members of the party's institutions whose votes were or will be needed on one issue or another, or for some candidate. More crucially, it is likely that the party leadership approved, or at least did not veto, the appointment of these individuals. We are talking of a process of severe selection in which those who come to make the case of the kibbutzim are not anonymous farmers from the back country but leaders of the kibbutz or moshav movements whose interests often defined the actions and policies of the labor parties. What is more, these movement leaders may one day become important party influentials.

This process occurs even in the army. At the highest levels of the army, meetings may be between politicians serving as government ministers and officers who are potential and even aspiring politicians. The military has always been an important recruiting ground for party politicians, and it is likely that the politicians at the meeting will on some occasion be consulted about the promotion or appointment of these senior military leaders to their next military or political position. As in all other social situations, people tend to like those who agree with them and agree with those they like. A community of interest builds up based on a communality of positions and lifestyles. Interest-group activists are often the product of the process of selection that will determine the cast for years to come. The point is that the cast is limited in number, in background, and in social class. Once, the member of the cast was born in Europe and was an immigrant of the second or third *aliyot;* today he is likely to be Israel-born and university educated. Efforts are increasingly being made to increase the number of Sephardim in this group, but overwhelmingly it is still Ashkenazi. Women and Arabs are almost totally absent from this group.

It is useful to think of Israeli politics as being of the closet and not of the caucus. Then it will be easier to understand that surface motion is not motion, that basic policies are set far from the displays in the Knesset or the headlines of the papers. Important policies are set and important groups operate without fanfare, without headlines, without the public knowing about it. For most groups with economic interests, publication of their victories is counterproductive. If the pilots win concessions that are likely to upset the delicate balance of wage differentials in the country, neither the pilots nor the government wants to broadcast this fact—the pilots because they want to retain their relative advantage, the government because they want to prevent others from knowing about it. If the kibbutzim win favorable water allocations, they are not likely to gloat in public over their achievement. Most interest-group activity is covert; an interest group often in the news is likely to be an indicator of setbacks to their interests (perhaps temporarily) and not a sign of strength.

Notice how different this description is from the pluralistic theory of interest-group representation alluded to earlier. Absent is the assumption that these groups provide a key linkage between the people and their government or that groups compete with one another. There is no safeguard against one group's interest becoming dominant, and it is not at all clear that resources are substitutable, with, for example, numbers taking the place of budget in the case of a poor group with a popular cause. Most important, the definition of the "public interest" that emerges from pluralistic interest-group theory must be changed in a basic sense: If the competition among groups competing fairly for policy goals is the best assurance that the public interest will be served, in the Israeli system the game is clearly stacked in favor of the ruling parties, allowing them to define the public interest if they have the will to do so.

Based on this analysis of the role of interest groups in setting public policy in Israel, it is clear that questions that might be important to scholars in other settings are less important here. For example, whether Israelis join voluntary groups to a great or a limited extent becomes a moot point. Voluntary organizations, when not party affiliated, tend not to be crucial in setting public policy. The numbers themselves do not provide an indication of political power. An estimated 600 public organizations exist in Israel, and 30 percent of Israeli adults belong to a voluntary organization other than the Histadrut.[3] About two-thirds of the adult population belong to the Histadrut, and about three-quarters receive medical treatment from its sick fund. But these figures tell us little about the contours of policy making in Israel.

In Israel, as in any other country, nonformal, nongovernmental processes play a role in decision making, and in this field the role of the interest group looms large. A useful typology has been put forward by Gabriel Almond and James Coleman.[4] They identified interest articulation as one of four input functions into the political system (along with interest aggregation, communication, and recruitment and socialization), arguing that in many political systems this function of formulating and expressing political demands would be performed by organized interest groups. They identified four major kinds of groups:

1. *The institutional interest group,* which is a formal organization or a long lasting informal group within a social institution whose manifest function is something other than interest articulation. A group of military or bureaucratic leaders who are formally authorized to undertake some task but who include in their activities influencing policy outputs would be an example of this.

2. *The associational interest group* is constituted in order to express the interests of the group it represents. To do this it usually develops a staff and orderly procedures for achieving the goal for which the group was established.

3. The *nonassociational group* would include kinships and ethnic, regional, or status groups which lack formal organization and through which interests are articulated on an intermittent basis by individuals, family heads, and other spokesmen.

4. The *anomic interest group* is of shortest duration and is not characterized by formal organization or long-range planning. Examples of it would be riots, demonstrations, assassinations, and other more or less spontaneous penetrations into the political system from the society.

Almond and Powell use this list to distinguish various means of access, styles of articulation, and environmental factors affecting articulation patterns.[5] Their basic concern is with political modernization, and they use the list and these areas of concern to explore differences in interest articulation in developing and developed polities. The emergence of differentiated infrastructures, such as in associational interest groups, indicates higher degrees of political development. As the polity becomes more complex and issues increase in volume and severity, the more institutionalized articulation of interest is seen as more important.

It is instructive to think of Israeli politics in terms of these four interest groups. While we can certainly think of instances of all four types, most interest articulation—and certainly most influence—is institutional and associational. For example, when we consider the penetration of the defense ministry in spheres of activity only peripherally related to defense, we comprehend the potential role of an institutional interest group. Associational interest groups such as the Histadrut are also very important. It seems reasonable to speculate, although no empirical work on the subject has been done, that two kinds of groups (institutional and associational) are the most active and the most successful in the Israeli decision-making process. Nonassociational and anomic interest groups are observed only rarely, although their occurrence is more likely to be noted in the newspapers than is the mundane, day-to-day operation of the first two groups. A demand for ethnic representation or a sit-in in apartments by young couples or a demonstration in support of some foreign policy are all more unusual—and therefore more likely to appear in the news—than a report by a committee of experts or a secret political twist of the arm by a Histadrut official to a senior civil servant. But the latter are likely to have the political weight necessary to influence policy; the others probably do not.

There is a close link between political parties and interest groups in all political systems. The Israeli case supports the contention, if only by negation, that a weak party system facilitates a strong pressure-group system.[6] Since the basic argument of our analysis is the primacy of party, an apparent corollary is the relative weakness of an autonomous system of interest groups. If a fragmented decisional system is widely thought to encourage associational groups, a centralized hierarchical one is likely to discourage them. Israeli political culture tends to prefer absolute value orientations. Pragmatic bargaining is permitted and even desirable behind closed doors; at the public level the pragmatic style that values bargaining is denied, and hence much of the legitimacy of interest groups that espouse that style is also denied.

In the compact conditions of the Israeli political and bureaucratic cultures, those groups do best in terms of policy outcome that are closest to decision-making bodies or decision makers themselves. Lobbying, the effort to secure specific policy decisions or the appointment of favorably disposed government personnel, is undertaken in discreet, covert ways as opposed to the more overt methods that characterize a more open system. One example of "painless lobbying" is the existence in Israel of multiple officeholding in which it is possible for a legislator to simultaneously hold an executive position in a major decision-making organization such as the Histadrut or the Jewish Agency. Mayors are sometimes elected to the Knesset, thus affording the municipal interests an ideal carrier and object for lobbying efforts. Levi Eshkol, while serving as prime minister and defense minister, retained for a time the post of chairman of the settlement division of the Jewish Agency, a politically sensitive post, but hardly one demanding the attention of the prime minister. But it is reasonable to assume that the head of the division had a good deal of access to the very highest decision makers in the land.

Elite interaction is usually a little less intense than the previous example, but it exists nonetheless. Keeping in mind the pyramidal structure of Israeli political life and the relatively small numbers of people at the apex of the pyramid reminds us that the probability of elite members meeting often—formally and informally, in official capacities and socially—is very high. And if these individuals also belong to the same party, the interaction is likely to be frequent and cooperative. The informality and ambiguity attendant on an "off the cuff" conversation between a mayor and a minister introduce severe analytic difficulties for the student of interest groups, but they are likely to be more frequent and significant in terms of policy outcomes than many more overt kinds of pressure.

Activities such as formal lobbying and mobilization of the public are not infrequent occurrences, but it is reasonable to suppose that their impact is slight. Lobbying as a recognized institution does not exist in Israel; there are no requirements to register, nor are there legal limitations on activities such as there are in the United States. Demonstrations, hunger strikes and petitions are regular occurrences in Israeli politics, but they are generally conducted by groups at the fringes of the power network and not by significant ones. If a group such as the Histadrut or Gush Emunim calls for a mass rally or march, it is likely to be for purposes of group arousal as much as for direct influence on a specific policy area. Demonstrations for these broad, politically well-connected groups have more of a symbolic role to play than a policy role.

In the British House of Commons a substantial proportion of the members have explicit and acknowledged ties to organized groups and the groups perceive the election of their members as advantageous to their general policy interests.[7] This condition sometimes exists in Israel as well; the election of an "interested member" is yet another indication of the group's connection with the party involved. A kibbutz member, a leader of the Histadrut or some cooperative, a rabbi, or a leader of a trade organization indeed represents the interests of his constituency, but the connections between his organization and his party are pervasive and continuous. Groups are often active at the party level campaigning for the election of their leader to the party list. The efforts of the group for the leader and the efforts of the leader for the group are often either side of the same coin because sometimes the leader speaks for his group on his own behalf in seeking election.

Perhaps the most important mechanism used by groups in attaining access and influence is influencing the appointment of officials on bureaucratic and statutory boards, including key civil service or political appointments. Groups utilize their proximity to party leaders to try to influence these appointments. During the three decades of Labor dominance it was well understood in Israeli politics that the way ahead led in some fashion through the parties of the Alignment or the parties in coalition with them. Such membership was an important, necessary, although not sufficient, condition for appointment and power. Individuals could be sponsored by groups close to the parties; if an endorsement could not be had, the absence of a veto was also occasionally sufficient. In the first period of Likud rule a good deal of carryover of Labor appointments was in evidence. This was attributed to a desire on the part of the Likud to adopt a merit civil service philosophy or, less kindly, to a paucity of candidates who could pass the Likud loyalty test after its long period in opposition. With their second victory in 1981 it was more evident that Likud appointments were influenced by endorsements of groups close to Likud parties, although business groups regularly complained that they had no influence on Likud economic policy.

Independent groups that organize to influence policy are generally short-lived and unsuccessful unless coopted by some party-affiliated or government-affiliated group. More important, in the Israeli system the number of groups proves nothing because of their extreme inequality in terms of power. Power in the system is in the hands of leaders of the party or parties in the government coalition. This power is fortified by an extensive system of interlocking directorates with these leaders or their chosen proxies, in this way concentrating power in the key organizations.

Keeping in mind the difficulties attached with the interest-group concept, we next consider some major areas of interest-group activity. While there are hundreds of groups in Israel, four areas are discussed, although no one area is easily identified with a single group. Analyzing these areas allows us a clearer picture of the issues that excite the political system and the ways these issues are handled and influenced by interest groups operating in each area. The four areas to be discussed are defense, the Histadrut, agriculture, and religion.

Defense

Defense policy provides the best example of an institutional interest in the Israeli political system. Defense is the policy area that commands the most attention, the largest concentration of budget and years of active service of most Israelis. This policy area has overshadowed all others in Israel's existence, often recruiting top-level individuals to serve its demands and rewarding many who have reached the top of its hierarchies with prominent second careers in politics, business, and administration.[8] Placing a priority on defense has become part of the Israeli way of life with an overwhelming proportion of the population agreeing time after time that this is the central issue facing Israel. The defense issue penetrates the value system of the country; symbols of military strength, self-sacrifice, and heroism are given positive recognition in the culture. Complex political issues of international relations are often simplified, and military aspects of problems are often stressed at the expense of the political. Borders and settlements are often the focus of the debate regarding Israel's future, with issues such as the Middle East and superpower considerations given a minor role.

For all its importance, however, defense is dominated by leaders of the major government party and is rarely permeated by groups outside the organizations set up to deal with this subject. Groups outside the defense establishment — even the Knesset Committee for Foreign Affairs and Security not to mention Peace Now or Gush Emunim — play only a minor role in determining Israel's defense policy, although the latter two may influence political parties. The defense challenges facing Israel are of course enormous, and Israel's success in this field has become legendary. The prolonged state of conflict that Israel has been in has shaped its perception of reality and has influenced its societal and economic arrangements as much as any other factor. It is precisely because the topic is so salient and the issue boundaries tend to be so impermeable that it is so central to understanding the political system.

The impact of the defense issue is clearly seen in the arrangements that have been worked out regarding national service. For many, it is a major form of identification with the country; for others, it signifies their being apart from the mainstream of Israeli life. The defense issue segregates the Jewish from the Arab population by requiring army service from the former while denying it (except for the Druze and Bedouin) to the latter. Having served in the army is an important requisite to most positions of power and importance in Israeli life, and non-Jews are effectively shut out from them. Veteran status is also a necessity for certain welfare benefits. Arabs are excluded for security reasons; given their choice, it is likely that many would not be willing to risk their lives for the Jewish state. Two Jewish groups are exempted from army service for political reasons: The conscription of some yeshiva students is formally deferred (in effect they are exempted) while they are studying, and religiously observant women may avoid active service. Both groups are regularly attacked for shirking their duty, and alternative forms of national service are often suggested for religious women and Arabs, but these have never been implemented.

Service is nearly universal among Jews and is a long-term undertaking. Most men serve in reserve units into their fifties; women are exempted after having borne a child. The pervasive structure of the military enterprise assures that all families have a connection—some more direct than others—with the army. The universality assures a high level of salience for military matters and tends to lend implicit public support to the policies followed. The military, certainly until the Yom Kippur War, enjoyed a very high level of prestige in the society, partially because of the sacrifice inherent in the job and partially because of the successes of the military since independence, especially in 1967. This combination of high participation, high prestige, and the admitted importance of the issue made the defense establishment one of the most important areas of interest-group activity in the country.

No area of Israeli public life is immune from its impact. Major economic decisions in such varied fields as industrial infrastructure and natural resource development and urban planning take defense considerations into account. The number of buses available in the country, the future of an airport close to the heart of a city, the routing of roads and their capacity, and the kinds of industries to develop are specific examples of this range of concerns. The defense issue also has an impact on cultural matters ranging from religious law to the development of an army slang that makes the army one of the most fertile areas of the development of the Hebrew language. The structure of the education system is influenced by the demands of defense ranging from the curricula of vocational high schools to the fact that Israeli university students tend to begin their studies after a number of years of army service and are likely to be called up for reserve service, along with many of their teachers, during their years of study. The impact of this reality on Israel's youth is a topic of justified concern among parents, educators, psychologists, and philosophers. Can moral, humanistic values be glorified in an environment of training to kill and destroy? Can the value of life be upheld in a structure calculated to bring death? The answers are not simple, and no single type has emerged as the Israeli soldier; but the dilemma provides the backdrop for the attempt to merge the rich morality of Judaism with the historical developments of Zionism.

The successes of the Israeli army must be seen against the backdrop of the Holocaust and the image of the defenseless Jew being led meekly to death. The trauma of that image undoubtedly goes a long way to explain the primacy of the military in Israeli thought and life. The objective challenges the country faces from a hostile environment complete the picture. For unlike other wars, Israel's has proven to be thus far a permanent state of conflict rather than a supreme effort to be expended for a limited time before returning to more normal patterns. For Israel, the normal pattern is a nation in arms, a nation besieged. Few modern polities have been called upon to maintain democratic and liberal traditions under conditions so continuously and so enormously working against those traditions.

Considering the enormous economic, psychological, and cultural burden of defense, Israel's record in maintaining democratic forms and civil rights (at least within the pre-1967 borders) is admirable. Part of the explanation for this success is the small size of the country. Israel's army depends on a vast reserve of manpower that is continually called up and trained. The aphorism that Israelis are soldiers on 11 months' leave catches the spirit of the situation. The values of the country are reflected in the army, and vice versa. No isolated class has developed, no feeling of being aloof or different from the rest of the population. While the image of the army may be one of great efficiency and having high levels of pride for past achievements, these feelings tend to be dissipated throughout the army and society and not concentrated in a narrow class of officers.

The dilemma posed by the military forces of any nation is clear. Since the state is supposed to monopolize the use of violence and since military might rests with the army, it is essential that the army be under the control of the civilian authorities of the state. Both democratic and communist regimes desire the subjugation of the military to the civilian forces, for fear of being replaced by those officers to whom the means of violence have been entrusted. Embuing a "professional" commitment in the army to obey the duly elected leadership is not only a matter of empty ideological posturing but also a matter of neutralizing a dangerous potential source of threat to the continuation of the regime.

In Israel the army was seen as a partner with the political forces in bringing about the national revolution of independence of statehood and not as a competing power. Yoram Peri points out that the pattern of dual control during the Yishuv period emerged with the Haganah responsible to the dominant party, Mapai, and to the voluntary national institutions that were the functional equivalent of civilian authorities of the state. Upon achieving statehood this dual pattern of loyalty to party and state persisted and prevented the emergence of an instrumentalist army solely controlled by the civilian branch of the state—the ideal model of liberal democracies.[9]

The existence of separate armies with competing political loyalties was a major problem resolved by Ben-Gurion in 1948 when separate commands of the Haganah, Palmach, Irgun, and Lehi were abolished and the Israel Defense Force (IDF) established. But because Ben-Gurion feared that the new army would be open to the same kind of coalition pressures as were other aspects of Israel's public life, the army was never domesticated in the sense of being controlled by the civilian ministry of defense. Ben-Gurion wanted to keep control in his own hands, and while he served as both prime minister and defense minister (1948-53 and 1955-63) this arrangement was possible. But when Ben-Gurion's personal stature was removed from the equation it became clear that the subordination of the military to the civilian government had not been properly institutionalized.

It was fashionable to talk of the depoliticization of the army, and there was much evidence of this new instrumental pattern emerging. But the basic flaw in the process was the attempt to devise a nonparty solution to a political problem in Israel's political culture, which rests squarely on political parties. Who can keep the army under civilian control and yet away from the politicians and their party interests? Ben-Gurion's answer was to extol the virtues of civilian control while keeping personal control over the major decisions of the IDF. All three times that Ben-Gurion retired (1953, 1954, and 1963) from the dual roles of prime minister and defense minister, he suggested that the roles be filled by two separate individuals. During his tenure he tried to make the defense sphere autonomous of the civilian sphere and in so doing ultimately made their interpenetration inevitable. "The end result was, therefore, that the dual control failed to achieve either of Ben-Gurion's aims. Though deprivatized, the IDF did not develop into an apolitical, instrumentalist army under the absolute supervision of the state institutions. Instead it ultimately became an army working as a partner in the political process, integrated with the civil power even beyond the national-security field."[10]

The nominal civil control instigated by Ben-Gurion largely succeeded in keeping other parties' influence out of the IDF but made the interpenetration of the highest echelons of Mapai and the highest echelons of the army very intimate. No strong autonomous civilian ministry was set up to oversee the functioning of the military. Since Ben-Gurion the civilian was in charge of the IDF, his oversight was deemed sufficient. The defense ministry became a civilian aide for the army, with all major functions of budgeting, procurement, and military strategy situated in the army itself or duplicated in the defense ministry. At certain levels, internal party developments influenced the army. Senior ministers would court army leaders for support in conflicts with other ministers regarding policy. The support of the officers was important not just in the sense of professional advisers but as the opinion of the major interest group involved in the area. In periods of generally accepted leaders such as Ben-Gurion and Begin the role of the military was more similar to that of the professional adviser, but when the role of leader was less secure, as with Eshkol and Rabin, the position of the military leadership was an important part of the political calculus.

After Ben-Gurion, the fact that civilian control had not been institutionalized became obvious. Daniel Shimshoni categorizes relations between the defense minister and the political system as follows: Ben-Gurion had almost complete authority over the IDF and the defense ministry. Lavon, his successor as defense minister, had almost none, and not surprisingly from this perspective, the Lavon affair (discussed in chapter 5) occurred during this period. Levi Eshkol is called a "representative" defense minister. Between 1963 and 1967 he held both positions of prime minister and defense minister, and represented the demands and programs of the military to the political leadership. This is hardly control. The period between 1969 and 1974 had Golda Meir as prime minister, Moshe Dayan as defense minister, and Pinhas Sapir as finance minister. Dayan and Sapir differed over economic and defense matters; also, Dayan had split from Mapai with Rafi while Sapir was leader of the Mapai political machine. This left Golda Meir in the role of arbiter, balancing between the two prominent ministers in her government. The period between 1974 and 1977 in which Yitzhak Rabin was prime minister and Shimon Peres defense minister was characterized by cabinet rivalry between the two and by professional control by Peres of the military.[11] Begin's experiences were more varied. With Ezer Weizman as defense minister, Begin tended to support a harder foreign policy line than Weizman, especially regarding Egypt, leading to a tacit coalition between Begin and Chief of Staff Rafael Eitan and ultimately bringing about Weizman's resignation. After the resignation in 1980 and until Sharon was appointed defense minister in 1981, Begin also served as defense minister. In that period he was slightly more actively involved in defense matters than when he had a defense minister, Eitan playing a dominant role. Ariel Sharon's appointment after the 1981 elections removed the political conflict within the triad because all three (Begin, Sharon, and Eitan) were hard-liners. Sharon tended to dominate the army as well as government policy until he was forced to resign from the defense ministry as a result of the Kahan Commission report concerning his role in the events in the Palestinian refugee camps of Sabra and Shatilla.

The pattern that has emerged is that top government leaders (by definition politicians) are very active in army policy, especially relating to procurement and personnel appointments. Top military leaders have also been known to be very active in matters of policy that, according to a purist model, should be the exclusive area of the politicians. The boundaries between the civilian and military in Israel are not clear; there is no civilian counterpart in the Israeli defense establishment to the military.

The problematic nature of civil-military relations is seen more clearly during periods of crisis and war. During the War of Independence, Ben-Gurion had to contend with a revolt among his generals, who were opposed to his proposed appointments, which were intended to purge the high command of officers who were not Mapai members. Ultimately Ben-Gurion won the battle by compromising with the generals while demanding total political support from his cabinet in such matters. In the Sinai Campaign of 1956, the army was well under way before Ben-Gurion appraised his government of the plan of war. Civilian control, yes, but not governmental control. In the days before the 1967 Six Day War, intense political negotiations were conducted that ultimately led to Dayan's appointment as defense minister after Eshkol removed himself from the position. Not only were other political parties active in this negotiation but the leadership of the army also took part in it.

In the 1973 crisis of the Yom Kippur War the porous relations between the civilian and military were most obvious. Ministers were given military appointments, and generals publicly criticized political decisions. The Agranat Commission ultimately focused blame on the military, largely ignoring the acts of omission and commission of the political leadership.[12] In the 1982 Lebanon war the military was divided on the goals and the tactics of the war, as was the civilian community. The lack of a national consensus split the military as well; crises of morale and resignations, demonstrations, and petitions swept the army. The lines of demarcation are not clear partially because the army is such an integral part of Israeli society and partially because basic institutions of civilian control have never been established. With the army being so esteemed, so prominent, and so important, it is not surprising that it is also so powerful.

Even in a constitutional sense civilian control over the military is blurred. We know who the chief of staff is, but it is more difficult to determine who the commander-in-chief is. Collective responsibility lies with the government and often many ministers speak out on military matters to the discomfort of the minister of defense and the prime minister. The Basic Law: Israel Defense Force, passed in 1976 after the evidence of a lack of clear lines of authority in the 1973 Yom Kippur War, formalized the constitutional responsibility. The army is under the authority of the cabinet, and the chief of staff is the commander. The minister of defense acts through authority of the cabinet in defense matters. The chief of staff is appointed by the cabinet on the recommendation of the minister of defense. While this better defines the relations, the roles of the prime minister and the other ministers are still left vague. The defense minister's role is defined neither as delegate of the cabinet nor as leader of the army. It could be both or neither depending on the circumstances.

The appointment of the chief of staff must incorporate both professional and political considerations. At that highest of levels, not even the strongest proponent of civilian-military separation would pretend that a complete divorce of the two is possible. But which quality should be prominent: professional competence or political loyalty? Leaders such as Ezer Weizman and Ariel Sharon have been candid in expressing their opinions that they were best qualified, but they were passed over because the Alignment leadership did not trust them politically. They both became defense ministers without being chiefs of staff. Chiefs of staff have done very well politically. The list includes Yigael Yadin, Moshe Dayan, Yitzhak Rabin, and Haim Bar-Lev, but only Yitzhak Rabin ever became prime minister. The fact that the chief of staff is so important in the political system both during and after his tenure indicates how close the apexes of the political and military pyramids are.

The civilian ministry of defense is eclipsed by the IDF. Yitzhak Rabin, former chief of staff and former prime minister, called the ministry of defense a ministry of supply for the army. Veteran military analyst Zeev Schiff writes that "the ministry exists in the heavy shadow of the IDF, and even in those spheres in which its formal authority is recognized, it does not succeed in exerting it."[13] It was Ben-Gurion who made the double decision that the ministry of defense would be separate from the army but that it would not supervise the army. The ministry tends to be an appendage of the general staff because later defense ministers have followed Ben-Gurion's practice of utilizing these uniformed officers extensively in the decision-making process and in his practice of choosing not only the chief of staff but other senior officers. Ben-Gurion's practice of keeping research, manufacturing, procurement, finance, and conscription under civilian management has been maintained, but in many of these spheres the dictates of the IDF carry the day, and the civilian defense ministry is swept along.[14]

The defense minister is an extremely important actor in Israeli politics because of the centrality of the defense issue, but the defense ministry as an implement of civilian control is relatively unimportant. The topic was so sensitive that the statement by a senior civil servant to the effect that "the army dominates the defense establishment" was banned by the censor.[15] The rationale of the concentration of power in the hands of the military is that the army, as the body responsible for implementation, must also be responsible for planning, procurement, and deployment of the arms and forces. This may be based on a naive belief that Israel is immune from social forces that have led to military takeover in other countries or it may be an expression of the high esteem that many Israelis have for their army. While there exists the formality of separation, and while the minister of defense and the cabinet have dominated military planning and moves, Israel lacks the patterns of civilian control in a more institutionalized sense that exist in other countries.

A good example of this is the defense budget. As we saw in chapter 3, the defense budget in effect defines Israel's budget both in terms of domestic spending and its reliance on funds from foreign sources to offset the purchase of weapon systems abroad. The military, in turn, defines Israel's defense needs. The head of the budget division of the ministry of defense (who also holds the title of financial adviser to the chief of staff) prepares a proposal after extensive consultation. His task is made easier in the sense that the army works on a five-year plan, which in effect means that the plan must be updated from year to year. In the case of major change—redeployment of forces as a result of political negotiations or military readjustments—a new plan might be needed. But the budget process takes last year's budget as a given and tends to grow from that point. No zero-based budgeting methods are used to attempt to determine what is really needed to achieve the desired results.

If a single budget proposal emerges from the whole process, it is forwarded through the defense minister to the finance ministry and the cabinet. If there are disagreements among general staff members or between the army and the ministry, the matter is brought to the minister. In such a case, however, his is the role of judge rather than leader. When brought to other civilian leaders, the tendency has been to give as much as possible. Eshkol tended to press the officers to ascertain that their budget was sufficient, and Sapir perceived his role as cashier for the defense establishment. Resources have always been in short supply in Israel, but in general a permissive atmosphere has existed in discussions of the defense budget. The cabinet was actively involved in the process usually only when the defense and finance ministers disagreed. While budget decisions need cabinet approval, these tend to be formal decisions ratifying decisions made elsewhere.

The Knesset has developed a special procedure for working on the defense budget. Since it is a secret subject, the entire Knesset is not involved. Instead, a special subcommittee composed of members of the Finance Committee and the Committee for Foreign Affairs and Security scrutinizes the budget in closed session and approves it item by item, while the whole Knesset approves the total sum as part of the national budget. The structure of its preparation and the political process it undergoes assure that the defense budget approved will be quite close to the proposals approved by the general staff and the defense minister. Only those groups at the heart of the preparation stage have a realistic chance of affecting it. Matters as important and far-reaching as the production of a new tank or a new jet aircraft are for all intents and purposes decided in the defense establishment. The finance ministry, the cabinet, and the Knesset, in decreasing order of effectiveness, may slow the decision-making process, but it is unlikely that they can turn it around. Arguments made about the tremendous expenses involved and the alternatives that might be economically more sound can be made, but they usually do not, at so late a date, abort the decision. If indeed the Israeli system is a partnership between civilian and military spheres, there is at least some evidence that the military partner is more senior than the civilian one.

The pattern of civil-military relations in Israel is complex. In a formal sense the civil branch dominates. In a deeper sense the military is not segregated in its barracks but is active in the political life of the country at its highest reaches. What is more, some military leaders enter active political life after retiring from the army. The boundaries are porous and shifting, and this very feature may allow Israel to retain formal civilian control over the military.

The Histadrut

If politics plays an important role in an institutional interest group in the defense field, party politics is even more prevalent in an associational interest group such as the Histadrut. The Histadrut was conceived as the organization of the workers' movement run by the labor parties, which would compete among themselves in elections. The Labor party has always been clearly dominant in the Histadrut, so the organization has become an important staging ground for political fights within the Labor party, an important aid to power when Labor ran the government and an important source of opposition when it did not. Jockeying for power within the Histadrut has been a major preoccupation for ambitious groups and individuals within the Labor party because the resources that the Histadrut controls are considerable, and the jobs that can be allocated are numerous.

The Histadrut is a voluntary organization of workers that functions as a trade union, but it is also much more than that. As we saw in chapter 3, the Histadrut played a key role in the pre-state period in building the infrastructure of the country's economy, in absorbing immigrants, and in preparing for the political and military challenges that Israel would face. With more than 1.5 million members the Histadrut includes about 80 percent of the Israeli work force. Obviously, such an organization must be taken into account when policies important to it are being considered. The Histadrut has three major functions: trade union activity, economic activity, and social services.[16] The ideology of the Histadrut has it that it represents the interests of the workers; in reality, the Histadrut represents the interests of the party that controls the Histadrut. Since its inception in 1920, that party has been the Labor party. Whether or not the interests of the Labor party are identical to the interests of the workers is a political and ideological question; suffice it to say that Labor presents itself as representing the workers' interests, while those parties who oppose Labor reject this contention.

Socialist parties are often associated with labor unions. The support may be more direct, as in West Germany and Great Britain where the unions actively support a labor party, or less direct, as in the United States where organized labor generally supports the Democratic party. Often in continental countries each political party has its own trade union and recruits labor's support in that way. Israel's pattern is unique; the Histadrut fits none of these descriptions. The Histadrut is made up of workers who elect their governing officers from competing parties. Until the 1960s the parties that competed were workers' parties or parties that did not reject socialist ideals. But since the 1965 Histadrut elections and the participation of a Herut-Liberal list (Gahal), the full spectrum of parties that competes for the Knesset elections also competes for the Histadrut elections. And since three-quarters of the Knesset electorate in Israel are Histadrut members, Histadrut elections are an important stage in Knesset elections.

The Histadrut member votes many times. He (or she) votes for the membership of the national convention, the workers' council in his city or region, the trade union council in his craft or prefession, and his workers' committee at his place of employment, among others. (Women, for example, also vote for the women's workers council, Naamat.) For the four elections, two distinctions are critical. First, there is a geographical as opposed to a functional base of representation. The elections for the convention are based on a single national constituency, and that is usually the case with the trade unions. The workers' committee is limited to place of work, and the workers' council includes the workers in a specific geographical area regardless of occupation. A second important difference among these elections is the system used. The national convention and the workers' council are elected on a fixed-list system, much the same as is used in Knesset elections. Some of the national trade unions and most of the workers' committees, however, are elected on a plurality basis. This latter system promotes the election of visible and popular leaders; the former system retains the processes of selection and promotion in the hands of the labor leaders. No clearer sign of the growing disparity between the labor leadership and the rank and file is needed than the different composition of the leadership elected by the different electoral systems. The national list of the convention and councils has tended to retain older Ashkenazi leaders in power, while the plurality votes of the workers' committees has tended to place younger and increasingly Sephardi leadership in the spotlight. In 1984, Israel Kaisar, of Yemenite extaction, was chosen Secretary-General of the Histadrut.

The older Ashkenazi Alignment leadership of the Histadrut long retained control, but seemed to be slipping. In the national convention the Alignment has always won an absolute majority, winning 62, 58, 55, and 63 percent respectively in the four elections between 1969 and 1981. The 1981 figure seems to change the pattern of loss generated by the other numbers, but it must be recalled that the 1981 elections took place before the Likud gained the momentum that was to lead to their 1981 Knesset victory and that the voting rate was low at about 56 percent. Moreover, the Likud held its own, growing from 17 percent in 1969, to 23 percent in 1977, and to 28 pecent in 1981. Council leaders (mostly Sephardi) in development towns have become more militant in their style and their demands.

The hierarchical structure of the Histadrut and the control of this structure by Alignment labor leaders are major explanations for the continued dominance of the established elite and the relatively conservative image of the Histadrut in the public mind. While more dynamic and younger leadership may emerge in the workers' committees, in the national bodies and the important workers' councils this is unlikely. The power of the leaders at the national level rests in their ability to nominate. In 1981, more than 825,000 Histadrut members elected 1501 delegates to the 14th Histadrut convention. The Histadrut council, elected by the convention, had 501 members; the executive committee, elected by the council, had 195 members. The executive committee meets regularly and is parallel to a Histadrut parliament. From it emerges the central committee (42 members), which can be likened to the Histadrut government. The higher up this hierarchy one goes, the higher is the concentration of loyal Alignment activists; and the higher up the scale of power, the more likely that they will be of the dominant elite. All parties that won representation participate in the executive committee, but only Labor and a few smaller parties such as

Shinui and the Independent Liberals participated in the central committee. The major positions of power were firmly in the hands of Labor party members.

This control would be an extremely important resource if we were discussing a monolithic party. But the Labor party is not monolithic; many competing groups and leaders exist, making the functioning of a hierarchical elite even more crucial to Labor's internal conflicts. In national politics the Histadrut is important because it is a partner to the national wage agreements that set the framework for wage and conditions of work negotiations. If the Histadrut is cooperative with the leadership of the ministry of finance, the process of wage negotiation can be smooth. If the Histadrut is not, the negotiations may be long and stormy. Much depends on the relations between the government and the Histadrut. After the establishment of the state, the Histadrut lost much of its power and leading personnel to the newly formed government. By and large the Histadrut was relegated to a second-rank status in terms of setting social and economic policy, although its ideas and leaders were often heard and sometimes promoted to more prominent positions. In the Likud era the Histadrut became a major focus of opposition to the government for the Labor party. There were two major reasons for this. First, the long years in government had weakened the party as an effective organization, and the Histadrut was more able to fill the gap. Second, the important base of power and patronage for Labor after 1977 was the Histadrut and its related enterprises. Paradoxically, the Histadrut and its leadership were strengthened as a result of the 1977 Likud victory over Labor.

The appropriate way to conceptualize labor relations in Israel in general is by seeing the Histadrut trying to further the interests of the workers and its own interests as well. In the period of Labor rule it was most likely for the Histadrut and government to resolve labor friction through compromise. When arguments developed they were due to differences over implementation, not over policy. Or, and this happened not infrequently, a group of workers' leaders would strive for concessions above and beyond what the Histadrut agreed to. Then, without the support of the Histadrut, these wildcat strikes or work actions would wreak havoc on a sector or function. What is fascinating to observe is how much more effective Histadrut leaders were in communicating with the government and/or the employers than they were with the workers. Under the Likud, the government and Histadrut seemed to perpetuate the kind of relations that existed under the Alignment in the field of labor relations, but in more general topics—such as social-economic policy or proposals for legislation regarding compulsory arbitration, national health insurance, or state pensions—the differences between the Histadrut and the government leaders were great.[17]

Within the Labor party the Histadrut is an important resource in another sense. The local leadership often uses the office of secretary of the local council as political patronage. If it wants to reward an active member, the party may provide him with that job. If, on the other hand, a member achieves prominence within the council and becomes its secretary, he almost automatically acquires an important position in the local party branch and possibly beyond it as well. It is the nature of the extended scope of the Histadrut in Israeli labor relations that the secretary of the workers' council has the potential to help solve individual as well as collective grievances and has the potential for patronage within the Histadrut network.

That network extends far beyond labor union activities. The two most important activities besides trade unionism are industrial enterprises and social welfare services. The Histadrut's industrial enterprises are concentrated in the Hevrat Ovdim (see chapter 3) and make the Histadrut the country's largest civilian employer as well as the representative of most of the nation's workers. Hevrat Ovdim's myriad operations provide organizational opportunities for developing managers as well as recruiting managers for a second career after army officer service; they provide the economic base that allowed the Histadrut to pioneer in industrial and agricultural areas that other investors would not enter; they allowed the setting up of factories and settlements in distant locations so that the population could be dispersed and so that pockets of unemployment could be relieved. These activities also brought criticism and objections. The Histadrut came to be perceived as a largely Alignment/Ashkenazi enterprise, even though the membership was much more varied. Charges were levied that the Histadrut's Hevrat Ovdim profited from itself, and the workers did not benefit enough from its profits; the slow pace of population dispersal and the concentration of Sephardim in lower-status positions were also blamed on the Histadrut.

Hevrat Ovdim and its related enterprises and industries are important actors in the economy. Within the Histadrut community they provide sources of patronage and resources. Charges are regularly made that Histadrut enterprises and their personnel, money, and resources (such as cars and telephones) aid the Alignment during election time without this aid being calculated in the party's expenses. The leadership often considers these enterprises as party related; the opposition within the Histadrut and some of the membership do not accept this attribution.

That the Histadrut membership is pluralistic in its party affiliation is evident from election results. But even within that part of the work force employed in Histadrut enterprises, the rank and file is less solidly labor than the leadership is or than the leadership would like it to be. In a 1981 preelection survey of Hevrat Ovdim workers it was determined that 45 percent favored Labor and 25 percent the Likud. These figures are much higher than the national average but indicate that not all Histadrut workers identify the interests of the Labor party with the interests of Histadrut. Even in Histadrut elections, the same sample reported giving 55 percent of its vote to Labor and 21 percent to the Likud.

The third major area of Histadrut activity, besides trade union activity and economic enterprise, is social services. By far the most important among these in terms of the scope of the activity and its role in the country's life is the health service provided by Kupat Holim. The Histadrut's Kupat Holim sick fund (there are four others sick funds in the country) provides services for 75 percent of the citizenry. About a third of the hospital beds are in Histadrut hospitals.[18]

The fund not only provides services for its members but also for members of the religious parties. In 1979 those affiliated with the NRP accounted for 6.7 percent of the insured and those of Agudat Israel 1.2 percent. These religious party members received services by virtue of their membership in *organizations* affiliated with the sick fund, although they themselves are not individual members of the Histadrut. These special relations prevented the religious parties from competing in Histadrut elections and was one of the bases of the long-term political cooperation between the religious parties and the labor movement. One of the important reasons why the religious parties oppose nationalization of the health services (as promoted by the Likud and opposed by the Alignment) is the historic connection these parties have with Kupat Holim.

The total expenditure on health in Israel is large and growing; in 1977 it accounted for 7.4 percent of the GNP, compared with 6.1 percent in 1975. Kupat Holim played a primary role in the delivery of services but increasingly had to rely on state funds to meet its deficits. Half of the ministry of health budget is earmarked for transfer to the sick funds, and other monies are added indirectly. During Alignment governments, ministers of finance were known to provide direct support to the Histadrut's sick fund above the 10 percent of budget received from the ministry of health. The health ministry opposed these added funds provided by the finance ministry because they wished to maintain control over the health field even though it has a small budget. (In the 1983 doctors' strike similar interdepartmental tensions were evident.) The Kupat Holim also competes with other Histadrut functions for budget. By the late 1960s the proportion of Histadrut dues allocated to the sick fund increased to almost 60 percent. A further source of income is the regular sum paid by Hapoel Hamizrachi (a religious party) in return for providing its members with health services. Another source of income is an employers' contribution paid to the sick fund for their workers. Since 1973, this employers' contribution has been paid to the National Insurance Institute, which apportions it among the different sick funds. As the payment to the Histadrut fund incorporates a contribution to the Histadrut, this arrangement in effect obliges employers to contribute to a trade union.

With almost 3 million insured and almost 30,000 employees, Kupat Holim is a major force in Israeli social life and economy. There is a widely held feeling that the prime motivation of many members in remaining in the Histadrut is to benefit from the health services it provides. Complaints are often heard about the bureaucratic problems attendant upon health care delivery, but there is general agreement that quality is relatively high. Proposals to transfer the delivery of health care to a national status (discussed in chapter 11) have been stymied over the years, although they recur. Leaders of the Histadrut are not anxious to lose control over the many jobs that a complex bureaucracy such as Kupat Holim controls. The supplying of medicines, linen, food, forms, and other goods needed to run such an operation is also a consideration. Not least, there is a deeply held belief that the organizational affiliation of millions with the Histadrut will ultimately accrue to the advantage of the Labor party on both ideological and organizational levels.

Another social service of considerable importance is the Histadrut's pension plans. In addition to providing for pensioners, the funds aggregate great sums of money that can be used to finance other Histadrut projects. The ability of the Histadrut to contain within itself so many important economic and social functions makes it a potent political force in the country.

In sum, the Histadrut is a world unto itself in many ways, concentrating economic, social, and political power. Its many functions and the ambitions of its leaders provide fertile ground for competitive relations. Its power and the scope of its membership make it a formidable organization in Israel's political life, although obviously it is much more than a pressure group.

Agriculture

Agriculture is an excellent example of an important policy area in which interest-group activity is more covert than overt, relying on party, parliamentary, and government contacts available because of the strategic location of the pro-agriculture persons in the system. Agriculture was a penultimate value in the period before the establishment of the state. Through agriculture the Zionist movement could realize two of its major goals: returning to the land of Israel in the most literal sense, and making the Jewish people productive rather than centering their economic activities on trade, craftsmanship, and scholarship.

Over time, especially since the 1930s, agriculture was also identified with defense imperatives because it allowed for spreading the population and establishing a physical presence and a kind of military early-warning system.

The earliest traces of modern Jewish agriculture go back to the first *aliyah* and the plantations set up by Baron de Rothschild. These efforts permitted Arab labor and discouraged Jewish labor because the former was cheaper and more experienced. The second and third *aliyot* pioneered new forms of agricultural settlement including the kibbutz and the moshav, and based their program on using Jewish labor while avoiding the exploitation of others by employing only members in their enterprises. These pioneering ventures became the ideological and organizational strongholds of the labor movement, and even though most of the Jews of Eretz Israel were always urban dwellers, agriculture became associated with the highest ideals of the system of values that existed before independence. Agriculture was perceived as a mission of the movement and the nation. It was fruitless to search for the boundary of agriculture's "lofty" influence because the leadership, ideology, and organization of the entire labor movement presented themselves as stemming from the agricultural sector.

The organization of bourgeois farmers and plantation owners associated with nonsocialist ideas was extraordinarily ineffective in opposing the socialist organization of agriculture. They were divided among themselves, and after the 1930s became more and more marginal in the politics of the country. One of their leaders, Yosef Sapir, even argued that only with decentralized organization could they be true to the ideals of the "free" farmer.[19] The right accepted the socialist ideology, seeing in agriculture a way of life that would lead to national rejuvenation. For the Alignment parties, these settlements and their leadership became leaders of the entire movement and ultimately of the nation, while the agriculturalists of the Likud parties were soon eclipsed and could do little more than make feeble attempts at interest-group activity.

The supremacy of the Alignment parties is obvious when the matter of land allotment is considered. Israel did not have a history of large landowners, and so it faced no necessity of agrarian reform. Land was purchased by the World Zionist Organization through the Keren Kayemet and distributed or leased by it primarily to settlements organized in the Agricultural Center. The Agricultural Center incorporated settlements (kibbutzim and moshavim) affiliated with the Histadrut. This arrangement gave the Histadrut enormous power, and in the early years it was the kibbutzim that won the battle, receiving preferential treatment at the hands of the Agricultural Center over resources provided to it by the Keren Kayemet.[20] The kibbutzim were preferred over the moshavim (the private farmers of the right were almost totally ignored) because the kibbutzim were more closely associated with the dominant party, while the moshavim had their closest contacts with a rival party. The kibbutzim were dominant in the Agricultural Center, and that made all the difference.

The interpenetration was so complete that various kibbutz movements, affiliated with different socialist parties, competed with one another within the Agricultural Center. The settlement division of the Jewish Agency handled training, research, and budget but left the allocation of land to the settlement movements, which set up a committee consisting of leading activists. When control was won over the WZO and the Jewish Agency by Mapai, it quickly took advantage of the resources placed at its disposal to further national, party, and sectoral goals. Since decision-making positions had been "colonized" by the kibbutz, there was no need to exert great amounts of pressure to secure favorable policies.[21]

After independence, the dominance of agriculture continued. Huge sums were poured into settlement movements, resulting in impressive achievements in agriculture; in addition, the settlement movements provided organizational strength and a supply of party activists and leaders to Mapai and the other parties. This was especially sensible for the kibbutz movement whose life style provided for the member's and his family's needs and could allow him to absent himself from work on the kibbutz to further the interests of the nation, the party, and the kibbutz. The national federations could recruit members from the federated kibbutzim for work within the movement or in national capacities. This ranged from 5 to 7 percent of the membership.[22]

Independence and the establishment of the agriculture ministry decreased the autonomy of the Histadrut and the Agriculture Center in agricultural matters and ultimately led to substantive changes. But at least in the first decade of independence the dominance of the Agriculture Center remained intact. Most of the ministers came from agricultural backgrounds in the settlement movements and usually from the kibbutz movement affiliated with Mapai. The organizational and ideological strength of the settlement movement prevented Mapai from actively interfering in agricultural policy; the opposite was true—leaders of the agricultural movements achieved prominent roles in the party and dominated in party affairs out of all proportion to their numerical size. Looking just at kibbutz members, we find that in 1965, six of Ahdut Haavoda's eight-member delegation, six of nine from Mapam, and eight of 42 from Mapai were from kibbutzim.[23]

Four of those who served as agricultural ministers—Pinhas Lavon, Levi Eshkol, Moshe Dayan and Ariel Sharon—eventually became ministers of defense. Especially in the case of Sharon, agriculture was defined by his activities and concern for settlement of the territories, thus continuing the tradition of the pre-state era, which equated agriculture with settlement and defense needs.

The ministry was dominated in its early years by ministers favorable to the kibbutz movement, and this expressed itself in both policy and appointments.

In the dominant party, Mapai, agricultural interests were assured because of the ideological tone of the era and the leadership positions that members of the settlement movement attained. This also meant that the party refrained from interfering in the affairs of the agricultural movements. Party interference was greatest in the agricultural organizations of the smaller parties, set up to try to compete with the successes of the organizations of the labor movement. This included the minuscule movements of Herut, the Liberals, and the Independent Liberals, and the slightly larger movements of the NRP and Poalei Agudat Israel (see table 10.1). These agricultural movements often achieved representation within party institutions but never achieved the importance of labor movement organizations.

In 1959 Moshe Dayan was appointed minister of agriculture. This shocked the political establishment because Dayan was young and many faithful politicians were itching to be appointed, because Dayan had only recently completed his turn as IDF chief of staff, but mostly because Dayan was seen to represent the moshavim and not the kibbutzim.

Dayan changed the sectoral outlook of Israel's agriculture ministers and adopted a statist approach (see chapter 11). This was upsetting to the old order whose interests were secured by having their men appointed to key positions. Dayan rejected the practice of having the agriculture ministry deal with the old-time settlements established before the state was founded and the Jewish Agency deal with the new ones founded after the state. The new settlements were predominantly populated by new immigrants from Asia and Africa untrained in agricultural ways and largely without the accompanying ideology with which the early European settlers had begun their settlements. The new settlements were generally set up on poorer land and were very dependent on the bureaucracies, which issued credit, training, and marketing. These bureaucracies tended to be run by veteran Europeans. When Dayan took over the agriculture ministry, he found the average kibbutz landholding unit was 105 dunams compared with the average 36.7 dunams for moshavim. The average water quota for the kibbutz unit was 24,300 cubic meters compared with 10,600 for the moshavim. Dayan undertook major changes in this balance. He allocated 100,000 dunams to the new kibbutzim, lowered the kibbutz water quota to 17,100 cubic meters, and raised that of the moshavim to 13,500.[24]

Competition in agriculture between the kibbutzim and the moshavim was not new. Historically the kibbutzim had dominated the party and hence policy. The other source of conflict that would fester over the years and become more and more evident as the ethnic polarization of the country grew was between

TABLE 10.1
AGRICULTURAL SETTLEMENTS BY ORGANIZATIONAL AND PARTY AFFILIATION AND 1981 VOTE

	Number of settlements	Population (thousands)	Party affiliation	Percent of vote for affiliated party, 1981 elections
Moshavim				
Moshav Movement	248	90.3	Alignment	56
Hapoel Hamizrachi	72	31.0	NRP	47
United Farmers	44	12.9	Alignment	52
Haoved Hatzioni	24	5.9	Independent Liberals	30
Poalei Agudat Israel	12	3.6	Poalei Agudat Israel	36
Herut	19	3.8	Likud (Herut)	81
Farmers' Association	5	1.5	Likud (Herut)	41
TOTAL MOSHAVIM	435	151.8	Alignment	43
			Likud	28
Kibbutzim				
Ihud	88	35.3	Alignment (Labor-Mapai)	92
Kibbutz Haarzi	78	37.0	Alignment (Mapam)	95
Kibbutz Hameuhad	65	29.3	Alignment (Labor-Ahdut Haavoda)	94
Hapoel Hamizrachi	15	6.4	NRP	68
Haoved Hatzioni	5	1.8	Independent Liberals	40
Poalei Agudat Israel	2	1.2	Poalei Agudat Israel	6
TOTAL KIBBUTZIM	255	111.2	Alignment	89
			Likud	2

NOTES: Those not affiliated are included in totals.
SOURCES: *Statistical Abstract, 1981*, 40-41; *Results of the Elections to the Tenth Knesset*, 50-57.

the kibbutzim and veteran moshavim, which were mainly Ashkenazi, and the moshavim peopled by Sephardi immigrants. The older settlements did not lead the community in absorbing immigrants who came soon after the state was founded. Whereas they had pioneered in statesmanship, diplomacy, agriculture, and security, they absented themselves from the effort of absorbing the new immigration. This may be understood as fatigue or overload. Regardless of the explanation offered, the veteran kibbutzim and moshavim take on the image of the landed gentry in the 1970s and 1980s. This group was characterized by others as affluent and arrogant, and as thinking that the leadership of the country was its natural and indispensable role. These people are most easily singled out in the anti-establishment, anti-Labor campaigns of the period. Their previous image of folk hero became tarnished and their political power dissipated.

Voting patterns are reported in table 10.1. When we consider data in addition to that reported in the table, the different political orientations become clear. The three kibbutz federations associated with the Alignment continue to support their party at rates above 90 percent regardless of when the kibbutz was established. In the moshav movement the picture is different: 76 percent of veteran settlers, compared to only 49 percent of new settlers, support the Alignment. Of the latter group, a third vote for the Likud. In the United Farmers and Hapoel Hamizrachi, about 60 percent of veteran moshav settlers (but only 46 percent of new settlers) support the Alignment and the NRP, respectively. When we recall that age of settlement is associated with ethnicity and that Sephardim supported the Likud heavily in 1981, it becomes clear that the forces at work that polarized the national vote worked in the moshavim as well.

The labor settlement movements abandoned the absorption of new waves of immigrants to the bureaucracies they had helped set up. By thus depersonalizing the process they accelerated feelings of alienation on the part of the new immigrants toward the more established farmers.

Dayan was the first minister who did not perceive himself as a representative of the settlement movements, although he was born in the first established kibbutz and raised in one of the pioneer moshavim. During his term the bulk of the country's land was formally nationalized with the passing of the Basic Law: Lands of Israel in 1960. The law regulated the allocation of land and made the Lands Administration (and not Keren Kayemet) responsible for the national lands, which comprised about 90 percent of the country's land. The minister of agriculture became chairman of the Lands Administration.

The production commissions were expanded during Dayan's term as minister. Commissions for the control and marketing of citrus fruit had existed since the 1940s.[25] Dayan introduced commissions in all branches of agriculture; they were empowered to oversee production, to assure regular supply of the product, to facilitate its marketing, and to deal with surpluses. Today the eight commissions are statutory authorities that can enter into contracts and enterprises (six other commissions relating to agriculture have been incorporated). The composition of these commissions represents those involved in the branch; the government has no more than 25 percent of the membership (with representatives of the agriculture, finance, industry, and commerce ministries and sometimes the ministry of health); the producers (represented by settlement groups) with 50 percent, the marketers 15 percent, and the rest, retailers and consumers. The commissions have a great deal of authority and can set quotas, minimum prices, surplus policy, subsidies and incentive bonuses, funds to encourage export and industrial usages, and they even deal with packaging and categorization.

Under the Alignment the settlement movements could greatly influence government policy because they could count on majority representation on the commissions that interested them. (The commissions for tobacco and olives had a majority of Arabs since much of the production of these items is in Arab hands.) Most of the settlement representatives came through the Agricultural Center, and the government representatives were also favorable to the sectoral demands of agriculturalists. Even in the Likud years the federations affiliated with the Alignment are well represented on the commissions because most of the agriculture of the country is organized by them (see chapter 3). Although the government representatives tend to be less cooperative in following the sector's demands, the influence of the settlements on agricultural policy is still very large.

Religion

The clearest case of political parties reflecting and promoting a set of interests is the religious parties and the role of religion in the state. For both the NRP and Agudat Israel, the first a Zionist and the second a non-Zionist party, the major plank of political ideology is to have the State of Israel organize its public life in accordance with Jewish religious law, Halakah. This is the overriding concern of both parties; after that, issues of economic policy, the future of the territories, and all other matters with which a political party concerns itself are addressed. In these parties the religious lobby and the party are synonymous. They have been successful in at least partially creating in Israel a Jewish state that adheres to orthodox rabbinical law. This has been achieved not through an articulate lobby impressing legislators with its vision but by succeeding in the game of coalition politics.

Religion is a central issue in Israeli political life. It is crucial because of the broad consensus within the Jewish population that Israel should be a Jewish state. The conflict is over the degree to which legislation and civil life in Israel should reflect the norms and decisions of established (orthodox) religious authorities.[26]

The issue is made more complex because of the various meanings of Jewishness. Judaism may be thought of as a religion, a nationality, a culture, or all of these. For orthodox Jews, religion and nationality are one and the same. Religious behavior and belief, while desirable, are not essential criteria for membership in the community.

Israelis are split over these matters, as is demonstrated in table 10.2. It is fascinating to note the degree of relative stability over time in the distribution of answers to questions regarding public life and personal religious behavior. About half of them agree to having public life conducted in accordance with tradition; about half disagree. Between a quarter and a third observe none of Jewish religious law, about the same percent observe all or most. More than 40 percent are somewhat observant. We have before us a picture of a symmetrically divided polity in terms of desired public behavior and in terms of private

TABLE 10.2

PUBLIC LIFE AND JEWISH RELIGIOUS TRADITION;
OBSERVANCE OF JEWISH RELIGIOUS LAW

Should the government see to it that public life is conducted in accordance with Jewish religious tradition?

	1962	1969	1981
Definitely	23%	27%	27%
Probably	20	16	23
Probably not	16	14	23
Definitely not	37	42	26
Number of respondents	1170	1240	1225

Do you observe Jewish religious law?

	1962	1969	1973	1977	1981
To the letter	15%	12%	14%	14%	9%
Quite a bit	15	14	17	12	14
Only somewhat	46	48	43	44	43
Not at all	24	26	26	29	34
Number of respondents	1170	1241	1877	1366	1212

NOTE: Deviations from 100 are the result of "no response" answers and/or rounding.

observance. The issue is a major one and splits the population. The cause is promoted by a number of religious parties; most other parties are secularist or noncommittal, but an antireligious party has yet to emerge. The issue of promoting religion is legitimate in the Israeli polity in a way that promoting antireligion or ethnicity is not. Forces that champion antireligion are as unpopular among the electorate as are forces that outrightly promote one ethnic group over others. The norm of the Israeli political system has been to legitimize both the role of religion and the ethic of a single Jewish people regardless of ethnic background.

The call for the separation of religion and the state has never had wide appeal for at least four reasons. First is the political reason. Religious parties have been active in the ruling Zionist and Israeli coalitions since the 1930s. This cooperation gave rise to the concept of the status quo when the state was founded; this meant that arrangements in effect during the pre-state period regarding religion and religious practice would be extended into the state period. And so it has been. Second is a symbolic-ideological reason. With the exception of a few groups, most Israelis support the notion of Israel as a Jewish state and wish to see this notion put into practice in everyday life.

To be sure, there are other than religious options open to the question of how to express the Jewishness of Israel, but once the premise is accepted, the status quo version becomes at least appropriate if not exciting. Even when the socialists ruled and preferred a different form of expression of the Jewishness of Israel, their coalition calculations and obligations led them to accept the status quo arrangements. Third is simply a matter of habit. For many Israelis, the arrangements in effect appear natural because they are the only ones they have known.

Besides, for most Jews in Israel, the arrangements pose no serious burden or inconvenience. Most marriages pose no problem, most children born are legitimate, and most rituals can be ignored if one so chooses. Only a small minority is affected negatively by rabbinical rulings, and its anguish has never catalyzed a mass movement for alleviating the situation.

Fourth, the call for the separation of religion and the state is foreign to much of the experience of Jewish history and the people of the Middle East. The focus of religion on the individual is a modern, Western notion, especially evident in Christian contexts. Religion in the traditional sense was a community undertaking, and the individual was identified by his membership in the community. The Yom Kippur service recites that "we have sinned," not that *I* have sinned. Jews were dealt with as members of a community throughout their history of dispersion, sometimes achieving large measures of communal autonomy. The Ottoman Empire recognized communities, and this millet system became the basis of practice during the British Mandate and ultimately within the State of Israel.

From this heritage it is a natural development to have marriage and divorce and other matters of personal law regulated by the religious community to which one belongs. Religion, then, connotes social belonging and jurisdiction, not only theological belief. Accordingly, notions of individual choice have never taken hold in Israel. While one might not believe in God, one's personal status would still have to be settled by the religious court. Political authorities and religious authorities have worked hand in hand to strengthen the power of each other. Rules of inclusion and exclusion in the community—that is, who is a Jew?—became questions given religious answers with the authoritative backing of the secular state.

Israel is not a theocracy; it is a modern parliamentary regime that has opted to allocate decisions on certain aspects of public and private life to religious authorities. For the Jewish population it is the orthodox rabbinate whose interpretations are binding; for members of other religions, it is the recognized religious authority of the other recognized communities whose rules are binding: Muslim, Druze, and almost a dozen Christian sects.

In regulating religious affairs in Israel the Knesset did not give the Jewish religious courts superior status to the courts of other religions, but it did give the orthodox religious courts a monopoly within the Jewish community regarding marriage and divorce. The 1953 law gives the rabbinical courts complete jurisdiction over marriage and divorce of the Jews in the country, whether citizens of Israel or not. Up until then, membership in Knesset Israel was voluntary, but from that point on, jurisdiction over all Jews was in the hands of the rabbinical courts. The various solutions to which Jews denied the right to marriage by the religious courts have turned—marrying in Cyprus or marrying through mail to Mexico or other places—are permitted not by Halakah but by the secular state and its rules of registering the marriage of citizens.

The registration of one's personal status is in the hands of the ministry of the interior. Control over this ministry has become extremely important for religious circles, and indeed two NRP leaders, Haim Moshe Shapira and Yosef Burg, held the post for most of the governments and most of the years of the country's existence. The ministry registers both "religion" and "nationality." According to Halakah, the two categories are interchangeable, "Jew" being a connotation of both religion and nationality. This interpretation is not the only one possible with, for example, atheists claiming that they are Israeli nationals with no religion or extreme antinationalists claiming that they are Jews with no special connection to the secular state of Israel. The result has been a standoff with an inclination to little or no modification of past practice. It is only when hard cases are introduced that the authorities must grapple again with these difficult questions.

Such a case was that of Brother Daniel. Brother Daniel was born, reared, and educated as a Jew in pre-World War II Poland. He even spent a number of years in training to immigrate to Eretz Israel. He converted and became a Catholic Carmelite monk but claimed the right under the Law of Return to come to Israel. The Law of Return, passed in 1950, grants Israeli citizenship to any Jew coming to Israel. Rufheisen, Brother Daniel's name before conversion, claimed that he was a Jew who had converted to Catholicism and was entitled to the same status and privileges granted other Jewish immigrants. In 1962 the Supreme Court ultimately backed the position of the religious parties, namely that Brother Daniel was no longer a Jew because he had converted.[27] But the court distinguished between Halakah, which regards him still as a Jew by virtue of the fact that he was born of a Jewish mother, and the secular usage, which recognized a convert to another religion as no longer a Jew. The court's support of the religious position denying Brother Daniel's request was based on secular grounds.

Another hard decision was made in the two cases brought by Benjamin Shalit in 1968 and 1972.[28] Shalit, an Israel-born Jew and naval officer, married a non-Jewish woman abroad. When they tried to register their two children as Jews under the nationality category, the request was denied. The NRP-run interior ministry wanted to leave both the religion and nationality category blank; Shalit, an atheist, was willing to leave the religion category blank but wanted his children registered as being of the Jewish nation. The Supreme Court, by a 5-4 majority, agreed to his request. This was an important decision and different from the Brother Daniel case. In the Daniel case the status of the plaintiff was cloudy according to Halakah; in the Shalit case the children were not Jews according to Halakah but the court ruled that they must be registered as of Jewish nationality. The Knesset, under NRP pressure, amended the law to read that a Jew is one born of a Jewish mother or converted. When the second Shalit case arose regarding their third child, the court denied the request, and the child was not registered as a Jew.

The "Who is a Jew?" issue did not end with that legislative change. Because of the fact that many conversions to Judaism (especially in the United States) are performed by conservative or reform rabbis, the religious parties have labored to have the law changed again, recognizing only conversion according to Halakah. This would mean limiting legal conversion only to orthodox rabbis. Although most secular politicians oppose these changes, whether they will be accepted depends on coalition calculations and not on philosophical or theological considerations.

The actors that determine developments in this issue area are the religious political parties, the factions within them, and the rabbis affiliated with them. These groups compete with one another, often attempting to win public support (within the religious community) by being more exacting in their interpretations of current events in terms of the Halakah. This is especially convenient with the more dogmatic. It is more desirable to be in a position of calling into question groups that are more lenient, and this is exactly the tactic used by the opposition factions within each party, by the more ultra-orthodox parties against the orthodox (usually the Aguda against the NRP), and by rabbis affiliated with one party against rabbis of another. The other political parties are absorbed in these dilemmas because of their desire to have the coalition support of the religious parties or to prevent religious parties from supporting the rival secular political party. Thus the government budget becomes a political football with religious parties pressing for added funds for their pet projects.

When the election of the president of Israel can be determined by religious party votes in the Knesset, political deals are rumored. Or when religious legislation might be defeated because antireligious members of the coalition threaten to vote against the bill or abstain, the leaders of the secular party heading the coalition have been known to put tremendous pressure on the upstarts, including threatening the downfall of the government if the bill fails. The point is that much of the activity in this issue area is motivated by purely political considerations. Israel is divided on the religious issue, but it would be inappropriate to measure that division by the legislation passed on the subject.

The clear political success that the religious parties have had rests on their pivotal role in coalition formation. The results of this success are obvious in law: a series of laws and administrative rulings that have, on the whole, gone in the direction desired by the religious parties on such questions relating to abortion, marriage and divorce, public transportation on Sabbath and holidays, enforcement of the Jewish dietary laws, and the definition of who is a Jew. From the point of view of the religious parties there are many matters yet to be settled as they would wish, but no one can disclaim the achievements they have made.

The background to their success is cultural and has to do with the symbol system and the basic premises on which the society rests. But would things change drastically if the religious parties were no longer needed in the government coalition? To what extent is the Jewish character of Israel one of political expediency and to what extent is it part of the civic culture? There is no certain answer to this hypothetical question but my own guess is that the forms regarding religion and religious usage that have evolved in Israel are more permanent than many secularists would like to think.

The arrangements perpetuated as a result of the status quo are more flexible than is commonly thought. Local authorities have leeway in how strenuously they apply laws concerning commerce or entertainment on the Sabbath and holidays. The local strength of the religious parties plays an important role in the matter. On national issues, a great deal more visibility and uniformity are maintained. All institutions that receive monies from the government are expected to observe Jewish dietary laws. This includes the army, schools, hospitals, and government missions abroad. The issue whether El Al, the national airline, would operate on the Sabbath and holidays occupied the country's attention in 1982 until the government decided in accordance with the demands of the religious parties to stop these operations. The list is a long one, not long enough for some, too long for others, and always changing.

One fascinating dilemma concerned television on the Sabbath. The secularists saw television as an extension of radio, which existed before the establishment of the state and hence was continued into the state period as part of the status quo. (Indeed, early Israeli television was not much more than radio with pictures.) The religionists saw television as especially insidious on the Sabbath and interfering with family solidarity, to say nothing of enticing weaker souls from endeavors of prayer and study. In 1969 the Broadcast Authority Executive Committee approved television broadcasting seven days a week (except for Yom Kippur). The minority appealed the decision to the prime minister, who decided to bring it before the government. In the meantime, the Supreme Court ruled that there was no reason to suspend the decision until the government met, and Sabbath television began on November 7. Other legal arguments regarding the legality of work permits issued to those who were to transmit the broadcast also failed in court. In this case it was the court which spared the politicians from facing the decision of how to interpret the status quo.

The religious parties, especially the NRP, have been constant partners in the ongoing story of Israeli politics. While the parties as a whole have had to straddle the fence that divides principle and pragmatism, the NRP in particular has had to guard its flank from the political sniping of the Agudat Israel; the NRP is a firmly Zionist party, the Aguda is non-Zionist. For both ideological and practical reasons, the NRP became the champion of the movement that summarizes developments since the founding of the state—the nationalization of religion.[29] The goal of the NRP was to have religious institutions, which might have been temporary or voluntary in the past, become permanent fixtures of the religious community by having them created by law. The NRP has invested great efforts to influence this legislation and to dominate these institutions. They include the ministry of religious affairs, the chief rabbinate, the rabbinical courts, and the religious councils. Through these efforts, the NRP hoped to establish itself as the major representative of the Jewish religious community.

The institutional instincts of the NRP were excellent. The web of relations between the party and these religious institutions has provided budget and patronage for the party's leaders. Their electoral fortunes, however, have come on hard times. Between 1977 and 1984 the NRP lost two-thirds of its Knesset delegation, going from 12 to four seats. Both ethnic and nationalist challenges have taken their toll. Abu-Hatzeira's Tami won one seat in 1984, the nationalist Tehiya won five. It is reasonable to speculate that many of these votes came at the NRP's expense. Tami's ethnic, especially North African, appeal and the Tehiya's link with Gush Emunim cost the NRP many votes. Gush Emunim had emerged from the Bnei Akiva youth group affiliated with the NRP. The future of the NRP at the polls is likely to determine whether it can continue to control the institutional arrangements it worked so hard to create.

The most important political institution of those mentioned above is the ministry of religious affairs. It has almost always been headed by a prominent NRP leader. The ministry has important administrative, legal, and political functions. It supervises and provides technical services for all the various religious sects in Israel. The ministry, along with the chief rabbinate, is very active in the Jewish community. It supervises Jewish dietary laws for public institutions not under the supervision of a local rabbinate and oversees the ritual purity of imported food, especially meat. It provides grants for the building of synagogues and ritual baths, supervises the activities of burial societies, administers holy sites such as the Western Wall, and encourages the development of yeshivas. On the legal level, the ministry initiates legislation on religious affairs and implements legislation after it is passed. This gives the NRP tremendous influence on such legislation.

The ministry of religious affairs is most important because of the patronage it affords the NRP. The selection of personnel of almost every religious institution in the state, Jewish and non-Jewish, involves the ministry. This includes the chief rabbinate and the local rabbinates, the rabbinical courts and the religious councils, as well as the state religious school system. Budget growth is also obvious in good political years. In the proposals for fiscal year 1982, for example, the finance ministry notes that the coalition agreements called for an increase in the support of yeshiva students, and accordingly that item grew in the budget of the ministry of religious affairs by 25 percent *after* controlling for inflation.[30]

There are two chief rabbis in Israel, an Ashkenazi and a Sephardi. Both of these developments—the fact that there is a chief rabbinate at all and the fact that there are two of them—stem from historical considerations; neither is mandated by Jewish tradition. Judaism does not require a rabbinical hierarchy; the chief rabbinate emerged more for purposes of managing contacts with those outside the Jewish community. In 1921 a rabbinical council was convened applying the principles of the millet system which allowed religious communities to manage their own affairs. This council was ultimately recognized by the mandatory power, and the chief rabbinate was institutionalized. Only in 1972, however, was its existence and the rules for its election mandated in law by the Knesset. The chief rabbinate was recognized as the supreme authority regarding Halakah, although with the establishment of a hierarchy of religious courts it ceased to double as the Supreme Rabbinical Court of Appeals. The electoral college to select the chief rabbis was to be composed of 80 rabbis and 70 laymen, equally divided between Ashkenazim and Sephardim, with the mayors of the country and the heads of local religious councils playing a role in the election. There have been appeals to abandon the practice of having two chief rabbis, but the practice persists more for political and personal reasons than for philosophical or theological ones.

The manner in which the electoral college is constructed was meant to ensure the joint influence of the NRP (through the rabbis appointed) and the Alignment, by virtue of their influence in local government when the law was passed. This joint influence has persisted despite the emergence of the Likud as a major political force at the national level. As in the past, the election of the chief rabbis in 1983 was accompanied by intense bargaining between the NRP and the Alignment; although the ballot was secret, the results showed that the parties had high levels of influence on the rabbis. The Aguda, which rejects the religious authority of the chief rabbis, occasionally calls for the abandonment of the institution and at other times backs candidates of its own.

The rabbinical court is another institution that the NRP has successfully brought under the jurisdiction of the law of the state, thus perpetuating it. While formally separate from the chief rabbinate, the chief rabbis serve as presidents of the Supreme Rabbinical Court of Appeals. The chief rabbis must approve all religious judges before their appointment. The Religious Judges Law of 1955 is similar to the Judges Law of 1953 with the exception that the latter sets out the qualifications for judges, whereas qualifications for religious judges are set by the chief rabbinate. A further difference is that judges swear allegiance to the state and its laws, whereas religious judges must swear allegiance to the state only. There are 20 district courts and the Supreme Rabbinical Court of Appeals in Jerusalem. The Israeli Supreme Court, in its capacity as the High Court of Justice, retains the right to determine whether the religious courts have jurisdiction in a given matter, and by precedent it has also intervened when it finds that principles of "natural law" have been violated by the rabbinical courts. The rabbinical courts have exclusive jurisdiction over all Jewish citizens in the area of personal-status law.

The local religious councils were established to provide services funded by the public treasury. After much party bickering, a Religious Council Law was passed in 1967 and calls for the religious councils to be recomposed every four years. The law provides that 45 percent of the members be appointed by the minister of religious affairs (usually NRP), another 45 percent by the local authority (in the 1960s usually Alignment), and 10 percent by the local rabbi (usually NRP). The members are to be personally religious, but the appointment system was meant to reflect the ethnic and political composition of the community. Whereas the NRP has dominated, it has been forced to share power and patronage with other religious parties as well as secular parties.

Religion is a potent issue area in Israeli politics. However, the density of action within the area makes it unlikely that groups from outside will successfully penetrate and win influence within it. The political parties have large stakes invested and are committed to compromises developed over the years. Many of these compromises have been enacted in law by the Knesset, a fact that makes it even more difficult to alter past practice. The NRP has had to pay a political price for the nationalizing legislation by sharing power with other religious parties and with secular parties. But this "price" has worked both ways: The secular parties also committed themselves to structures that enhanced the *weltanschauung* of the NRP, not to mention its political power and patronage.

Rather than think of competing interest groups, it is best to think of political parties attempting to "colonize" bureaucracies or public policy issues or both. The ruling party has dominated defense, the Alignment has run the Histadrut and has "colonized" the agriculture bureaucracies, and the NRP has nationalized the religious issue and has made it its own. Pluralism is not in evidence; competing political parties are.

11. Statism, Public and Local Administration

Statism

Many of the services in the pre-state era were provided by voluntary organizations; the largest and most resourceful of these groups was the Histadrut. The services proved important in establishing the Histadrut and its ruling party in a dominant position throughout the pre-state period and the first generation of the independent state. With independence came a wave of nationalization of these services. The ideology was called *statism,* and Ben-Gurion was its major champion. The call was taken up by sections of his Mapai party before he left it in 1965, and it was a major plank in the Rafi platform, the party he founded after leaving Mapai.

After most of the members of that party returned to the Labor fold in 1968, Ben-Gurion persisted in rejecting the Labor party and in maintaining his call for statism. His State List of 1969 even included the idea in its name, and when that party became part of the Likud, it brought Ben-Gurion's call more forcefully to that part of the spectrum. There were two elements to the idea: One stated that "services required by all citizens must be provided by the state";[1] the second argued that the Labor party was unable to separate party interests from national interests and that the latter must prevail.

The process of nationalization of services in Israel is a long and incomplete story. Perhaps the major conclusion of the story is that the incompleteness of the transfer has caused the administration of public services to face unique challenges. The incompleteness must be explained by (1) the complexities of the political system and coalition politics, and (2) the fact that because these processes of nationalization were not completed, they reinforced the structural complexities that characterize the system. This closed circle is not easily penetrated; interests, symbols, and careers are all involved. The tension between those who attempt to achieve a more complete transfer and those who support a partial transfer (or no transfer at all) is likely to continue to be a major theme in the country's story. Four areas indicate the complexities: defense, education, employment, and health services.

DEFENSE

After independence in 1948, there was no question about Israel's need for a single national defense force. Immediately after the state was established, the Haganah (the largest military organization in the Yishuv, controlled by Mapai) became Israel's army; the future of the other military organizations—Irgun, Lehi, and the Palmach—was in doubt.

The Irgun (also known as Etzel) and Lehi were underground organizations that sprang from the Revisionist movement. The Irgun, headed by Menachem Begin, was the larger and had the support of most Revisionists. When the state was established, the Irgun was dominated by the Herut movement. Lehi was smaller but more extremist in its methods of activity against the British. It had split off from the Irgun in 1940 and was less strongly identified with the Revisionists. The Palmach was identified with the Kibbutz Hameuhad (the kibbutz branch of Ahdut Haavoda) and, to a lesser extent, with Hashomer Hatzair.

Disbanding the Irgun and Lehi can be seen as part of the struggle to ensure the legitimacy of the regime. Neither organization was represented in the provisional government, and thus Mapai had no need to compromise with them. Disbanding the Palmach was more problematic because Mapam, to which the Palmach owed its allegiance, was an integral part of the labor movement and was Mapai's partner in the government when the Palmach command was disbanded. At that time, however, the composition of the coalition was such that Mapam did not have the power of veto, because it could not leave the government and abandon Mapai in a minority position. Nevertherless, disbanding the Palmach formations was postponed until Mapam was in opposition. Disbanding the Palmach did not threaten the organizational infrastructure of either the labor movement or the Histadrut. Mapai thus had the support of the party machinery on this issue. The Histadrut, firmly in Mapai's control, also supported its dissolution. The dissolution of the Palmach also had economic benefits for the Histadrut, which had funded it, as monies were released for other activities. Disbanding the Palmach is best considered as the means by which the dominant party prevented other political bodies from retaining their own militias within the newly formed sovereign state.

EDUCATION

The nationalization of the education system in 1953 did not create a unified school network. The state system was broken down into a general and a religious (Jewish orthodox) subsystem. In addition, Agudat Israel and the kibbutz movements retained autonomy over the educational systems of their members' children. Today most Jewish children in Israel attend government schools, with about a third of them attending within the religious subsystem. Mapai/Labor controlled the ministry of education from 1948 to 1977, along with other key posts of dominance and governance (the prime ministry, finance, foreign affairs, and agriculture). In 1977 the National Religious party won control of the education ministry, which had always been considered a crucial focus of power in the Labor party.

The labor movement entered the field of education at a relatively late stage in the development of the educational system of the pre-state period. It developed a socialist track that existed in competition with the "general" track (identified with the General Zionists) and the religious track. After the establishment of the state and with the advent of massive waves of immigrants from Europe, Asia, and Africa, education became a prime political issue. The socialist track experienced pronounced growth compared with the general track. In 1948-49 only 29.3 percent of pupils were registered in socialist schools; 43.8 percent were enrolled in general schools. Three years later the general schools accounted for only 27.4 percent of all pupils, while the share of the socialist schools had increased to 42.6 percent.[2] The labor schools movement achieved outstanding success in the settlements of the new immigrants, but this was the cause of a bitter struggle with the religious parties, which at one stage even boycotted government meetings because of the dispute.

The transfer of the education system to the hands of the government in 1953 did not generate a coalition crisis because Mapam was then in the opposition, and thus effectively isolated and prevented from allying with possible sympathizers in Mapai. The leaders of Mapai knew that Mapam would be satisfied with a guarantee of educational autonomy for its kibbutzim, and when the support of the religious factions was obtained in return for strengthening the influence of the religious faction (Hapoel Hamizrachi) in the religious state schools, no real opposition remained. Thus, in 1953 the particularist school movements were abolished. The socialist and general tracks were, in effect, merged into the national secular subsystem controlled by the ministry of education, which in turn was controlled by the labor movement. The NRP retained effective control over the national religious subsytem, and both the ultra-orthodox party and the kibbutz movement had their own autonomous schools. Of the parties that had been active in education during the pre-state period, only the General Zionists did poorly. This is especially ironic since they strongly supported the idea of statism and the State Education Law.

EMPLOYMENT

Labor exchanges run by the labor ministry were set up by law in 1959 after a long history of party competition over the provision of employment.[3] Labor exchanges were politically important in the pre-state period and the first years of nationhood, during which unemployment was widespread; their importance decreased once the service ceased to be required by the majority of the population. Cooperation of sorts even existed among the parties. Ben-Gurion reached an agreement with Jabotinsky and the Revisionists with regard to job allocations in 1935 (due to the scarcity of jobs at this time), but Ben-Gurion's premature statism was defeated in a referendum of Histadrut members. Still, other joint ventures were pursued in the labor field, and by statehood cooperation was widespread. A Labor Exchange Center was established and gradually concentrated on employment, despite frequent squabbling among the groups involved. Mapai gave silent consent to the nationalization of the employment service because it was already dominant in the Labor Exchange Center and felt that other parties had achieved overrepresentation there.

HEALTH SERVICES

There are five sick funds in the country, but the sick fund (Kupat Holim) belonging to the Histadrut is by far the most important. Opposition to nationalizing health services is very strong in the Histadrut, in part because of the feeling that the other episodes at nationalization were poorly conceived at best, or took place at the Histadrut's expense at worst. To this day one can hear heated debates in Israel about the disbanding of the Palmach or the nationalization of the education system. Ideologues as well as pragmatists argue that the movement toward statism was one factor that brought about the downfall of the Labor party in the 1977 elections; bases of spiritual and political dominance had been relinquished over the years to anonymous forces opposed to the continued rule of the left.

The Labor party and the Histadrut have always opposed national health insurance; in the past they have supported proposals for making health insurance compulsory but leaving the provision of services to the existing sick funds. Sick fund, Histadrut, and Labor party leaders appreciate the enormous financial power and patronage opportunities they would lose if sick fund activities were nationalized. In addition, ideological arguments for the present arrangements extolling the virtues of mutual aid, self-help, and worker solidarity are voiced. It is clear to all that the sick fund is the labor movement's main source of strength and that its abolition would mean the collapse of the movement's organizational and financial base. Only parties that did not have their own health schemes—the General Zionists, the Progressives, and Agudat Israel— supported the introduction of a national health insurance law, a movement that started in the 1950s and continued through the defeat of the Labor party in the 1977 elections.

Attempts at complete nationalization have been thwarted regularly. The terms of reference for a governmental commission set up in 1957 called for general health insurance preserving the multiplicity of sick funds and the autonomous management of the insurees' organizations. The majority report complied; the minority report claimed that the terms of reference were inconsistent with the principles of good management and financial efficiency and proposed a unitary structure. The debate heated up and suggestions were even made by party leaders keen on statism (including Ben-Gurion) that the sick fund and the Histadrut should be separated and the sick fund left on its own.[4]

Much of this debate coincided with the split in Mapai in 1965. After the elections in which Rafi took 8 percent of the vote (disappointing for it, but heartening for Mapai, headed by Eshkol), another committee was set up to plan for general health insurance "provided by the insurees' sick funds," in the words of the letter of appointment. The committee again split between those who were loyal to the needs of the government and those who felt that the goals of supervision, avoidance of duplication, planning, and compulsory insurance were not attainable by the proposed method. It was a standoff between the professionals and the politicians.

Within the Labor party the argument centered on the way in which the sick fund's organizational and budgetary independence could be ensured after the enactment of such a law. All factions of the labor movement were interested in weakening the smaller sick funds by demanding that funds not operating in the more remote settlements would have to subsidize the provision of health services in those areas. Since the Histadrut sick fund is the only organization that does so, this would mean a significant weakening of the smaller sick funds. If such a national health scheme was introduced, the labor movement intended to exploit it for its own ends, namely, to ensure its fund's dominance in the field of health care while ensuring a substantial budget from the national treasury that would both reduce the pressure on the Histadrut and ensure the sick fund's organizational independence. In the ministerial committee that discussed the whole issue in 1968, the labor ministers were united in their opposition to the demand made by the NRP and the Independent Liberals to channel the collection of sick fund dues through the National Insurance Institute.

Minister of Labor Yosef Almogi suggested the compromise mentioned above. By it, members' contributions would be paid directly to the sick funds, while employers' contributions would be collected by the National Insurance Institute, which would make the allocation to the different funds. The labor movement wanted to be sure that Histadrut members knew their contribution was going to the Histadrut and that it could continue to use the collection offices for patronage; with regard to the employers' contribution, the fund's only concern was to guarantee its income. The sick funds and the Histadrut were prepared to accept a certain degree of state supervision in return for an expansion in the scope of their activities and an increase in their power. In this case the banner of statism was used as a camouflage for trade union and party interests.

In 1973 the Medical Insurance Law was proposed to the Knesset by the government. It had been developed during the previous two years largely to meet the needs of the Histadrut sick fund and without excessive consultation with the other funds or the ministry of health. The proposal was presented a few months before the elections with the hope of impressing the electorate with the legislative activity of the Alignment, although it was uncertain that there was enough time to enact the proposal into law. Items on which the Histadrut sick fund was not prepared to compromise included service provision by the many sick funds, collective membership, and dues collection. No single fund was to be established, although principles for supervision and standardization were proposed. Membership was compulsory, but the Histadrut refused to agree to freedom of choice of sick fund by employees who belonged to organizations (mainly the Histadrut) that had collective affiliation contracts with a sick fund. The proposal to have fees collected by the National Insurance Institute was resoundingly rejected by the Histadrut and its sick fund for fear of losing control of the funds and the patronage of the jobs involved.

The proposed bill included a division of responsibility between the ministries of health and labor in providing different elements of the health service. This was crucial, for while the Labor party never deemed it important enough to control the health ministry, it almost always controlled the labor ministry for both practical and ideological reasons. At subsequent stages the bill was stalled by opposition from those who feared reduction in their influence following the passage of the bill in its proposed form—the smaller sick funds, the ministry of health (which basically objected to the role proposed for the ministry of labor), and the Histadrut, which feared that the proposed law would lead to an increase in the sick fund's membership and increase its autonomy within the Histadrut.

The ascension to power of a non-Labor government in 1977 raised expectations that legislation would be quickly forthcoming in the health field. But the government soon became deeply involved in negotiating a peace treaty with Egypt and controlling runaway inflation. The health ministry went ahead with preparations for national health insurance legislation based on two concepts: organizational unification and administrative regionalization.[5] The plan was to divide the country into regions and "provide health services based on the facilities available in the region—sick funds, public hospitals, institutes, laboratories, etc." No nationalization of health facilities was foreseen; agreements would be arrived at between the health authority and the providers of health services. But most significant, "there [would] be no more membership and no more membership fees, rather residents [would] be eligible to receive all health services by virtue of their being insured by National Insurance." It was not at all surprising that even without seeing the detailed proposal, the Histadrut, its sick fund, and the Labor party immediately and emphatically rejected the proposal. The legislation was abandoned.

Public Administration

Israel's public administration reflects many elements of the country's political culture. There is a plethora of rules, bureaucrats, and committees; but the political element is never far from the surface, especially if the issue is considered an important one. Lip service is paid to professionalism and nonpartisanship, but these values are likely to weaken the higher up the civil service ladder one climbs. There is a pretense of modern rational structure, and increasingly computerized techniques have been introduced; still, a solid core remains of a more personal and traditional form of dealing with the citizenry by the administration. Outright corruption is relatively rare or small in scale, but *protektzia*—the use of pull or personal acquaintance to speed up processes or obtain favorable treatment—is rampant.

Israel's administrative culture is composed of four strands. The first is the Middle Eastern style in which there is "deference to authority and status, bargaining skills and displays of bureaucratic officiousness." At the same time there is the British legacy, which "is a no-nonsense, orderly, condescending, bureaucratic approach, with little room for bargaining, local initiative or disruption." Third is the strand of traditions brought by Jewish immigrants: "Paranoic ghetto attitudes mingle with dynamic, cosmopolitan, liberal entrepreneurship." The fourth strand—the Israeli—uses the experiences with which the people grew up. The older ones, "skilled in political infighting and insurgency tactics, affirm their inherent visionary powers, their pragmatic 'feel' of things, and their confidential, in-group decision-making." Their children, more middle class and likely to be native born, turn more to models experienced in military service or learned in the university.[6]

The public administration is a direct extension of the pervasiveness of bureaucracy. Bureaucracy is a feature of the modern state everywhere, but in Israel it seems even more prevalent. Part of this impression stems from the fact that such a large portion of the population is employed in jobs related to one bureaucracy or another. This is enhanced by the extremely large role of government and its related agencies in the economy and society. This employment pattern fortified the inclinations of the Jews who came to Israel to continue living in urban areas and make their livings in commercial or service sectors.

Bureaucracy is important in a modern society because it provides for a division of labor and is immune from reliance on a single individual. As transactions are based on written rules and records, it allows for neutrality and constraint. These positive features also provide the background for bureaucracy's limitations and perversions: too much paperwork, too many authorizations needed, too many organizations involved, too little coordination. The proper functioning of the bureaucracy is as much an art form as any human endeavor; ultimately it depends on the people involved, their motivations, and their attitudes. Faults are rarely to be found in the instrument but in the way the instrument is employed.

Bureaucracy is seen as a neutral form that facilitates executing policies. In this theoretical world politicians *set* policy; the public administration and its civil servants merely *execute* policies. In the real world, relations are not nearly that simple. Politicians usually lack expertise in highly complex and technical areas such as welfare delivery, water distribution, or defense allocations, so they turn to senior civil servants for advice and opinion. Civil servants often present to the decision maker a choice between various alternatives, but the structuring of the problem and the implications of the policy are in their hands. Politicians have been known to prefer one policy over another for political reasons; bureaucrats have been known to promote one policy over another because they think that the policy better meets the political goals of the politician. Not least important in this list that confounds the line between administration and politics is the fact that administrators tend to remain, but politicians rotate out of office if their party loses or they move on to other positions.

These considerations point to two major questions regarding the civil service. The first has to do with the degree to which it is motivated by professional as opposed to political considerations. Looked at from another angle, to what extent do appointments and promotions result from merit considerations as opposed to a spoils system in which the victors divide jobs and privileges among their camp followers? The second question has to do with the degree to which the civil service is responsive to public demands and responsible in its actions to the executive, legislature, and ultimately, the voters.

The answers to these questions in Israel are not straightforward.[7] Certainly much lip service is paid to creating a professional, nonpolitical, responsive, and responsible service. And there is evidence that progress has been made. But the evidence is mixed. For example, merit considerations are often spoken of, especially at the lower ranks of hierarchies. But as we move up the ladder of power and prestige, the prevalence of extraprofessional considerations grows.

Israel is a small country, and among the few candidates for a senior position, the front runners are likely to be known. Past performance and the groups to which a candidate is affiliated cannot easily be separated in the minds of an appointment committee. Charges of politicization have frequently been heard from various sides of the political fence.

The dilemma is not an easy one to solve. It is important that years of service in the public administration be rewarded with promotion; on the other hand, politicians in decision-making positions must be able to work with and trust the judgment of senior civil servants. Obviously, this trust will be facilitated by appointing people known to the politicians and who have demonstrated their loyalty. For most of the bureaucrats, professionals, and clerks in public administration (close to 100,000 without the army and teachers), these considerations are not relevant, but they may be very relevant in determining who will lead their ministry, department, or regional office. The specter of politicization has grown more acute as each political party accuses the others of indulging in political appointments. For our purposes there is no better indicator of the problems of the public administration than its failure to develop as a neutral, professional arm of government.

It is a rule of thumb that when a civil service is strong, it is a meritocracy; when it is weak, it is not. In Israel the civil service is neither very strong nor is the system exclusively meritocratic because the political element is never far from the surface in matters of policy, appointment, and execution. So much of economic and social policy is traceable to the centralized control of the finance minister, and so much of the foreign and defense policies to the prime minister and defense minister, that seeking an independent and autonomous civil service is futile. The control of the finance ministry is evident from the structure of the arrangements: the Civil Service Commission is a department of the finance ministry and thus control tends to be centered in the ministry and not at the cabinet level. Many career bureaucrats made the transition in 1977 from Labor to Likud without difficulty, but since this was Israel's first transition it was more of a personal feat than a characteristic of the system.

The relative weakness of the Israeli civil service is obvious from the career compartmentalization that characterizes the system. There is very little real mobility in the Israeli civil service, although almost everyone is rewarded with occasional promotions within the department, division, or ministry. In the United Kingdom it is relatively easy to move horizontally within a department; in the United States it is easy to move vertically from department to department. Both systems provide training for senior civil servants in a variety of tasks and fields. In Israel neither movement is widespread. Everyone in the system crawls forward together, everyone receiving gradual promotions but rarely breaking the pattern of employment into which he or she began work. The lack of lateral transfer promotes inbreeding, which ultimately works to the detriment of the organization.[8]

One group spared the dilemma of having secure tenured positions without much chance of getting beyond their department or ministry includes those few individuals who are in direct contact with the minister: the director general of the ministry, the minister's secretary and driver, and various aides. These are really political appointments. The future of these people depends on their ability and perseverance, and on the political fortunes of their minister. Young aides have been known to use the protégé relations that develop to enhance their career mobility. Successful director generals have been known to use their experience and connections to good political advantage in promoting their careers. Two examples are Levi Eshkol and Shimon Peres, both of whom served as director general of the defense ministry.

It would be too narrow an understanding to think of the public administration as obediently administering policies made elsewhere. The ministries are the major repositories of knowledge and the major collectors of data regarding the topics under their control. As we have seen, most legislation originates in the ministries. Recommendations may or may not be adopted, but that is likely to be a political or budget issue as much as an administrative one.

The role of the minister in the political system is the key to determining how strong the ministry will be. It works the other way as well: Top political leaders head the important ministries. A small ministry such as welfare might become important if the minister holds the balance of power in coalition calculations in the government and Knesset. The major point is that the public administration is an extension of the political system. The organization of the government is primarily affected by political considerations and not by abstract models of rational public administration. There is usually an inverse relationship between the number of ministers and the size of Knesset support for the government coalition. Yitzhak Rabin's government between 1974 and 1977 was one of the largest in the country's history and yet was supported by a bare majority of the Knesset. In 1983 there were 21 ministers in Begin's government, and it faced constant threats of removal of support from coalition partners. The National Unity Government of 1984 had 25 ministers. These situations reflect problems within the ruling party and other parties making up the coalition. After the Likud assumed power in 1977, the leaders declared they would streamline the ministries and reduce the number of ministers. There was some reshuffling (the police ministry was merged with the interior ministry) and some new names were attached to old functions (energy and infrastructure, building and housing, transportation and communication). What should be clear is that these rearrangements were temporary and could be revised if political demands required, in this way providing other politicians with ministries.

The number of ministries is not the only thing determined by politics. That is true of deputy ministers and ministers without portfolio as well. The former may fill roles in the administration. When the education ministry was in the hands of the Labor party, for instance, it was usual to have a religious party deputy minister to handle religious schools' affairs. Other deputy ministers may be appointed as part of the delicate political balance within coalition parties. This is also the case with ministers without portfolio who participate in government meetings but have no direct responsibility for the administration of a ministry. This was the role Menachem Begin filled in the National Unity Government between 1967 and 1970. The National Unity Government of 1984 had four ministers without portfolio.

The fact that the minister's political clout is often a key to the ministry's success gives him (or her) the potential for prestige within his ministry. On the other hand, since the minister is often an outsider to the subject matter of the ministry and dependent on professionals in the ministry to aid him, and since his success as minister is partially connected with the cooperation he receives from his ministry, the minister may become a captive of his ministry. He quickly finds himself representing not only the ministry's policies but also its interests. He becomes the major force in the government committed to retaining or even enlarging his ministry's budget and areas of activity.

Decision making in Israel tends to take one of two forms. One is the crisp, often surprise, decision made by a handful of people that effectively bypasses the public administration. Decisions such as these reflect the centralized nature of the system and the enormous political power implanted in the hands of a few. The second form is one of organized randomness with myriad sections and departments within ministries often expressing conflicting points of view, and fights between ministers and ministries regarding policies. In these latter situations the system is the opposite of hierarchical; it is chaotic. Either no clear policy is articulated because of the conflicting demands or a series of contradictory rules emerge that tend to defeat the policy purpose of any one group.

Perceived centrality to the system is the difference between issuing clear-cut edicts or allowing a situation to develop haphazardly. Michael Brecher has studied foreign policy decisions in times of crisis, and his figures illustrate the situation in Israel. Of the crucial decisions regarding the Six Day War in 1967 and the Yom Kippur War in 1973, Brecher documents the concentration of decision-making power in the hands of the prime minister and a small number of handpicked politicians and senior officials. By way of illustration we may consider the following figures: In the 1967 crisis, Brecher identifies 97 consultative meetings. Of these, 31 had two participants, 23 had three or four, and 24 had five to ten participants. Of these meetings, 65 were of an ad hoc nature, with only 13 being institutional. In 1973 Brecher counts 111 meetings, 42 attended by two participants, 8 by three or four, and 25 by five to ten. Of these, 25 were of an ad hoc nature, and 50 were institutional.[9]

There tends to be a reverse relationship between the importance of the issue being discussed in terms of national security and the number of people involved in the decision-making process. The Sinai Campaign of 1956 and the destruction of Yamit before withdrawing from Sinai in 1982 are examples of decisions taken by Ben-Gurion and Begin respectively, with minimal if any consultation preceding the decisions. In many other areas, however, the effort that would have to be made to coordinate policy or the political capital that would have to be expended to sort out conflicting interests and goals would be greater than it seems to be worth. Israeli public administration has learned to live with this duality of sometimes being ignored in influencing policy and sometimes being frustrated in achieving clear-cut policy.

Planning exists in the system, but it is often irrelevant to the political exigencies in force when projects are actually implemented. Planning demands an assumption of stability regarding the future environment, and that is precisely the characteristic that is lacking in Israel. Parties in power shift, influence within the coalition changes, a new administrator is more important than his predecessor, new interests must be placated—all of these things and others are insidious to the planner. Besides political surprises, there are other uncertainties that interfere with planning. Large-scale immigration, a war, a peace treaty, or an economic crisis can all have devastating effects on plans.[10]

Another problem is bureaucratic conservatism. In-place structures generate interests and jobs and a built-in inertia. Conditions often change more quickly than structures do. Yitzhak Galnoor documented the national bureaucratic structures planned and implemented for the creation of water supplies. When that challenge was successfully faced with the establishment of a national water carrier, water distribution became the pressing bureaucratic problem, and the old structures persisted even though they were clearly unequipped to handle the new challenge.[11]

Overseeing the activities of the public administration is quite developed. The state controller regularly probes into the practices and policies of ministries and other organizations that receive state funds. These reports are presented to and responded by the finance minister (more recently the minister in charge of coordinating economic affairs)—a sure sign of where the power lies. While reports tend to be professional and unbiased, their impact is negligible—serious failures are reported year after year. There must be a formal, ministerial response to the report, but many of the problems remain. The very act of revealing is important, but it is a giant step from controlling.

Another institution that has achieved public acceptance is the commission for citizens' complaints, or the ombudsman. In 1980-81 almost 8000 complaints were heard, and in more than a third of the cases the ministry or other authority was found at fault. Either the ombudsman is becoming less strict or the public administration is improving because in the mid-1970s the percentage of complaints justified out of those decided was almost 50 percent.[12]

Israel's public administration, like many of the country's other institutions, has many rules that indicate the intention of the lawmaker was that it be run in a modern, apolitical, and detached fashion. Unfortunately, rules are not enough to determine the outcome. The human element—the kind of people attracted to the civil service, their motivations and professional competence, the satisfaction they have in their jobs—influences the way in which the administration operates. Add to this the political dimension that always must be taken into account in Israel, and the resulting picture is one of an administration that does not live up to the lawmaker's original intention.

Local Government

Local government and the quality of the services it provides affect every citizen directly. In Israel local government is highly dependent on the national government ministries, but it would be an unfortunate oversight to ignore local government completely. Local government is important because it was in municipal elections that much-discussed electoral reform was achieved. Local government is important because it has become a major source of recruitment of young and promising leaders. Although the national government is dominant, local government provides services, and the local government budget provides a vehicle for redistribution among communities.

The municipal elections of November 1978 were the first to be held using two separate systems: direct election of mayors and proportional election of the council. Until then the proportional system was used exclusively, and the mayor was elected by the council. The selection of the mayor became political with coalition maneuvering within the council. More than that, it was not unknown for national parties to take an interest in the selection of the mayor; parties sometimes used coalition negotiations, especially in the bigger cities, to achieve added leverage in the national negotiations for the composition of the coalition.

In addition to being a pawn in national negotiations, local policy sometimes displays acts that may be interpreted as promoting a politician's status.

The exploitation of a political situation to further personal goals is not unknown in politics. In Israel it has a special name: Kalanterism. The name comes from a municipal crisis that occurred in the Jerusalem city council in August 1956. A majority of the city council decided to remove Mapai Mayor Gershon Agron from the mayor's seat. At that time mayors were elected by the city council in much the same way that prime ministers were elected by the Knesset. The religious parties were displeased with Mayor Agron's support for establishing a Jewish Reform institute of architecture (and attached chapel) in Jerusalem. The opposition General Zionists denounced the economic policies of Agron's administration. Rahamim Kalanter, a member of Hapoel Hamizrachi, defected from the anti-Agron group, voted for Agron, and was subsequently appointed deputy mayor in charge of religious affairs and responsible for the sanitation department. Kalanter's defection was attacked by his political opponents (and former allies) as treason and was defended by his new allies as civic-minded behavior. Kalanter bettered his immediate political fortunes and became immortalized in Israeli political vocabulary.

After years of effort, and at a time of growing popular support for electoral reform before the elections to the Knesset of 1977, a new law regulating municipal elections was passed in 1976. The mayor is now elected by direct vote, the winner being the candidate who receives the most votes providing that he achieves at least 40 percent. If no candidate achieves 40 percent, a second round is held two weeks after the first. In the second round the two biggest vote-getters of the first round compete with each other.[13] In the 1983 municipal elections, about a third of the mayoral contests were decided by a second round. The council is still elected using proportional representation and a fixed list; the minimum required for representation is three-quarters of one percent. The possibility exists for clashes between the popularly elected mayor and the municipal party activists on the council, but except for isolated cases, no major difficulties have yet been encountered under the new law.

Until its assent to national power in 1977, the major political base of the parties of the Likud was in local government. The General Zionists (later the Liberal party) controlled major cities such as Tel Aviv, Ramat Gan, and Netanya. Haifa, Holon, and Bat Yam were long considered safely in the Alignment camp. In 1959 the Mapai candidate became the Tel Aviv mayor; the party held the post until 1973. Competitiveness has become the characteristic of local elections, especially since the advent of local lists that have often shifted the distribution of the vote between the major parties within a locality.[14] The 1983 municipal election results did not clearly indicate whether popular support resided with the Likud or the Alignment; both parties found hopeful signs in the results.

The change in the electoral system captured the spirit of a process that was developing and helped perpetuate it. Young and ambitious politicians, especially from the development towns, emerged in local politics and used this exposure as a base to enter national politics. The young generation of Sephardi Knesset members, especially in the Likud, is the best example: David Levy of Beit Shean, Meir Shitrit of Yavne, Moshe Katzav of Kiryat Malachi, and David Magen of Kiryat Gat. These politicians have counterparts in the Alignment, but those in the Alignment have not reached the levels of visibility and power enjoyed by those in the Likud. Part of the explanation is that being in the party in power allows more exposure; but there is also a feeling that Likud leaders of this type are more "authentic" because they have been active and successful in electoral politics for years, whereas many of their opposite numbers in the Alignment were drafted as pseudo representatives without the same roots in local politics.

The pioneering aspect of electoral reform and the generating of political leadership notwithstanding, the proper perspective for understanding Israeli local government is its extreme dependence on the center. The legacy of Ottoman rule, the British Mandate, and Yishuv politics created a heavy bias toward politics from the capital. The politics of independent Israel reinforced this tradition, and the center retains a vital role in the budgeting, planning, and development of local affairs.

It is not that local authorities are unimportant, but that government ministries are so dominant in determining what goes on at the local level. Past practices of overt favoritism and postponing money transfers have largely disappeared as the system has become more rationalized and bureaucratized. But the political element has not been eradicated. Local governments succeed when they are adept at the political tasks of bargaining and applying political leverage. For it is the ministry of the interior (which is in charge of local authorities) and the ministry of finance (which releases the money) that must be penetrated if a municipality or local council is to enjoy a budget for developing beyond the minimum required by law and regulation.

The most important actor in determining local government affairs and the clearest indication of the retention of the forms of the British Mandate is the district field officer. He is appointed by the interior ministry and has wide-ranging discretionary power regarding local governments, up to and including dismissal of the elected councilors and the appointment of administrators to run the affairs of the local authority. This is in the tradition of direct rule as practiced in British colonies. That the Israeli system carried over this tradition seemed natural given the pressing problems of the independence period, but it has become an important instrument of central control over local affairs and a symbol of the dominant status of the central government and its interior ministry.

The bargaining that can be entered into concerns the size of budget, the programs to be supported, and the timing of program execution. The services the local government provides are varied, and the forms of payments are complex. What determines the success of the local authority, especially the mayor, is access to and influence with bureaucrats, ministers, and party politicians active in the decision-making process regarding local affairs. Mayors who are also Knesset members may have special leverage; perhaps these Knesset members are also mayors because of their political traits. Going beyond the authorized plans demands special approval, which cannot be divorced from the political process.

The functions of local government, including education and health services, are closely monitored and influenced by national rules. The budget and the number of approved job slots are determined by the size of the community and its past activities. Education is a good example of the relation between central and local governments. This is the biggest item for most local authorities, yet most of the important decisions regarding education come from Jerusalem. Teachers are paid by the municipal authority, but the budget to pay them comes from the center. Some local discretion on the part of parents is permitted in the formation of the curriculum, but mostly it is dictated by the ministry of education. Teachers are hired, trained, and licensed by national supervisors. The local government is left with the administration of buildings (which must meet nationally dictated standards), the administration of the payroll, and tasks like hiring guards and nurses for the schools. Teachers throughout the country are paid according to the same contract.

Between one-half and two-thirds of the budget of a local authority comes from the central government. The amount varies by community and type of service. For example, in Kiryat Shmona, a town close to the Lebanese border and made up of many Sephardi families, as much as 90 percent of the welfare budget comes from central authorities. In Givatayim, a middle-class suburb of Tel Aviv, the figure may be a third of that of Kiryat Shmona. Not only are there fewer welfare cases in Givatayim, but the authorities are anxious to bolster the social fabric and morale of the border town, which became the symbol of vulnerability to PLO shelling before the Lebanese war of 1982. Money channeled to the local authorities plays a redistributive role because block grants are used to encourage poorer local authorities to provide better services, though uniformity of service is not sought.[15]

Local governments finance the rest of their activities by collecting taxes, especially property taxes. Two other methods developed over the years are the special municipal endowment funds, especially for cultural purposes, and Project Renewal. The endowment funds, usually collected from wealthy contributors outside Israel, allow mayors to be more flexible and more creative in handling the affairs of the city. The most successful use of this method has been by Teddy Kolleck, mayor of Jerusalem, whose initiatives have been widely acclaimed. Tel Aviv and Haifa have also been successful. But having mentioned Israel's three biggest and most important cities, as we continue down the list the record of success using this method dwindles. Most local authorities cannot compete with the historical and emotional attraction of Jerusalem or the appeal of large cultural, business, and industrial centers like Tel Aviv and Haifa. Thus the funds at their disposal are relatively smaller.

Project Renewal was an attempt to help local authorities by raising funds from Jewish communities abroad. The funds were earmarked to renew neighborhoods that had deteriorated and were becoming slums. The money was to be spent on housing, ecology, and cultural and educational projects. Despite a slow start occasioned by a complex method of coordinating the desires of the citizens with the plans of the local authority, the various government ministries involved, and the Jewish Agency, Project Renewal has begun to help communities and to give a psychological lift to many of their residents.

The role of local government is relatively weak. This is obvious when one considers the structure of the planning and zoning process in Israel. Local, regional, and national commissions must approve plans. The local level plays an important role because its city council, which is popularly elected, must first approve plans. But the approval of local government is not sufficient; local government shares this function with the central government. Plans are then forwarded to the regional commission and in some cases to the national commission. These last two are composed of members who represent government ministries and major local governments. This composition obviously reflects the strength of the political parties in the government, in ministries involved, and in the local councils.

Planning is hindered because of the lag between approval and performance. Sometimes well-placed politician-mayors ignore plans and "create facts." Large projects have at times been approved by various commissions well after the projects were complete. Illegal constructions are widespread; even minor changes in a building often demand a license, and licenses are often not obtained. Enforcing these laws is done sporadically. Rather than force compliance with the plans, fines are usually assessed, and the infraction is not corrected.

The dilemma between lawmaking and law enforcement on the one hand and the provision of services on the other is nowhere better seen than in regard to parking in the large cities. Business, commerce, and entertainment are encouraged to draw customers, clients, and spectators to the cities, which quickly become snarled because the streets and parking lots are inadequate for the growing number of cars in the country. Parking on the sidewalks has spread. This is a clear violation of city laws and a hindrance to residents of the neighborhoods. The municipality is incapable of solving the problems of traffic congestion and parking; instead, it fines the sidewalk parkers and simultaneously encourages them to continue to come to the city.

Local government plays an important role in setting the cultural atmosphere of the city or town. The uneven enforcement of laws prohibiting entertainment on the Sabbath provides a good example. In Tel Aviv, movies operate in some neighborhoods, although no theaters do, and buses do not run. In Haifa some buses run (supposedly because of the Arab population and in accord with the rule of maintaining the status quo), but movies are not permitted. In Jerusalem there are no movies and no buses. Yet the police is a national force and might be expected to use universal rules in law enforcement. What is obvious is that the political climate of the city (especially the size and concentration of the religious population and its political power) influences law enforcement. In the power-sharing balance between national and local government, the former is clearly dominant, but the latter must not be ignored.

12. Ideology, Communication, and Socialization

An ideology is a system of ideas that is normative in nature in that it depicts and justifies an ideal, is based on assumptions concerning the nature of man and social reality, and is action oriented. Politics, being a normative activity, must be accompanied by guidelines against which the actors gauge their behavior. Political ideology is a set of attitudes employed in answering questions of political priority.[1]

Ideology, much like politics, is a concern of the elite. Members of the elite not only produce ideology but are also its largest distributors and consumers. They distribute it to their constituents in programs and statements; they consume ideological output because, trained in the language of ideological discourse, they tend to communicate with their peers in that idiom and are alert and sensitive to messages that have an ideological cast.

In ideological intercourse the elite tends to be active, the people passive. Since ideology is less than salient to the population at large, deviations from ideological purity by the elite are accepted by the electorate. Ideologues in power invariably find that they must modify and adjust ideological pronouncements to fit policy imperatives. Both phenomena can exist simultaneously: Ideology may be modified, yet ideological discourse continues at a high level of intensity.

Two principles to be kept in mind are that ideology is largely an elite affair and that ideology is not necessarily a good predictor of policy. Political communication in Israel tends to be highly ideological, public policy much more pragmatic. Israel has developed a form of mixed economy with elements of capitalist and socialist policies and with a very high level of government activity. This basic form has been developed by ministers of the Alignment left and augmented by officials of the Likud right. The rhetoric of their parties still identifies them as socialist and capitalist, respectively.

Left-Right Continuum

Political discourse, and the ideologies and parties associated with it, is generally based on the assumption that political groupings can be ordered on a continuum from left to right. The concepts left and right (or liberal and conservative in the American version) are common terms in politics. Nevertheless, their meaning is multifaceted at best, elusive at worst, and divergent over time and across polities.

Most often in political discourse the left-right continuum has been given economic meaning, referring to equality as opposed to inequality, government intervention as opposed to free enterprise, tolerance of change as opposed to adherence to the status quo. Other issues, such as abortion, foreign aid, and integration, have all been subsumed under these headings in their time. On closer examination, however, it becomes clear that notions of left and right are too simplistic to capture the complexity of reality. It is important to consider the problems related to a left-right continuum.[2]

First, the assumption of unidimensionality is explicitly made in discussing a left-right continuum, yet it is questionable whether so simple a concept is adequate. The test is whether the continuum provides an ordering of parties such that if we know, for example, that a party is on the right of the continuum, we then know its views on the issues of the day. Clearly this is not the case. The positions of Israeli parties on issues raised by the role of religion in the state, for example, are not related to the locations of the party on the continuum when arranged by social welfare policy or foreign policy. The left would be expected to be least amenable to the religious position, the right more so. Yet much of the Liberal party takes a "leftist" position on these questions, and many Labor party leaders accepted religious policy positions to maintain the coalition and their power. Different issues are salient for various parties. In Israel at least two, and possibly more, dimensions are needed for making sense of the orderings of political parties.

A second problem relating to the left-right continuum has to do with the meanings of *left* and *right*. Broadly, the left represents the socialist values of equality, social justice, and international cooperation and brotherhood. The right has historically been associated with capitalist values such as freedom of opportunity, competition, restricted government activity, and nationalism. In certain senses this description fits Israel, but in other important senses it is incomplete. For many years, and certainly since the Six Day War, the major Zionist parties have competed in their nationalism. The highest values have been security and Israel as a Jewish state. The Likud has concluded that these goals can be achieved using a firm, nonconciliatory policy, and the Alignment has tended to favor more flexibility and concession. But the Alignment began the policy of settling the territories, and the Likud ceded the Sinai to the Egyptians. Neither of these government actions could have been anticipated if only the left-right continuum were our guide. Being a party of the "left" did not

TABLE 12.1
PARTIES ACCORDING TO POSITIONS CONCERNING
THE ARAB-ISRAELI CONFLICT

		1, 2	3, 4, 5	6	7, 8, 9	10, 11, 12	13
Left	Extra-Parliamentary Left (Matzpen, etc.)	+	+	+	+	+	+
	Democratic Front for Peace and Equality (Rakah)	–	+	+	+	+	+
	Shelli	–	–	+	+	+	+
	Mapam, Independent Liberals, Civil Rights Movement	–	–	–	+	+	+
	Labor, DMC, Agudat Israel	–	–	–	–	+	+
	Likud, NRP, Poalei Agudat Israel	–	–	–	–	–	+
Right	Extra-Parliamentary Right (Rabbi Meir Kahane, etc.)	–	–	–	–	–	–

KEY 1. In favor of a "secular, democratic Palestinian state" or the imposition of the 1947 UN partition plan.
2. Willing to return to the pre-1967 cease-fire lines.
3. Willing to return Jerusalem to its pre-1967 status.
4. Willing to define peace in terms that are not absolute.
5. Willing to form an independent Palestinian state on the West Bank and in Gaza.
6. Willing to negotiate with the PLO without preconditions.
7. Ready to negotiate with the PLO on the condition that it renounces terrorism and formally recognizes Israel.
8. Supports special arrangements in Jerusalem on the basis of "religious autonomy" within the framework of a final peace agreement.
9. Rejects settling the West Bank for reasons other than security.
10. Ready for territorial compromise on the West Bank.
11. Rejects the relinquishing of sovereignty over the West Bank, and rejects giving full citizenship to its inhabitants.
12. Ready to compromise on the Golan Heights and in Sinai.
13. Objects to planning for and encouraging Arab emigration.

SOURCE: Party publications and official platforms for the 1977 elections; and A. Diskin, "The 1977 Interparty Distances: A Three-level Analysis," in *The Elections in Israel—1977,* ed. Asher Arian (Jerusalem: Jerusalem Academic Press, 1980), 215.

prevent Ahdut Haavoda in the 1950s from taking a very strong militant line against neighboring Arab states. And it was on this very issue that the party split from Mapam in 1954.

Table 12.1 presents differences among the parties concerning the Arab-Israeli conflict. The table indicates that it is the parties of the extreme left of the continuum in which there are differences, that the four largest parties of the 1977 elections (Labor, DMC, Likud, and NRP) are in the middle tending toward the right, and that the left-right continuum fails to distinguish among the parties on this most critical issue. The major parties are close on this issue with the extremes, especially the left, much more spread out.

This phenomenon would hold as well for social and economic issues such as compulsory arbitration in public-sector labor disputes or welfare benefits to the underprivileged. Again, the large parties would cluster toward the center; variation would be evident among extreme, and weaker, political groups. On religious matters, the problem is more complex. Almost all secular parties stress the importance of religious freedom and civil rights, and the religious parties promote the importance of behavior in accordance with Jewish religious law. Secular parties tend to release their Knesset members from the obligation of party discipline on Knesset votes on these issues by referring to such issues as matters of personal conscience. Often, however, the coalition needs of the party in power offset the principle of freedom of conscience and the Knesset member finds himself in the dilemma of choosing between his personal views, his party's ideological stand, and his party's political needs.

A third difficulty has to do with the lack of a fixed structure in the continuum. The meaning of left and right may well change over time. The ranking provided by the continuum today may well be different from that of earlier years. Party positions change. The NRP was much less militant in its foreign policy before the 1967 war than after it. Since then, it has become a prominent spokesman for the positions of Israeli settlement on the West Bank of the Jordan and Greater Israel. This stunning change must be understood in terms of the changes in the mood of the times, the ascension of a young generation of leaders in the NRP, and the increased salience of these issues in the public mind.

The difficulty of fixed structure is also demonstrated by the lack of necessary connection between party platform and policy when that party is in power. Power tends to modify extreme positions because responsibility is more keenly felt as problems are confronted. Opposition affords a politician the luxury of being judged by his words and not by his deeds. The economic policies followed by Pinhas Sapir when he was finance minister in the 1960s would not have been anticipated by a student of socialist economic theory. But for a dynamic leader faced with difficult problems, Sapir's program was conceived as an answer to national needs; only then was the question of ideological purity addressed. His socialist party could encourage private investment and even subsidize it to achieve goals thought important. Leaders such as Sapir have no problem with ideology because ideology is never rigid; only some ideologues are.

The surprise that followed Prime Minister Begin's turnabout on the question of the peace negotiations with Egypt that culminated in the Camp David agreements is a good example of the inadequacy of the continuum to provide precise indication of the behavior of the politician in a given situation. Begin had been associated with tough, nationalist stands throughout 29 years of parliamentary opposition. Upon achieving power and following Sadat's visit in November 1977, Begin altered many of his views. Consider also the opposition of the Labor party to settle Jews in densely populated Arab areas in the territories. Histadrut economic concerns run by Labor are active there. While the continuum implies fixed structure, political reality is much more fluid.

A fourth problem of the left-right continuum is the difficulty in determining what a party's position is on a given issue. Larger parties have increasingly refrained from clearly stating ideological positions in order to include diverse elements. The two biggest groupings, the Likud and the Alignment, themselves comprise separate and autonomous political parties. Often the platforms of the Herut and Liberal parties (or the Labor party and Mapam) are not identical. There is a great pressure to generalize ideological positions and make them lose specific meaning.

A good example of this is the party platforms prior to the 1969 elections, which took place after the Six Day War. *Alignment:* Until peace comes, our forces will remain on all the cease-fire lines. . . . Israel will never return to the armistice lines used before the Six Day War. . . . Additional settlements will be established in the border areas. *Gahal:* Our security requirements in peace treaties with Arab states, stemming from our experience, demand our ruling in areas that served as the basis of our enemies' aggression. . . . Large-scale Jewish settlement . . . must be given priority in the development plans of the state. *NRP:* . . . will work for continued large-scale, speedy urban and rural settlements in the liberated areas.

The most striking feature of these excerpts on security policy from the platforms of the country's three strongest parties is their similarity. Both the Alignment and Gahal platforms were straining toward the middle. Within the Labor party there was considerable difference of opinion regarding security policy, Eban and Sapir supposedly being much more dovelike than Dayan, Allon or Golda Meir. As if these differences were not enough, the platform committee had to attend to the demands of Mapam, the group farthest to the left in the Alignment. That the final document turned out as tough as it did caused much ill feeling among Mapam members. The possibility of returning territory (the word "retreat" is never used) is only mentioned in a positive form: "Until peace comes, our forces will remain on all the cease-fire lines." But the next sentence, "Israel will never return to the armistice lines used before the Six Day War," quickly recovers the momentarily lost initiative of the more hawklike.

It used to be that you could tell a person's position by whether he talked about the "conquered territories" or the "liberated territories." Both Gahal and the NRP used the phrase "liberated territories." The Alignment talked only of the "territories." When speaking of settlements, it could not bring itself to use the word "territories"; instead, it stated that "additional settlements will be established in the border areas." Gahal too strained a bit toward the center, but not nearly as hard. Those looking for the statement "not one inch of land will be returned" will look in vain. Deleting this line was in deference to the more centrist Liberal party, many of whose leaders became uncomfortable when categoric language was used.

By the 1980s some movement was evident. The Likud government spoke only of Judea and Samaria instead of the West Bank territories, thereby annexing them semantically. The Alignment approved a platform calling for territorial concessions for a true peace, placing themselves in firm opposition to the Likud government. The NRP, after losing half its electoral strength in 1981, attempted to moderate some of its more extreme statements on the territories.

All these changes indicate the election platform is a compromise among the factions of a party and the constitutent parts of a list. On very difficult issues the surest formula is not to mention them. According to an old saying, party platforms are like train platforms—something to get in on, not to stand on. In addition, a party platform does not commit the party in any legal sense. If a party wishes, it may ignore part of its platform entirely. A good example of this is the recurring commitment of the platform of the Democratic party in the United States to move its embassy to Jerusalem from Tel Aviv. Just as consistently as the platform has promised it, Democratic Presidents have ignored it.

A fifth problem relates to how the continuum is perceived and understood by the electorate. In Israel, as in other countries, only people with high levels of sophistication in conceptualizing politics concern themselves with the left-right continuum. For most people, politics is a matter of parties and leaders. The images of parties and leaders are no less important than ideological issues of left and right. Alternately, some think of politics in terms of specific questions facing the polity or in terms of the ability of a party to satisfy group demands. The left-right continuum in Israel plays more of a political function than an ideological one. That is the topic of the next section.

Left-Right, Attitudes, and the Vote

The left-right continuum is a useful shorthand for the initiated to understand and order the political scene.[3] But it is misleading to expect the parties on our man-made continuum to conform in their behavior to our expectations. For most people, left and right are political labels used to make sense of the party system. The left-right label is part of one's political vocabulary, of one's political education. It is learned the way one learns about other labels, being Jewish or being Israeli. Behavior reinforces this labeling. The process seems to work this way: Having voted Likud and learned that it corresponds with "right," one identifies with that label. Most people do not start by being for a certain policy, identifying that policy with left or right, and then searching for the appropriate party. The left-right label seems to be related and probably stems from one's party identification.

The best evidence of this is to consider the distribution of left and right in the Israeli population over a 22-year period. It is often observed that Israel has moved to the right; the data presented in table 12.2 bear out this contention. The right has increased almost fivefold, from 8 percent in 1962, to 16 percent in 1969, to 39 percent in 1984. Not only has the answer become more legitimate in the system—so too has the word. When the Israel Institute of Applied Social Research ran a pre-test before the 1962 study, the "right" political trend was found to be so discredited that it was decided to substitute the political party of the right—Herut—in the questionnaire. The final version of the question had as its extremes "Marxist left" and "Herut," with "moderate left" and "center" as the other two categories. By 1969 this problem had disappeared, and the terms left and right were used for the extreme responses. By 1981, some studies began splitting the "right" response into "right" and "moderate right" because the distribution had so shifted over time.

If the left-right continuum were a representation of ideological differences in Israel, we would expect that as the right grows, so too should the distribution on attitudes identified with a "right" ideology. The fascinating finding is that although the country has moved to the right politically, there is a stability of attitude over time in the society. For example, 90 percent in 1969 favored returning none of the territories or only a small part, and 92 percent in 1981, after most of Sinai had been returned.

This attitudinal stability even as the political continuum is moving to the right is more confounding because the population has not become more capitalist in economic matters, as might be expected from the "right" label. Almost 60 percent favor socialism in the surveys. Government intervention is often de-

TABLE 12.2
LEFT-RIGHT TENDENCY, 1962-84[a]
(in percent)

	1962	1969	1973[c]	1977	1981	1984
Left-Right Label[b]						
Left	31	6	3	4	4	5
Moderate Left		19	19	14	13	18
Center	23	26	33	29	39	21
Right	8	16	23	28	32	39
Religious	5	6	7	6	6	2
No interest in politics; no answer	33	27	15	19	6	15
Economy						
Capitalist	7	10		11	10	7
More capitalist	19	24	not	18	25	28
More socialist	39	38	asked	31	40	50
Socialist	15	19		25	20	6
No answer	20	9		15	5	9
Return the Territories						
None		38	31	41	50	41
A small part	not	52	52	43	42	44
Most	asked	5	10	7	4	6
All		1	2	7	3	8
No answer		4	5	2	1	2
Sample size:	1170	1314	1939	1372	1249	1259

a. From 1962 through 1977 the surveys were conducted by the Israel Institute of Applied Social Research; the 1981 and 1984 surveys were by the Dahaf Research Institute.
b. The question was "With which political tendency do you identify?" The first four responses were read, the last two were not.
c. The 1969 "return the territories question" was posed in August to a sample of 380 respondents.

cried and the economy has been liberalized, yet the movement to the right is not reflected in this important attitude. The stability of these attitudes over time forces us to consider the sense in which the system has changed.

What has happened in Israel over the last few decades is a process of political change, not ideological change. The growth of the Likud and the growth of the right must be understood as a reaction to the years of dominance of the Alignment and the left. The terms are important as labels but not necessarily as instructors of ideological content. Likud means not only "right," it also means non-Alignment and hence non-"left." Left-right has a greater importance in its labeling function than its ability to instruct regarding ideological questions. Beyond the aggregate stability of attitudes and simultaneous movement to the right of party fortunes and labels, another good example of this labeling function is the very stable "religious" response. A category not offered to the respondents in the surveys, a steady 5 to 7 percent of the samples through 1981 volunteered the "religious" answer when asked to identify the political label with which they identified, and those are the religious parties' voters. In 1984, the rate fell to 2 percent, probably because the religious parties were so fragmented and because many religious voters chose to vote for the rightist Likud and Tehiya.

Most people do not impute issue meaning to left and right. When asked about its meaning, 70 percent mentioned nothing. Of the 30 percent who did respond, the farther to the right one is, the more likely there will be a response. This seems to indicate that the former dominant left is in retreat ideologically as well as politically and that its adherents are less equipped to confront the issues than the more assertive voters of the right. The political pendulum in Israel at the beginning of the 1980s was swinging in their favor, and the respondents of the right were more prone to talk about it. These data are similar to findings for the United States, Britain, and other countries regarding the prevalence and function of ideology and the left-right continuum.[4]

The interrelations among vote, left-right label, and attitudes provide further evidence for the contention that political change—and not ideological change—is the major feature of the shifting fortunes of political life in Israel and that left-right labels are partisan rather than ideological. Between 1969 and 1981 the Alignment lost support and the Likud gained. More important, the correlation between vote and political label tended to rise during this time, indicating that the distribution of the left-right label became more important in a political context of competition than when the plurality of most groups supported the same party. Both the right and the Likud have grown; only the percentage of those who report they will vote Alignment was in decline. The portion of the Alignment voters who identified themselves as left was constant. The shrinkage of the left was a result of the decline of the Alignment; the growth of the right stemmed from greater legitimacy and increasing political power of the Likud.

That political labels should fill a function of veto by pointing out whom we want to avoid is not surprising to observers who know the nature of political communication in Israel. This function was filled by the left in the pre-state and early state eras—the period of dominance—when the left was widely considered as the appropriate legitimate authority in the system. As that basic understanding is now being overturned, the term "right" fills the role of identifying the bad guys (the left) as much as it does of identifying the group with which one might wish to identify (the right). The prime motivator is the identification with one of the political parties; from that flows identification with one of the political labels.

The explanation for the pattern of increasing correlation between vote and label is the shift from dominance to competitiveness. In a dominant-party system, the clarity of signal of the dominant party is less crucial because most groups support it anyway. No political cues are needed, no ideological labels are necessary to more clearly identify the object of the vote. The message can remain fuzzy as long as political dominance is not at stake. The more competitive the system, the more important the ideological labels and the cueing function of the campaign. This interpretation seems to fly in the face of the inherited wisdom that says that competitive systems, especially if two large parties are competing between themselves, will work to blur the ideological message in order to appeal to the center. In reality, no contradiction exists here. The party competing in a two-party system will not strive for ideological clarity but will endeavor to accurately cue its supporters, using labels such as left and right, and thereby strengthen their decision to vote for the party. The cue is important as an additional support for the voting decision, not as a correlate of ideological context. This explains why in Israel, in the long term, the correlation between left-right tendency and vote tends to increase as the system passes from dominance to competitiveness.

In a basic sense all politics in Israel are ideological. Messages are packaged in ideological containers, codewords are frequently attached. "Isms" and phrases such as fascism, socialism, Revisionism, and the basic values of the labor movement abounded in the campaigns of the 1980s; yet for many of the voters they were empty sounds. The style of Israeli political communication has overshadowed the importance of the substance.

Ideological differences among the parties in Israel have diminished over time, and campaigns have become less ideological. Elections have turned on party image and leader popularity, with ideological themes providing a muted accompaniment to the main melodies. Attitudes do not predict voting behavior well, nor do they predict left-right labeling well. In the five elections since 1969, the correlations of attitudes and foreign policy and the economy tend to be weakly related with vote and political label, and never reach the level of the correlations between vote and political label.

The process of filtering, or the use of selective perception in handling political cues, is also evident. The images of the ideal party and of the two major parties on the right-left continuum were measured over time using semantic differential questions. In May 1973, before the October Yom Kippur War presented the Alignment with a fatal blow to its dominance, the ideal party was already perceived to be the right; the Likud was thought of as strongly right, but even the Alignment was more right than left. By 1981, the passing of dominance and advent of competitiveness had clearly emerged. While Alignment voters perceived things much as they did in 1973, Likud voters suddenly perceived the Alignment as much more left than in the past. The cue had been received! The Alignment was to be rejected. The Likud cue to its voters to strengthen their vote was that the Alignment is now left and must be rejected not only on political grounds but on ideological ones as well. Whereas Likud voters perceived their party as right over time, they perceived the Alignment as moving to the left. In a relative sense, then, they too have moved to the right.

Political Communication

A free press is a major prerequisite of a democratic system, and Israel's record on this score is a good one. The dilemmas posed by the difficult security problems Israel faces make its tradition of having a lively press even more impressive. Two conflicting sets of priorities lie at the base of the dilemma. On the one hand, there are the values of free speech, freedom of the press, and the right of the people to know. All of these are basic democratic rights. On the other hand, there is the legitimate demand to prevent publication of information that will be of use to the enemy. Some cases are clear-cut: Divulging information about troop strength and location may legitimately be suspended; quoting an opposition politician who thinks the government's policy is wrong must be allowed. The difficulties are at the borderline: Should stories that morale is low or emigration rising or that a minister says he has no faith in the senior army command be permitted or not?

The answer to the question of a free press in Israel is difficult; its implementation even more so, since freedom of the press is not safeguarded by constitutional or legal provisions. On the contrary, almost all of the legislation enacted enables the prevention of publishing or broadcasting news. In fact, the Israeli press operates freely because the authorities allow it to do so through voluntary arrangements worked out by them and the editors of the largest daily newspapers. The State Security Ordinance (Emergency Regulations) is the legal basis for the military censorship of news published in Israel or abroad that could "endanger the defense of Israel, or the well-being of the public, or public order." Appeals may be heard by a special committee of three, representing the press, the military, and the general public. While unanimous decisions are final, majority decisions can be appealed to the chief of staff. The Press Ordinance of 1933, issued during the Mandate and still in effect, requires licensing of all newspapers and printing houses by the interior ministry. The license may be revoked for incitement "endangering public order."[5]

Israelis consume news at very high rates. More than three-fourths of the Jewish population over the age of fourteen read a newspaper at least one day a week, and about two-thirds read one daily; almost half the population reads two or more papers daily.[6] Ninety-six percent of the population view television on a regular basis, with 81 percent watching the nightly news program.[7]

The Hebrew press is active and competitive. The two largest newspapers are *Yediot Aharonot* and *Maariv*. Both papers are mass-circulation afternoon tabloids. In 1981, *Yediot* was read by 45.6 percent of the reading public, *Maariv* by 28.4 percent.[8] Both papers are independently owned and present a wide range of opinions in their signed columns. The editorial tone of both papers tends to be right of center. The important Hebrew morning paper is *Haaretz,* with 10.6 percent of the market. It is probably the most prestigious of Israel's papers, blending liberal values and pragmatic Zionism in its editorial columns.

Newspapers affiliated with political parties were much more important during the Yishuv and in the early state years. They provided the political line to activists and served as important channels of communication among segments of the party. With statehood, their partisan function was eclipsed by the more general mass-circulation papers. These appealed to the growing market and downplayed political and ideological matters. The one party paper that is still important in a national sense is *Davar,* the Histadrut newspaper, with a readership of 3.4 percent of the reading public. In recent years its editorial staff has tended to be free from political inference, but the newpaper is heavily subsidized by the Histadrut and is identified with the Labor party.

Newspapers depend on good reporting, and reporters are only as good as their sources. Even reporters for independent newspapers must enter tacit agreements with politicians to receive information. The politician's interest is to have his name in print, preferably with his point of view as well. The reporter wants to know what is really going on. Symbiotic relations are bound to develop. And in Israel, a small country where everyone who counts knows everyone else, and a country with a competitive press and a news-attentive population, these symbiotic relations are useful to both reporter and politician. Information or opinions that it would be inappropriate to have the minister reveal can be released through the friendly reporter. This may be for public consumption or as part of the intragovernment or intraparty battle taking place at the moment, or for international targets.

Leaks are generated the same way. Reporters do not create leaks from government meetings or secret deliberations. Leaks are fed reporters by ministers who take part in these consultations and have an interest in having information that may be helpful to them or harmful to their opponents brought to public attention. Periodically there is a public uproar regarding the secrecy of deliberations and the lack of professional discipline on the part of the newspapers. The real culprit is, of course, the minister who provides the information. In the debate over the role of the press in the Lebanese war, for instance, it was maintained that the antigovernment position expressed by the Alignment opposition was detrimental to the morale of the troops and the civilian population. Reports of dissent within the government itself were even more harmful to public morale. Note that the source of these reports was not the opposition but members of the government.

Preventing leaks is a matter of concern to all governments. In the 1950s Ben-Gurion resigned the premiership over leaks in his government and returned to the job only after extracting support for legislation making all cabinet proceedings secret. That was not as successful a solution as the arrangement worked out in 1966 in which deliberations of the Cabinet Security Committee were defined as "state secrets," which meant that unauthorized publication could be punished as "severe espionage." Since the 1970s, a practice has developed of declaring cabinet meetings special sessions of the Security Committee, thus achieving total secrecy. This practice can easily be abused. The Begin government attempted, unsuccessfully, to consider settlement policy under these total blackout rules. The line that protects the government's right to keep its secrets safe is also the line that may infringe on the public's right to know. The balance is a difficult one, but one that is crucial to maintain in a democracy.

The competition of the published word is sharply contrasted by the monopoly enjoyed by radio and television. Although there are a number of radio stations, including one run by the IDF, radio news broadcasts all stem from the same organization. There is only one television channel, although there has been talk of establishing a second one. Radio and television operate under the Israel Broadcasting Authority, set up in 1965, which is patterned on the British Broadcasting Corporation. Before the law was passed, radio was located in the prime minister's office (television did not yet exist), and political interference in broadcasting was not unknown. The Broadcasting Authority brought much more autonomy to the world of the airwaves but did not divorce programming and news broadcasting from the political sphere. The plenum of the authority has 31 members, the board seven. The plenum meets three times a year, the board weekly. Members are appointed to a five-year term by the government according to a party key that assures coalition control of the authority, at least at the moment of appointment. The British model calls for nonpolitical appointments based on ability, professional expertise, and independence; the Israeli system clearly deviates from that norm. The director general is appointed by the government in Israel and by the board in Britain. Again, political rather than professional considerations predominate.[9]

The composition of the authority and its exposure to the political process mean that the staff has to keep political considerations in mind, even if it is not given clear-cut political dictates. Deliberations within the authority often reflect the political debate in the country. Members from parties participating in the government coalition are likely to argue that the authority emphasizes negative aspects of life in Israel, while its mandate should call for encouraging the public by emphasizing the positive. Opposition party members are likely to be critical of reporting they perceive as propaganda for the party in power. Who should be interviewed, how much weight should be given to a story, and what is news are not only professional questions of radio or television journalism. In Israel they are very important political questions.

While the Broadcasting Authority law affords Israeli television and radio a monopoly on news broadcast in Israel, in a wider sense there is competition. It comes from the foreign journalists who cover stories in Israel, foreign television and radio signals received in Israel, and foreign publications distributed without restriction. Other points of view are available. When the security forces prohibited coverage of the early phases of the Lebanese war, international coverage originated from the Lebanese side of the battle lines. Inevitably reporters saw the war, and reported it, through the perspective of the Palestinian forces and the Lebanese civilians. No countervailing reporting was permitted at first. This inflicted severe damage on Israel in Western public opinion.

In internal politics Israeli journalists can be as inquisitive and courageous — few are — as any in the world. In most security areas they are more restrained than foreign journalists. This stems from national loyalty, a desire to maintain good relations with sources, and a self-imposed mechanism of self-censorship. Foreign correspondents usually work without these restraints, sometimes leaving the impression that Israeli journalists are lackeys of the government. In the government's attempt to win the battle of public opinion it must walk the hazardous line between controlling the news and those who report it and respecting the right of the people — and the world — to know. The more controversial the policy that lies at the heart of the story (Israel's policy regarding the territories, for instance), the harder this dilemma is.

Public opinion is a phantom often worshipped by politicians and the press. Public opinion is of course more than simply a computation of the attitudes of members of the population. Public opinion must be understood in terms of the distribution of opinions within the population, the intensity with which they are held, their stability, and the organizational means used to translate the opinions into actions that will have an impact on policy.[10] Demonstrators outside Mapai party headquarters in 1967 are said to have had an impact on the decision to appoint Moshe Dayan minister of defense before the Six Day War. The mass rally of hundreds of thousands in the summer of 1982 preceded the government's decision to reverse itself and set up a commission of inquiry into the events that occurred in the Palestinian refugee camps of Sabra and Shatilla in Beirut. These were expressions of "public opinion," but they were also carefully organized demonstrations in support for ideas frequently expressed in the press.

Television has become a major focus of the electoral campaign. In the past the mass rally or the visit of politicians to the neighborhood or place of work were ways that the public was exposed to competing politicians. During the month preceding the elections, no candidate's picture may be shown on television in order to prevent giving unfair advantage to one side or the other. Broadcast time for the parties on radio and television during the campaign, however, is provided free of charge and is allocated in proportion to the party's strength in the outgoing Knesset. Each list competing was provided with a base of ten minutes on television in the 1981 campaign with six additional minutes for each member in the outgoing Knesset. Thus the Likud, which had a much bigger delegation in the outgoing Knesset than did the Alignment, had more television time during the campaign. Small parties and new ones had very little.

The impact of the medium on the electorate is hard to determine but we know that in 1977 about half the population viewed most of the party political broadcasts. Nevertheless, only 7 percent of the sample reported in 1981 that television helped them very much in deciding how to vote, a third said somewhat, almost 60 percent said that it did not help at all. These figures are similar, if a bit more favorable to the impact of television, than the figures for newspapers and radio.

Newspaper advertising is extensive during the campaign. A major party can limit a paper's income by not advertising or advertising little in it. The Likud never emphasized advertising in *Davar,* the paper identified with the Labor party. But in the 1981 elections it also advertised very little in *Haaretz* as a protest against that paper's editorial policy, and evidently under the assumption that readers of *Haaretz* were unlikely to vote for the Likud or would be exposed to its campaign in one of the mass-circulation afternoon papers.[11]

Political Socialization

Political socialization refers to the process in which values important to the political system are internalized. The way a person responds to authority, the way he (or she) perceives his responsibility toward the collectivity, whether he sees himself as active or passive in the political system—these are all topics affected by one's political socialization. More party-specific and issue-specific dimensions are also involved: For whom should I vote? What is my attitude regarding the territories?[12]

Political socialization studies place great emphasis on the formative years of childhood, adolescence, and early adulthood in determining one's political outlook and later behavior. Any individual is influenced both by early experiences (the primacy hypothesis) and by current political developments and issues (the recency hypothesis).[13] No thorough research has yet been done in Israel to throw light on the primacy/recency argument. There is no doubt that one's primary reference groups in the formative years influence one's political ideas. Most Israelis report that they vote as their families do, and this is true in other countries as well. The exact rate of congruence between the voter and his or her family is difficult to ascertain because "one's family" may be understood to include only spouse or parents or a much more extended group. In 1981 the question was put whether "your family" votes as you do; 55 percent said yes, 25 percent said no, 18 percent reported that they did not know how their family votes. (An interesting aspect of this matter points to the independent temperament of Israelis. When the question was phrased "Do you vote as other members of your family?" a much lower agreement rate was recorded. The respondent is the leader, and the family acts as he does, not vice versa.)

Schools and the youth culture are important sources of influence in political socialization. The inherited wisdom regarding the Israeli polity is that in the pre-state period and in the first years of statehood, schools and youth movements were influential agents in the hands of political parties. As such, it is not surprising that much of the curriculum dealt with material that could be used to strengthen identification with Zionism and with the political struggle that the Yishuv had undertaken.[14]

After independence and the changes in the school population as the result of mass immigration, the school curriculum began more fully to represent the complexity of Israeli society. Schools, especially high schools, were no longer treated as sources of elitist education but stressed public and mass education, and achieved almost universal attendance through the age of sixteen. This change is clear in high school civics instruction. Early texts barely mentioned political parties, although the role of the political party was dominant in almost every sphere of life. Over time, issues that were salient in public life were discussed in the schools, and representatives of various points of view were invited to speak.

The decline of the youth movements paralleled the general decline of party-related activity after the founding of the state. Alternative frameworks within the school system competed with the particularistic youth movements. Nonetheless, peer-group pressure remains strong among Israeli youth in general. One discerns high levels of conformity in dress, entertainment, leisure-time activity, and life style. These are direct carryovers of the more organized pressures of youth movements, even though fewer youths are organized in these political and ideological movements.[15]

The army service of young Israelis coincides with their entrance into active participation in politics by virtue of their right to vote, and with the period in which historical events can have their strongest ongoing impact on the future political behavior of an individual. A good case in point is the vote of the army in 1973. Some two months after the Yom Kippur War, army voters supported the Likud at a higher rate than did the general population. For some time, the young had tended to support the Likud at higher rates, but evidently the war accelerated this phenomenon.[16] Army service is not only important in terms of specific acts of voting. Perhaps more crucially it is in the army that the young citizen receives his first independent taste of the systems of hierarchy and bureaucracy that are such important features of Israel's political culture.

The agents of socialization—family, friends, schools, army—are usually crucial for relatively set periods of time. The system also acts to reinforce attitudes and predispositions. The most obvious examples are the national pageants associated with events such as Holocaust Day and Independence Day, which tug at the collective memory and attempt to rekindle feelings of collectivity, shared destiny, and patriotism. More subtle are the presentation of Jewish holidays in ways that reinforce national and patriotic feelings. In these efforts the governing system—ministries, television and radio—play a central role.[17]

Political socialization leads to the internalization of values and attitudes, but it does not occur in a vacuum. It is clear that the family and its social environment will be important conditioners of the results of political socialization. In Israel's varied society, different patterns are obviously at work on different parts of the population. Extreme examples are provided by groups that are relatively isolated from general society, such as kibbutz members and the ultra-orthodox, who live in relatively hermetic quarters. Both groups seem relatively successful in socializing their later generations politically if we use community perpetuation and voting patterns as indicators. There are many cases of people leaving these groups and out-voting, but compared to the general society, rates of conformity there are high.

Leonard Fein studied political socialization in Israel in the early 1960s and distinguished among moderns, transitionals, and traditionals. The distinctions were made according to education, orientation toward change, empathy, and religious orthodoxy. He found that most moderns were Westerners, and most traditionals were Easterners, with the transitionals being more heterogeneous but dominated by Easterners.[18] High levels of support for democratic processes, tolerance of other political groups, frequent discussion of politics, and participation in the system characterize the modern; the traditional is characterized by the opposite, with the transitional a composite. The typology is still relevant, but it is obvious that the dimensions of the groups have changed. In the early 1960s the traditional family with its strong patriarch was likely to be dominant in traditional groups; today, the authority of the patriarch has been displaced in many cases by his Israel-born or Israel-trained sons. The decline of the patriarchical family was a sharp blow to large groups of immigrating traditionals, but in their place has emerged a generation of their sons who are in command of more modern ways without totally rejecting traditional patterns.

As a country of immigration, Israel has had experience with the resocialization of immigrants, usually adults. Adult immigrants arrive after the early phases of their political socialization are over. Their experiences before arriving in Israel may be thought of as important in determining their political predispositions in Israel. For many, especially Europeans, the various Zionist parties were active and exposed the potential immigrants to the ideological differences among them well before their arrival in the country. For many others, Israel was a place of refuge after the displacements caused by the war in Europe. Ideological issues were not really at stake. For many Sephardim who arrived in Israel in this period, religious motivation and messianic vision were more central than earthly divisions among competing political groups. Almost all these groups came from political systems that lacked democratic traditions. Being introduced to a democratic regime was as novel for Russian immigrants in 1980 as it was for Poles or Moroccans in the 1950s. After carefully studying the political resocialization of Soviet and American immigrants to Israel in the early 1970s, Zvi Gitelman concluded that the process "affects attitudes toward specific issues most, abstract political ideas less, and fundamental orientations to politics least."[19]

The children of Israel who wandered in the desert for 40 years before entering the promised land were a transitional generation, not capable, we are told, of independence. As Israel approaches its 40th anniversary of independence the transitional generation is becoming smaller in number, and the population is dominated more and more by citizens born in Israel. Those born and raised in Israel have known no other, predemocratic or nondemocratic, experience. Unlike their forefathers, they were born to democracy. They have witnessed the institutionalization of democratic processes in the country despite the severe challenges that have faced the system and the rotation of power from one party to another.

Democratic Norms and Political Tolerance

Israelis support abstract democratic norms at very high rates. The belief in majority rule, in freedom of expression, in the right of the citizen to criticize the government, and in equality before the law is supported by between 80 and 90 percent of the population.[20] But when the question becomes less abstract and more salient in the political context, the rate of democratic support falters. Only two-thirds agree that minority-opinion groups should be allowed to operate freely to gain majority support for their positions. The disparity between abstract norms and practical tolerance is seen even more clearly when the problem is concretized by referring to the group least liked by the respondent. In Israel in the 1980s the "least liked" groups most often mentioned were on the political left and outside the Zionist consensus. Seventy-three percent of the sample mentioned these groups, with "groups linked to the PLO" getting 35 percent of the mentions, Rakah 30 percent, and groups such as Peace Now, Shelli, and Matzpen 8 percent. Seven percent chose right-wing groups such as Gush Emunim and Rabbi Meir Kahane's Kach, and 13 percent mentioned the ultra-orthodox anti-Zionist Naturai Karta. When the abstract norm of free speech (supported by 83 percent) was applied to the least-liked group, only 38 percent supported it.

Michal Shamir and John Sullivan have found that the overall levels of political tolerance in Israel, while not high, are similar to levels found in the United States in the 1980s.[21] Moreover, they find that in Israel crucial variables such as ethnicity, religiosity, and social status relate to the selection of the least-liked group but not to the level of tolerance. More closely related to political tolerance, they find, are such factors as psychological security, political ideology, and the threat that the least-liked group is perceived to pose to the individual and the political system.

POLITICAL EFFICACY

The feeling that you have influence in the political system, or can have if you choose to, is generally considered an important feature of a democratic system. Israelis are interested in politics, discuss it quite a bit, vote in great numbers, and believe in the potency of elections to change policy;[22] but they do not have much faith in their own ability to influence policy (see table 12.3). What is more, this rate has dropped from 1969 to 1981. In 1969, 51 percent reported that they had little or no power to influence policy; by 1981, those pessimistic responses had risen to 61 percent.

Based on the 1969 data, it appears that the *lower* on the social scale the Israel citizen was, the more likely he or she was to feel efficacious. The Asian- or African-born were most efficacious, the European- or American-born least efficacious. Looking at those who claimed no efficacy, the pattern was even more striking. Those born in Asia or Africa and their Israel-born children stood out as being least influential, with the Europeans and Americans, and expecially

TABLE 12.3

POLITICAL EFFICACY BY PLACE OF BIRTH, 1969 AND 1981

"To what extent can you and people like you influence policy?"

Place of birth	N	Very great deal	Great deal	Somewhat	Little	Not at all
1969						
Asia-Africa	296	5%	14%	26%	23%	32%
Europe-America	629	4	11	34	27	24
Israel (father Asian- or African-born)	89	7	8	23	26	37
Israel (father European- or American-born)	213	3	11	43	29	14
Israel (father Israel-born)	68	3	2	39	29	26
TOTAL	1295	4	11	33	26	25
1981						
Asia-Africa	316	6	16	18	28	33
Europe-America	321	3	7	24	29	38
Israel (father Asian- or African-born)	190	6	12	22	22	38
Israel (father European- or American-born	196	3	9	26	28	35
Israel (father Israel-born)	127	2	8	20	28	43
TOTAL	1150	4	11	24	24	37

their children, having the lowest nonefficacious rate. The inverse relationship between efficacy and social status (place of birth, education) was explained by greater sophistication in understanding the essentially closed nature of the Israeli political system. As the Israeli moved up the social ladder, he became more realistic and realized that his chances of penetrating it were slight.

By 1981 changes had taken place. Efficacy on the whole declined and it fell most dramatically among those European- or American-born groups that evidently perceived most clearly their loss of power with the ascent of the Likud in 1977. This analysis is strengthened by the relatively high levels of efficacy reported by Asian- or African-born and their children. The data are especially fascinating since no real change of political power in ethnic terms was evident in Israel between the two time periods. But the high rates of low efficacy, especially among the Israel-born whose fathers were also Israel-born, is striking. There has been little evidence of alienation from the system, but the fact that the second-generation Israeli feels least efficacious is not an encouraging sign for Israeli democracy.

PARTICIPATION

The tension between high rates of support for democratic norms, high rates of voting turnout, and low levels of efficacy is further complicated by high levels of participation in politics. Israelis have high levels of political information with 87 percent knowing the correct answer (compared with 53 in a comparable American sample). Israelis live politics with 57 percent (compared with 33 percent in the United States) reporting that they talk about politics at least once a week.[23] We have already observed the high rates of news-media consumption and are told by more than a third of the respondents of a survey before the elections (June 1981) that they read election advertisements in the newspaper "often."

Sam Lehman-Wilzig claims that participation is not only high but is also changing its nature from being party based to being centered in extraparty protest.[24] According to his figures, more than 20 percent of the Israeli public has participated in demonstrations, a high figure by international standards. In addition to that, the rate of party membership (see chapter 6) has been declining. What is important to note is that although the major parties seem to have become ossified, the political system is vibrant and dynamic. Protest groups and movements arise and activists find ways of making their demands felt. The responsiveness of the system is another matter. But even here the data are far from conclusive. Groups such as Gush Emunim and Peace Now, which are formally outside the party system, have certainly had an impact on policy in the 1970s and 1980s. On the other hand, the voting public has concentrated its votes in the two party-conglomerates as never before. Jonathan Mendilow has suggested that conglomeration does not encourage specific messages, and therefore extraparty organization results.[25]

STRONG LEADERSHIP

A different question generated when the low-efficacy-high-participation dilemma is considered is whether politicians pay attention to the opinions of the ordinary citizen. In 1969 a quarter of the sample thought they did, a third thought that perhaps they did, and 38 percent were convinced that they did not. By 1981 a picture of greater responsiveness on the part of politicians emerged. Forty-two percent of the sample thought that politicians paid attention to the opinions of ordinary citizens, 23 percent thought that perhaps they did, and a third thought they did not. The data for both time frames seem to indicate that the Israeli citizen is very attentive and interested in politics; both citizen participation and lack of efficacy seem to be rising. Perhaps one is influenced by the other: The more frustrated you are, the more you participate; and the more you participate, the more frustrated you become. In addition, the citizen seems more convinced than before that the politician is attentive to demands.

The consistent result of this skein of conflicting patterns is the desire for assertive political leadership. This pattern was noted in the 1960s, and it persists.[26] If in 1969, 64 percent of a national sample preferred strong leadership to "all the debates and laws," by 1981 the percentage was 72 percent. In 1984, after Begin's resignation, it was 50 percent. Despite the surface support for democratic norms, there is a stubborn respect for the strong personality in Israeli politics. This explains at least in part the overwhelming popularity of leaders like Ben-Gurion and Begin. Impressive achievements in military and other areas have fashioned a nation that seems to be impressed with doing, creating, action. The élan of a leader is compared very favorably against the humdrum of the cumbersome parliamentary process with its weak personalities and compromising atmosphere. In comparison with magnetic leadership, the political system seems inefficient; politicians appear to lack imagination and resourcefulness.

We must seek an explanation for these findings by noting that Israel is a nervous, energetic nation. The doers—pilot, manager, builder, settler—are rewarded heavily both materially and symbolically. Much of this nervous energy is evident in the army or in more anonymous moments, such as on the highways and in buses. There, Mediterranean friendliness merges with this nervousness to produce a fundamental Israeli characteristic. Hemmed in on many sides by bureaucratic regulation and feeling trapped by international isolation, this condition expresses itself in less formal, less structured situations. Yet the need for guidance, for structuring, and for leadership remains strong.

The resulting syndrome appears paradoxical, but its elements actually mesh nicely. On the surface there is a cockiness and self-assurance about running the country—and many less important issues, for that matter. At a more fundamental level there is also a desire for order, for security, and for leadership. The former provides the semblance of the latter: In place of the desired authority comes an assertive dogmatism. Whether this fundamental insecurity has its roots in the individual psyche or the educational system—or in one of any number of other sources—is unclear. At the public level, however, it provides a very fertile soil for cultivating widespread support for positions associated with leaders invested with legitimacy. Public opinion in Israel is unstable and can be brought to support the dominant position of the appropriate leaders when the proper symbols and appeals are applied.

Notes

All voting statistics are from official publications of the Central Bureau of Statistics. *Maariv, Haaretz,* and *Yediot Aharonot* are Hebrew daily newspapers; *Otot* is the Hebrew journal of the Israeli advertising assocation; and *Megamot* is a Hebrew social science quarterly.

CHAPTER 1. Introduction (pp. 1-10)
1. Giovanni Sartori, *Parties and Party Systems* (Cambridge, England: Cambridge University Press, 1976); Arend Lijphart, *Democracy in Plural Societies* (New Haven: Yale University Press, 1977); Amos Perlmutter, *Military and Politics in Israel* (London: Cass, 1969); Gabriel Ben-Dor, "Politics and the Military in Israel," in *The Elections in Israel—1973,* ed. A. Arian (Jerusalem: Jerusalem Academic Press, 1975), 119-44; and S. N. Eisenstadt, *Israeli Society* (London: Weidenfeld and Nicolson, 1967).
2. Simon N. Herman, *Jewish Identity in the Jewish State* (Beverly Hills: Sage, 1977), 175, 184.
3. Yitzhak Samuel and Ephraim Yuchtman-Yaar, "The Status and Situs Dimensions as Determinants of Occupational Attractiveness," *Quality and Quantity* 13 (1979): 485-501; *Haaretz,* 9 March 1983.

CHAPTER 2. People of Israel (pp. 11-24)
1. Data on Israeli and Jewish population are plentiful. An authoritative source, from which most of the data in this chapter are taken, is Dov Friedlander and Calvin Goldscheider, *The Population of Israel* (New York: Columbia University Press, 1979). For material on world Jewish statistics, see Roberto Bachi, *Population Trends of World Jewry* (Jerusalem: Institute of Contemporary Jewry, Hebrew University, 1976); and for material on Israeli population statistics see Roberto Bachi, *The Population of Israel* (Jerusalem: Institute of Contemporary Jewry, Hebrew University, 1977).
2. See, for example, Joseph Gorni, "Changes in the Social and Political Structure of the Second Aliya, 1904-1914," in Hebrew, *Zionism* 1 (1970): 204-46.
3. Cf. Drora Kass and Seymour Martin Lipset, "America's New Wave of Jewish Immigrants," *New York Times Magazine,* 7 December 1980.
4. Good discussions of the Zionist idea are found in Ben Halpern, *The Idea of the Jewish State* (Cambridge, Mass.: Harvard University Press, 1961); Arthur Herzberg, *The Zionist Idea* (New York: Meridian, 1960); and Shlomo Avineri, *The Making of Modern Zionism: The Intellectual Origins of the Jewish State* (London: Weidenfeld and Nicolson, 1981).

5. Important treatments of the pre-state period include Yonathan Shapiro, *The Formative Years of the Israeli Labor Party* (London: Sage, 1976); S. N. Eisenstadt, *Israeli Society;* and Dan Horowitz and Moshe Lissak, *The Origins of the Israeli Polity: Palestine under the Mandate* (Chicago: University of Chicago Press, 1978). For good overall historical treatments, see Walter Laqueur, *A History of Zionism* (London: Weidenfeld and Nicolson, 1972); and Noah Lucas, *The Modern History of Israel* (New York: Praeger, 1974).
6. The clearest statement of this position is found in Shapiro, *The Formative Years.*
7. Anita Shapiro, *The Frustrated Struggle: Jewish Labor,* in Hebrew (Tel Aviv: Hakibbutz Hameuhad, 1977).
8. See Gorni, "Changes in the Structure of the Second Aliya."
9. Friedlander and Goldscheider, *The Population of Israel,* 16.
10. Yonathan Shapiro, "Generational Units and Inter-Generational Relations in Israeli Politics," in *Israel—A Developing Society,* ed. A. Arian (Assen: Van Gorcum, 1980), 161-79.
11. See Shabtai Tevet's discussion in his *David's Jealousy: The Life of Ben-Gurion,* vol. 1, in Hebrew (Jerusalem: Schocken, 1977).
12. See Dan Giladi, *The Yishuv at the Time of the Fourth Aliyah (1924-29): Economic and Political Aspects,* in Hebrew (Tel Aviv: Am Oved, 1977).
13. Cited in Friedlander and Goldscheider, *The Population of Israel,* 97.
14. For a thorough discussion see Zvi Gitelman, *Becoming Israelis: Political Resocialization of Soviet and American Immigrants* (New York: Praeger, 1982).
15. Drora Kass and Seymour Martin Lipset, "Jewish Immigration to the United States from 1967 to the Present: Israelis and Others," in *Understanding American Jewry,* ed. Marshall Sklare (New Brunswick, N.J.: Transaction, 1982); and Dov Elizur, "Israelis in the United States: Motives, Attitudes and Intentions," Bar Ilan University Monograph, 1979.
16. Cf. Friedlander and Goldscheider, *The Population of Israel,* 27, 28.
17. Salo Wittmayer Baron, *The Social and Religious History of the Jews,* vol. 2, 2nd ed. (New York: Columbia University Press, 1952).
18. Figures cited from a poll of the Israel Institute of Applied Social Research, in Kass and Lipset, "America's Jewish Immigrants."
19. *Statistical Abstract, 1983,* 60.
20. *Statistical Abstract, 1981,* 90.
21. For a thorough discussion, see Raphael Patai, *Tents of Jacob* (New York: Prentice-Hall, 1971).
22. *Encyclopedia Judaica,* s.v. "demography." For a broader analysis, see Sammy Smooha, *Israel: Pluralism and Conflict* (Berkeley: University of California Press, 1978).
23. *Statistical Abstract, 1983,* 60.
24. *Statistical Abstract, 1981,* 90.

CHAPTER 3. Political Economy (pp. 25-46)
1. Reviews of Israel's economy can be found in Nadav Halevi and Ruth Klinov-Malul, *The Economic Development of Israel* (New York: Praeger, 1968); Abba Lerner and Haim Ben-Shahar, *The Economics of Efficiency and Growth* (Cambridge, Mass.: Ballinger, 1975); Michael Michaely, *Foreign Trade Regimes and Economic Development: Israel* (New York: Columbia University Press, 1975); and Don Patinkin, *The*

    Israel Economy: The First Decade (Jerusalem: Falk Project for Economic Research in Israel, December 1980).
2. Zvi Gitelman and David Naveh, "Elite Accommodation and Organization Effectiveness: The Case of Immigrant Absorption in Israel," *Journal of Politics* 38 (November 1976): 973-79.
3. Background material on the Histadrut can be found in Rachel Tokatli, "Political Patterns in Labor Relations in Israel" (Ph.D. dissertation in Hebrew, Tel Aviv University, 1979); Shapiro, *Formative Years of the Israeli Labor Party;* and Horowitz and Lissak, *Origins of the Israeli Polity.*
4. More up-to-date material on the Histadrut can be found in Tokatli, "Political Patterns in Labor Relations"; and Gavriel Bartal, *Histadrut Structure and Activities,* in Hebrew (Tel Aviv: Histadrut Executive Committee, 1981).
5. Ira Sharkansky, *Wither the State? Politics and Public Enterprise in Three Countries* (Chatham, N.J.: Chatham House, 1979), 75.
6. Yair Aharoni, *State-Owned Enterprises in Israel and Abroad,* in Hebrew (Tel Aviv: Gomeh, 1979), 22-23.
7. Yair Aharoni, *Structure and Performance in Israeli Economy,* in Hebrew (Tel Aviv: Gomeh, 1976), 222-63.
8. Richard F. Nyrop, ed., *Israel: A Country Study* (Washington, D.C.: Foreign Area Studies, 1978), 179.
9. Efraim Tzur, "Political and Social Sources of Inflation," in Hebrew, *Economic Quarterly* 22 (April 1975): 18-28.
10. Haim Barkai, "The Public Sector, the Histadrut Sector and the Private Sector in the Israeli Economy," *Sixth Report 1961-1963* (Jerusalem: Falk Project for Economic Research in Israel, 1964), 28-30.
11. *Statistical Abstract, 1979,* 292.
12. Ministry of Finance, *The Budget Proposal for 1980,* in Hebrew, 28.
13. Gideon Doron and Boaz Tamir, "The Electoral Cycle: A Political Economic Perspective," *Crossroads* (Spring 1983): 141-52, table 5.
14. Nyrop, *Israel,* 185.
15. *Statistical Abstract, 1981,* 190.
16. *Yediot Aharonot,* Economic Supplement, 11 June 1982, 5.
17. Assaf Razin, "American Aid to Israel," *Haaretz,* 23 November 1982, 11.
18. Haim Ben Shahar, "How We Lost Our Way," *Haaretz,* 26 November 1982, 14.
19. *Statistical Abstract, 1981,* 198-99.
20. Razin, "American Aid."
21. *American Jewish Yearbook, 1980* (Philadelphia: Jewish Publication Society of America, 1980), 151. See also Gabriel Sheffer and Yohanan Manor, "Fundraising: Money Is Not Enough," in *Can Planning Replace Politics? The Israeli Experience,* ed. Raphaella Bilski et al. (The Hague: Martinus Nijhoff, 1980), 283-319.
22. *Statistical Abstract, 1983,* 356.
23. Aharoni, *Israeli Economy,* 116-19.
24. *Statistical Abstract, 1983,* 602.
25. Ibid., 356-57.
26. Ibid., 378; and Nyrop, *Israel,* 181.
27. Yoram Ben-Porath, "The Years of Plenty and the Years of Famine—A Political Business Cycle?" *Kyklos* 28 (1975): 401.

28. Doron and Tamir, "The Electoral Cycle," 27, table 4.
29. Eli Arom, "Economic Motivation for DMC Support" (Graduate paper, in Hebrew, Political Science Department, Tel Aviv University, 1978).
30. *Statistical Abstract, 1983,* 310.
31. Zvi Zussman, *Differential and Equality in the Histadrut,* in Hebrew (Ramat Gan: Massada, 1974).

CHAPTER 4. The Political Elite (pp. 47-70)
1. Gaetano Mosca, *The Ruling Class* (New York: McGraw-Hill, 1939), 50.
2. See Robert D. Putnam, *The Comparative Study of Political Elites* (Englewood Cliffs, N.J.: Prentice-Hall, 1976).
3. Shapiro, "Generational Units and Inter-Generational Relations in Israeli Politics," 161-79.
4. Mosca, *The Ruling Class,* 144-45.
5. Avraham Brichta, "Social Political and Cultural Background of Knesset Members in Israel" (Ph.D. dissertation in Hebrew, Hebrew University, 1972), 201.
6. Emanuel Gutmann and Jacob Landau, "The Political Elites and National Leadership in Israel," in *Political Elites in the Middle East,* ed. George Lenczowski (Washington D.C.: American Enterprise Institute, 1975), 166-67.
7. Walter Laqueur, *A History of Zionism* (New York: Schocken, 1976), 308-9.
8. For the judiciary, see Elyakim Rubinstein, *The Judges of the Land,* in Hebrew (Jerusalem: Schocken, 1980), chap. 6; for the army, see Yoram Peri, *Between Battles and Ballots* (Cambridge, England: Cambridge University Press, 1983), chap. 5; and for the mass media, see Yitzhak Galnoor, *Steering the Polity: Communication and Politics in Israel* (Beverly Hills: Sage, 1982), 250-53.
9. Avraham Brichta, "The Social and Political Characteristics of Members of the Seventh Knesset," in *The Elections in Israel—1969,* ed. A. Arian (Jerusalem: Jerusalem Academic Press, 1972), 123.
10. Max Weber, "Politics as a Vocation," in *From Max Weber: Essays in Sociology,* ed. H. H. Gerth and C. Wright Mills (New York: Oxford University Press, 1946), 84.
11. Zbigniew Brzezinski and Samuel Huntington, *Political Power: USA/USSR* (New York: Viking Press, 1963), 150-73.
12. "The Cincinnatus and the Apparatchik: The Israeli Case," *Jerusalem Quarterly* (Winter 1984): 105-12.
13. Horowitz and Lissak, *Origins of the Israeli Polity,* 159.
14. Emanuel Gutmann and Jacob Landau, "The Israeli Political Elite: Characteristics and Composition," in *The Israeli Political System,* in Hebrew, ed. Moshe Lissak and Emanuel Gutmann (Tel Aviv: Am Oved, 1977), 192-228.
15. Peter Medding, *Mapai in Israel* (Cambridge, England: Cambridge University Press, 1972), 158-60.
16. Shevah Weiss, *Israeli Politicians,* in Hebrew (Tel Aviv: Ahiasaf, 1973), 51.
17. Aharon Lapidot, "Informal Election: Predicting the Results of the Election of the Fifth President," in Hebrew, *State, Government and International Relations* 13 (1979): 111-13.

CHAPTER 5. Political Parties (pp. 71-94)
1. See Maurice Duverger, *Political Parties* (New York: Wiley, 1963).

2. See the sources listed in chapter 2, note 5, especially Lucas, *Modern History of Israel*.
3. See Zvi Even-Shushan, *The History of the Workers' Movement in Eretz-Israel*, in Hebrew (Tel Aviv: Am Oved, 1963).
4. Michael Bar-Zohar, *Ben-Gurion: A Biography* (London: Weidenfeld and Nicolson, 1979); Medding, *Mapai in Israel*.
5. Natan Yanai, *Split at the Top*, in Hebrew (Tel Aviv: Lewin-Epstein, 1969).
6. See Yonathan Shapiro, "The End of a Dominant Party System," in *The Elections in Israel—1977*, ed. A. Arian (Jerusalem: Jerusalem Academic Press, 1980), 23-38; and Ariel Levite and Sidney Tarrow, "The Legitimation of Excluded Parties in Dominant Party Systems: A Comparison of Israel and Italy," *Comparative Politics* 15 (April 1983): 295-327.
7. See Joseph B. Schechtman, *Rebel and Statesman, Vladimir Jabotinsky: The Early Years* (New York: Thomas Yoseloff, 1956); and Menachem Begin, *The Revolt* (London: W. H. Allen, 1951). See also Rael Jean Isaac, *Israel Divided: Ideological Politics in the Jewish State* (Baltimore: Johns Hopkins University Press, 1976).
8. See Jonathan Mendilow, "Party Cluster Formations in Multi-Party Systems," *Political Studies* 30 (December 1982): 485-503.
9. Nakdimon Rogel, *Tel-Hai*, in Hebrew (Tel Aviv: Yariv, 1979).
10. Miriam Geter, *Haim Arlozoroff, A Political Biography*, in Hebrew (Tel Aviv: Kibbutz Hameuhad, 1978); Shabtai Tevet, *The Murder of Arlozoroff*, in Hebrew (Jerusalem: Schocken, 1982).
11. Yaacov Shavit, *The Season of the Hunt: The "Season"—The Confrontation between the "Organized Yishuv" and the Underground Organizations, 1937-1947*, in Hebrew (Tel Aviv: Hadar, 1976).
12. Shlomo Nakdimon, *Altelena*, in Hebrew (Jerusalem: Idanim, 1978).
13. Efraim Torgovnik, "Likud 1977-81: The Consolidation of Power," in *Israel in the Begin Era*, ed. Robert Freedman (New York: Praeger, 1982), 7-27.
14. Gary Schiff, *Tradition and Politics: Religious Parties of Israel* (Detroit: Wayne State University Press, 1977); and Menachem Friedman, *Society and Religion: Non Orthodoxy in Eretz Israel, 1918-1936*, in Hebrew (Jerusalem: Ben-Zvi Institute, 1978).
15. See Ehud Sprinzak, "Gush Emunim: The Tip of the Iceberg," *Jerusalem Quarterly* (Fall 1981): 28-47; and Danny Rubinstein, *Gush Emunim*, in Hebrew (Tel Aviv: Kibbutz Hameuhad, 1982).
16. For information on Rafi, see Yanai, *Split at the Top*. For information on the DMC, see Amnon Rubinstein, *A Certain Political Experience*, in Hebrew (Jerusalem: Idanim, 1982); and Nachman Orieli and Amnon Barzilai, *The Rise and Fall of the DMC*, in Hebrew (Tel Aviv: Reshafim, 1982).

CHAPTER 6. Party Organization (pp. 95-119)
1. Amitai Etzioni, "Alternative Ways to Democracy: The Example of Israel," *Political Science Quarterly* 74 (1959): 196-214.
2. Duverger, *Political Parties*, 308.
3. Ibid., 312.
4. Harry Eckstein, *Division and Cohesion in Democracy* (Princeton: Princeton University Press, 1966).
5. For a discussion of political parties see Duverger, *Political Parties;* and Sartori, *Parties and Party Systems*.

6. Medding, *Mapai in Israel,* 88.
7. Yaacov Shavit, *From Majority to State—The Revisionist Movement: The Settlement Program and the Social Idea, 1925-35,* in Hebrew (Tel Aviv: Yariv, 1978), 101-3.
8. Amnon Barzilai, "The Fight of the Factions in the NRP," *Haaretz,* 28 September 1976, 9; and Schiff, *Tradition and Politics,* 104-5; and Yael Yishai, "Factionalism in the National Religious Party: The Quiet Revolution," in *The Elections in Israel—1977,* ed. A. Arian (Jerusalem: Jerusalem Academic Press, 1980), 57-74.
9. Robert Michels, *Political Parties* (New York: Hearst, 1915).
10. Ibid., 391.
11. Ibid., 56.
12. Ibid., 228.
13. Medding, *Mapai in Israel.* The quotations are from pp. 301-5
14. Duverger, *Political Parties.* The quotations are from pp. 140-41.
15. Most of the examples are from Natan Yanai, *Party Leadership in Israel* (Ramat Gan: Turtledove, 1981).
16. Weiss, *Politicians in Israel.*
17. Myron J. Aronoff, *Power and Ritual in the Israeli Labor Party* (Assen: Van Gorcum, 1977), chaps. 2 and 6.
18. Schiff, *Tradition and Politics,* 91.
19. Giora Goldberg and Steven Hoffmann, "Nominations in Israel: Politics of Institutionalization," in *The Elections in Israel—1981,* ed. A. Arian (Tel Aviv: Ramot, 1983).
20. Medding, *Mapai in Israel.* Quotations are from pp. 122-24.
21. Michels, *Political Parties,* 407-8.

CHAPTER 7. The Electoral System (pp. 120-32)
1. Shlomo Deshen, *Immigrant Voters in Israel* (Manchester, England: Manchester University Press, 1970).
2. Amnon Rubinstein, *The Constitutional Law of Israel,* 3rd ed., in Hebrew (Jerusalem: Schocken, 1980), 237-55.
3. Moshe Atias, *Knesset Israel in Eretz Israel,* in Hebrew (Jerusalem: The National Committee, 1944), 20-21.
4. *Yediot Aharonot,* 1 January 1974.
5. Avraham Brichta, "1977 Elections and the Future of Electoral Reform in Israel," in *Israel at the Polls: The Knesset Election of 1977,* ed. Howard R. Penniman (Washington, D.C.: American Enterprise Institute, 1979), 39-57.
6. Harry Eckstein, "The Impact of Electoral Systems on Representative Government," in *Comparative Politics—A Reader,* ed. Harry Eckstein and David E. Apter (Glencoe, Ill.: Free Press, 1963), 247-54.
7. Douglas Rae, *The Political Consequences of Electoral Laws* (New Haven: Yale University Press, 1967).
8. Goldberg and Hoffmann, "Nominations."
9. A. Brichta, *Democracy and Elections,* in Hebrew (Tel Aviv: Am Oved, 1977), chap. 4.

CHAPTER 8. Electoral Behavior (pp. 133-54)
1. All voting statistics are from official publications of the Central Bureau of Statistics.
2. Uri Avner, "Non-Voting in the Elections for the Tenth Knesset (1981) and its Causes," *Statistical Monthly of Israel,* appendix 5, in Hebrew (1982): 79-101.

3. A. Arian, *The Choosing People: Voting Behavior in Israel* (Cleveland: Press of Case Western Reserve University, 1973), chap. 6.
4. The literature on voting is extensive. Among the important contributions are Bernard Berelson, Paul F. Lazarsfeld, and William N. McPhee, *Voting* (Chicago: University of Chicago Press, 1954); David Butler and Donald E. Stokes, *Political Change in Britain* (London: Macmillan, 1969); Angus Campbell, Gerald Gurin, and Warren E. Miller, *The Voter Decides* (Evanston, Ill.: Row Peterson, 1954); Angus Campbell, Philip E. Converse, Warren E. Miller, and Donald E. Stokes, *The American Voter* (New York: Wiley, 1964); Morris P. Fiorina, *Retrospective Voting in American National Elections* (New Haven: Yale University Press, 1981); and Norman G. H. Nie, Sidney Verba, and John R. Petrocik, *The Changing American Voter* (Cambridge, Mass.: Harvard University Press, 1976).
5. Moshe Lissak, *Social Mobility in Israeli Society* (Jerusalem: Israel Universities Press, 1969); and Judah Matras, *Social Change in Israel* (Chicago: Aldine, 1965).
6. Hanna Herzog, "The Ethnic Lists to the Delegates' Assembly and the Knesset (1920-1977)—Ethnic Political Identity?" (Ph.D. dissertation in Hebrew, Tel Aviv University, 1981).
7. Michal Shamir and Asher Arian, "The Ethnic Vote in Israel's 1981 Elections," *Electoral Studies* 1 (1982): 315-31.
8. Butler and Stokes, *Political Change in Britain,* 293.
9. See H. Smith, "Analysis of Voting," in *The Elections in Israel—1969,* ed. A. Arian (Jerusalem: Jerusalem Academic Press, 1972), 63-80.
10. V. O. Key, Jr., "A Theory of Critical Elections," *Journal of Politics* 17 (1955): 4. See also V. O. Key, Jr., *The Responsible Electorate* (Cambridge, Mass.: Harvard University Press, 1966); and Angus Campbell, "A Classification of Presidential Elections," in *Elections and the Political Order,* ed. Angus Campbell, Philip Converse, Warren Miller, and Donald Stokes (New York: Wiley, 1966), 63-77.
11. Duverger, *Political Parties,* 307.

CHAPTER 9. The Knesset, the Government, and the Judiciary (pp. 155-85)
1. Walter Bagehot, *The English Constitution* (London: Watts, 1964); and Ivor Jennings, *The British Constitution* (Cambridge, England: Cambridge University Press, 1966).
2. Material for this section is from Basic Law: Knesset. Other sources are Shevah Weiss, *The House of the Elected,* in Hebrew (Tel Aviv: Ahiasaf, 1977); Asher Zidon, *Knesset* (New York: Herzl Press, 1967); and Amnon Rubinstein, *The Constitutional Law of Israel,* 3rd. ed., in Hebrew (Tel Aviv: Schocken, 1980).
3. Rubinstein, *Constitutional Law,* 225.
4. William H. Riker, *The Theory of Political Coalitions* (New Haven: Yale University Press, 1962); and David Nachmias, "Coalition Politics in Israel," *Comparative Political Studies* 7 (October 1974): 316-33.
5. Basic Law: Government; and Gad Yaacobi, *The Government of Israel* (New York: Praeger, 1982).
6. R. T. McKenzie, *British Political Parties* (New York: Praeger, 1963).
7. Rubinstein, *Constitutional Law,* 275, n. 28.
8. Yonathan Shapiro, *Democracy in Israel,* in Hebrew (Ramat Gan: Massada, 1977).
9. *Knesset Proceedings* 5, in Hebrew, 1721-22.
10. Rubinstein, *Constitutional Law,* 280-81.

11. *Bergman v. Minister of Treasury,* Israeli Supreme Court 23 (1) 693.
12. Rubinstein, *Constitutional Law,* 380. See also Baruch Bracha, "Restriction of Personal Freedom without Due Process of Law According to the Defence (Emergency) Regulations, 1945," in *Israel Yearbook of Human Rights, 1978,* 296-323.
13. See J. E. Baker, *Legal System of Israel* (Jerusalem: Israel Universities Press, 1968).
14. Rubinstein, *Judges of the Land,* chap. 5.
15. Ibid., chap. 6.
16. Ian Lustick, "Israel and the West Bank after Elon Moreh: The Mechanics of De Facto Annexation," *Middle East Journal* 35 (1981): 557-77.
17. Amos Shapiro and Baruch Bracha, "The Constitutional Status of Individual Rights," in Hebrew, *Legal Discussions* 2 (1971): 20-53.
18. Shalev Ginossar, "Access to Justice in Israel," in *Access to Justice,* vol. 1, ed. Mauro Cappelletti and Brian Garth (Milan: Giuffre, 1978), 627-48.

CHAPTER 10. Interest Groups and Public Policy (pp. 186-225)
1. David Truman, *The Governmental Process* (New York: Knopf, 1951). A good summary of the field is to be found in "Interest Groups," by Robert H. Salisbury, in *Nongovernmental Politics,* vol. 4, *Handbook of Political Science,* ed. Fred I. Greenstein and Nelson W. Polsby (Reading, Mass.: Addison-Wesley, 1975), 171-228.
2. Sam Lehman-Wilzig, "Public Protests Against Central and Local Government in Israel, 1950-1979," *Jewish Journal of Sociology* 14 (December 1982): 99-116.
3. Yael Yishai, "Interest Groups in Israel," *Jerusalem Quarterly* (Spring 1979): 130; and Eliahu Katz and Michael Gurevich, *The Secularization of Leisure: Culture and Communication in Israel* (London: Faber and Faber, 1976), 135.
4. Gabriel Almond and James Coleman, eds., *The Politics of Developing Areas* (Princeton: Princeton University Press, 1960).
5. Gabriel Almond and G. Bingham Powell, *Comparative Politics: A Developmental Approach* (Boston: Little, Brown, 1966).
6. E. E. Schattschneider, *Party Government* (New York: Farrar and Rinehart, 1942); and L. Harmon Ziegler, *Interest Groups in American Society* (Englewood Cliffs, N.J.: Prentice-Hall, 1964).
7. Samuel Finer, *Anonymous Empire: A Study of the Lobby in Great Britain* (London: Pall Mall Press, 1966).
8. Peri, *Between Battles and Ballots,* chap. 5; and Dani Zamir, "Generals in Politics," *Jerusalem Quarterly* (Summer 1981): 17-35.
9. Peri, *Battles and Ballots,* chap. 2.
10. Ibid., 50-51.
11. Daniel Shimshoni, *Israeli Democracy* (New York: Free Press, 1982).
12. Gabriel Ben-Dor, "Politics and the Military in Israel: The 1973 Election Campaign and its Aftermath," in *The Elections in Israel—1973,* ed. A. Arian (Jerusalem: Jerusalem Academic Press, 1975), 119-44.
13. Zeev Schiff, "The New Man in the Defense Ministry," *Haaretz,* 27 May 1977, 13.
14. Shimshoni, *Israeli Democracy,* 189; and Peri, *Battles and Ballots,* chap. 9.
15. Dina Goren, *Secrecy, Defence and Freedom of the Press,* in Hebrew (Jerusalem: Magnes Press, 1976), 203-6, cited by Peri, *Battles and Ballots,* 200.
16. On the Histadrut, Tokatli, "Labor Relations in Israel"; Shapiro, *Israeli Labor Party;* and Horowitz and Lissak, *The Israeli Polity., See* also Arye Globerson and Ozer

Carmi, *People in Organization: Managing Human Resources,* in Hebrew (Tel Aviv: Administration Library, 1982); and Joseph Glatt, "The Historical Development of the Histadrut: An Evaluation of the Post-State Wages Policy, 1948-1967, and Its Impact on the Economic Independence of Israel" (Ph.D. dissertation, Columbia University, 1976).

17. Yoni Reshef, "The Impact of the Political Change in Israel on the Patterns of Political Exchange between Government, Histadrut and Workers — October 1973 to June 1981" (MA thesis, Department of Labor Studies, Tel Aviv University, 1981).
18. A. Arian, "Health Care in Israel: Political and Administrative Aspects," *International Political Science Review* 2 (1981): 43-56.
19. Yosef Sapir Institute, *Yosef Sapir,* in Hebrew (Tel Aviv: Yosef Sapir Institute, 1977), 125.
20. Horowitz and Lissak, *The Israeli Polity.* For later developments, see Jay Abarbenel, *The Co-operative Farmer and the Welfare State: Economic Change in an Israeli Moshav* (Manchester, England: Manchester University Press, 1974); and Alex Weingrod, *Reluctant Pioneers* (Ithaca, N.Y.: Cornell University Press, 1966).
21. The term is developed in Brian Chapman, *The Profession of Government* (London: Allen and Unwin, 1959); and by H. Gordon Skilling, "Groups in Soviet Politics: Some Hypotheses," in *Interest Groups in Soviet Politics,* ed. H. Gordon Skilling and Franklin Griffiths (Princeton: Princeton University Press, 1971), 19-45.
22. A. Arian, *Ideological Change in Israel* (Cleveland: Press of Case Western Reserve University, 1968), 87; and Neal Sherman, "The Agricultural Sector and the 1977 Knesset Elections," in *The Elections in Israel—1977,* ed. A. Arian (Jerusalem: Jerusalem Academic Press, 1980), 149-70.
23. Arian, *Ideological Change,* 81-82.
24. Moshe Dayan, *Pathmakers,* in Hebrew (Tel Aviv: Idanim, 1976), 379.
25. Aharoni, *State-Owned-Enterprise,* 24.
26. Differing viewpoints may be found in Charles Liebman and Eliezer Don Yehiya, "Israel's Civil Religion," *Jerusalem Quarterly* (Spring 1982); Gershon Weiler, *Jewish Theocracy,* in Hebrew (Tel Aviv: Ofakim, 1975); Yeshayahua Leibowitz, *Judaism, the Jewish People and the State of Israel,* in Hebrew (Jerusalem: Schocken, 1976); and Amnon Rubinstein, "State and Religion in Israel," *Journal of Contemporary History* (October 1967): 107-21.
27. *Rufheisen* v. *Minister of Interior,* High Court of Justice 62/72, decision XV 2428.
28. *Shalit* v. *Minister of Interior,* High Court of Justice 68/58, decision XXIII (2) 477; and *Shalit* v. *Minister of Interior* 72/18, decision XXVI (1) 334.
29. Schiff, *Tradition and Politics.*
30. Ministry of Finance, *Budget Proposal for the Ministry of Religious Affairs—1982,* in Hebrew, 21.

CHAPTER 11. Statism, Public and Local Administration (pp. 226-43)
1. David Ben-Gurion, *Eighth Histadrut Convention,* in Hebrew (Tel Aviv: Histadrut Executive, 1956).
2. A. Shmaltz, ed. *Educational and Cultural Statistics,* in Hebrew (Tel Aviv: Histadrut Executive, 1956).
3. On the establishment of the Labor Fund for Israel and the political debate that followed, see Giora Goldberg, "The Labor Exchanges as a Political Instrument in

a Developing Society," in Hebrew (MA thesis in Hebrew, Tel Aviv University), 114-17.
4. H. S. Halevi, "The Pluralistic Structure of Health Services in Israel," in Hebrew, *Social Security* 17 (n.d): 5-50.
5. Ministry of Health, "Principles for a National Health Insurance Law," in Hebrew, 1978.
6. Gerald E. Caiden, *Israel's Administrative Culture* (Berkeley: Institute of Governmental Studies, 1970), 18-19.
7. On the Israeli civil service, see Jacob Reuveny, *The Israel Civil Service* (Ramat Gan: Massada, 1974); and David Nachmias and David H. Rosenbloom, *Bureaucratic Culture: Citizens and Administrators in Israel* (New York: St. Martin's Press, 1978).
8. Arye Globerson, "The Bureaucratic Elite in the Israel Civil Service," in Hebrew, Faculty of Social Sciences, Tel Aviv University, 1970, chap. 8. Mimeographed.
9. Michael Brecher, *Decisions in Crisis: Israel, 1967 and 1973* (Berkeley: University of California Press, 1980), 239.
10. Benjamin Akzin and Yehezkel Dror, *Israel: High-Pressure Planning* (Syracuse, N.Y.: Syracuse University Press, 1966).
11. Yitzhak Galnoor, "Water Planning: Who Gets the Last Drop?" in *Can Planning Replace Politics?*, 137-215.
12. *Statistical Abstract, 1981*, 599.
13. Mordecai Ben-Porat, "The Election System for the Local Authorities," in Hebrew (Jerusalem: Ministry of Interior, 1978). Mimeographed.
14. Shevah Weiss, *Local Government in Israel*, in Hebrew (Tel Aviv: Am Oved, 1972).
15. Efraim Torgovnik and Yeshayahu Barzel, "Block Grant Allocation: Relationship between Self-Government and Redistribution," *Public Administration* 57 (Spring 1979): 87-102.

CHAPTER 12. Ideology, Communication, and Socialization (pp. 244-65)
1. Arian, *Ideological Change in Israel*.
2. Donald E. Stokes, "Spatial Models of Party Competition," *American Political Science Review* 57 (June 1963): 368-77.
3. This section is based largely on A. Arian and Michal Shamir, "The Primarily Political Functions of the Left-Right Continuum," *Comparative Politics* (January 1983): 139-58.
4. Philip E. Converse, "The Nature of Belief Systems in Mass Public," in *Ideology and Discontent*, ed. David E. Apter (New York: Free Press, 1964), 206-61.; Butler and Stokes, *Political Change in Britain;* Ronald Inglehart and Hans D. Klingemann, "Party Identification, Ideological Preference and the Left-Right Dimension among Western Mass Publics," in *Party Identification and Beyond*, ed. Ian Budge, Ivor Crewe, and Dennis Farlie (London: Wiley, 1976), 243-73.
5. Daniel Shimshoni, *Israeli Democracy* (New York: Free Press, 1982), 83-84.
6. The former figure is from *Statistical Abstract, 1982*, 720; the latter, based on 1970 data, is from Katz and Gurevich, *Leisure*.
7. Of those who watch television on Sabbath, almost 80 percent view the news. Sabbath television watchers are 87 percent of the total television audience. These data are from *Statistical Monthly of Israel, 1981*, in Hebrew, appendix 3, 30; and *Statistical Abstract, 1982*, 722-23. For a detailed report on television viewing, see mim-

eographed report (in Hebrew) of Israel Institute of Applied Social Research, March 1983.
8. *Otot* 40 (February 1982), 8.
9. William Frankel, *Israel Observed* (London: Thames and Hudson, 1980), 138.
10. V. O. Key, Jr., *Public Opinion and American Democracy* (New York: Knopf, 1961); Bernard C. Hennessy, *Public Opinion* (Belmont, Calif.: Wadsworth, 1965); and Arian, *Choosing People,* chaps. 2 and 7.
11. Judith N. Elizur, "The Role of the Media in the 1981 Knesset Elections," in *Israel at the Polls,* ed. Howard Penniman (Washington, D.C.: American Enterprise Institute, forthcoming).
12. David O. Sears, "Political Behavior," in *The Handbook of Social Psychology,* vol. 5, ed. Gardner Lindzey et al., 2nd ed. (Reading, Mass.: Addison-Wesley, 1969), 315-45.
13. David Nachmias, "A Temporal Sequence of Adolescent Political Participation: Some Israeli Data," *British Journal of Political Science* 7 (1977): 71-83; Orit Ichilov and Nissan Naveh, "The Perception of the 'Good Citizen' by Israeli Adolescents," *Comparative Politics* 13 (1981): 361-76; and Eva Etzioni-Halevy with Rina Shapira, *Political Culture in Israel* (New York: Praeger, 1977).
14. Yonathan Shapiro, *An Elite Without Successors,* in Hebrew (Tel Aviv: Sifriat Hapoalim, 1984).
15. Rina Shapira, *Blue Shirt and White Collar,* in Hebrew (Tel Aviv: Am Oved, 1979).
16. A. Arian, "Were the 1973 Elections in Israel Critical?" *Comparative Politics* (October 1975): 152-65.
17. Charles Liebman and Eliezer Don Yehiya, *The Civil Religion of Israel* (Berkeley: University of California Press, 1983).
18. Leonard Fein, *Politics in Israel* (Boston: Little, Brown, 1967), 113.
19. Gitelman, *Becoming Israelis.*
20. Michal Shamir, "The Lack of Political Tolerance," *Haaretz,* 22 February 1983, 12.
21. Michal Shamir and John Sullivan, "The Political Context of Tolerance: A Cross-National Perspective from Israel and the United States," *American Political Science Review* 77, no. 4 (December 1983): 911-28.
22. Arian, *Choosing People,* 27.
23. Shamir and Sullivan, "Political Context of Tolerance."
24. Sam Lehman-Wilzig, "The Israeli Protester," *Jerusalem Quarterly* (Winter 1982): 127-38.
25. Mendilow, "Party Cluster Formations."
26. Arian, *Choosing People,* 28.

Glossary

AGUDAT ISRAEL (also AGUDA). Ultra-orthodox religious political party with a non-Zionist ideology.

AHDUT HAAVODA. *(a)* Political organization founded in 1919 and dominant in the politics of the Yishuv; *(b)* left-wing party that joined Mapai and Rafi in 1968 to form the Israel Labor party.

ALIGNMENT. *(a)* Name of election list in 1965 composed of Mapai and Ahdut Haavoda; *(b)* name of election list between 1969 and 1984 composed of Labor and Mapam.

ALIYAH (plural ALIYOT). Waves of mass immigration to Israel. Literally, going up.

ASHKENAZIM. Jews whose background was generally from the countries of Europe.

BADER-OFER AMENDMENT. Law that sets the method of distributing the last seats to be allocated in Knesset elections.

BALFOUR DECLARATION. Statement by British Secretary of State for Foreign Affairs in 1917 supporting the establishment of a Jewish national home in Palestine.

BASIC LAW. Legislation of constitutional stature. Collection of Basic Laws to form the Israeli constitution.

BEITAR. The youth group of the Revisionist movement and later of the Herut movement.

BLACK PANTHERS. Jewish protest movement to better social and economic status of Sephardim. Affiliated in electoral list with Rakah.

CIVIL RIGHTS MOVEMENT. Small party of the left led by Shulamit Aloni.

COUNCIL OF TORAH SAGES. Committee of rabbis that provides political and religious instruction to Agudat Israel.

DEMOCRATIC MOVEMENT FOR CHANGE (DMC). Party headed by Yigael Yadin; ran only in 1977 and won 15 seats.

D'HONDT SYSTEM. Allocation of seats in parliament taking into consideration the relative strength of the competing lists.

DMC. *See* Democratic Movement for Change.

DOMINANT PARTY. A political party in power for some time with spiritual and wide-ranging dominance.

EDA HAHARIDIT. Ultra-orthodox group that rejects Zionism.

EL AL. National airline of Israel.

ELECTORS' COUNCIL (ASEFAT NIVHARIM). Elected assembly of the Yishuv.

ERETZ ISRAEL. Land of Israel, denoting the biblical Promised Land.

ETZEL. *See* Irgun.

FREE CENTER. A splinter group from Herut in 1967, a part of the Likud between 1973 to 1977, and a component of the DMC in 1977. Headed by Shmuel Tamir.

GAHAL. Acronym for the Herut-Liberal bloc. Established as a joint list in 1965; expanded in 1973 and called the Likud.

GENERAL ZIONISTS. Right-of-center bourgeois party that joined with the Progressives between 1961 and 1965 and was known as the Liberal party.

GREATER ISRAEL. Notion of completeness and indivisibility of Eretz Israel.

GUSH EMUNIM. Settlement movement, largely religious, active in the territories acquired after the 1967 war and staunchly opposed to any territorial compromise.

HAGANAH. The defense force of the Yishuv.

HALAKAH. Jewish religious law.

HAPOEL HAMIZRACHI. Religious workers' movement and a major component of the National Religious party.

HAPOEL HATZAIR. A political party in the Yishuv period representing labor.

HASHOMER HATZAIR. The settlement movement and youth group of Mapam.

HERUT. A political party with a nationalist ideology and the major component of the Likud.

HEVRAT OVDIM. The Histadrut's holding company.

HISTADRUT. The General Federation of Labor and a key economic and political force in Israel.

HOVEVEI ZION. First organized national Jewish groups that encouraged immigration to Eretz Israel at the end of the nineteenth century.

IDF. Israel Defense Force. Israel's army.

INDEPENDENT LIBERALS. Formerly the Progressive party. Part of the Liberal party between 1961 and 1965. Since 1984, part of the Alignment.

IRGUN. Also known as the Etzel, the Irgun Zva Leumi, the National Military Organization. A pre-independence military organization associated with the Revisionist movement.

ISRAEL LABOR PARTY. *See* Labor-Mapam Alignment.

JEWISH AGENCY. Executive body of the World Zionist Organization.

KACH. List of the Jewish Defense League headed by Rabbi Meir Kahane.

KALANTERISM. The exploitation of a political situation to further personal goals, in particular switching support form one party to another, thereby deter-

Glossary

mining the party that will be able to form the governing coalition.

KEREN HAYESOD/MAGBIT. An institution of the World Zionist Organization charged with raising funds for the movement.

KEREN KAYEMET. Institution of the World Zionist Organization charged with purchasing and reclaiming land in Eretz Israel.

KIBBUTZ. Communal settlement sharing production and consumption.

KIPAH. Skullcap, worn for religious purposes.

KNESSET. Israel's parliament with 120 members.

KNESSET ISRAEL. Communal organization of Jews in the Yishuv in which membership was voluntary.

KUPAT HOLIM. The sick fund that provides health insurance and treatment.

LA'AM. A political party that developed from the Rafi faction of Mapai; in 1968 it refused to support the Labor party, then joined the Likud.

LABOR ALIGNMENT. *See* Labor-Mapam Alignment.

LABOR-MAPAM ALIGNMENT. List that included the Labor party and Mapam; 1969-84.

LADINO. Language combining Spanish and Hebrew; spoken by many Sephardim.

LAMIFNE. Faction within the National Religious party headed by Dr. Yosef Burg.

LAVON AFFAIR. Political conflict in Mapai with far-reaching implications within the party. Conflict began as a question regarding the role Defense Minister Lavon played in a security mishap in 1954.

LAW OF RETURN. Law passed in 1950 by the Knesset granting to every Jew in the world the right to immigrate to Israel.

LEHI. Extreme rightist pre-state underground organization opposed to cooperation with the British.

LIBERAL PARTY. Middle-class party; a member of Gahal and Likud. Formerly the General Zionists.

LIKUD. Joint list of Herut, Liberal party, La'am, and others founded in 1973; ruling party between 1977 and 1984.

MANDATE. The British administration of Palestine by a decision of the League of Nations after the First World War until 1948.

MAPAI. Acronym for Israel Workers' party. Created in 1930, it was the dominant party in Israel until its merger in 1968 with Ahdut Haavoda and Rafi to form the Israel Labor party.

MAPAM. Acronym for the United Workers' party. A left-wing socialist-Zionist party, Mapam was part of the Alignment between 1969 and 1984.

MIZRACHI. A major component of the National Religious party.

MORASHA. Religious party established before 1984 elections.

MOSHAV. Cooperative settlement in which production (but usually not consumption) is collective.

MOSHAVOT. Small agricultural towns.

NAAMAT. Women's branch of Histadrut labor federation. Formerly Pioneer Women.

NATIONAL COMMITTEE (VAAD LEUMI). Executive committee of the Yishuv.

NATIONAL RELIGIOUS PARTY (NRP). Historically Israel's most powerful religious party and a constant coalition partner in government.

NATURAI KARTA. Anti-Zionist ultra-orthodox Jewish religious group.

NEW ZIONIST ORGANIZATION. Established in 1935 by Revisionist movement led by Jabotinsky after splitting with the World Zionist Organization.

PALMACH. Elite striking force of the Yishuv's military arm, the Haganah.

PARTY KEY. Distribution of resources based on the proportional strength of the parties.

PEACE NOW. Movement formed after the 1973 Yom Kippur war active in urging policies of conciliation and moderation toward Arabs and Arab states. Opposes most settlement in the territories that resulted from the 1967 Six Day War.

POALEI AGUDAT ISRAEL. Ultra-orthodox religious party with a workers' orientation. In 1984, a component of Morasha.

POALEI ZION. A major socialist political party in the Yishuv period.

POGROM. Organized massacre, especially of Jews.

PROGRESSIVE LIST FOR PEACE (PLP). Established in 1984 as a joint Arab-Jewish list supporting the creation of a Palestinian state alongside Israel.

PROGRESSIVES. Political party originally supported and dominated by German immigrants. In 1961, merged with General Zionists to form the Liberal party. This party split in 1965 and the Progressives took the name Independent Liberals. In 1984, part of the Alignment.

PROTEKTZIA. Political pull; favoritism shown or access achieved because of informal connections with an official or clerk.

RAFI. Party founded by David Ben-Gurion and others who split from Mapai. Ran once in 1965 and won 10 seats. In 1968, most of the activists (excluding Ben-Gurion) returned and formed the Labor party along with Mapai and Ahdut Haavoda.

RAKAH. Acronym for the New Communist list, a Moscow-oriented party that appeals to Arab nationalist sentiment. Most important component of list that includes opposition groups including the Black Panthers.

SEPHARDIM. Jews whose background was generally from the countries of Asia and Africa.

SHAS. Ultra-orthodox religious party established in 1984 with special appeal to Sephardim. Split from Agudat Israel.

SHELLI. Leftist group that split before the 1984 elections. Part of the group

Glossary 281

ran in the elections with the Civil Rights movement and part with the Progressive List for Peace.

SHINUI. Centrist political party whose name means "Change." Established as a protest movement after the 1973 Yom Kipopur war; part of the DMC in 1977.

SHLAMUT HAARETZ. The notion of the completeness or indivisibility of Eretz Israel.

SIAH B: Leftist opposition faction in Mapai.

SIX DAY WAR. 1967 war between Israel and Arab states resulting in Israeli capture of East Jerusalem, West Bank of Jordan, Gaza Strip, Sinai Peninsula, and Golan Heights.

SMDS. The single-member district system of electoral representation.

STATE OF ISRAEL. Founded in 1948.

STATE LIST. A political party made up originally of Rafi members who refused to reunite with Mapai in 1968.

STATUS QUO. Regarding the role of the Jewish religious law in Israel, perpetuating the arrangements that existed in the Yishuv period.

TAMI. A political party set up in 1981 after its leader, Aharon Abu-Hatzeira, split from the NRP. Its appeal is ethnic, especially to Israelis of North African descent.

TEHIYA. An extreme party of the right whose platform rejects the Camp David accords, the Israel-Egypt peace treaty, and the return of the Sinai to Egypt.

TORA VEAVODA. Hebrew for religious law and toil.

TORAH RELIGIOUS FRONT. Joint list of Agudat Israel and Poalei Agudat Israel.

WESTERN WALL. Sometimes known as Wailing Wall. Remnant of outer wall of the Second Temple in Jerusalem. Considered most holy site in Judaism.

WHITE PAPER. Policy statement of the British government. Used during the Mandate period to announce restrictions on Jewish immigration.

WORLD ZIONIST ORGANIZATION (WZO). Established by Theodore Herzl in 1897 to promote plans of Jewish nationalism.

YAACOBI PROPOSAL. Plan for electoral reform in Israel.

YAHAD. List established in 1984 and headed by Ezer Weizman.

YERIDA. Out-migration from Israel. Literally, going down.

YESHIVA (PLURAL YESHIVOT). Seminars of higher learning of Jewish religious law and ritual.

YIDDISH. Language combining German and Hebrew; spoken by many Ashkenazim.

YISHUV. Jewish settlement and communal organizations in the pre-state period.

YOUTH FACTION. Group within the NRP.

ZIONIST CONGRESS. Governing body of the World Zionist Organization.

Index

Abdullah (kind of Jordan), 64
Abu-Hatzeira, Aharon, 54, 57, 94, 107, 142-43, 167, 223
Agranat Commission, 166, 201
Agricultural Center, 30, 211-12, 216
Agron, Gershon, 239
Agudat Israel, 54, 227
    coalition, 92, 160, 175
    platform, 86-89, 168, 229, 246
    religious issues, 108, 216, 221, 222, 224
Aharoni, Yair, 32, 36
Ahdut Haavoda (est. 1919), 50, 62, 63, 67, 72, 74. *See also* Mapai
Ahdut Haavoda (est. 1944), 51, 74-78 passim, 161, 214, 227, 247. *See also* Alignment, Mapam
Ahimeir, A., 101
Alignment (1965-69), 77, 82, 91, 151. *See also* Ahdut Haavoda, Mapai
Alignment (1969-84), 3, 72-79, 123
    decline, 30, 252-54
    elite, 54, 55, 60, 64, 69-70, 89, 93, 224, 225, 239
    ended, 79
    and ethnicity, 139-44
    floating vote, 144-51
    formed, 71
    government, 35, 58, 86-88
    and Histadrut, 28
    ideology, 248, 249
    images, 152-54
    membership, 102-3
    settlers, 214-16
    voters, 43-44, 135-39
    See also Labor, Mapam
Aliyah, 5-7, 11-24, 49, 50, 77, 78, 211
Allon, Yigael, 52, 61, 78, 248

Almogi, Yosef, 230
Almond, Gabriel, 192, 193
Aloni, Shulamit, 55, 93-94
Altelena, 81, 82
Amidar, 28
Arab-Israeli conflict, 246-47
Arabs, 75, 216
    civil liberties, 184-85
    economic gap, 45-46
    integration, 5, 6-7, 197
    participation, 133
    population, 16-18, 20-21
Aranne, Zalman, 50
Arbeli-Almozlino, Shoshana, 142
Arens, Moshe, 83, 174
Aridor, Yoram, 35, 43
Arlozoroff, Haim, 63, 80
Aronoff, Myron, 114
Arrow paradox of voting, 69-70
Ashkenazim, 22-24, 262-64
    chief rabbi, 223-24
    elite, 55-57
    immigration, 6
    income, 45
    party images, 152-54
    settlers, 213-15
    voting, 137-44
Avneri, Uri, 94

Bader, Dr. Yohanan, 82
Bader-Ofer Amendment, 123-24
Balfour Declaration, 15, 66
Bank Discount, 31-32
Bank Hapoalim, 28, 29
Bank Leumi, 28
Bank of Israel, 31, 32, 43
Bar Association, 182, 185
Baram, Moshe, 52

Barkai, Haim, 35-36
Bar-Lev, Haim, 175, 202
Bar-Yehuda, Israel, 161
Basic Law, 178-80
  Government, 178-79
  IDF, 202
  Knesset, 122-24, 178-79
  Lands of Israel, 215
Begin, Menachem
  biography, 64-65
  Herut, 82-84, 101, 113, 227
  leadership, 52, 53, 79, 134, 151, 200-201, 237
  National Unity Government, 77, 163, 236
  prime minister, 3, 7, 35, 58, 61, 62, 69, 70, 85, 92, 94, 160, 164, 248
Beitar, 65-65, 79
Ben-Aharon, Yitzhak, 110
Ben-Gurion, David
  biography, 62
  leadership, 14, 17, 53, 61, 62, 82, 110, 163, 229, 237
  Mapai, 75-75, 116, 226
  military, 163, 199-201, 202, 227
  prime minister, 63, 64, 74-77, 81, 126, 160, 161, 164, 256
  Rafi, 50-51, 66, 67, 68, 79, 90, 91, 151
  World Zionist Organization, 22, 73
  Yishuv, 2, 12, 18, 80
Ben-Meir, Yehuda, 54, 162
Ben-Porat, Mordecai, 94, 143
Ben-Porath, Yoram, 43
Ben-Zvi, Yitzhak, 14, 62, 66-67
Bergman, Aharon A., 179, 184
Berman, Yitzhak, 166
Biltmore Program, 74
Biton, Charlie, 94
Black Panthers, 122, 143, 190
Bnei Akiva, 223
Brecher, Michael, 236-37
Broadcasting Authority, 31, 222, 256-57
Brother Daniel, 220
Brzezinski, Zbigniew, 58
Bureaucracy, 100, 232-38

Bureaucratic politics, 9, 95
Burg, Yosef, 54, 58, 107-8, 219

Canaanites, 4
Central Elections Committee, 121
Civil liberties, 177-78, 183-85
Civil Rights movement (CRM), 55, 93-94, 147, 149, 162, 246
Civil Service Commission, 43, 234
Coalition, 157, 159-66
Coalition politics, 9, 95
Cohen, Geula, 83, 113
Cohen, Haim, 76
Coleman, James, 192
Commissions for production and marketing, 31, 215-16
Communist party, 101
Constituent assembly, 178
Constitution, 177-80
Council of Torah Sages, 89, 168
Courts, 181-82

Dan, 29
Davar, 29, 63, 67, 100, 255, 258
Dayan, Moshe, 50, 58, 75, 76, 92, 94, 143
  and agriculture, 212-16
  and defense, 35, 51, 77, 163, 166, 200, 201, 202, 248, 257
  and Rafi, 61, 68, 90, 151
Declaration of Independence, 18, 56
Defense budget, 36, 203-4
Defense minister, 201-2
Defense ministry, 200-204
Democratic Movement for Change (DMC), 69-70, 89-93, 123, 160
  electoral reform, 125, 131
  elite, 60-61, 173-74
  formed, 52
  membership, 103
  platform, 246-47
  primary, 92, 129
  voters, 43-44, 86, 139, 147-49, 152
  See also Shinui
Democracy, 96, 117-19, 144, 177, 254, 256, 261-64
Deputy ministers, 236

d'Hondt system, 123
Dominant party, 7, 71-72, 75, 96-103 passim, 160, 227, 253
  and voting, 136-37, 140
Doron, Gideon, 43
Druckman, Haim, 54, 88
Duverger, Maurice, 97, 99, 112, 146

Eban, Abba, 248
Eda Haharidit, 87
Egged, 29
Egypt, peace treaty, 65, 98
Ehrlich, Simha, 35, 85
Eichmann, Adolf, 185
Eitan, Rafael, 200-201
El Al, 22, 28, 31, 173-74
Electors' Council (Asefat Nivharim), 27, 80, 155
Elections
  call for new, 120, 121, 157-58
  and economy, 43-44
  Histadrut, 28, 92-93, 205-6
  in 1951, 84
  in 1961, 76
  in 1965, 63, 65
  in 1969, 64, 248-49
  in 1977, 44, 52, 54
  in 1981, 7, 43
  participation rates, 133
  provisions, 122-24
  and television, 258
Electoral politics, 9, 95
Electoral reform, 161, 188, 238, 239, 240
Eliav, Lova, 94
Elite
  judicial, 183
  political, 244
  from military, 53
  in Yishuv, 59
Emergency regulations, 177, 178, 180, 254
Eshkol, Levi, 35, 61, 63, 64, 76-77, 82, 163, 194, 200-203 passim, 212, 230, 235
Ethnicity. *See* Arabs, Ashkenazim, Sephardim

Etzel, 227. *See also* Irgun
Etzioni, Amitai, 96

Fein, Leonard, 260
Feisal (king of Jordan), 66
Finance minister, 27, 43, 63, 237-38
Finance ministry, 33-35, 240
Flatto-Sharon, Shmuel, 167
Floating vote, 144-51
Free Center, 79, 83, 92, 147
Freidman, Avraham, 41
Freidman, Marsha, 55

Gahal
  elections, 147, 151
  formed, 65, 79, 82, 84, 91
  in Histadrut, 205
  National Unity Government, 77, 166
  platform, 83, 248-49
  See also Herut, Liberal party
Galili, Israel, 52
Galnoor, Yitzhak, 237
General Zionists, 79, 80, 84, 85, 103, 104, 228, 229, 239. *See also* Liberal party
Germany, 37-38, 65, 82
Gitelman, Zvi, 261
Government, 158-66 passim
Government corporations law, 31
Gross national product, 32, 36, 37
Gush Emunim, 54, 87-88, 195, 196, 223, 262

Haaretz, 255, 258
Hadassah, 85
Haganah, 63, 65, 81, 199, 227
Halakah, 89, 216, 219, 220, 221, 224
Hamashbir Hamerkazi, 29
Hammer, Zevulun, 54, 58, 107-8, 162
Haolam Haze, 94
Haoved Hatzioni, 86, 214
Hapoel Hamizrachi, 86, 105, 107, 112, 209, 214, 215, 228, 239
Hapoel Hatzair, 80, 100
Harari decision, 178
Hashomer Hatzair, 64, 74, 75, 227
Hasneh, 29

Hebrew, 4, 22
Herut, 65, 75, 79-84, 151, 227
  electoral reform, 131
  elite, 35, 52, 69-70, 82-83, 101
  as illegitimate, 2, 7, 72
  organization, 112, 113, 213-14
  platform, 19, 83-84, 248, 250
  selection of candidates, 115
  See also Gahal, Likud
Herzl, Theodor, 26, 49
Herzog, Haim, 68, 90
Herzog, Hanna, 143-44
Hevra Leisrael, 31
Hevrat Ovdim, 28, 208-9
High Court of Justice, 179, 181, 182, 183, 224
Histadrut, 8, 50, 84, 204-10
  in economy, 35-36, 42, 72-73, 190, 208, 211, 248
  elections, 92-93, 205-6, 208-9
  elite, 56, 62, 63, 67, 116, 206
  Kupat Holim, 108, 209-10, 229-32
  services, 59, 100, 102, 104, 226-31
  structure, 28-30, 206-7
  Yishuv, 80, 81
Hovevei Zion, 13
Huntington, Samuel, 58
Hurewitz, Yigael, 34, 35, 43, 94

Ideology, 8, 134-35, 244, 253-54
Ihud, 214
IDF, 53, 65, 81, 199-204, 256
Import capital, 13, 36, 37-40
Independent Liberals, 57, 84, 86, 113, 147-48, 207, 213, 214, 230, 246.
  See also Progressives
Inflation, 32
Interior ministry, 240, 254
Interest group, defined, 186-88
Irgun Zva Leumi, 65, 80-81, 82, 101, 199, 227
Israel Institute of Applied Social Research, 250
Israel Labor party. See Labor party

Jabotinsky, Vladimir (Zeev), 49, 65, 74, 77, 79-80, 81, 84, 101, 229

Jerusalem Post, 28, 29
Jewish Agency, 16, 19, 26-28, 36, 41, 62, 63, 67, 212, 213, 242
Jewish aid, 38-39
Johnson-Lodge Immigration Act, 12
Judges, selection of, 182
Judicial review, 179, 184

Kach, 262
Kahan Commission, 201
Kahane, Meir, 94, 246, 262
Kaisar, Israel, 206
Kalanter, Rahamim, 239
Kalanterism, 239
Kanovitz, Shimon, 172
Kaplan, Eliezer, 35
Katz, Israel, 92
Katzav, Moshe, 240
Katzir, Efraim, 62, 67, 68, 69
Keren Hayesod/Magbit, 27
Keren Kayamet, 27, 211, 215
Kibbutz, 8, 29-30, 72, 74, 78, 88, 107, 191, 211-16 passim, 227, 228, 260
  political elite, 59
  voting, 134, 214-16
Kibbutz Haarzi, 74, 112, 214
Kibbutz Hameuhad, 74, 214, 227
Kissinger, Henry, 168
Klal, 31
Knesset, 3, 82
  chairman, 65, 170
  defense budget, 204
  delegation, 167-69
  elections, 92-93, 124
  legislation, 171-77
  origins, 155
  private member's bill, 170, 172-73
  question time, 170
  relations with government, 157-58
  structural features, 155-56
Knesset committees, 173-77
  finance, 33, 35, 173-74, 175, 176, 182, 204
  Foreign Affairs and Security, 76, 173-74, 196, 204
  House, 167, 172, 173, 174

Law, Constitution, and Justice, 173, 178
Knesset Israel, 27, 62, 219
Knesset members, 9, 49, 129, 166-71
  ethnic origin, 55-67
  immunity, 166-67
  occupations, 59, 60
  sex, 55
Kolleck, Teddy, 242
Koor, 29, 41
Kupat Holim, 29, 41, 72, 105, 108, 192, 209-10, 229, 232

La'am, 69, 79, 90
Labor exchanges, 228-29
Labor movement, 59, 72-79
Labor party
  decline, 7, 98
  elite, 52, 62, 228, 236
  formed, 51, 63, 77, 151
  and Histadrut, 204-8
  and Kupat Holim, 229-32
  organization, 112, 114
  platform, 246-47
  selection of candidates, 115
  settlers, 214
  voting, 136-37
  See also Ahdut Haavoda, Alignment, Mapai, Rafi
Ladino, 22
Lamifne, 107
Landau, Haim, 58
Landau, Justice, 179
Lands Administration, 27, 215
Lavon, Pinhas, 63, 75-76, 116, 200, 212
Lavon Affair, 63, 64, 75-77, 200
Law of Return, 5, 18, 162, 220
Lebanon War, 7, 201, 257
Left-right continuum, 71, 89-90, 244-54
Legitimacy, 2, 71, 72
Lehi, 65, 80-81, 82, 101, 199, 227
Lehman-Wilzig, Sam, 264
Levy, David, 52, 57, 142, 240
Liberal party, 84-86, 151
  elite, 69-70, 168, 239
  in Likud, 35, 52, 79
  membership, 103, 213
  organization, 112-15
  platform, 248
  See also Gahal, General Zionists, Likud
Lijphart, Arend, 1
Likud, 7, 65, 71, 75, 79-86, 98, 123, 226
  elite, 54, 55, 58, 60, 83, 89-93, 240
  and ethnicity, 139-44, 240
  floating vote, 144-51
  formed, 79
  in government, 86-88, 160, 173-74, 235
  in Histadrut, 30, 206-7
  images, 152-54, 253-54
  membership, 102-3
  platform, 246-49, 252
  settlers, 214-16
  voters, 43-44, 136-39, 150-52, 239, 260
  withdrawal from Sinai, 3, 169-70
  See also Gahal, Herut, La'am, Liberal party
Lists, 71, 115, 121

Maariv, 255
Maccabee, 85
Machiavelli, Niccolo, 110
Magen David Adom, 31
Magen, David, 240
Mandate, 15, 16, 26, 181, 219, 240
Mapai, 226, 229, 230
  and defense, 199-200, 227-28
  as dominant party, 96, 98, 100
  and electoral reform, 126
  elite, 50, 52, 59-60, 62, 63, 78, 90, 239, 257
  in government, 75-77, 161
  in Labor, 51, 77, 79
  organization, 110-11, 113-17
  settlers, 214
  in Yishuv, 27, 72-75, 80, 212-13
  See also Alignment, Labor
Mapam, 151
  in Alignment, 64, 78-79
  coalition, 227, 228

Index

elite, 54, 168
formed, 74
organization, 101, 112, 114
platform, 246, 248, 249
voters, 214
See also Alignment
Mass party, 99-103
Matzpen, 246
Mayors, direct election of, 238, 239
Medding, Peter, 100, 110-11
Meir, Golda, 50, 55, 61, 63-64, 68, 77, 110, 134, 162, 164, 165, 166, 200, 248
Mekorot, 28, 63
Mendilow, Jonathan, 264
Michels, Robert, 108-11, 118
Minister
of immigrant absorption, 20, 27
of religious affairs, 219, 222-25
See also defense minister, finance minister
Ministers of government, 164
deputy, 163
removal, 165
resignation, 166
without portfolio, 236
Mizrachi, 86, 105
Modai, Yitzhak, 35
Morasha, 86, 88
Mosca, Gaetano, 47, 51, 53
Moshav, 8, 29-30, 72, 107, 211-12, 213-15
voting, 214-16
Mossad, 65
Moyne, Lord, 81

Naamat, 205
National Committee (Vaad Leumi), 56, 67
National Insurance Institute, 210, 230-32
Nationalization
of defense, 227
of education, 227-28
of employment, 228-29
of health, 229-32
of religion, 222-25

National Religious party (NRP), 86-89 passim, 213
in coalition, 64, 92, 94, 123, 160, 161, 162, 168
education, 228
electoral reform, 125, 131
and Kupat Holim, 209, 230
leadership, 53-54, 69
membership, 102, 103, 105, 107-9
organization, 112-15
platform, 246-49
religious issues, 216-25
and Tami, 55, 143
voting, 139, 214-15
Youth Faction, 54, 88, 89, 107-8, 162
National Unity Government (est. 1967), 51, 63, 65, 77, 84, 163, 166, 236
National Unity Government (est. 1984), 35, 61, 65, 66, 67, 78, 83, 86, 163, 235, 236
Naturai Karta, 2, 4, 87, 262
Navon, Yitzhak, 61-70 passim, 90, 142, 151
New Zionist Organization, 80, 84
Nissim, Moshe, 57

Ofer, Avraham, 52, 91
Oligarchy, 109-11
Ombudsman, 238
Ottoman Empire, 14, 15, 180-81, 218-19, 240

Pail, Meir, 94
Palmach, 64, 75, 199, 227
Peace Now, 196, 262
Peres, Shimon, 35, 50, 52, 61, 65-66, 68, 75, 76, 78, 90, 113, 126, 142, 151, 163, 175, 200, 235
Peri, Yoram, 199-200
Planning, 237, 242
Pluralism, 186, 188-89, 192
Poalei Agudat Israel, 86, 87, 88, 160, 213, 214, 246
Poalei Zion, 62
Political party
defined, 95

discipline, 169-70
financing, 106, 175, 179
key, 16
machine, 50, 51, 104
membership, 102-9
platform, 248-49
Porat, Hanan, 88
Powell, G. Bingham, 193
Presidents, 61-62, 157, 159
    biographies, 66-68
    election, 68
Prime ministers, 61-62, 164-66
    biographies, 62-66
Progressive List for Peace, 94
Progressives, 57, 84, 229. *See also*
    Independent Liberals
Project Renewal, 242
Proportional representation, 124-30,
    238, 239
Protektzia, 232
Provisional State Council, 56
Public opinion, 96, 257, 265

Raasco, 28
Rabbinate, chief, 162, 222-25
Rabbinical courts, 222-25
Rabin, Yitzhak, 52, 61, 62, 64, 66, 78,
    92, 94, 113, 126, 162, 175, 200,
    202, 235
Rabinowitz, Yehoshua, 35, 52
Rafael, Yitzhak, 54, 107-9, 165
Rafi, 79, 89-93, 151, 152, 230
    formed, 50, 62, 66, 77
    leaders, 35, 67, 68
    National Unity Government, 163
    platform, 131, 226
    returned to Labor, 51, 78
Rakah, 57, 94, 168, 246, 262
Rechtman, Shmuel, 167
Religion in state, 245, 247
Religious councils, 162, 222-25
Religious parties, 86-89, 139, 147-51
Revisionist movement, 2, 65, 74, 79-80,
    82, 101, 227, 229
Rimalt, Elimelech, 69-70
Rogers, William, 77, 166
Rothschild, Edmond de, 13, 211

Rubinstein, Amnon, 91, 131, 156, 178
Rufheisen, 220

Sabra and Shatilla, 166, 201, 257-58
Sadat, Anwar, 84, 248
Sapir, Pinhas, 35, 51, 64, 78, 200, 203,
    247-48
Sapir, Yosef, 211
Sartori, Giovanni, 1
Schiff, Zeev, 202
"Season," 80-81
Sephardim, 6, 262-64
    chief rabbi, 223-24
    elite, 55-57, 83, 94, 240
    party images, 152-54
    population, 22-24, 241
    as president, 68-70
    settlers, 213-15
    social gap, 29, 45-46
Shaki, Avner, 143
Shalit, Benjamin, 220
Shamir, Michal, 262
Shamir, Moshe, 83
Shamir, Yitzhak, 52, 61, 62, 65, 83
Shapira, Haim Moshe, 219
Shapiro, Yonathan, 177
Sharett, Moshe, 27, 61, 62-63, 64, 68,
    75, 76, 116, 117, 160
Sharf, Zeev, 35
Sharon, Ariel, 52, 85, 151, 200-201,
    202, 212
Shas, 86, 143
Shaveh, Yitzhak, 69
Shazar, Zalman, 67, 68
Shelli, 94, 246
Shemtov, Victor, 79
Shikun, Ovdim, 29
Shimshoni, Daniel, 200
Shinui, 91-92, 131, 149, 207
Shitrit, Meir, 240
Shlamut haaretz, 83
Shprinzak, Yosef, 14
Siah B, 74
Sick fund. *See* Kupat Holim
Sinai campaign, 63, 164, 201, 237
Six Day War, 64, 75, 201, 236-37
Sollel Boneh, 29, 73

State controller, 106, 237-38
State list, 62, 147, 226
Statism, 89, 106, 213, 226-32
Status quo, 4, 218, 222
Stern, Abraham, 81
Stern Gang, 65
Sullivan, John, 262
Supreme Court, 179, 182-84, 220, 222, 224
Surplus vote, 123

Tahal, 28
Tami, 54, 57, 86, 87, 94, 142-43, 158, 223
Tamir, Boaz, 43
Tamir, Shmuel, 83, 92
Tehiya, 83, 87, 88, 113, 149, 223, 252
Telem, 92, 94
Television, 106-7, 222, 255, 258
Tnuva, 29
Torah Religious Front, 86
Truman, David, 186
Trumpeldor, Joseph, 79

Unemployment, 42
United Farmers, 215
United Jewish Appeal, 40
United Religious Front, 86
United States aid, 38-39, 40
Uzan, Aharon, 143

Vaad Leumi, 27
Voting
  Arab, 133
  in army, 146, 149, 260
  dominant party, 136-37, 140, 146-47
  and ideology, 134-35
  kibbutz, 214-16
  left-right continuum, 250-54
  moshav, 214-16

Wadi Salib, 190
Wahrhaftig, Zerah, 107
Weber, Max, 57, 58
Weizman, Ezer, 53, 58, 83, 85, 94, 200, 202
Weizman, Haim, 62, 66, 67, 84
White Paper, 17, 81
Who is a Jew, 161, 162, 219, 220, 221
WIZO, 85
World Zionist Organization (WZO), 14, 16, 26-27, 39, 62, 66, 73, 79, 80, 84, 85, 211-12

Yaacobi, Gad, 130-32
Yaad, 168-69
Yad Vashem, 31
Yadin, Yigael, 91-92, 131, 202
Yadlin, Aharon, 52
Yahad, 83, 94
Yamit, 237
Yariv, Aharon, 52
Yediot Aharonot, 255
Yeshiva, 87, 108, 175, 197, 223
Yevin, Y. H., 101
Yiddish, 22
Yishuv, 2, 80, 100, 104, 240
Yom Kippur War, 64, 201, 202, 236-37

Zim, 28
Zionism, 3-4, 11, 12, 26, 27
Zionist Congress, 26, 155
Zoning, 242

About the Author

ASHER ARIAN was born in Cleveland, Ohio in 1938. He studied in Cleveland and received an A.B. degree from Western Reserve University. His graduate work was completed at Michigan State University where he received his doctorate in political science in 1965.

Since 1966 he has been at Tel Aviv University where he is professor of political science. He has served as chairman of the Political Science Department and as dean of the Faculty of Social Sciences. In addition to Tel Aviv University, Arian has had visiting appointments at the University of California at Berkeley, Columbia University, Brandeis University, University of Minnesota, Hebrew University, New York University, and Queens College of the City University of New York.

Arian's professional writing has concentrated on Israeli politics, especially elections, public opinion, and political parties. He is the author of many books, including *Ideological Change in Israel* and *The Choosing People: Voting Behavior in Israel*. Since the 1969 elections Arian has edited the series titled *The Elections in Israel*. His articles have appeared in journals such as *Comparative Politics, Journal of Politics, Western Political Science Quarterly,* and the *International Journal of Political Science*.

Arian has served as president of the Israel Political Science Association and in 1979 and 1982 he was elected to the Executive Committee of the International Political Science Association.